VERSO
CLASSICS

The last few decades have seen an immense outpouring of works of theory and criticism, but, as the number of titles has increased dramatically, it has become more and more difficult to find one's way around this vast body of literature and to distinguish between those works of real and enduring value and those of a more ephemeral nature. The Verso Classics series will rise to the challenge by taking stock of the last few decades of contemporary critical thought and reissuing, in an elegant paperback format and at affordable prices, those books which genuinely constitute original and important intellectual contributions.

Many of these works are currently out of print or difficult to obtain: Verso Classics will bring them back into the public domain, building a collection which will become the 'essential left library'.

A Theory of Capitalist Regulation

The US Experience

*With a new postface
by the author*

◆

MICHEL AGLIETTA

Translated by David Fernbach

VERSO
London · New York

First published as *Régulation et crises du capitalisme* by
Calmann-Lévy, 1976
First published by Verso 1979
© Verso 1979
Verso Classics edition first published by Verso 2000
© Verso 2000

Verso
UK: 6 Meard Street, London W1V 3HR
USA: 180 Varick Street, New York, NY 10014–4606

Verso is the imprint of New Left Books

ISBN 1–85984–268–2

Printed and bound by
WS Bookwell Ltd, Finland

Contents

5. General Rate of Profit and Competition among Capitals

Introduction

The Need for a Theory of Capitalist Regulation

1. Regulation, Equilibrium and the Concept of Reproduction

At the present time, dissatisfaction with the body of doctrine that the academic establishment considers 'scientific economics' is expressed with growing intensity by an ever greater number of theorists.[1] This dissatisfaction bears on two major failings of the dominant economic theory: firstly, its inability to analyse the economic process in terms of the time lived by its subjects, in other words to give a historical account of economic facts; and secondly, its inability to express the social content of economic relations, and consequently to interpret the forces and conflicts at work in the economic process. These two aspects are certainly not independent of one another or simply juxtaposed. But their essential unity is often inadequately grasped by contemporary critics, thinking as they generally do within the conceptual universe of the very theory they are seeking radically to criticize. The greater part of the time they use the language of this theory, which either vitiates their conclusions, or at best merely questions the correspondence of the orthodox theory to reality. What is seldom challenged, however, is the logic by which the concepts of the theory are developed.

There is indeed something fascinating about the monumental

---

[1] Texts which represent widespread positions, and develop far-reaching critiques of the prevailing, 'neo-classical' conception, include: Joan Robinson, *Economic Heresies*, London, 1971; Nicholas Kaldor, 'The Irrelevance of Equilibrium Economics', in *Economic Journal*, December, 1972; G. Destanne de Bernis, 'L'équilibre général', *Revue économique*, November 1975.

edifice constructed by the neo-classical theorists of a century ago. The attraction it can still exercize today is a function of its totalizing and totalitarian character. The theory is totalizing inasmuch as it is entirely geared to the elaboration of a single concept, that of *general equilibrium*. It is totalitarian because it reduces and excludes from its ambit economic phenomena identified from observation of real practices as 'imperfections', rather than dialectically transforming its concepts by incorporating a more concrete content into them. This is why the term 'regulation' needs no definition in orthodox economic theory. In its universe, regulation is nothing other than the set of overall properties of general equilibrium. Conventional economic science presents itself as a set of coherent precepts which can be neither extended nor diminished; hence the inflexibility of doctrine that generally characterizes the high priests of equilibrium theory.

If this theory has exercized such a dictatorship over economic thought, it is because it supplies a reassuring vision of society and a justification for the profession of economist. General equilibrium is seductive because it suggests the collective harmony of a community whose subjects preserve their absolute autonomy yet where all conflict is excluded. The normative character of this theoretical project does not in any way diminish its prestige. Its protagonists claim to elaborate rules of efficiency which the economic system must obey so that all subjects can act rationally and their actions be mutually compatible. They compare existing economic systems according to these norms of absolute efficiency and conclude that capitalism is both the least bad alternative and the only system amenable to advance towards an optimal configuration. It should not be surprising that this double achievement has brought the profession of economist honour from the established social order. 'Reform without risks' is underpinned by this 'normative science'.

Yet the dissatisfaction that we mentioned persists and even grows. This is particularly so in periods of crisis, where the scale of the 'disequilibria' of the real economy casts doubt on the validity of the concept of time with which general equilibrium theory operates. Keynes accomplished a profound theoretical renovation by turning for the sources of his inspiration to the troubled history of a capitalism torn by gigantic conflicts and weakened by deep depression. But Keynesian theory failed to extend its criticism of the neo-classical conception of market adjustments to a criticism of the neo-classical conception of economic subjects and relations, and so was to be reabsorbed in the process of reduction characteristic of the totalitarian procedures of general equilibrium doctrine.[2] This recuperation was facilitated by the fact that Keynes confined his theoretical horizon to the short run. For if there is one field in which equilibrium theory has found itself in serious trouble, and has made little headway on daunting problems, it is that of long-run economic movements. The very notion of equilibrium is put in question here, in an irrepressible way. In their desire to reconcile the concept of equilibrium with that of dynamic development, the neo-classical theorists caricature their own reductive procedures, putting the very notion of equilibrium blatantly into question. A host of macro-economic models of development has mushroomed, all seeking the conditions for balanced or harmonious economic growth.

The failure of these countless models, which differ among themselves only by mathematical refinements of the same normative procedure, is particularly patent in the practical advice they have sought to offer the under-developed countries. Yet their inadequacies are no less at the theoretical level. Any treatment of growth that evacuates history leads to a conception of time that renders dynamics a mere variant of statics – in effect, a logical time which is not the expression of any real movement. A variable called 'time' is introduced into the characteristic multi-dimensional parameters of equilibrium, such that the representation of equilibrium conditions lays down 'paths of growth'. The variable of time is not constructed;

[2] As early as 1937, scarcely a year after the publication of Keynes' *General Theory*, J.R. Hicks attempted such a recuperation in his essay 'Mr Keynes and the Classics', reprinted in *Readings in the Theory of Income Distribution*, London, 1946. This was no isolated effort, but the initial act of a steady reabsorption of Keynesian thinking by neo-classical schemas. A new academic school was born from this falsification. Its high priests were Hansen, Allen, and Samuelson, whose textbooks have swept the world. Harrod's attempt in 1939 to generalize Keynesian theory to the disequilibrium conditions of a growth economy was similarly recuperated by Solow as an investigation of the conditions for balanced growth. Harrod himself was a party to this stifling of his initial project.

it is one of the independent variables of the model. But dynamics is etymologically the study of forces. It necessarily involves the construction of a 'temporality', as the characteristic of a real movement. The study of a movement, moreover, is the study of changes of state. If a system is described as dynamic, then the constitutive relationships of this system must have a logic of internal transformation. To conceive of the regulation of a system transforming itself in this way is to see the changes that occur in its relationships as such that these relationships can always be organized into a system. This raises two methodological problems.

On the one hand, we deny that what exists does so automatically. The notion of *reproduction* then becomes necessary. To speak of reproduction is to show the processes which permit what exists to go on existing. In a system whose internal relationships are in course of transformation, not everything does continue to exist. It is thus necessary to study the way in which innovation appears in the system. There is no *a priori* reason why a transformation must be no more than a 'plastic deformation' of the relationships that structure the system; if this were so, then continuity would be assured and the concept of reproduction would be simple. But when actual social systems are studied, historical experience confirms that *transformation means rupture, qualitative change*.

On the other hand, these two notions of reproduction and rupture confront one another in sterile opposition, each simply excluding the other, as long as the system is defined in the manner of the various conceptions of equilibrium as a network of relations between economic agents and activities which display *a priori* types of specified rationality. The attempt to define the regulation of a system in movement leads to a different conception of the system. It implies the conception of a *hierarchy* in the constitutive relationships of the system, and not merely a functional interdependence.

These methodological indications pose the question of the analytical tools needed to establish the concept of mode of production. For the study of a mode of production will seek to isolate the determinant relationships that are reproduced in and through the social transformation, the changing forms in which these are reproduced, and the reasons why this reproduction is accompanied by ruptures at different points of the social system. To speak of the regulation of a mode of production is to try to formulate in general laws the way in which the determinant structure of a society is reproduced. The object of the present work is the regulation of the capitalist mode of production. Our investigation will base itself on a long-run historical analysis of the economy of the United States of America.

2. The Role of Historical Analysis in a Theoretical Elaboration

The arguments so far are designed to indicate that a theory of social regulation is a complete alternative to the theory of general equilibrium. If we are to contribute to the construction of this alternative, then we cannot seek to dispel the characteristic hypotheses of general equilibrium theory by adopting the language of the latter or its criteria of scientificity.[3] All critical studies that still orient themselves towards this theory adopt the basic principle that is at the root of its reductive procedures: the *a priori* postulation of economic subjects defined by a rational conduct that is alleged to be a characteristic of human nature, a permanent datum taken as self-evident; economic relations are then defined as modes of coordination between the predetermined and unalterable behaviour of these subjects. Theoretical debates revolve around these modes of coordination and tend towards the definition of an equilibrium configuration of an ever more general scope. Hence the need these theorists feel to lend their equilibrium a dynamic character. The need would not exist if the basic concepts of economic theory were those of relationship and process, incorporating an internal principle of transformation in their very definition, instead of subject and state. But in that

---

[3] Attempts to amend general equilibrium theory have given rise to some remarkable intellectual contributions, which seek to extend the concept of equilibrium in two directions. The first introduces the concept of *information* in its representation of the functional relationships between subjects. One of the most advanced examples of this type is the work by J. Kornai, *Anti-Equilibrium*, North Holland, 1971. The second introduces the concept of *power*, to denote an asymmetry in the relationships between subjects. The chief exponent of this tendency is F. Perroux, *Pouvoir et Économie*, Paris, 1974.

case the concept of equilibrium itself would lose its foundation and make way for the concept of reproduction.

Notions of time, as we have already said, are closely dependent on more fundamental conceptions of the object of the theory, the criteria of scientific procedure, and the role of abstraction in the creation of concepts. From this point of view, general equilibrium pertains to an idealist philosophy of abstract man, based on the notion of a 'state of nature'.

This is why the field of economic science is not defined in this theory by a division between various social activities, but rather by a principle that makes universal claims. Any human action is economic as long as it is governed by the principle of rationality – that is, by a logic of choices that satisfies certain axioms of formal coherence.[4] Once defined as a science of human behaviour detached from any social conditions, the dominant economic theory cannot but be altogether foreign to history. It can only proceed normatively. The apparently rigorous character of the theory should not deceive us here. It is not the rigour of an experimental science, increasing the explanatory power of its concepts by an ever closer interchange between the development of knowledge and practical action on the object of analysis. It is rather the rigour of a theological construction, confined purely to the world of ideas; the stricter its logic, the more divorced from reality. Such is the fate of general equilibrium theory as it refines its theorems to adjust to criticisms made on its own ground. The final outcome is in no way paradoxical, but already implicit at its point of origin. For the concept of the rational and sovereign subject, free of any social tie, introduces an absolute opposition between theory and experience, necessity and contingency, essence and phenomenon. The goal of theory is to express the essence of its object by stripping it of everything contingent; institutions, social interactions, conflicts, are so much dross to be purged to rediscover economic behaviour in its pure state. Purity is finally attained in the concept of price, as the sufficient and exclusive bond between all rational subjects under the uniform constraint of scarcity.

[4] The significance of the principle of rationality, its emergence with the development of commodity exchange and its ascendancy under capitalism, have been analysed by Oskar Lange in his *Political Economy*, Vol. 1, London, 1963.

Economists confronted with the transformations and crises of contemporary Western societies, and with the troubling future of the capitalist system as a whole, can find no foothold in general equilibrium theory. To take refuge in partial investigations, half empirical, half theoretical, only compounds the confusion. The way forward does not lie in an attempt to give a better reply to the theoretical questions raised by the orthodox theory, but rather in an ability to pose quite different theoretical questions. This means a collective effort to develop a theory of the regulation of capitalism which isolates the conditions, rhythms and forms of its social transformations.

The term 'regulation', whose concept it is the task of theory to construct, denotes the need for an analysis encompassing the economic system as a whole. This analysis should produce general laws that are socially determinate, precisely specifying the historical conditions of their validity.

For reasons already outlined, our project will be sustained by a procedure quite different from the reductive process characteristic of idealism. This procedure finds its logical foundations in dialectical materialism. The method elaborated by Marx has important consequences, both for the proper order of research and exposition and for the fundamental concepts from which it is possible to develop a theory of the regulation of capitalism.

Marx's refusal to postulate an immutable essence underlying the variability of phenomena means that for him the tension characteristic of every process of knowledge does not take the form of an opposition between the theoretical and the empirical, external to the theoretical construction itself. This tension is expressed instead by the relationship between abstract and concrete within the development of theory itself. Abstraction is not a return of thought into itself in order to grasp its real essence (the rational subject); it is rather an exclusively experimental procedure of investigation of the concrete (historically determinate social relations). It follows that concepts are not introduced once and for all at a single level of abstraction. They are transformed by the characteristic interplay which constitutes the passage from the abstract to the concrete and enables the concrete to be absorbed within theory. Theory, for its part, is never final and complete, it is always in the process of development. The progression of thought does not consist simply of hypothetico-deductive phases; these rather alternate with dialectical phases. It is the dialectical phases that are most important, and make theory something other than the exposition of conclusions already implicitly contained in an axiomatic system. The transformation of concepts means the creation of new forms and consequently the negation of limits within their previous formulation. If this transformation is effectively achieved by an experimental procedure, a concatenation of concepts can become a representation of a historical movement.

In order for the transformation of concepts to correspond to the representation in thought of a real historical movement, these concepts must be social in nature from the outset. Such is in fact the nature of the concepts introduced by Marx. They are representations of the relationships that structure society, and not systematizations of individual choices. The object of economic theory then becomes the study of the social laws governing the production and distribution of the means of existence of human beings organized in social groups.

The definition of the field of economic science does not derive from a universal principle that founds a pure economy. It is solely a methodological demarcation within the field of social relations, one perpetually probed and shifted by the development of theoretical analysis itself. The study of capitalist regulation, therefore, cannot be the investigation of abstract economic laws. It is the study of the transformation of social relations as it creates new forms that are both economic and non-economic, that are organized in structures and themselves reproduce a determinant structure, the mode of production. As such, it will elucidate the general lesson of historical materialism: the development of the forces of production under the effect of the class struggle, and the transformation of the conditions of this struggle and the forms in which it is embodied under the effect of that development. In this perspective, history is no longer an alibi designed to justify certain abstract schemas. It is an indispensable component of the experimental procedure, which must orient the tension between abstract and concrete towards the following questions: What forces transform the social system and guarantee its long-run cohesion? Are the conditions and modalities of this cohesion capable of evolution? In what conditions and by what processes are qualitative changes in the relations of production induced? Is it possible to identify stages in the development of capitalism and can such an identification interpret the structural crises of this mode of production? Is the present crisis a sequel to other historical changes internal to capitalism, and does it offer a basis for hypotheses about future class struggles? These are the questions at issue for a theory of capitalist regulation.

3. The General Plan of This Work

The present work is designed to make a modest contribution, in the perspective that has just been outlined, to the renovation of positive research and the deepening of critical enquiry that have already begun in economic science in the course of the last few years. Its ambition, which it seeks to realize by way of a systematic analysis of the history of American capitalism since the Civil War, is chiefly theoretical. The objective of this work, in other words, is to develop the potential of Marx's concepts by deploying them in a critical study of the major social transformations of the past century. This aim can only be attained by proceeding with maximum rigour: it is important not to be confused about the precise meaning of the basic concepts of Marxism. We shall therefore draw on the results of contemporary debates within historical materialism. But in order to concentrate on our own project in a work which has to remain of reasonable size, we shall refrain from detailed commentary on these debates, as well as from any extended exposition of the basic concepts on which we plan to build.

The central issue of controversy over the Marxist conception of the capitalist system is the articulation of the laws of capital accumulation and the laws of competition. This problem will be at the core of our study, and we shall show that it is in fact the nodal point of a theory of capitalist regulation. But our approach can be properly understood only if it is appreciated that the real terms of this problem have nothing in common with the formulation given it by certain neo-classical economists who seek to assimilate Marxism into a version of general equilibrium theory, with its reductionist procedures.[5] For the latter, the key question is whether there exists a system of equilibrium prices, compatible with the technical conditions of commodity production and incorporating rules of distribution of the net product, which can be derived from the amounts of labour necessary to produce these commodities. There can be no doubt that this question is quite foreign to the developmental logic of the basic concepts of Marxism. To study the articulation between the laws of capital accumulation and the laws of competition means to elucidate the contradictory process of the generalization of the *wage relation* and the stratification of the two polar social classes (bourgeoisie and proletariat) constituted by it.[6] It means to ask what determines the hierarchy of social relations and the mode of social unification engendered by the accumulation of capital. It means to subordinate analysis of the movement of individual capitals to that of the social capital, defined by the wage relation or the social relation of the appropriation of both the products of labour and labour-power itself as commodities. It means, therefore, to pose a problem amenable to an experimental method that gives a large place to historical analysis (the study of laws of the social division of labour), instead of a metaphysical problem (the existence of harmony between subjects who are oblivious of one another and are endowed with pre-existing resources and a pre-established rationality).

This book is therefore divided into two major sections: the first part explores the laws of capital accumulation through a study of the transformations of the wage relation; the second explores the laws of competition through a study of the transformations of inter-capitalist relations. These two themes are in no way simply juxtaposed. We shall show, on the contrary, that the competition between autonomous capitals issues from the fundamental antagonism of the wage relation that is the motive force of capital accumulation. We shall see more precisely that the major social transformations of the 20th

---

[5] A critical survey of the attempts to construct a functional relationship between value and price can be found in C. Benetti and J. Cartelier in *Économie classique, économie vulgaire*, Paris, 1975, text no. 3 and appendix.

[6] The central problem of historical materialism is rigorously defined by Étienne Balibar in his essay 'Surplus-Value and Social Classes', in *Cinq études du matérialisme historique*, Paris, 1974.

century, which tend to unify the wage-earning class by the universal extension of the wage relation, also lead to a deep division within the capitalist class by accentuating the uneven development of capitals and reinforcing the concentration of capital. The forms of competition are historically modified to the extent that the expanded reproduction of capital in general imposes its demands on social relations as a whole. This contradictory process does not take place without transforming the structure of the state itself. The more the capitalist class is divided by the changing forms of competition, the more it is impelled to seek its unity in the framework of the state and to consolidate its domination by enmeshing the entire society in state-governed relationships.[7] This leads to both economic and ideological practices of state intervention which constitute a development of basic social relations. We shall use the term *structural forms* for the complex social relations, organized in institutions, that are the historical products of the class struggle.

We intend to show, therefore, how the regulation of capitalism must be interpreted as a social creation. This theoretical position will enable us to conceive crises as *ruptures* in the continuous reproduction of social relations, to see why periods of crisis are periods of intense social creation, and to understand why the resolution of a crisis always involves an irreversible transformation of the mode of production. The concept of a rupture only makes sense in a theory that takes qualitative changes into account – an indispensable condition in the social sciences, where the systems under study cannot be represented by systems of equations whose variables can be continuously differentiated. A social system constitutes a *morphology*, in other words a space structured by relationships subject to the principles of qualitative difference and unequal influence. Such systems develop in a way that reproduces a basic invariant element in each of their component parts, thát is, a determinant relationship whose presence is what assures the system its integrity and cohesion. So long as the reproduc-

---

[7] This is true even when these relations retain a private statute in law (cultural institutions, press, religious and educational organizations, etc.). They form ideological state apparatuses, structures unifying the capitalist class and legitimizing its leading role over society as a whole.

tion of the fundamental invariant is not put in question, the quantitative parameters of the system can develop continuously. But there exist weak points, or zones where corrective mechanisms can break down. In that event a direct threat is posed to the reproduction of the invariant element, and hence to the existence of the system itself. When this happens, the system reacts as a totality to plug the gap by modifying the form of regulation. A change of regime takes place, in a morphological transformation that may be more or less considerable. Ruptures are one such transformation. They cannot be studied by the analytical tools used to scan the stability of an equilibrium in a homogenous space where the possible states of the system are known in advance and its movement is represented by continuously differentiable functions.

Both Parts One and Two contain three chapters. In Part One, the first chapter studies the production of capital – that is to say, it analyses in what way capital is a fundamental social relation denoting a mode of division of labour. The proposition that capital arises from social labour finds its precise expression in the Marxist concept of surplus-value. The analysis of surplus-value in its two modalities, absolute and relative, leads to the formulation of the law of capital accumulation. At this level of abstraction, the law enables the long-run tendencies of capital accumulation in the United States to be surveyed in a general overview. The second and third chapters make the analysis of surplus-value deeper and more concrete by investigating the general meaning of the transformations in the wage relation over the last century. These chapters also enable us to give a theoretical foundation to the periodization of capitalism into successive stages of historical evolution. The criterion for this periodization is furnished by the changing content of relative surplus-value: in the first stage, the transformation of the labour process without major alteration in the conditions of existence of the wage-earning class; in a second stage, the simultaneous revolutionization of both the labour process and the conditions of existence of the wage-earning class.

In Part One of this book, therefore, we reject the idea that the concentration of capital is the most fundamental process in the history of 20th century capitalism. The key theoretical process rather lies in a radical change in the conditions of reproduction of capital in general: hence the theoretical importance of Chapter 3, where we study the transformation in the conditions of existence of the wage-earning class. But as already indicated, the interaction between this transformation and the change in forms of competition is at the heart of the problems of capitalist regulation. Chapter 4 therefore analyses the causes and forms of the centralization of capital. For it is this centralization which determines the fault-lines along which social capital divides into fractions and the structural forms (giant corporation and financial group) in which the control of property is exercised. On the basis of the findings of the first four chapters, the two final chapters tackle the formulation of the laws of regulation proper. Their crux is an analysis of the constitution and operation of the monetary system. The formation of prices can only be adequately interpreted on the basis of a qualitative theory of money, as the expression of the totality of social relations of exchange. We shall show that the concentration of capital provokes an implosion of the forms of competition. There results a coexistence of different price systems representing different modes of transformation of value according to the nature of the constraints that the division of capital into different fractions imposes on exchange relations.

These constraints can only be rendered compatible with one another by an adaptation of the monetary system. But this adaptation in no way follows automatically, given the autonomy of the monetary form of value from the valorization of productive capital. Study of the relationships between money and credit elucidates the conditions of this adaptation, and conversely, the origin of the financial crises characteristic of capitalist regulation. The nature of these financial crises in turn provides an overall perspective on inflation. For it is necessary both to link inflation to its most fundamental determinants, in the transformations of the wage relation and the forms of competition they engender, and to take due account of the protracted and insoluble nature of it as a crisis. In the course of deepening our reflection on the phenomenon of inflation, we shall examine the standpoint that considers it as a crisis of capitalism rather than a crisis that expresses a modality of capitalist regulation. In the process of inflation, in effect, the development of capitalism weakens, and possibly even puts into ultimate question, the laws of commodity exchange on which it is based.

4. Spatial and Temporal Delimitation of the Field of Analysis

As we have indicated already, this essay on the theory of capitalist regulation will proceed via an interchange between conceptual elaboration and historical analysis of the economy of the United States since the Civil War. The selection of this concrete field of reference for our analysis calls for a few remarks.

In the first place, the choice of the economic history of a single country as our starting point, rather than that of the world, is motivated by reasons of convenience as well as principle. Precise conclusions can be reached only after assembling, classifying and interpreting a vast number of data. A work on world economic history with a similar aim to our present study would be beyond the capacity of a single individual. It is certainly necessary, in the interests of theory, to take stock of works on segments of world economic history. Yet there are fundamental reasons for thinking that the cohesion of social relations under the rule of the wage relation necessarily involves the framework of the nation. Contrary to the illusions fostered by the theorists of general equilibrium, the antagonism of the wage relation and the competition between capitals that follows from it cannot be regulated simply by the laws of exchange. The organization of the capitalist class within the bourgeois state, and the development of the structural forms in which it is expressed, are indispensable for the expanded reproduction of capital across society as a whole. It remains no less true that the international expansion of capital forms part of this expanded reproduction, and that a gap is left if this is not studied in detail. Such a study, however, demands knowledge of the general tendencies of capitalist development within the different nations, and careful attention to the relations between states. The gap in question is a sign of the dialectical character of the theory developed here – the fact that it in no way represents an axiomatic system posited *a priori*.

In the second place, the particular selection of the United States is designed to highlight the general tendencies of capitalism in the 20th century. The USA, in effect, experienced a capitalist revolution from the Civil War onwards. The extension of the wage relation brought about a unification of the nation by its own internal dynamic alone. Capitalism developed on the basis of commodity relations without having to combine with archaic social structures foreign to it, which elsewhere acted as a brake on its impetus that had to be overcome for it to advance. We shall certainly have occasion to indicate the peculiarities of American capitalism as we encounter them. But there is no need to fear that these specificities will bring us back from the general to the particular. They have rather an exemplary character for capitalist regulation. For they express the most adequate structural forms for perpetuating capitalist relations of production that the class struggle has yet created anywhere. It is in this sense, in fact, that the United States constitutes a model for all contemporary capitalist countries. The generalization of this model, moreover, in other words the degree of universalization of the structural forms created in the United States, was a decisive aspect of the global domination of American capitalism after the Second World War, and of its most privileged regions of geographical expansion. The study of US capitalism, therefore, affords the best vantage point for developing a theory of capitalist regulation and at the same time throws a sharp light on contemporary European societies.

In the third place, our study is a long-run analysis. This does not mean we have sought, in the manner of statisticians, the longest possible series of data to analyse the inertias in them. It would be a sad error if we were to denounce the reductionist procedures of general equilibrium theorists only to fall into a purely empirical process of reduction of our own. We have already remarked, in fact, that historical time is not a linear temporality in which the variables empirically selected progress mutely forward; it is rather a time that has to be constructed by theory, whose substance is determined by changes in the form of social relations. It is essential, therefore, to accord major importance to qualitative changes, for the interest of a theory of regulation is not so much that it tells us that a

structure is perpetuating itself as that it furnishes the analytical elements for assessing the significance of that which is
new to it. The long-run perspective has sense only in this
context. To interpret what is new, it is necessary to insert it in
the contradictory movement of its formation: we must be able to
account for the ruptures in historical evolution and the genesis
of new social forms, before we can show how these alter the
expression of the fundamental laws of capitalism.

Any scientific study of capitalist development must necessarily start from the production of the material conditions of
social life. The lessons of history, the practices of mass
organizations and the most everyday experiences all combine to
demonstrate that the manner in which material wealth is
produced stamps quite irrevocably the lives of individuals,
social differences, and opportunities for self-development. But
there are snares in the analysis of production which lead the
majority of economic schools to abandon this task. For it
involves an analysis that deals with the meaning of labour in its
most fundamental aspects. Labour is a human activity, and
therefore a temporal process through which human beings form
definite relationships among themselves in the course of transforming their material conditions. Production is always the
production of social relations as well as of material objects. To
take these activities and relations as the starting point of
scientific research in economics, instead of simply subjects,
functions and goods, has a decisive bearing on the field of this
discipline, its object and criteria of scientificity, and its connections with other fields of social science.

The aim of the first part of this book is to establish in what
respect contemporary capitalism reveals the general determinants of capital: a social structure that is produced by labour, but
which subjects labour to the logic of its own reproduction. We
shall see that, far from attenuating this social necessity, the
evolution of capitalism in the 20th century has generalized it to
encompass the totality of social relations. The extension of
wage-labour has made society homogenous as never before, and
yet the enormous growth of the productive forces of collective
labour remains entirely dependent on the accumulation of
capital. The antagonism that this polarization of social activity

engenders is nowadays more and more clearly displayed, and affects every phase of the cycle of daily life in which the reproduction of the wage-earning class is inscribed.

Our study will proceed in several steps. Chapter 1 sets out a general formalization of the law of capital accumulation. This inevitably involves a high degree of abstraction. The results gained at this degree of abstraction are still meagre, but they make it possible to present an overview of the historical evolution of capitalist accumulation in the United States. For the moment, this is still an abstract confrontation between theory and empirical reality. It is not yet an explanation, but it generates a cluster of questions which set the directions for the concretization of concepts in the subsequent chapters. The two chapters that follow deepen the analysis of surplus-value by studying the transformations of the wage relation in its dual aspect as both a relation of exchange and a relation of production.

Chapter 2 analyses the meaning and trend of the collectiviz-ation of the labour process under capitalism. It shows how the abstract character of labour, as the creation of value, pro-foundly transforms its concrete characteristics as the creation of objects. It also shows how labour-power in the wage system is absorbed in production as an element of capital, and why the production of surplus-value leads to far-reaching changes in the organization of the labour process.

Chapter 3 studies the decisive features of capitalist develop-ment in the 20th century. Capitalism consolidated its domi-nation over society and reached its most rapid impetus in a very specific phase of history. This was the phase in which it transformed not only the labour process but also the process of reproduction of labour-power. The social revolutions through which capitalism succeeded in producing the characteristic mode of consumption of the wage-earning class, and in integrat-ing this mode of consumption into the conditions of production, are the chief elements needed to explain the great disturbances of the first half of the 20th century and the exceptional growth that followed the Second World War. In the course of these revolutions, the wage relation developed all the characteristic features that are implicit in its concept. This is why we shall analyse in this context the formation of wages, the link between the evolution of forms of wages and the socialization of consumption, and finally the long-run trends of wages.

5. The Difficulty of Analysing the State and its Theoretical Consequences

Analysis of the state has always been the Achilles' heel of the social sciences. The very division of these sciences into distinct domains, each with very little reference to the others, is itself a token of an inability to constitute the omnipresent yet ungraspable reality of the state as an object for theoretical analysis. As far as economists are concerned, their naïvety vis-à-vis anything that involves the state is a notorious fact. If economists of the classical or neo-classical tradition either ignore the state completely or else reduce it to the role of a palliative agency in relation to the market, writers claiming allegiance to the Marxist tradition also display a theoretical incapacity that reveals major difficulties. Yet historical materialism does provide an explanation of the necessity of the state as a mode of social cohesion required by relations of production that divide society into conflicting groups with heterogeneous objectives and unequal possibilities of action. This starting point, however, has not led to the development of a positive theory of the capitalist state, its historical transformations, national specificities or proliferation of economic functions. It is well known that Marx's own work does not contain a finished theory of the state, but only sparse indications, critical analyses and texts of political intervention. This is undoubtedly where the main difficulty lies. Marxism sees itself as a practice whose aim is to transform society, and yet nowhere more than in connection with the state is a divorce between scientific investigation and practical action more pronounced. A contemporary example is the doctrine of state monopoly capitalism, which assumes as a starting point what might be produced as the result of a theory. The state is seen as an entity that is at once objective and subjective, devoid of internal contradiction, composing a single system together with the 'monopolies'. It is the progressive instrument of the socialization of productive forces, but is also subordinate to the monopolies. This is the system's sole contradiction. The state must therefore be 'freed' from the grip of the monopolies so that the forces of production can also be liberated and a gradual transition to socialism can ensue. Keynesianism, meanwhile, has exercised an influence on Marxist economists in the Anglo-Saxon countries. Here the analysis of the state is entirely subordinated to the problem of effective demand, reinterpreted in a long-run perspective. The result is the well-known problematic of the surplus and its absorption. In this respect there is no substantial difference between Sweezy, an avowed Marxist, and Kaldor, a celebrated neo-Keynesian, except for the pessimism of the former, contrasted with the optimism of the latter, as to the ability of the state to overcome the supposed tendency of modern capitalism to engender a larger surplus than the market can absorb.

In both of these doctrines, the state is defined by its functional purpose or instrumental role. No direct analysis is undertaken of the nature of the social relations that have to generate the specific form known as the state in order to ensure their reproduction. More fundamentally still, economic discourse on the state can be no more than a simulacrum of theory so long as internal analysis of the wage relation is neglected – the essential determinant of the development of the capitalist mode of production. If our aim is to construct a theory of the state, it is necessary first of all to forget the apparent unity of its manifestations, exhibited by the centralized direction of the government, and investigate in what way the most fundamental relations of capitalism involve a separation between the private and the public. We shall see that these relations are the monetary relation and the wage relation. It is then necessary to show why and how the inherent contradictions of these relations give rise to a process of institutionalization, or, as we put it in this work, to the creation of structural forms. The type of sociality that forms the state must thus be conceptualized from within the logic of exposition of the general tendencies of capitalism. For want of research in this direction, the typical economist's vision of the state involves the artificial construction of a global overview on the basis of a very partial foundation. In the Keynesian logic, pushed to its extreme by Baran and Sweezy, it is correctly held that the determination of money wages is not a commodity relation, and that this quantity is the pivot of the circuit of value in its monetary form. An essential feature of capitalist social relations is thereby certainly grasped. But the formation of money wages is not related to the development of mass consumption. The absence of an analysis of the network of social relations that comprises the mode of consumption of the wage-earning class makes it impossible to take into account the reasons that lead to a socialization of the financing of consumption, of the functional usage of the objects produced as commodities, and of expenditures on protection and insurance. Since the structural reasons for the tendential growth in public expenditure fall outside the field of macro-economic arguments, the state figures merely in the form of an autonomous and undifferentiated total expenditure, amenable to manipulation for the purpose of stabilizing cyclical fluctuations. In the logic of the doctrine of state monopoly capitalism, structural aspects are certainly given far greater prominence, but consideration of the wage relation is totally lacking. The state is envisaged simply as a means of regulating inter-capitalist competition and favouring the monopolies. Analysis here is based on the fundamental process of concentration of capital, but it reduces this to the question of whether profit rates are standardized or differentiated, without being able to tell us what the forces are that determine the level of the general rate of profit. The *leitmotiv* of the argument is that by valorizing public capital at a reduced rate of profit or by financing capitalist production in the most concentrated sectors at low cost, the state contributes to raising the rate of profit for the monopolies. This thesis, which has been very widely diffused in France, is represented in the United States chiefly by Victor Perlo.

The theoretical reasons just adduced should make it clear why we dispense in this book with a special chapter on the role of the state. The conception of the state that I share is located in the theoretical tendency represented by James O'Connor in the United States, Manuel Castells in France, Tony Negri in Italy and Joachim Hirsch in Germany, as far as the institutionalization of the wage relation is concerned. I also advance a theoretical analysis of the transformation of monetary conditions, to render contemporary inflation intelligible. Rejecting the idea of a superstructure that acts from outside on a similarly autonomous infrastructure, I shall seek to show rather that the institutionalization of social relations under the effect of class struggles is the central process of their reproduction. The analysis of the state undertaken in this book, therefore, must inevitably be incomplete, since it is restricted to the field of the relations whose historical transformations are the object of its study. But a procedure of this kind, the principle merit of which is that it does not arbitrarily slice social reality into instances, can readily engage with those disciplines that make up the social sciences. Contrary to the economic analyses of the state that rest on a rationalization of the apparent characteristics of economic policy, this approach is open to internal analyses of the political field such as those of Ralph Miliband, which study in detail the organization of the state apparatuses, their penetration by the forces that represent social groups, and the relationships that form within them. The unification of these valuable descriptive investigations with more fundamental analysis of the determinants of social institutionalization should probably take its concepts from the work of Gramsci. By developing the Gramscian concept of the hegemony of a social class in the specific conditions of each nation, it may be possible to overcome the various traps of a structuralism of instances, a sovereign state manipulating macro-economic variables, or an instrumental state in the hands of the monopolies.

6. Imperialism, an Ambiguous Notion Not Studied in this Work

Imperialism is a terrible reality, experienced by millions of people in the world and described in hundreds of books. It is also a term that unleashes political passions without to date ever having unified struggles against the dominant centres of capitalist decision-making. But it is not always a theoretical notion. For here again, dogmatism has long sterilized theoretical research. Imperialism is typically seen in an reductively economistic perspective that distorts its significance. There is hardly a domain in which unswerving fidelity to Lenin has been more damaging. The canonical text in which Lenin formulated what he deemed to be the five defining characteristics of imperialism was essentially a political intervention against his opponents in the Marxist movement of the time. Swiftly written, its economic content resumed results reached by Hobson in his historical analysis of developments on the world market at the end of the 19th century. Essential as they are for the historian, these conclusions are nonetheless simply empirical observations on the international circulation of commodities and capital at a certain epoch in the international division of labour. Like every other empirical phenomenon, they have not survived the conditions that underlay them. Yet the economism that pervades them has persisted, although for Lenin the function of his economic analysis was largely to sustain his immediate political positions of the time. Today, the common feature of economic studies devoted to a positive analysis of imperialism is an eclecticism in which no convergence can be detected. For writers such as Magdoff, imperialism could be described as the extension of a theory of oligopoly onto a global terrain. For others, such as Emmanuel, it is unequal exchange. For others again, distinct national spaces no longer exist from an economic point of view; the internationalism of the technical conditions of production is sufficient to establish a homogeneous world economy in which the capital of the multinational firms is free to seek valorization. Finally, there are those for whom imperialism resides in the exploitation by capital from the 'centre' of the retardation of the societies of the 'periphery', in their destructuration and integration into the world market.

All these viewpoints can legitimately claim to account for one aspect or another of existing international relations, and yet none of them can grasp the full significance of imperialism. Like the power of which it is the most global expression, imperialism is not a notion that can form the object of any explicit definition that originates from economic concepts. Imperialism can only be grasped on the basis of a fully developed theory of the state, capable of studying the significance of inter-state relations in all these mediations and showing that these express the most complex form of capitalist socialization. Henri Lefebvre's recent work goes furthest in this direction. He postulates a basic historical tendency that would invalidate all economic interpretations of imperialism. For Marx, the international solidarity of the proletariat was the process by which a universal society would emerge, inasmuch as the bourgeoisies of different countries were incapable of rising above conflicts of private interest. Marx's interpretation of the wage relation predicted a frontal struggle between bourgeoisie and proletariat that would spill over national frontiers and break up state institutions. Lefebvre, on the contrary, contends that the universalization of humanity has taken the form of the establishment of a *system of states*. On this point, he sees Hegel as correct rather than Marx – an ineffectual superiority, since Hegel believed inter-state relations would realize absolute harmony. The global hold, however, of the state form of institutionalization of social relations reinforces existing antagonisms and gives them the tremendous violence of a conflict of state powers. Consequently a study of imperialism must involve analysis of the network of asymmetrical political influences between states, the conditions of their reproduction or disappearance, and their roots in the most general determinants of the wage relation.

The great movement of decolonization that followed the Second World War has seen the total triumph of the state, and the weakening rather than the strengthening of proletarian internationalism. This was no accident. For the effect of decolonization was basically to remove obstacles to the development of the wage relation. Now this wage relation is not a private transaction that can be interpreted in commodity terms. It denotes the dispossession suffered by a class in a society dominated by private property. This is not a commodity relation. It is the logical contrary to a commodity relation, for it does not involve any exchange of equivalents. It is curious that Marx maintained the classical fiction of labour-power as a commodity in his own conceptual system, even though his decisive pages on primitive accumulation abundantly proved that it was the very opposite. This fiction is abandoned in the conceptual framework used in this volume, in which the wage relation directly gives rise to a division in the abstract space of value. The essential point, as we shall see in the first section of this book, is that the wage-earning class is involved in a mode of access to labour and a condition of life whose continuity goes far beyond the relations of commodity exchange that are reflected in the costs of reproduction borne by capitalist firms. Without a set of social norms, which are always relative and remoulded by class struggles, the conditions of capitalist accumulation would have no regularity. It is true that capitalism, which can be reduced in the pure state to the abstraction of value relations, makes use of the tissue of solidarity and reciprocal obligation of traditional societies. But the capitalist dynamic tears apart this social ethos which forms the substance of an older civil society. It does so precisely to the extent that it extends the wage relation to the detriment of all other relations of production, and transforms the mode of life of the wage-earning class by destroying all communal conduct. New social norms must be centrally instituted, and these take on a state form. The state thus develops by penetrating civil society and profoundly restructuring it. This penetration and restructuration show that *the state forms part of the very existence of the wage relation.* This is why the generalization of the wage relation on a world-wide scale is accompanied by the consolidation of a system of states. We can now catch a glimpse of the full meaning of imperialism: a hegemony difficult to exhibit through which one state manages to influence a series of other states to adopt a set of rules that are favourable to the stability of a vast space of multilateral commodity relations guaranteeing the circulation of capital. It is not the multinational firms that give rise to imperialism. Their existence would be impossible without a system of states maintaining stable relations of unequal influence. It is this system as a whole which is imperialist. It provides the structural conditions thanks to which the logic of accumulation of the transnational firms produces the economic effects that are now so well known.

When we take into account what was said earlier of the difficulty of analysing the state, it will readily be seen that there could be little question of analysing in the present work the system of contemporary states and the transformation that the crises of the 20th century have produced in inter-state relations. It should never be forgotten, however, that the rise of the United States to world hegemony forms an integral part of the social transformations that we are going to study in more detail below. From the formulation of the 'Open Door' doctrine at the turn of the century, through Bretton Woods and the Marshall Plan to Nixon's monetary manoeuvres of 1971, the strategic concern of the US financial community and those industrial interests with an overseas orientation has always been to deploy political influence to ensure the prevalence of those types of social organization in other nations and procedures for settling international conflicts that would safeguard the expansion of American capital. That is why the United States fought so bitterly in Vietnam. It fought not just for certain limited economic aims, but against the danger of a deterioration in the set of rules that had stabilized the system of states since the establishment of 'détente', the creation of the EEC and the extension of Japan's economic influence. If this aspect of American history is ignored, the militarization of the US economy cannot be granted the importance that it deserves. Yet militarism should not be interpreted simply as a convenient means of absorbing a surplus with which the market is unable to cope. It acquires its full meaning only in an analysis of the modalities of American hegemony within the system of states. Yet however major the importance of militarism in this perspective, it should not lead us to forget American monetary domination, which requires protracted theoretical treatment of its own. Rather than superficially treating all these problems together, I have chosen to return to the sources of Marxism in order to construct a set of concepts as a precondition of such investigations.

Part One

The Transformations of the Wage Relation: The Laws of Capital Accumulation

1

The Production of Capital

I. The Creation and Accumulation of Surplus-Value

The central concept giving theoretical expression to capitalist relations of production, central because it defines the economic form in which the labour of society is appropriated, is the concept of *surplus-value*. The starting point of any investigation of the law of capital accumulation is therefore an analysis of the creation of surplus-value and the limits that this encounters. But surplus-value itself depends on a more general concept, that of *value*, which expresses the relations by which particular labour performed in different sites where productive forces are gathered together becomes social labour. These relations are those of the commodity economy. It is essential therefore to define precisely how capital depends on the commodity and how it introduces new determinations in the general field of value. We shall therefore proceed from concept to concept, aiming to show their precise order of logical dependence, in order to identify the whole set of relations which constitute the invariant kernel of the capitalist mode of production, defining it as a mode of organization of social labour. This procedure is necessary if we are not to be deceived as to the significance of the historical changes we intend to study. One essential aim of a theory of regulation, in fact, is to provide a scientific interpretation of the appearance of novelty in the social realm. The theory must seek to answer the question as to whether a new phenomenon is a change in form of the determinant relationships or instead the emergence of relations which can, if they develop, transform the mode of production itself. There is scarcely any need to emphasize the scientific and political importance of this question. But we cannot embark on it without having at our disposal a solid theoretical foundation which is the synthesis of a long collective experience and a longstanding critique of political economy.

1. Abstract Labour and the General Equivalent

For science to be experimental, it must be able to measure the phenomena it studies. The act of birth of a scientific discipline consists in the identification of certain general properties that make of the object to be studied a measurable space. It is its failure in this initial task of abstraction that has rendered neoclassical theory incapable of dealing with concrete phenomena and condemned it to offer us simply a general equilibrium established from all eternity, since for it prices are homogeneous variables for all economic subjects only on condition of a general equilibrium.[1] In economics, the task of abstraction is possible because a process of homogenization exists in the reality to be studied, making the objects under investigation commensurable elements in a space to which a measure can be applied. This process of homogenization is known as *value*, and its concept was first produced by Marx.

(a) Definition of abstract labour. The process of homogenization of economic objects is a social relation. It is the general characteristic of commodity-producing societies, and denotes a mode of division of labour that transforms the products of labour into *commodities*. These products of labour are commodities when they are the products of private labour intended for society in general, whose underlying social character is acknowledged only in an operation of exchange. The exchange transaction realizes the uniformity of products as commodities by establishing an *equivalence* in which private labour appears simply as a fraction of the overall labour of society. This uniform character of labour, as a fraction of overall social labour, is what is known as *abstract labour*. The products of

---

[1] For the inability of neo-classical theorists to confront the problem of value as the construction of an objectively measurable economic space, see the critique by J. Fradin, *Les fondements logiques de la théorie néo-classique de l'échange*, Paris, 1976.

labour are commensurable only from this standpoint. Abstract labour is a social relation that transforms the products of labour into equivalent categories, known as commodities, in a homogeneous space to which a measure known as value can be applied. It is quite correct, therefore, to say that commodities have a value, just as it is correct to say that material bodies subject to universal gravitation have a weight. The utility of a commodity has no more to do with its value than the colour of an object has with its weight. Finally, it is as absurd to speak of the value of labour as to speak of the weight of gravity. It is only their empiricist tradition and their ignorance of the conditions of the mathematical operation of measurement, conditions that require the measurable space to be constructed before it is possible to measure, that have led economists to such aberrations.

In order to understand the significance of abstract labour, let us examine the following formal system, called a system of values. Let there be n heterogeneous products of labour. Let q_{ij} be the quantity of product j needed for the production of quantity q_i of product i. These quantities are heterogenous as soon as different products are considered. No mathematical operation can be performed on these numbers considered by themselves; they do not belong to any measurable space. The homogenization of products as commodities is then expressed by the following system of equations:

$$q_{11} \ VE_1 + q_{12} \ VE_2 + \ldots + q_{1n} \ VE_n + VA_1 = q_1 \ VE_1$$
$$q_{21} \ VE_2 + q_{22} \ VE_2 + \ldots + q_{2n} \ VE_n + VA_2 = q_2 \ VE_2$$
$$\ldots \ldots \ldots \ldots \ldots \ldots \ldots \ldots \ldots \ldots \ldots \ldots \ldots \ldots$$
$$q_{n1} \ VE_1 + q_{n2} \ VE_2 + \ldots + q_{nn} \ VE_n + VA_n = q_n \ VE_n$$

where $VE_1, VE_2, \ldots, VE_n$ are the values of commodities. These values are determinable because the space is rendered homogeneous by the abstract labour $VA_1, VA_2, \ldots, VA_n$, which fulfils the condition:

$$VA_1 + VA_2 + \ldots + VA_n = VA;$$

where VA is the total labour of the society over a certain period. It is essential to bear in mind that these quantities are homogenized by values which themselves flow from a uniformity resting on abstract labour.

(b) Exchange relation and general equivalent. In order for the commensurability of commodities to be completely defined, it is necessary to know the unit by which value is measured. This might seem to be the working hour, as the 'natural' unit of homogenized labour. But it should not be forgotten that the unit of measurement is in no way something to be arbitrarily chosen; it is created by social practice. Abstract labour is an operator expressed in practice in the process of commodity exchange. It is therefore by analysing the form that equivalence takes in this exchange that the unit of measure can be elicited.

Let us consider an exchange effected between two commodities A and B. Let a and b be the quantities exchanged. Examining the exchange equation: $a \cdot VE_A = b \cdot VE_B$, we can convert this into:

$$\frac{b}{a} = \frac{VE_A}{VE_B} = v(A/B).$$

Only actual exchange makes these quantities homogeneous. The meaning is contained in this particular relation, and not in any other. But the equivalence is not symmetrical. It expresses the realized value of A *relative* to B, which plays here the role of representative of abstract labour because the act of exchange is the process by which products are recognized as commodities, i.e. as bearers of a fraction of society's total labour. The ratio $v(A/B)$ is thus the *exchange-value* of A in terms of B. Commodity B, a quantity b of which has enabled the value of A to be realized through an act of practical exchange, is the equivalent commodity. It plays here the role of the measuring unit of value.

Naturally, when the exchange equation refers simply to a single isolated act it might seem possible to reverse the preceding argument and say that it expresses the value of B in terms of A, considering A as the equivalent commodity. But this position would be incorrect. For exchange is not in fact a confrontation of subjectivities, it is rather a social process by which the products of independent private labours are integrated with one another and form fractions of society's overall labour. The universal alienation of these products as commodities is necessary to the manifestation of this integration. The exchange equation is thus the formal representation of the elementary act of exchange as a link in *general commodity circulation.* The law of value, or the general law of equivalence, is the formal representation of the process of homogenization of economic objects. Its field is the general circulation of commodities as the homogeneous social space of abstract labour. This is why the representation of abstract labour is fixed on one single commodity that becomes the general equivalent and is known as *money.*

As the permanent and exclusive representative of abstract labour, money is expelled from the set of commodities proper. Every commodity always expresses its exchange-value in money. Money, for its part, never expresses its value relative to any other commodity, since it never faces any equivalent. It is because it is the pivot of relations of equivalence that the measuring unit for values is expressed in this commodity. If we call the money commodity A and fix a unit to which a name is given (for example the dollar), then the exchange ratios of the infinite series of particular commodities $C_1, C_2, \ldots, C_n$ take the form:

$$v(C_1/A) = a_1, \ v(C_2/A) = a_2, \ \ldots, \ v(C_n/A) = a_n, \ \ldots$$

Exchange values are expressed by positive real numbers which are 'quantities' of money, because money is the homogeneous commodity which is the explicit form of abstract labour. This status of money has an implicit corollary; it is *the monetary expression of the working hour* that indicates of how many monetary units the quantum of abstract labour, the homogeneous element of society's overall labour, is the equivalent. This quantity is in some respects the synthesis of the relationships of equivalence. It is only fixed for certain given conditions of commodity production, a general commodity equivalent determined by the repeated practice of exchange, and a unit of this selected commodity – in fact the sum total of equivalence relations which enable the realization of the total abstract labour by the universal alienation of stabilized commodities. The description of these conditions is already sufficient to show that money is a unit for measuring values which is variable over time. In the total set of conditions, we can define the *monetary system* as the sub-set of those conditions affecting the formation of the general equivalent and the choice of the measuring unit. This definition refers to the variability of the value measurement that is caused by the instability of conditions of commodity production and exchange processes. It is evident that this formal definition is in no way sufficient to characterize capitalist inflation. But we shall see when we come on to investigate this phenomenon later on in this book that it can only be rendered intelligible on the basis of the general determination that follows from the nature of the commodity economy.

(c) Monetary constraint and the definition of total income. Let us return now to the exchange process and study the modalities of realization for the value of a commodity *C*, money being commodity *M*. This problem brings us to the organization of exchange and introduces the notion of utility, which has no place in the definition of value. There should be nothing surprising in this. To understand the position better, let us take an example from outside economics. The laws of motion in Euclidean space are determined by the fundamental equation of Newtonian dynamics. They owe nothing to the reasons we might have for moving around. But if the problem to be investigated is the organization of a traffic system, it is necessary to take into account not just these laws of motion but also the number and the frequency of journeys, which depends on a network of connections in space and does involve the motives behind the journeys.

What we are concerned with here is the system of exchanges, and we know that the principle of exchange is a relationship of equivalence in which value is preserved. Every agent of exchange is equipped with a value materialized as a product of labour, and must find in the general commodity circulation, by means of the exchange transaction, a commodity (one or more) that has some utility for him. This utility has nothing in common with some mythical and generic ophelimity, the phantom of a human nature. It is rather a social utility characteristic of the division of labour. It indicates that each isolated private producer has to find the conditions for the reproduction of his activity in the general circulation. These conditions are both personal, for his labour-power must be sustained, and directly dependent on the production process that he sets in motion.

The relationship of exchange equivalence, as it operates in an organized system, realizes this condition by developing into a

process that Marx calls *the metamorphosis of the commodity*.
This metamorphosis is the unity of a sale and a purchase. The
exchange agent, owner of commodity *C*, sells this commodity,
i.e. there is an exchange against money, which must therefore
be a means of effective exchange and not simply an ideal
equivalent. This is the act *C – M*, the first phase of the
metamorphosis, and at the end of it the value has taken for him
the form of money. In this form he possesses an element of
abstract labour which is by nature a value that remains
constant as long as the monetary expression of the working
hour is unchanged. He can therefore expect to find in the sphere
of circulation a commodity *C'*, the utility he requires, and thus
realize the sale *M – C'*, the second phase of the metamorphosis.
The complete metamorphosis *C – M – C'* thus involves a double
change of form for the value, a change which is realized by
means of a *separation between sale and purchase*. This separation is made possible by the status of general equivalent
possessed by money. It is this separation that makes the
universal alienation of commodities intelligible as a social
process of circulation capable of reproducing the entire set of
conditions of production. By this we can well measure the
absurdity of the neo-classical view which would have us believe
that exchange is a simple process of barter *C – C'* between
subjects each provided with a pre-established and ophelime field
of choice, money being no more than a merely technical
intermediary.

We can now grasp the unity of the social process of exchange.
When all the commodities in the system of values whose
production flows from the division of the overall labour of
society *VA* have completed their metamorphoses, the abstract
labour *VA* has been realized in money. The amount in money
VP, as thus defined, is *the total income of society*. This is
therefore the exchange-value of the net product created by
social labour, known as value added. If the abstract labour is
completely realized in the exchange, and if we call the monetary
expression of the working-hour *m*, then the total income must
satisfy the equation:

$$m = \frac{VP}{VA}$$

This equation is *the monetary constraint*. It is a constraint for the realization of value and not a defining equation. In actual fact, there is a formation of monetary income whenever there is production for exchange. But production and exchange are two separate processes in the social division of labour. If the general commodity circulation does not succeed in realizing the full series of metamorphoses, then one portion of the labour concretely spent in production does not fulfil the conditions of equivalence. This labour then does not form part of social labour. Some products are not sold, they do not become commodities and their producers incur corresponding losses.

One essential point must still be stressed. Social labour is an activity constantly recreated by production. When commodities have completed their metamorphoses and leave the circulation sphere to be destroyed by consumption, they are also annihilated as values. The social income thus disappears as soon as it is realized. There is no way exchange can preserve incomes over time.[2] It is the continuity of production that determines a new total income as the realized monetary form of a new expenditure of social labour. It would be ridiculous to believe that today's income contains a certain fraction that existed in the days of Julius Caesar and has been preserved down to the present. This fantastic notion derives from an inability to conceive of labour as an activity that creates value on the basis of a specific social organization. The economy is seen solely as an exchange, in which labour itself is viewed as a commodity.

Conceptions of time are very closely bound up with those of the social system and the role that exchange plays in it. In the classical and neo-classical conceptions alike, if in different forms, the existence of both commodities and capital are seen as self-evident facts that require no further explanation. Capital stands on its own footing, because it fills the entire social space. The irreversibility of economic time is inconceivable, since everything is homogeneous and no qualitative change exists to create any temporal rhythm. In the general equilibrium, the present is distinguished neither from the past nor from the future. Time is simply one exchangeable good among others whose equilibrium is what determines 'price'. This confusion

[2] On this point, see the critique of the multiplier by B. Schmitt, *L'analyse macroéconomique des revenus*, Paris, 1971.

between present and eternity is expressed by the concept of *discounting*. The logical time of discounting is that of an automatic valorization of capital. It is claimed that what exists today has existed before and will exist for all time.

The conception of time that abstract labour implies is radically different. It is only the time of socially necessary labour that is homogeneous, underlining the predominance of the present conditions of the division of labour. The distinction of production and exchange in the process of socialization of private activities generates the qualitative problem of the social validation of private labours. There is no necessary correspondence between past labour and present abstract labour. This non-correspondence, which issues from the transformation of the conditions of production, is the characteristic feature of a social organization in which private labours can acquire a social character only *a posteriori*. It generates that irreversibility of time that is manifested by a social non-validation, in other words a devalorization, of greater or lesser scope, of the past labour embodied in the means of production. So far as the future is concerned, it exists only at the level of projects, imaginary spaces of private economic agents which are by nature heterogeneous and incommensurable with the space of value.

2. Rate and Mass of Surplus-Value

We shall now introduce the fundamental relation defining the capitalist mode of production by a specification of the general space of value. This relation is the *wage relation* that makes labour-power a commodity. Social labour thereby becomes wage-labour. This relation has a double condition of existence: on the one hand the society in question must be commodity-producing; on the other hand a cleavage must take place within the community of independent producers such as radically to change their situation vis-à-vis production. New relations of production are then created, those capitalist relations of production that we shall study in more detail in Chapter 2. The fundamental constituent of these relations is the appropriation of the ensemble of conditions of production by one section of society, and the correlative transformation of the other section into a wage-earning class. The wage relation thus fully defines social capital, i.e. capital in its most general determination. Capital is the *social relation of appropriation*, as *commodities*, of products of labour and labour-power sold by *free* individuals. Defined in this way, capital polarizes society into two social classes whose situation in production is qualitatively different.

(a) The effect of the wage relation on the field of value. It follows immediately from the preceding argument that labour-power is not a commodity like all others. If labour-power is a commodity, and consequently has a value, its use is labour itself. This is why the wage relation is both a relation of exchange and a relation of production. The use of labour-power in production under the wage system is the creation of abstract labour VA, and this use proceeds under capitalist direction. We may conclude that the wage relation effects a *division* of the general space of value by dividing total abstract labour (VA) into value of labour-power (V) and surplus-value (SV):

$$VA = V + SV$$

This proposition is fundamental. The wage relation is defined in the homogeneous space of value. The cleavage that it introduces is defined directly, and only has any meaning at the macro-economic level. The process of homogenization that value involves is applied fully to the value of labour-power. It is important to pay particular attention to the significance of abstract labour in its application to labour-power. It is true that workers are heterogeneous in the concrete operations of production; this bears on the analysis of the labour process. It is further true that individual labour-power can perform work which is simpler or more complex; this bears on theories of wages and prices. But it is essential to see that these determinations do not affect the general space of value. They bear on transformations conducted in that space, which develop and specify its fundamental laws but are no substitute for them. These determinations will be investigated in due course as we progress from the abstract to the concrete. For the present, what is essential to note is that the division in the space of value effected by the wage relation in its general determination is the theoretical foundation of a macro-economics.

This caution applies equally to the analysis of surplus-value. The mass of surplus-value (SV) is appropriated by the capitalist class as a whole. This is the foundation for the solidarity between all members of this class, a solidarity imposed as a constraint on their divisions as commodity owners. The rate of surplus-value $e = SV/V$, a non-dimensional number as it is a ratio between two quantities defined in the same homogeneous space, is the ratio of its division. Many readers of Marx have been astonished to see him implicitly presuppose, without even justifying his assumption, the same rate of surplus-value in all branches of production. They should not be so surprised, for the problem does not even arise. The rate of surplus-value is a global concept defined in a homogeneous space. It precisely makes clear that capital arises from social labour through the mediation of the wage relation. If it is legitimate to speak of the rate of surplus-value for an elementary production process, it is so only to the extent that this process is an element in the valorization of capital in general, not in so far as it is specific and tied to an individual capital. It can never be repeated often enough that not all economic problems can be treated at the same level of abstraction. Value and the concepts directly bound up with it do not enable one to proceed immediately to the problems of competition.

(b) Relations of production and relations of distribution. Marx strongly insisted that relations of distribution are the reverse side of relations of production. This bears in particular on the division of the total income by the wage relation. We know in fact that this income is the monetary form of abstract labour. The division in the field of value necessarily confers on it this monetary form, which defines the unit of measurement. How does this take place? Here we can only offer the most formal and most general determination. As an exchange relation, the wage relation is expressed in a relation of monetary equivalence, the *wage*. The determination of wages is complex and will be investigated in Chapter 3. Here we can only furnish a formal expression which will suffice to indicate the principle of distribution, even if not its concrete content. In order to understand it, we must see how wages form a very special exchange relation, one completely dominated by the relations of production.

The qualitative difference between the positions of the capitalist and the wage-earner in exchange is as follows. For the capitalist the monetary sum paid as wages is *advanced* in the sense that labour-power is incorporated into the production process and produces value, which the capitalist has at his disposal in the form of the commodities produced; for the wage-earner, this sum is *spent* on the purchase of commodities which are destroyed in consumption. This difference is expressed in the metamorphoses of value. For the capitalist the pattern of metamorphosis is inverted. It is transformed from $C - M - C'$ into $M - C - M'$, with money appearing at the two extremes. The purchase precedes the sale, and not vice versa, because the phases of the metamorphosis are separated by production. It follows from this that the wage contract does not form part of the realization of value in general commodity circulation. It is only the expenditures of the wage-earners that form part of this realization. Now the monetary expression of the working hour takes shape in the general circulation that realizes overall value in proportion to its production. Its development over time evolves with the creation of value which is at the source of the new income which takes the place of that annihilated when commodities make their exit from the circulation sphere. Since it does not enter into relationships of equivalence that determine the present monetary expression of the working hour (m), the conversion of the value of labour-power into wages depends on a quantity $(\overline{m})$ which is a function of the past magnitudes of this variable. In order to study this function, it is necessary to analyse the concrete modalities of the wage contract and the constraints imposed by the reconstitution of labour-power, which we shall study in Chapter 3.

The preceding analysis leads to the following formalization. Let VA be the total mass of value that the society produces. The total revenue VP is linked to it by the monetary constraint: $m = VP/VA$. The wage relation determines a division in the value space which is defined by the rate of surplus-value $e = SV/V$, with $VA = V + SV$. Let us call the total wages paid S, and the wage related to the quantum of abstract labour $\overline{s}$. This we shall call the *nominal reference wage*.

The total wages $S = \overline{m} \cdot V$

The nominal reference wage $\bar{s} = \dfrac{S}{VA} = \dfrac{S}{V+SV} = \dfrac{\overline{m}\cdot V}{V+SV}$

$= \dfrac{\overline{m}}{1+e}.$

Profit is determined by the difference: $P = VP - S$. The resultant macro-economic theory of distribution presents a *division* of total revenue corresponding to the specific character of the wage relation. It is linked to a theory of value and to a conception of the wage relation that already enables us to draw two conclusions.

(1) The foundation of this division is a social relation of production. Its quantitative expression is the rate of surplus-value; but it arises from a qualitative difference in the positions of the two social classes vis-à-vis the conditions of production. This qualitative difference will enable us to analyse the factors determining the evolution of the rate of surplus-value, and thus to show that the overall distribution of revenue depends on the transformation of the conditions of production.

(2) The distribution of income depends crucially on the formative conditions of the general equivalent. We have already indicated that the most general determination of inflation was the instability of the relations of exchange equivalence under the impact of the transformation of the conditions of production and the characteristic properties of the monetary system. We can now confirm in more detail that this instability has a determining influence on the wage relation. The distribution of income is a function of the evolution of the monetary expression of the working hour, because a more rapid increase in m than $\overline{m}$ leads to a depreciation in the equivalence relations of exchange of those rights allocated to the wage-earners in monetary form.

(c) Absolute surplus-value and its limits. Let us start by offering an alternative formulation of the rate of surplus-value. Let N be the total number of workers sharing in the formation of the total value VA. The value space being homogeneous, we may write:

$$VA = N \cdot t_v, \text{ and } V = N \cdot t_n,$$

i.e. relating the magnitudes to the unit of social labour-power.

Let us take the working day, of apparent duration T, as representative of a uniform working period during which the total value VA is created. The time t_n is then to be interpreted as the time socially necessary to reconstitute labour-power, and the time t_v as the uniform time that produces value. The difference $t_v - t_n$ is the surplus labour-time. These times satisfy the double inequality in the working-day: $t_n < t_v < T$.

The rate of surplus-value can be written as: $e = t_v - t_n/t_n$. In this form it is readily apparent that the rate of surplus-value is defined by a relation of production. It is possible in fact to interpret it as the *rate of return* on social labour-power. Under given conditions of production, the duration of labour has to be T so that this rate of return can be obtained. The difference $T - t_v$ forms what might be called the 'pores' of labour. These are such losses of time as result from the organization of the labour process and the capacity of the workers to sustain the pace of work. The increase in the rate of return is thus a function of three factors:

— a decrease in t_n
— a rise in t_v by way of a rise in T
— a decrease in $T - t_v$ with T remaining constant: i.e. the attempt to make the entire working-day actually productive of value.

The set of procedures leading to a decrease in t_n is known as the production of *relative* surplus-value. The set of procedures that increase t_v with t_n remaining constant (whether by a rise in T or a fall in $T - t_v$) is known as the production of *absolute* surplus-value. Detailed analysis of these two types of surplus-value depends on an investigation of the labour process and the conditions of existence of the wage-earning class, which will be treated in Chapters 2 and 3. The present theoretical procedure is simply designed to articulate the necessary concepts which will enable us to proceed to more concrete developments. The creation of absolute surplus-value by the extension of the working day is the earliest method, and played an essential role during the first stage of capitalist industrial expansion. But it still has a role to play in later stages too, in the form of resistance to a shortening of the working day despite the immense growth in the social forces of production. It reminds us that the production of surplus-value is an internal necessity of capital, inscribed in the field of value. Capitalist production is not a production of predetermined utilities in a universe of heterogeneous and original needs.

It is somewhat more complex to interpret the method by which t_v increases while T remains constant. This is the phenomenon of the *intensification* of labour, a powerful method for raising the rate of return. The intensity of labour does not seem at first sight to be expressible in terms of abstract labour-time. Two different intensities are in fact two different densities in the expenditure of labour-power during each hour's work. An increase in labour intensity is obtained chiefly by subordinating labour-power to the continuous and uniform movement of the machine system and increasing the system's speed of operation. But the homogenization effected by exchange involves a reduction of labour periods to an average intensity. Intensity is transformed into extensity. In the overall system of commodity production, labours of different intensities and effected at different dates are distinguished in the different times of abstract labour t_v and t_v' performed in the same space of labour-time T. The intensification of labour can more than make up for a moderate shortening of the working day.

Absolute surplus-value in the strict sense, however, i.e. considered in the absence of any transformation of the labour process, encounters definite technical limits, since a given machine system can only operate within a relatively narrow range. It also and above all encounters social limits, when the working class succeeds in endowing itself with a permanent organization. So far as the intensification of labour is concerned, the possibilities open to workers in resisting a speed-up are far from negligible when the definition of job positions and their organic connection remain unchanged. But this resistance can be broken if the pace of work is increased for the individual worker by simplifying his motions and coordinating them more efficiently in a different allocation of jobs. Absolute and relative surplus-value are thus indissociable from one another. They are what compels capitalism to continuously revolutionize the conditions of production. In investigating the production of surplus-value as a permanent process, we shall study the direction in which technical progress develops, and show that this is subordinated to the extension of capitalist relations of production.

3. Productivity of Labour and Relative Surplus-Value

In studying relative surplus-value we shall be deepening our analysis of capitalist relations of production. This analysis raises new theoretical problems. Up till now we have operated in terms of the homogeneous field of value, in which we have demonstrated the general determination of capital. The problem now is to take into systematic account the transformation of the conditions of production, a material and therefore heterogeneous transformation, and to show how this forms part of a process that modifies value relations in the direction of an increase in the rate of surplus-value. We shall therefore be tackling the problem of the evolution of the standard of measure over time, and thereby will be led to identify the inmost causal sequences of the capitalist dynamic.

(a) Definition of labour productivity. In the production process labour-power appears as an element of capital, inasmuch as it sets material means of labour in motion within work collectivities. These collectivities are systems of productive forces whose cohesion derives from the *cooperation* of the labour-power involved. But this cooperation, which exists in any organized collective process, is only given a direction by the social determination on which it is based. Under capitalism, this is the subjection of the work collectivities to a uniform process of *valorization* that produces and reproduces the social relation of production. This latter is therefore a dialectical relation. On the one hand, the principle component of the relation, capital, arises from labour by way of valorization: the inherent antagonism between the two is conceptualized as the rate of surplus-value. On the other hand, the secondary component, labour-power, is incorporated into capital as wage-labour in certain definite labour processes, each of which is characterized by a particular technical composition of capital, i.e. a combination of means of labour designed for specific uses and labour-power that sets these in motion. For the neo-classical economists, only this secondary component exists, and

is referred to as 'technology'. The problem then is to define the economic categories of income on the basis of the heterogeneous technical combinations that are empirically observable. The Cambridge school has demonstrated that the attempt to do so runs into the obstacle of the standard of measurement, an obstacle that is immovable as long as the mathematical space of measurement adequate to the object under investigation has not been defined at the start. We can add that this defect is itself the result of an ideological refusal, a refusal to acknowledge the social nature of capital.

Marxist analysis has identified the space of measurement as the homogeneous field of value. In this field, the quantities that are measurable and have significance are exclusively those that have been made the object of effective exchange, and have thus been rendered homogeneous by the exchange equation. No scientific procedure could in any way conceive of technological systems, convex or otherwise, that were constructed on the basis of imaginary combinations of quantities. All that can be defined is the *organic composition of capital*. For any production process, the organic composition of capital is the aggregate expression of the technical composition reduced to abstract labour-time. This expression has a meaning because all the elements entering into it are commodities. The value of those commodities that are means and objects of labour is known as *constant capital*. These commodities form one section of the total set of commodities, distinguished by the fact that they are destroyed during the process of commodity production. As this production is a process of valorization, and valorization is the form taken by the division of labour under capitalism, each commodity owner must be able to purchase from among the mass of commodities in circulation the means of production that enable him to repeat his productive activity. This is why constant capital is a value transmitted to the value of the product in the course of production. It is transmitted in full when the means of production is entirely consumed and thus disappears as a value. This is because the social division of labour is a single process of valorization and realization of value that is partitioned into distinct commodities. As this social process continues, value is destroyed by productive consumption, but it simultaneously reappears in a different sector of the social process by the production of commodities designed to replace those consumed. As everything is homogeneous in the field of value, the fact that productive activity takes place in determinate conditions of production that have to be reproduced in conformity with the law of value presents itself as a process of transmission of value which is added to the new creation of value by social labour-power.

We are now in a position to give this analysis a formal expression. Let us consider social production as an overall process of valorization. We know that this process is the creation of a total abstract labour VA over a certain given period. Let us call C the constant capital which is the value crystallized in those means of production that take part in the production process and are consumed in it in the course of this period. The overall valorization is expressed as:

$C + VA = VE$, or alternatively

C	$+$	V	$+$	SV	$=$	VE
constant capital		variable capital		surplus-value		total value of the product

The structure of the social production process is expressed by the following value relations:

$$e = \frac{SV}{V} = \text{rate of surplus-value}$$

$$k = \frac{C}{V} = \text{value composition of capital}$$

$$q = \frac{C}{VE} = \frac{C}{C + V(1 + e)} = \frac{k}{k + 1 + e} =$$
$$\text{value composition of the product}$$

$$z = \frac{SV}{C + V} = \frac{e}{k + 1} = \frac{e(1 - q)}{1 + eq} =$$
$$\text{rate of return on capital}$$

All these relationships are defined in the homogeneous space of value, and have no meaning outside of this space. If the rate of surplus-value indicates the origin of capital, the rate of return reflects the nature of wage-labour, in other words the fact that labour-power is incorporated in the total capital as an ingredient of valorization according to the structure expressed by the value composition of capital.

Labour productivity is defined as those processes of transformation of productive forces over time that raise the rate of surplus-value by modifying the structure of the social process of production. This definition can be made more precise by two very important remarks.

(1) Labour productivity has a social significance in that it bears on the overall production of surplus-value and can only be measured at this level. It is a potential of the organized productive forces which the wage relation transforms into a property of capital in general. But it originates in local mutations of the systems of productive forces because capitalism is a commodity economy. Hence the centres of production are autonomous as far as the initiation of labour processes is concerned, though they are bound together by the general commodity circulation. Labour productivity thus only acquires its social character by provoking instability in the relationships of exchange equivalence. We may say that *labour productivity involves a continuous series of feedbacks from the set of exchange equivalence classes onto itself.* It defines an irreversible temporal transformation. It is possible for theory to conceive this real movement, rather than simply virtual displacements around a general equilibrium, because the value space is always a measurable homogeneous space. The transformation of equivalence relations in no way puts in question the concept of value itself.

(2) Labour productivity can be identified at the overall level with relative surplus-value, that is, an increase in the rate of surplus-value with VA being given. It is therefore a fall in V for a given quantity VA of abstract labour. The transformation of the productive forces which it betokens is thus necessarily *a modification of the technical composition of capital that economizes on labour-power*. This modification is translated into an increase in the organic composition of capital, that is the value expression of the technical composition according to the equivalence relations that prevail at the moment when the transformation of the productive forces occurs. But through general commodity circulation this transformation gives rise to

a disturbance in the equivalence relations. To the extent that this change goes in the direction of a *reduction in the unit value of commodities*, then the growth in the organic composition of capital, as measured in the initial state of the value system, may very well not be expressed by an increase in the value composition of capital once the distortion induced in the value system is taken into account. We are thus led to identify and pay close attention to the causal chain of processes that characterize the transformation of production conditions.

(b) Significance of relative surplus-value. To deepen our analysis of relative surplus-value, it is necessary to note that transformations of productive forces to economize labour-power are processes of *collectivization* of labour by the application of large-scale and indivisible means of production. Now the overall equation of valorization, $C + VA = VE$, leads us to distinguish between the combination of production processes that forms the department producing means of production (Department I) and hence those commodities that are elements of constant capital, and the combination of production processes that produces other commodities and forms the department producing means of consumption (Department II). To avoid any ambiguity it is necessary to note immediately that this theoretical distinction bears on the nature of the valorization of capital in general as we have analysed it above. It has nothing to do with the division into branches that bears on the mode of division and regroupment of individual capitals, and which can only be introduced in the investigation of competition.

The distinction between the two departments is of great importance for relative surplus-value, and consequently for the accumulaton of capital at the social level. The motive impulses in the transformation of the forces of production, in effect, derive from Department I. There is therefore a tendency for the two departments to develop unevenly, as a result of the accumulation internal to Department I. The increase in the organic composition of capital inscribes this tendency into the structure of social capital. But we know that relative surplus-value represents a raising of the rate of surplus-value by a reduction in the time t_n needed to reconstitute social labour-power. It can only be produced by transforming the conditions of production of the commodities produced in Department II. For this to happen, Department II must be able to absorb the commodities produced in Department I, and incorporate these as constant capital in those production processes that lower the value of means of consumption. The development of the two departments must thus necessarily proceed in a certain harmony. Yet the social conditions that promote the uneven development of Department I and those that make possible this harmonization are not immediately compatible, since they are spontaneously independent. They can only be made compatible tendentially, by way of a temporal development of the two departments in which this harmony is created by radical changes in the equivalence relations affecting exchanges between them. Social capital can only accumulate by such radical changes in the value relations that constitute it. We shall see that this theoretical model makes it possible to read the history of capitalist accumulation and interpret the major crises that punctuate it.

The profound significance of relative surplus-value is readily apparent. At the overall social level it represents an economization of the labour-time directly and indirectly necessary for the production of the sum total of all means of subsistence consumed by productive workers. The free time thereby released is transformed into surplus labour-time. This transformation in no way results from the choice of a society deciding, on the basis of an increase in the collective potential of labour, between an expansion of free time and an increase in the surplus commodity product. Capitalist relations of production can only lead to an increase in surplus labour-time. Moreover, the same transformations of the labour process which increase labour productivity are also those that permit its intensification. Time T remains constant or slightly declines, while there is a simultaneous fall in t_n and a rise in t_v. The return on labour-power thus increases very considerably, and with it the mass of surplus-value. But surplus-value must be incorporated into capital; it is capital's very sustenance. The more the socialization of the forces of production has expanded the share of past surplus-value in relation to the overall value of the labour-power producing surplus-value, the more capitalist relations of production demand that this expansion be continued into the future.

(c) Effects of labour productivity on the structure of social capital.
To formalize the causal connections constituting the process of relative surplus-value, let us distinguish three steps which we can denote on our variables by the indices 1, 2, 3. The first step defines the system of equivalence relationships as these exist prior to any change; the second is that immediately following from a change in the organic composition of capital; the third is that which takes into account the effects induced by the revolutionization of the equivalence relations. We shall start by considering the value composition of the product, $q = C/VE$. Our problem is to define the increase in the organic composition of capital as an autonomous increase in q, such that $q_2 > q_1$, and to determine the development of q_3 as a function of q_2, q_1 being a fixed parameter. By the definition of relative surplus-value, it is the overall structure of valorization that changes, the abstract labour that is newly produced remaining constant. We thus have $VA_1 = VA_2 = VA_3$. By the definition of labour productivity, we know that this involves a transformation of the equivalence relations of exchange that has an effect on the social process of valorization. We can represent this effect by a function $f(q_1, q_2 - q_1)$. For the problem we are concerned with here, the general laws of relative surplus-value and not the study of a particular rate of growth in productivity, it is unnecessary to specify f with any degree of precision. We shall consider a very general class of functions of q_2 – continuous, differentiable and increasing for all magnitudes of q_1 and q_2 such that $0 < q_1 < q_2 < 1$. We need only add the initial condition: $f = 1$ for $q_2 = q_1$. The results we shall now obtain do not depend on the precise form of f.

We have already seen why the overall effect of labour productivity passes by way of its influence on constant capital. Steps 2 and 3 are distinctive only by the incidence of this productivity on the value field, so that we can write:

$$\frac{C_3}{C_2} = \frac{1}{f}$$

It follows from this that:

$$q_3 = \frac{C_3}{VE_3} = \frac{\dfrac{C_2}{f}}{\dfrac{C_2 + VA_2}{f}} = \frac{q_2}{q_2 + f(1 - q_2)} < q_2$$

since $f > 1$ for $q_2 > q_1$.

We must stress that this formalization concerns social productivity, which has a rigorous meaning in the Marxist conceptual system. It is effected entirely within the measurement space. It avoids any reference to use-value, which always leads into the swamp of otiose debates over the *a priori* comparison of heterogeneous quantities independently of any process of homogenization.

We still have to see what analytical results can be obtained at this degree of generality. In capitalist production, subject as it is to the primacy of valorization, the resultant effect can be synthetically expressed by the evolution of the rate of return on capital in the value space. This can be written as:

$$z_3 = \frac{SV_3}{C_3 + V_3} = \frac{e_3}{k_3 + 1} = \frac{e_3(1 - q_3)}{1 + q_3 e_3}$$

The development of z_3, clearly enough, can only be analytically known if the function f is specified. But it is not a question of dreaming up mathematical expressions for this function. The problem is rather to descend to a more concrete level of analysis by investigating the historical movement of the forces of production and seeking to summarize their effect on the homogeneous value space. We can, however, establish the following general conclusions.

(1) The transmission of a local mutation in the productive forces is effected by a harmonization of the development of the two departments of social production. If the new productivity is exclusively a function of the development of the department producing means of production, then its only overall effect consists in reducing C_3 in relation to C_2. The rate of surplus-value remains unchanged: $e_3 = e_1$. The exclusive development of Department I, moreover, is also restrained by the market

demand for this department. The difficulties encountered in realizing the value of the new commodities brake the fall in their unit value. The outcome is that, apart from very specific historical periods when capitalist production is rapidly expanding geographically, the decline in value induced by labour productivity does not fully make up for the rise in the organic composition of capital which is at the root of this increased productivity. The situation is then certainly $q_3 < q_2$, but nevertheless $q_3 > q_1$. In this case z decreases. It is incorrect then to claim that technical progress is automatically favourable to capitalist accumulation. *The uneven development of the department producing means of production exercises a depressing influence on the rate of return to capital, despite the technical progress it engenders.*

When the development of the department producing means of consumption permits the new level of productivity to be generalized throughout the field of commodity production, two effects then make themselves felt. On the one hand, the flow of commodities from Department I undergoes massive expansion, with the result that the rise in q_3 above q_1 is greatly reduced and may even be cancelled altogether. Finally, and above all, the general change in equivalence relations leads to a fall in the value of labour-power such that $V_3/V_1 = 1/f$. Since $VA_1 = VA_3$, it follows that $1 + e_3/1 + e_1 = f$. The rise in the rate of surplus-value can counteract, and even more than counteract, the already reduced effect of the increase in q. The rate of return capital can then remain stable or even increase.

(2) The Marxist theory of accumulation is thus indeed a theory of the contradictory development of capitalist relations of production. It is quite contrary to any dialectical procedure to seek a general formal law of evolution of the rate of return. The conclusion we obtain here is far more significant as a guide to historical analysis. The development of the productive forces is, in effect, given a social rather than a technical content. Capitalist accumulation necessarily comes up against obstacles. It derives its impulse from the uneven development of Department I. But this uneven development meets a barrier in the course of accumulation. This barrier, which is always latent, can only be raised if *capitalist production revolutionizes the conditions of existence of the wage-earning class*. It is only by

this social transformation that commodity production can achieve a rhythm of expansion which permits at least a tendential realization of that harmonious development of the two departments which is a necessary condition for a regular rhythm of accumulation. As we shall show later on, this gives us a theoretical basis for characterizing the historical epoch that has arisen since the First World War as a new stage in the development of capitalism. It also gives us an analytical instrument for interpreting the cyclical crises of capitalist accumulation.

4. Accumulation of Capital and Growth in Social Labour-Power

The foundations of capitalist accumulation have now been conceptualized. To express the law of capital accumulation in the field of value, all that is further needed is to translate into a temporal dynamic the phases of transformation of the value relations that we have identified. This involves the construction of the temporality intrinsically characteristic of capitalist production, in a procedure radically opposed to any artificial 'dynamization' of an equilibrium state. This formalization of temporal evolution will enable us to define the rate of total capital formation in value terms, and so deduce the law of development of the value of social labour-power, i.e. the basis of those fluctuations in the labour market that are characteristic of the capitalist mode of production.

(a) The temporal dynamic of capital accumulation as a whole. In order to study accumulation as an on-going process, we need to add a further hypothesis to the results already established. This concerns the division of surplus-value into a portion $a \cdot SV$ which is accumulated and a portion $(1 - a)SV$ that is consumed by the capitalists or allocated to finance the general overheads of society. This is the only hypothesis that can be made at the present level of abstraction, but it is not satisfactory as it stands. While it is clear enough that surplus-value is indeed divided in the manner just indicated, it is no less clear that the coefficient of this division is endogenous and not exogenous. In point of fact, the division of surplus-value bears on the division

into fractions of the capitalist class itself. It has to be investigated in the space of monetary quantities and forms part of the transformation of value into price. The coefficient of division (a) is as it were the effect of an inverse transformation of the laws of distribution of total profit on the space of value. It is only the division of profit that expresses a social law. The image of this law within surplus-value is simply an *ex post* result without major significance.

To simplify the formalization we shall operate with discontinuous time. Let us assume that there exist unit periods of production separated by the dates of the realization of value in exchange. At date $t + 1$, commodity exchanges take place which incorporate the changes in the value relations deriving from increased labour productivity. These are superimposed on the growth in the organic composition of capital which is at the root of the gains in productivity of period $t + 1$. The relationship we have established between q_2 and q_3, at two successive steps in the modification of the value relations, consequently becomes the link between $q_{3,t} + 1$ and $q_{2,t}$ on which the increase in the organic composition between the periods t and $t + 1$ comes to operate, this being $q_{2,t} + 1/q_{2,t} > 1$. We then get the following laws for the evolution over time of the variables defining the value structure of total capital:

$$k_{3,t} = \frac{C_t}{V_t} = \frac{q_{3,t}(1 + e_t)}{1 - q_{3,t}}$$

$$q_{3,t+1} = \frac{q_{2,t}}{q_{2,t} + f_t(q_{2,t}) \cdot (1 - q_{2,t})} \cdot \frac{q_{2,t+1}}{q_{2,t}}$$

$$\frac{1 + e_{t+1}}{1 + e_t} = h_t(f_t),$$

where the function h denotes the degree of harmonization between the development of the two departments of production. In the general case, h is located between 1 and f; $h = 1$ in the extreme case where technical progress is exclusively located in Department I. When the conditions of production do not change, $f_t = 1$, and we then get $q_{3,t+1} = q_{2,t+1}$, since there is no modification in values resulting from productivity gains.

The above relationships determine the temporal profile of accumulation as a function of the increase in the organic composition of capital, once we know the functions f and h that summarize the effect of the development of the productive forces in the field of value.

(b) Rate of growth of capital in value terms. The rate of capital formation evidently forms part of the temporal pattern of accumulation, once the hypothesis concerning the distribution of surplus-value is introduced. Let us call $g_{k,\,t}$ the rate of growth of capital in value terms between periods t and $t+1$. This is defined in the following way:

$$g_{k,t} = \frac{\Delta C + \Delta V}{C_t + V_t}, \text{ with } \Delta C = C_{t+1} - C_t, \text{ and } \Delta V = V_{t+1} - V_t.$$

The distribution of surplus-value at the end of period t is then:

$SV_t = \Delta C + \Delta V + (1-a)\, SV_t$, or alternatively
$a \cdot SV_t = \Delta C + \Delta V.$

From this we derive:

$$g_{k,t} = a_t \cdot e_t \, \frac{V_t}{C_t + V_t} = \frac{a_t \cdot e_t}{k_{3,t} + 1} = a_t \cdot z_t.$$

As we have already explained, there is no reason why the rate of growth of capital should remain constant over time. The profile of capitalist growth is the pattern over time of a movement created by the interaction of the antagonistic forces which we have identified. It is only possible to speak of relatively balanced growth, as a moving average, for historical phases where the social conditions of production are transformed in a way that counteracts the tendency to uneven development of the department producing means of production.

(c) Evolution of variable capital. Let $g_{v,t} = \Delta V / V_t$ be the rate of growth of variable capital. We can dispense here with the index in the notation for the value composition of capital and write simply k_t instead of $k_{3,t}$. We have then:

$$g_{v,t} = \frac{\Delta V}{V} = \frac{V_{t+1}}{V_t} - 1,$$

or,

$$1 + g_{v,t} = \frac{\dfrac{V_{t+1}}{C_{t+1} + V_{t+1}} \cdot (C_{t+1} + V_{t+1})}{\dfrac{V_t}{C_t + V_t} \cdot (C_t + V_t)} = \frac{k_t + 1}{k_{t+1} + 1} (1 + g_{k,t})$$

Substituting for $g_{k,t}$, we get:

$$1 + g_{v,t} = \frac{k_t + 1 + a_t e_t}{k_{t+1} + 1}, \text{ and } g_{v,t} = \frac{k_t - k_{t+1} + a_t e_t}{k_{t+1} + 1}$$

Now, k_{t+1} is generally greater than k_t. From the relationship between k_t and q_t, in fact, we can deduce:

$$\frac{k_{t+1}}{k_t} = \frac{q_{t+1}}{q_t} \cdot f_t \cdot \frac{1 - q_t}{1 - q_{t+1}}$$

Each of the three ratios on which k_{t+1}/k_t depends is generally greater than 1. We also know that it is a sharp rise in f_t that tends to neutralize the increase in q_t. We can therefore conclude that apart from certain transient phases in which q_t undergoes a sharp decline because of the devalorization of constant capital, the value composition of capital rises in the course of accumulation. We shall see, moreover, in investigating crises, that the devalorization of constant capital represents a rupture in the structure of social capital, making it possible to find new relations which re-establish a viable rate of return on capital and set capital formation in motion again.

In the perspective of the law of accumulation as formulated up till now, the determination of $g_{v,t}$ leads to certain general conclusions concerning the tendential evolution of social labour-power.

(1) To the extent that the evolution of k_t may be accompanied by violent oscillations bound up with the uneven development of the two departments of production, these oscillations have their effect on the rate of growth of wage-labour. They create movements of relative expansion and contraction. It may even happen that in certain periods there is an absolute fall in the rate of growth of employment.

(2) The growth of employment is slower in tendency than that of social capital, reflecting a relative decline in the variable portion that follows immediately from the saving on living labour. This tendency cannot be fully compensated by the possibilities of expansion opened by increases in labour productivity. This is the foundation for the creation of a relative surplus population in industry on a growing scale, with ever greater labour being absorbed by unproductive employment created by non-accumulated surplus-value.

(3) The rate of growth in total capital forms an upper limit on the extension of the wage-earning class.

The specifically capitalist law of population is therefore in no way a natural law, but forms part of the law of capital accumulation, as Marx unambiguously maintained. 'The appropriate law for modern industry, with its decennial cycles and periodic phases which, as accumulation advances, are complicated by irregular oscillations following each other more and more quickly, is the law of the regulation of the demand and supply of labour by the alternate expansion and contraction of capital, i.e. by the level of capital's valorization requirements at the relevant moment, the labour market sometimes appearing relatively under-supplied because capital is expanding, and sometimes relatively over-supplied because it is contracting. It would be utterly absurd, in place of this, to lay down a law according to which the movement of capital depended simply on the movement of the population.' (*Capital*, Volume 1, NLR/Pelican edition, p. 790.)

II. An Overview of Capital Accumulation in the United States

By formalizing the law of capital accumulation in the first section of this chapter, we introduced the concepts needed for an overall perspective on its historical movement. These will now guide our investigation of 'stylized facts'. The task of the theorist in approaching historical analysis is to investigate what is fundamental in the evolution of a social formation over a certain historical period, the limits of which have themselves to be justified. Research of this kind does not start from raw

facts, but rather from an elaboration of results already produced by historians. There is therefore a dialectical relationship between different aspects of the scientific procedure, which
can be interpreted as a passage from the abstract to the
concrete. This is no royal road where the most abstract concepts
magically command the movement of society. There is rather a
two-way process marked by frequent mishaps, often uncertain
in its results, where the objective is the development of concepts
and not the 'verification' of a finished theory. This development
of concepts involves a permanent questioning of received
judgements on the facts. It rejects as illusory the claim that an
inductive procedure can 'go beyond the facts' and reach
concepts in a linear itinerary. The need for a dialectic in the
relationships between thought and reality arises because facts
are not atoms of reality to be classified, linked and assembled.
Facts must rather be treated as units in a process, or articu-
lations between relations in motion, which interfere and fuse
with one another. They can only be grasped by the collaboration of different modes of investigation, and this is why the
concrete can be reached in thought only at the end of a
globalizing procedure in which deductive and critical moments
interact.

These few methodological indications are intended to avoid
any misunderstanding in the pages that follow. The main aim of
our preliminary confrontation between the theory of accumulation and the general lessons provided by the history of US
capitalism is to generate questions that will enable us to
develop our theory and make it more concrete in the subsequent
chapters. This is a legitimate ambition, since our prior formulation of the law of capital accumulation already takes into
account the transformation of the productive forces as a
necessary component of the expanded reproduction of the wage
relation. This is the meaning of relative surplus-value. This
endogenous character of the productive forces arises from their
social determination. We saw that their transformation involved two different aspects: the transformation of the labour
process and its conditions, and the transformation of the
conditions of existence of the wage-earning class. These two
aspects are not brought into harmony by any social rationality;
it is rather the class struggle that here determines the actual

movement of history. This movement is all the more governed by the logic of accumulation, the more the class struggle occurs in modalities that are compatible with the extension of commodity exchange. The conditions for such a canalization of the class struggle involve the totality of social relations at any given time, and it is their study that forms the content of the theory of capitalist regulation.

The first task is to investigate whether it is possible to give concrete form to the principle of accumulation formulated in highly abstract terms in the first section of this chapter. Our aim will not be to periodize the history of the United States by identifying epochs that are allegedly homogeneous and separated by dates seen as marking events that induced irreversible changes. Such a claim would be ridiculous coming from a non-historian. It could only lead, moreover, to unending controversies among specialists lacking theoretical criteria. History as actually lived is infinitely prolific and heterogeneous. Historians have developed a method of scientifically investigating this reality, but in no way any overall principles of interpretation. Such principles, moreover, could only belong to the philosophy of history, since they necessarily involve judgements on the final goals of human societies. There can be little doubt that a vision of such a kind is contained in the work of Marx, for whom capitalism inevitably leads to the abolition of social classes, i.e. the end of history in general, since history is nothing but the history of class struggles. The present work does not keep faith with this philosophic vision. It simply accepts that the class struggle produces, transforms and renews the social norms which make economic relationships intelligible. These relationships have conditions of validity which are narrowly limited by the persistence of the norms which gave rise to them. At our present level of knowledge of the problems of social transformations, we can accept here that if the class struggle produces norms and laws which form the object of a theory of social regulation, it is itself beyond any 'law'. It can neither be assigned a limit, nor be confined by a determinism whose legitimacy could only be metaphysical. In a situation of historical crisis, all that a theory of regulation can do is note the conditions that make certain directions of evolution impossible, and detect the meaning of the actual transformations under way. Thereafter, however, the future remains open. Historical development is totally different from biological evolution inasmuch as it is governed neither by chance nor by a hereditary determinism. *History is initiatory.* But it is only possible to construct a theory of what is already initiated – which puts a decisive limit to the social sciences.

The reasons why it is impossible to reconstruct the movement of past history are therefore the same as those that prevent any prediction of history in the making. We can act in history, but not calculate it. Even though it is rooted in existing conditions, the class struggle goes beyond them in producing social institutions and procedures that are not rearrangements of these conditions. It is a process of creation in the strong sense. The object of theory cannot be to prescribe what is going to happen or what must happen in this creation, but rather to show how under capitalism this creation is a permanent process. Accumulation reproduces the relations of production by constantly transforming their operation. In order to achieve a precise analysis of the forms of regulation under capitalism, it is necessary first to define an intermediate concept, less abstract than the principle of accumulation so far introduced. This is the concept of the *regime of accumulation*. In the second section of the present chapter, we shall analyse the history of the United States not so as to periodize it, but rather to define a theoretical object, the regime of accumulation.

A regime of accumulation is a form of social transformation that increases relative surplus-value under the stable constraints of the most general norms that define absolute surplus-value. This definition requires us to deepen the concepts of absolute and relative surplus-value which we have distinguished analytically in the preceding arguments. It might be thought from these arguments, whose aim was to grasp the quantitative aspect of surplus-value, that absolute and relative surplus-value were two alternative modalities, forms that could be substituted one for the other in the production of a social surplus. This is in no way the case. The distinction between these two forms of surplus-value denotes an articulation of social relations that induce different but complementary practices.

Absolute surplus-value, as we have seen, is the effect in the homogeneous field of value of the wage relation as a general process of separation between individuals, and separation of the power of disposal over the means of producing their conditions of existence. Individuals are transformed into wage-earners, i.e. they are made indifferent and interchangeable as far as production is concerned. This is an abstraction engendered by social separation, an abstraction which alone makes it possible to speak of labour in general and not just some trade or other that is qualitatively defined, access to which derives from particular procedures that are ritualized and codified by craft organizations. Access to wage-labour, on the contrary, derives from general norms, the extent of whose application depends on the organization of political and judicial powers, but is in any case delimited by a national territory. The wage relation can be fully established in such a territorial space only if the sovereignty of the state comes to be identified with the nation. Such norms are inherent to the wage relation: they are social practices that are partially contractual and partially coercive. It is thanks to them that surplus-value can be produced as an on-going process. They are therefore the determinants of absolute surplus-value. In Chapters 2 and 3 we shall be studying the historical evolution of these norms and their organization into a wage system. For the time being, we formulate them simply so as to define more precisely the theoretical content of a regime of accumulation:

— With regard to the utilization of labour-power in production: the fixing of the legal duration of labour on which the basic hourly wage is reckoned, as well as the rate for overtime; maximum working hours; the limiting ages for individuals to enrol for wage-labour; the extent of capitalist freedom to hire and fire; and the regulation of legitimate trade-union practices.

— With regard to the determination of wages: general procedures for negotiation of the basic hourly wage; regulation of its application; and the arbitration of conflicts that arise.

— With regard to the socialized management of the reproduction costs of the wage-earning class: standardization of the insecurity due to mobility of individual labour-power by means of unemployment benefits and public job-creation or retraining programmes; standardization of risks of temporary disability by systems of insurance, whether compulsory or contractual;

standardization of deferred wages by retirement schemes.

Relative surplus-value is the concept that defines the unity of the relations which structure the concrete organization of the production and reproduction of the wage-earners. Based on the general principle of abstraction inherent in absolute surplus-value, a principle that involves a fundamental lack of differentiation between individual wage-labour units, relative surplus-value structures the wage-earning class according to a spectrum of desired differentiations that are purely *quantitative*: output norms for the work of specific collectives as divided up into branches of production, systems of grading for skill and wage hierarchies, rates of possession and thresholds of access for different types of use-values, etc. It is these differentiations within a measurable space inherent to the wage relation that make it possible to use statistical tools in the socio-economic analysis of capitalism. Yet such analyses do not yield the secret of its social dynamic. Their scientific interest is to give a representation of the influence of social norms of different degrees of generality, or their combination, which determine the official principles of classification of socio-economic categories. These latter are not living collectivities, but rather abstract groupings defined by statistical manipulations within the undifferentiated mass of the wage-earners. More fundamentally, the classificatory procedure that assigns social positions according to abstract criteria is the mark of the penetration of the state into civil society. This mode of state organization, in fact, extends to all enterprises that subordinate major work collectives to the abstract and exclusive objective of capital valorization. As we shall see in detail in the following chapters, *a classificatory and identificatory logic*, in other words abstract institutional codes for social positions, partakes of the very essence of capitalist social relations. It is the principle of the systematic institutionalization of society. It is radically opposed to the unification of so many traditional societies by way of myth, custom, and a tight network of interpersonal obligations, by a solidarity of community and neighbourhood. It is because capitalism does not simply utilize in its production workers who still continue to live according to the rules of a traditional community, but penetrates into their whole mode of life, that it necessarily breaks up civil society and recombines it according to the logic of abstract classification and stratification. It is the systematic operation of this logic that defines the production of relative surplus-value.

These explanations make it possible to indicate the argument that will follow in the second section of this chapter. We shall attempt to characterize two regimes of accumulation which we call the predominantly extensive and the predominantly intensive. It should be clear by now that these are concepts required for the development of a theory of social regulation, and not for a periodization of concrete history. Throughout the historical period under consideration, the two regimes of accumulation were combined together, and yet the process of capital accumulation assumed a different pattern according to whether one or the other dominated. There are theoretical reasons for this combination, since absolute and relative surplus-value are distinct but associated components of the system of social relations that makes up wage-labour. The combination of the two is effected in the organization of labour and the mode of life of the wage-earning class.

The predominantly extensive regime of accumulation is that in which relative surplus-value is obtained by transforming the organization of labour; the traditional way of life may persist or be destroyed, but it is not radically recomposed by the logic of utilitarian functionalism. Only agriculture is affected, by the formation of the agricultural-foodstuffs complex. The division of society effected by classificatory and identificatory logic operates on working time in production in the strict sense. Its material support is mechanization. The general movement of accumulation that follows from it is the build-up of industry in successive layers. The combined development of the two departments of production is achieved only with difficulty, the pace of accumulation encountering recurrent obstacles.

The predominantly intensive regime of accumulation creates a new mode of life for the wage-earning class by establishing a logic that operates on the totality of time and space occupied or traversed by its individuals in daily life. A social consumption norm is formed, which no longer depends in any way on communal life, but entirely on an abstract code of utilitarianism. This norm is stratified according to principles that closely correspond to the stratification of social groups within the wage-earning class. The intensive regime of accumulation accomplishes an integration of the two departments of production that makes possible a far more regular pace of accumulation and a far more rapid increase in the rate of surplus-value.

Before proceeding to detailed study of the different notions that have just been introduced, it must also be noted how this theory of accumulation is distinguished from the neo-classical conception of growth. The theory we shall seek to elaborate here is in reality a theory of development of the wage relation. Our aim is to grasp the source of this dynamic in order to be able to interpret the modes of societal cohesion from which economic relationships can be derived. The neo-classical conception of growth is devoid of any basis, since its theoretical schema is the general configuration of market adjustments from the starting point of rules of individual decision. Adjustments of this kind are only rational if the structural conditions of the choices involved are given and invariant. Now the transformation of these structural conditions is not only certain, it is the very rationale of capital's dynamic. This is why theories of markets are totally unable to account for processes of development. The cohesion of these processes cannot be found in the markets themselves, but only in a social logic, which we call here the regime of accumulation. For want of any direct analysis of these processes, models of growth are simply formal exercises in which technical progress has no concrete significance, social demand plays no role, and time itself has nothing in common with the specific irreversibility of a genuine social dynamic.

1. General Conditions of Development of the Forces of Production

The characteristic mode of existence of developed capitalism is large-scale industry with its mass production. Yet capitalist relations of production do not just arise from thin air. They derive historically from the formation of the wage-earning class by the gradual dissolution or destruction of previous modes of production. This movement, moreover, can never be the product of an exclusively economic logic. It requires political relations adequate to the domination of the industrial bourgeoisie, and decisively involves the role of the state. The conditions under which state power is exercised may be more or less favourable to the implantation of capitalist relations of production on the terrain of the commodity economy. The rhythm and forms of penetration of these capitalist relations of production form the specific infrastructure of a particular social formation. It is this social infrastructure that enables us to grasp the differences in the development of the productive forces between different social formations. From this point of view, the United States displays major originality.

(a) The frontier principle as a specific mode of capitalist penetration. All forms of precapitalist production have agriculture as their productive base. The fundamental economic condition for industrial capitalism to develop is the formation of a growing agricultural surplus product and its realization in commodity form. In the United States this condition was enormously favoured by the existence of an immense reserve of unappropriated agricultural land. Yet it was made a reality above all by the political origins of the American nation, which united petty producers with the commercial and financial bourgeoisie in a common struggle against English colonial rule. This struggle, whose aim was freedom of enterprise, left a permanent mark on the ideological representations of American social relations and created political institutions governed by those general principles that are the legal formalization of relations of commodity exchange.

The type of juridical subjectivity that reflects the general reification of commodity-producing societies was all the more decisively imposed within the new American nation inasmuch as there were no organic ties to precapitalist forms of production. This juridical ideology condensed the formal liberty and equality of individuals as economic subjects endowed with initiative, as political subjects electing their representatives, and as cultural subjects giving and receiving opinions. All social activities were conceived as exchange relationships formed and unformed by the will of the contracting parties. This conception of social relations involved an irreparable rift between theory and practice. At one pole there developed a positivism bearing within it economic utilitarianism and pragmatism, at the other an idealism which in the United States took an essentially religious form. This representation of society was able to impose itself so uniformly in the USA because it was not merely a static ideology, but was linked to the dynamic expansion of the frontier. The energy that individuals expended in their economic competition did not merely reproduce a stable social order, it actually created new social relations. The frontier principle was more than is implied simply by its literal content, in other words the mere domestication of a geographical space. It was rather an ideological principle expressing the ability of the American nation to polarize individual activity in a direction of progress. Indeed the industrial bourgeoisie was later able to get the whole of the nation to accept the technological transformations induced by relative surplus-value by presenting these as the building of a 'new frontier'. The development of capitalism and the construction of the nation were thus identified as one process in the popular consciousness. The ideological institutions of capitalism absorbed intellectuals originating from all social strata; bourgeois representations of the world were constructed without resistance; the juridical principles of the state took on a sacred and eternal character. Any questioning of free enterprise was perceived as a threat to the integrity of the nation.

Liberation from colonialism thus removed the political brakes from both geographic and economic expansion. Expansion became the dominant phenomenon of American life; it could almost be identified with the country's history. This expansion was the conscious work of broad masses of the population over successive generations. The community of petty producers who built up the frontier economy were never the agents of an agricultural economy geared to mere subsistence. As the frontier expanded, and the communications network became denser in the geographical space behind it, the relative economic conditions of the different regions underwent a change. The mobility and mutual competition of producers was sharpened by the permanent influx of new arrivals. Competition for the private appropriation of the best situated and most productive land lent extraordinary importance to speculation in real estate. Such speculation was fuelled by any major change in economic conditions, in particular irrigation projects and the construction of railways from the 1840s onwards. With the end of the Mexican-American war, the period 1846–48 saw the incorporation of California into the USA and the simultaneous discovery of gold there. These events unleashed an extraordinary wave of speculation, plunder and monopolization of land by every available means of violence. After 1848, moreover, the world capitalist economy embarked on a long phase of expansion which stimulated American agricultural production. The space of commodity circulation expanded, and agricultural prices rose. A massive wave of immigration and migration to the West in search of opportunities for profit shook frontier society. Land prices rose rapidly, and with them the sums paid in settlement of inheritances. The more land prices increased, the more monetary resources were needed by new would-be producers or old producers seeking to extend their holdings or move into regions where the possibilities of expansion were more propitious. The upshot was that in order to bring its owners the monetary yield they needed the agricultural surplus product had more and more to take commodity form and to circulate in a wider space, thereby stimulating the extension of means of transport.

These were the ideal economic conditions for capitalism to take hold in the new economic spaces in course of formation. Commercial and finance capital was already well established in the eastern states, where it flourished on the basis of international trade. From the 1850s onwards, the development of the transport system led to the creation of new urban centres to the west of the Appalachians, which became trading sites and foci for the formation of new capital, illustrated by the multiplication of banks. In California, mining operations and the expropriation of Mexican latifundists gave rise to an explosive centralization of capital. But the major part of this economic expansion, depending as it did right from the start on the centralization of financial resources for the extension of the railways network, was directed by the financial powers of the East. The spearhead of capitalist encroachment on agrarian property was the establishment of railway and mining companies, which were above all else capitalist associations for engrossing land. These companies obtained huge concessions for the construction of the transcontinental railways; the

Federal government made them gifts of immense swathes of land on either side of their lines. The railway companies were financed by vast share issues and state loans. The same enterprise that owned the railway thus typically also came to own all natural resources on the soil granted it. These lands, obtained gratis and now monopolized, were now increased in value by the railway line, whose construction cost the company's initial promoters nothing. They were subsequently sold off in small plots at very high prices, or alternatively leased.

In those regions where land was already apportioned, the companies managed to buy back the land that they needed at low cost, using every possible means of intimidation, one of these being to threaten the population of the towns and settlements along the proposed route that the railway would be diverted elsewhere if local authorities did not grant them the land they wanted on their own terms. The inhabitants of these towns were also forced to subscribe to loans issued by the companies and guaranteed by public authorities; municipalities likewise had to devote a good portion of their fiscal resources to railway finance. From the Mississippi to the Pacific coast, railway and mining companies, along with other financiers involved in monopolizing land, also had at their disposal the trusty weapon of water control. It was enough to seize the watersheds overlooking the rich valleys either side of the Rockies in order to ensure dominion over immense territories; it then became possible to buy up particularly profitable land, or land with a strategic importance, and to hold the rest to ransom. The western states passed very flexible legislation that closely met the requirements of the dominant financial groups. Eventually, the increase in land prices brought small-scale producers into intensified competition to sell their agricultural product. Local commodity circulation rapidly became insufficient. The mechanism by which petty commodity production was subordinated to capitalism was now clinched by several processes that supplemented the direct monopolization of the land which we have just outlined. Firstly the need to expand the circulation of agricultural products put small-scale producers at the mercy of the railway companies for transporting their goods; these appropriated a portion of the agricultural surplus

The Production of Capital 77

in the form of prohibitive and discriminatory tariffs, an additional arm in their strategy of expansion. Subsequently the growth of taxes and rents, and the need to take out loans to finance their own subjugation to the companies as the price of land purchase escalated, forced the small producers into debt vis-à-vis merchants and bankers. This led to the rapid spread of mortgages and increased indebtedness because mortgage loans had to be repaid. By the outbreak of the Civil War, capitalist domination over petty commodity production was already well established. The transport infrastructure that provided its precondition was in full development, and the monopolization of mining resources was also well under way. The Civil War was at once to accelerate and to modify the process qualitatively.

The American Civil War was the final act of the struggle against colonial domination. This is why it is legitimate to see it as the origin of the modern epoch in the overall trajectory of the American capitalist revolution. The slave form of production in the South owed its existence and its prosperity to its total integration into an English-dominated international trade. It blocked the unification of the American nation at every level, and threatened to put an end to the frontier expansion. The long phase of industrial growth in England after 1849, with its strong demand for agricultural raw materials, including cotton, incited the slaveowners to expand their territory. Hence slavery gained new footholds in the lands conquered in the Southwest. In this way slavery braked the expansion of the textile industry and other industries using sub-tropical raw materials, and prevented the exploitation of immense mining resources. The slaveowners also exercised a preponderant influence in Congress, sufficient to thwart any protectionist policy. Industrial capitalism thus suffered as a whole, for the pilot industries of the economic division of labour were unable to withstand English competition. What was at stake in the Northern war effort was thus simultaneously the direct penetration of capitalism to the entire territory of the Union, the establishment of tariff protection, and the political and ideological unification of the nation under the leadership of the industrial and financial bourgeoisie. The reasons for the political alliance between the capitalists and the small agricultural producers are clear enough. The latter feared above all else the extension of the slave system to the free lands of the West, and the blocking of the sale of public land by a Congress dominated by the slaveowners' representatives. Finally, these fiercely individualistic petty producers were also very strongly attached to the ideology and institutions of bourgeois democracy. Yet they were soon to find out to their cost that this was an alliance with the devil himself.

The Civil War gave a vigorous impetus to the development of the forces of production in the United States. Economic exchange between North and South was disrupted, and imports from England reduced. The war effort in the North mobilized all industrial resources and promoted accumulation in those branches of Department I involved in the production of armaments, explosives and weapons, as well as the extension of communications routes. There was also major military demand for the articles of the textile industry and for food products, while army recruitment led to a great scarcity of labour-power. This circumstance favoured a very rapid advance of capitalist methods of production in the department producing consumer goods. Mechanization was undertaken in the textile and leather industries, enabling women and children to be employed. In agriculture the increase in demand gave a bigger stimulus than ever to production for exchange-value. Producers became indebted to the banks, who lent them paper money (greenbacks) issued as legal tender to finance the public debt. The immediate post-war period saw expansion continue at a rapid rate, propelled by the construction of the transcontinental railways. Only with the outbreak of recession in 1873, and the long phase of depression that lasted until 1897, did it become evident that the articulation of modes of production in the social formation had been profoundly changed. *Petty commodity production had gradually been integrated into capitalist production.* This integration created a permanent tendency for labour productivity to rise in agriculture, and induced a major expansion in the output of agricultural equipment. There developed a strong tendency for farm prices to fall, settling at the minimum level required to provide sufficient money to maintain a farming family, plus the valorization of the capital lent by marketing firms and banks. The downturn in agricultural prices was in turn decisive in bringing about a fall in wages. It not only favoured accumulation in the department producing means of production; competition in agriculture also permitted the development of a powerful foodstuffs industry. One of the main patterns of interaction between the two departments of production thus found the conditions for its development much earlier and more thoroughly in the United States than in the major European capitalist nations. This interaction by way of foodstuffs reinforced the radical separation between town and country required for the extension of commodity circulation over a vast economic space, and for the deepening of the social division of labour in the USA.

(b) Transformation of the conditions of existence of the wage-earning class. A long historical process which began at the start of the 20th century has seen the penetration of capitalist production into the internal organization of towns, and into the production of means of individual consumption for the broad mass of wage-workers. These two accomplishments have been closely linked together. They enable us to understand how capitalist relations of production could spread over the entire field of social activities, and subordinate the rationality of these activities to the equivalence of commodity exchange – thereby realizing its full potential across the whole social formation. As long as capitalism transforms the labour process by the creation of collective means of production, but without reshaping the mode of consumption, accumulation still progresses only in fits and starts. The regime of accumulation is principally an *extensive* one, based on the build-up of heavy industry section by section. The resultant jerkiness is a function of the uneven development of Department I, which lowers the overall rate of return on capital and requires phases of depression in which the value composition of capital is reduced by the destruction of a portion of the capital invested in production.

In the United States, the most powerful heavy industry in the world was built up at an exceptionally rapid pace in the last third of the 19th century. The speed of this process resulted from the specific social conditions which we have briefly resumed as the frontier principle. It was also related to the peculiar modalities of the formation of the wage-earning class in the

United States, which we shall shortly examine. We shall see that these modalities favoured the historical transition of the USA to a regime of principally *intensive* accumulation, based on the transformation of the conditions of existence of the wage-earning class. Here we put forward the following proposition, to be demonstrated in the further course of this work: when the accumulation of capital finds its content no longer simply in a transformation of the reproduction of the labour process, but above all in a transformation of the reproduction of labour-power, a new stage in capitalist development has arrived. This stage bears with it quite new forms of the wage relation. It alters the stability of equivalence relationships in exchange, and modifies the monetary system. The precise operation of the law of value, therefore, the fundamental principle of commodity regulation, depends on the conditions in which the wage relation is generalized across the whole of society.

When capitalist relations of production spread by the manufacture of collective means of production, the resultant creation and expansion of the wage-earning class generates a double structural change: a separation between labour-power and means of production, which are combined solely in the labour process under the authority of capital, and a destruction of the spatio-temporal environment moulded by precapitalist forms of production. This environment is characterized by close relationships between town and country, by a rhythm of work punctuated by season and stabilized by custom, by an incomplete separation between productive and domestic activities, and by a *domination of non-commodity relations over commodity relations in the mode of consumption* – non-commodity relations finding the conditions for their existence within the extended family and neighbourhood community.

There is no reason why the two components of this dual structural change should occur together. Capitalism can implant itself for a long historical period without destroying traditional ways of life, indeed even benefiting from the reconstitution of labour-power by a non-capitalist environment in which it is still inserted. For the latter makes it possible to pay very low wages and impose very long working hours. In this period, however, the wage relation is not fully established. The destruction of the traditional social environment is only accomplished by the development of heavy industry, which enforces the total uprooting that is characteristic of the wage relation: the separation of labour-power from all its conditions of existence. The mode of life of the wage-earning class then suffers a deep degradation. This degradation is the basis of the gigantic structural transformation that all the capitalist countries experienced from the end of the 19th century through to the middle of the 20th, with the exception of England, which experienced it somewhat earlier and over a more protracted period. The logic of this structural transformation is the production of a new mode of consumption expressing the complete realization of the wage relation. This mode of consumption is characterized by the *domination of commodity relations over non-commodity relations*. There is no such thing as a consumer society, but there certainly is a universal extension of the capitalist mode of production in the social formations in which it is implanted. Capitalism can reproduce itself only by an incessant accumulation which develops as a mass production and consumption of commodities, a phenomenon generalized to embrace the sum total of activities of social life.

To develop the law of capital accumulation and interpret the fundamental characteristics of 20th century capitalism, we must analyse the transformations of the wage relation from a four-fold standpoint:

(1) The standpoint of capital – in other words the contradictory evolution of accumulation in its dual tendency to an uneven development in Department I and a deepening of the social division of labour in Department II, as the commodity consumption of the wage-earning class increases. This involves a study of the changing forms of competition in the context of the increasing density of exchange relations between the two departments of production.

(2) The standpoint of the productive forces – in other words, the transformation of the organization of production under the constraint of relative surplus-value, involving an interaction between the transformations of the labour process and the homogenization of the mode of consumption of the working class. We shall see, in fact, that the socialization of consumption

in the form of the generalization of commodity relations influences the formation of wages and the use of labour-power in production.

(3) The standpoint of wage labour – in other words, the production of infrastructures and the creation of new forms of the wage relation that enable the wage-earning class to purchase all the conditions of its existence in the general circulation of commodities. These transformations can be interpreted as the formation of a *social consumption norm*.

(4) The standpoint of the commodities consumed – in other words, the adaptation of the use characteristics of the objects of consumption to mass production, and the diffusion of a functional aesthetic that structures the consumption norm; the rate of penetration of new commodities as a function of income differentiation, and the socialization of consumption expenditure by the wage-earners through credit, to overcome the difficulties of wage-earning households in purchasing consumer goods whose exchange-value is relatively large in relation to their current income, and to regularize the renewal of these goods by a collective responsibility for those risks that give rise to exceptional expenses.

All these various processes will have to be thoroughly investigated if we are to develop the theory of capital accumulation into a general theory of capitalist regulation. Fortunately there are already several studies in the different fields listed above. In the remainder of this book, we intend merely to start to utilize them in the framework of the law of capital accumulation already formulated, with the aim of constructing the more concrete concepts needed to interpret the regulation of capitalism in the 20th century.

First of all, however, we must pursue our sketch of the specific characteristics of American capitalism. The frontier principle has already revealed that its peculiar traits made the United States the exemplary nation of capitalist development, justifying our selection of it for the construction of a theory of regulation. These peculiarities were compounded by the particular formation of the American working class and the very rapid dissolution of traditional ways of life in the Republic.

Between the Civil War and the First World War, the broad mass of unskilled labour-power in heavy industry was composed of successive strata of immigrants of quite disparate languages and cultures. When they joined the American wage-earning class, they had no roots in the country. Benefiting from the political and legal equality enshrined by the constitutional principle and American democratic tradition, these workers sought above all a cultural assimilation according to the ethical norms of the subjective idealism that was the common basis of ideological representation for all social groups in the United States. This aspiration was all the more intense in that these immigrants came to a large extent from the countries of Central and Southern Europe,[3] and were fleeing the oppression of absolutism. The norms that the immigrants had to internalize to accomplish their cultural assimilation were individualism, stable family life, and monetary gain as the mark of social success and the spur to labour discipline. But they also encountered extremely harsh conditions of economic exploitation which materially negated the perspectives offered them by political and religious liberalism. The resultant contradiction is fundamental for an understanding of the specific forms and objectives assumed by the American labour movement. This movement took root in a country where political democracy was far more advanced then anywhere else in the 19th century, and where working-class organization meant at the same time for the immigrants the awakening of their cultural identity as American citizens. The bitter class struggles of the 1890s were fought against the degradation of their living conditions, largely in the name of the principles of the commodity-producing society itself, rather than those of any proletarian ideology. Conducted on a strictly economic basis, these struggles gave a powerful impetus to the transformation of working-class living conditions in the direction of commodity relations.

Completely deracinated when they arrived, the workers of the new industrial centres had to struggle against conditions of life entirely imposed by capitalism, in towns where no previous urban community had ever existed. In the last three decades of

[3] Up till the Civil War most immigration had been Anglo-Saxon in origin, and equipped with a minimum of resources necessary for its settlement. After the Civil War the proportion of non-Anglo-Saxon immigrants increased rapidly, and consisted more and more of individuals possessing absolutely nothing, in general being unable even to pay the cost of their voyage.

the 19th century, the accelerated accumulation in Department I concentrated capitalist production around mining resources, waterways and railway junctions. Working-class concentrations were established at a rapid pace and in the greatest disorder. In general working-class housing was frightful: close to the factory, it typically belonged to the factory owners. The latter rented out these dwellings at prohibitive rents, and if dismissed, the workers lost their homes as well. In the 1890s, these special conditions of exploitation provoked very hard-fought strikes, and disturbances that seriously disrupted production (e.g. the Chicago Pullman strike of 1894). The unhealthy condition of the industrial slums also became dangerous for the industrial towns as a whole. Finally, the immediate proximity of working-class housing to the factories began to impede freedom of industrial location and time-saving concentration of interconnected production activities in single sites. There was also an acute need for services in the new industrial towns: sales outlets and urban transport, improvement of communications between business offices, and organization of commercial districts.

Towards 1900, working-class struggles for decent housing linked up with the political campaign of the new bourgeois strata produced by the industrial revolution for the creation of certain infrastructures which the large and rapidly developing American cities lacked. Despite resistance from the financiers and real-estate owners who controlled the municipal authorities and strictly limited local taxes, political pressure on the city and state assemblies of the major industrial states in the East and Midwest generated a beginning of public intervention in housing and urban amenities. The fruit of political compromise, public housing advanced in waves whenever movements of industrial activity and population necessitated building operations on a very large scale. Four major waves of expansion occurred: at the turn of the century, after each of the two World Wars, and at the beginning of the 1960s, when new households multiplied as a result of the rise in the birth rate from 1940 onwards. On top of this, the 1920s and the entire period after the Second World War saw a strong demand for business offices due to the growth in bureaucratic personnel caused by the increasingly complex administrative structure of big firms – and in the post-war period, the gigantic expansion of the Federal government. The extension of capitalist production of private consumer goods also posed other problems. The advance of the economic division of labour in this field certainly depended on the transformation of the housing situation and on the provision of urban infrastructures. But there were more direct constraints on it connected with the production of surplus-value. The material means of consumption produced on a capitalist basis are commodities resulting from a mass production process and designed for purchase by individuals. Their incorporation into the norm of working-class consumption is thus their contribution to the formation of wages. These commodities can only form part of the consumption norm if their unit exchange value is on the decline and already sufficiently low. The conditions in which these commodities are produced must therefore be those of the standardized labour process of mass production. For this to be the case, the social demand for these branches of output must be sufficiently large and rapidly rising.

The squaring of this particular circle occurs dynamically in a non-linear process of contradictions, with successive advances and blockages. The process is as follows. The social division of labour in Department II results from a differentiation of this department into a sub-department producing commodities bought by the portion of surplus-value consumed as revenue and a further sub-department producing commodities bought by the monetary equivalent of the value of working-class labour-power. This differentiation of Department II itself depends on a development of the division of labour. To the extent that capital is accumulated in Department I and the division of labour there progresses, a centralization of capital results. This makes the job of capitalist management far more complicated, creating new social functions both in industrial firms and in the autonomous activities of the service, commercial and financial sectors. These social functions are the basis for the increase in those salaried social categories who are paid in part from the appropriation of centralized surplus-value. To the extent that the centralization of capital progresses, so too does the sum of surplus-value that is not accumulated, and in particular the dispersion of this portion of surplus-value among a larger number of individuals. It is essential therefore to note that *the centralization of accumulated surplus-value has as its corollary the dispersion of the surplus-value spent as revenue.* This is how a growing social demand is created for consumer goods that were previously considered as luxuries, so that these goods can now be produced by capital. However, the movement of these branches from the sub-department producing for surplus-value consumption to Department II as a whole does not take place automatically. When it is realized, in other words when the consumption norm of the working-class successively incorporates commodities already in existence, then capitalist relations of production dramatically quicken. All technological progress can be deployed in the transformation of the social conditions of production. Advances of productivity in Department I find their outlets in the expansion of Department II. The fall in unit exchange-values in this department sufficiently increases the production of relative surplus-value to enable real wages to rise. Accumulation can thus progress at a rapid pace in both departments. Commodity production invades the entire life of society; all social relations become commodity relations. The limits to this accelerated and regular accumulation are those of the extension of capitalist relations of production to the whole field of social production.

It is to the generalization of capitalist production relations to the entire social division of labour that the United States owes the advanced social relations that we have analysed: the rapid integration of agriculture, the absence of cultural traditions of sedentary or subsistence production, the rapid formation of industrial towns unaffected by precapitalist forms of urban life, the homogenization of successive waves of immigrants on the basis of the living conditions of the wage-earning class in large-scale industry, the powerful centralization of capital that induced the early adoption of new methods of management and sales which then gave rise to intermediate wage-earning strata (the famous American middle class into which the whole population was supposed to melt!).

These structural conditions were further reinforced by the particular role played by the United States in the two World Wars. These military conflicts considerably enlarged the production capacities of Department I, brought new manufacturing methods to maturity, and forced rapidly growing incomes into savings, and hence into potential expenditure for post-war reconversion to civil production. The 1920s were years of expansion of the sub-department producing commodities absorbed by the various incomes issuing from surplus-value. This expansion was the work of the automobile, of electro-mechanical consumer durables, and of the first electronic products. The development potential of these branches was enormous, but from 1926 onwards threatening signs indicated that it was nearing the limits of social demand. The output of consumer durables started to stagnate. The working-class market could not yet be reached under the social conditions of production of the time. But the transformation of these conditions by the advent of the New Deal and the establishment of collective bargaining permitted capitalist accumulation to go forward on the entire front of Department II immediately after the Second World War (which created greater possibilities of subsequent development than did the First). This accelerated accumulation began to falter again in the mid 1960s. To explain this crisis, we shall analyse the limits to the saving of living labour and the extension of surplus labour in the framework of current labour processes, the increasing difficulties in further revolutionizing the conditions of existence of the wage-earning class in the direction of an ever more total dependence on commodity production, and the significant rise in social overheads that is linked with the generalization of commodity relationships.

2. General Tendencies in the Accumulation of Productive Capital

We know that the rate of surplus-value is the pivot of capitalist accumulation. We have also seen that this accumulation necessarily receives its greatest impetus when the two departments of production develop simultaneously through a transformation of the conditions of existence of the wage-earning class. We propose, as we have said, to make the advent of this process the criterion of a new stage in the historical evolution of capitalism. If this periodization is correct, it should be possible to observe an acceleration in the long-run rise in the rate of surplus-value. This will provide a starting point for a quantitative examination of the tendencies of accumulation.

At this point we come up against the delicate problem of constructing statistical indicators that are derived from our fundamental concepts and so able to represent their development. We know that the rate of surplus-value denotes a division in the field of value, the homogeneous space of measurement. But this measurement is realized in the process of exchange, i.e. in the form of monetary quantities. Now in studying the relationship between relations of production and relations of distribution we have already shown that the wage relation is such that when abstract labour is expressed in monetary terms the division of total income is not the same as the rate of surplus-value. The first indicator that suggests itself, therefore, the division between wages and profits, only indicates the rate of surplus-value in a biassed way. Is it possible to find a more faithful statistical indicator? It should be borne in mind that we are not seeking to measure the absolute magnitude of this variable, but simply its long-run trend.

To continue with the notation used in the previous section, when we investigated the formation of total income and its division into wages and profits, let us take two periods separated in time which we will denote by the indices o and t. The fundamental relationships are $VP = m \cdot VA$, where VP is the total income, VA the total abstract labour spent during this period, and m the monetary expression of the working hour as formed in the commodity circulation of the period; $S = \overline{m} \cdot V$, where S is the sum of wages and $\overline{m}$ the function of the past values of m that expresses the overall balance of forces contributing to determining the basic wage by way of the wage contract. The basic wage or nominal reference wage is itself determined by $\overline{s} = \overline{m}/(1 + e)$. This relationship involves both the influence of the contractual relation and the influence of the capitalist relation of production, i.e. the dual aspect of the wage relation.

Let us now investigate the change in the share of wages in value added. This is expressed as:

$$\frac{(S_t/VP_t)}{(S_o/VP_o)} = \frac{(\overline{m}_t \cdot V_t/m_t \cdot VA_t)}{(\overline{m} \cdot V_o/m_o \cdot VA_o)} = \frac{(\overline{m}_t/m_t)}{(\overline{m}_o/m_o)} \cdot \frac{1 + e_o}{1 + e_t}$$

It appears as the product of two indices. One of these is the inverse of the index of the rate of surplus-value. The other expresses the share of wages at a constant rate of surplus-value. In actual fact, $\overline{m}_t/\overline{m}_o$, on condition that e is constant, gives the change in the nominal hourly wage at a constant rate of surplus-value, and is therefore simply a function of the evolution of the contractual relation. Moreover,

$$\frac{m_t}{m_o} = \frac{VP_t/VA_t}{VP_o/VA_o}$$

is the index of the net monetary value added per hour of productive labour. But at a constant rate of surplus-value, the social productivity of labour is itself constant, as we have seen in studying relative surplus-value.

Let us then consider the following statistical indices:

$S_{r,o}^t$ = index of average real hourly wages
π_o^t = index of average hourly productivity
P_o^t = price index for value added
$P_{c,o}^t$ = price index for private consumption
$C_{s,o}^t = S_{r,o}^t/\pi_o^t$ = index of real social wage cost

The evolution of the monetary expression of the working hour is expressed as $m_t/m_o = \pi_o^t \cdot P_o^t$. With productivity constant, it is indicated by the general price level.

The evolution of the share of wages in value added is expressed in the following way on the basis of these statistical indicators:

$$\frac{(S_t/VP_t)}{(S_o/VP_o)} = \frac{P_{c,o}^t}{P_o^t} \cdot \frac{S_{r,o}^t}{\pi_o^t} = C_{s,o}^t \cdot \frac{P_{c,o}^t}{P_o^t}$$

Comparing this expression with the theoretical definition of the same index, it is possible to deduce that the rate of surplus-value changes inversely to the real social wage cost, on condition that the index of the share of wages at a constant rate of surplus-value can be represented by the index of consumer prices. This is a reasonable hypothesis if we consider that changes in the balance of forces that influence the wage contract are bound up with transformations in the conditions of production and in the conditions of existence of the wage-earning class which form the content of surplus-value. With the rate of surplus-value constant, the social consumption norm is maintained. Calculation of the evolution of the share of wages at a constant rate of surplus-value via the index of consumer prices reflects the conservation of this norm.

We are thus led to the following proposition: the statistical indicator most appropriate to represent the evolution of the rate of surplus-value is the *evolution of the real social wage cost*. This indicator varies in the opposite direction to the rate of surplus-value over the long run, but exhibits the same changes of rhythm. We shall now proceed to study the latter, in order to identify the successive phases of capital accumulation in the United States.

(a) The evolution of the real social wage cost. The evolution of the social wage cost and its statistical components, average hourly real wages and net value added per man-hour in real terms, is given by Diagram I for the period 1900 to 1972.

Calculations of this variable, however, have been extended forward to 1974. Moving backward, the evolution of value added per man-hour from 1850 can be sketched in from estimates made by Kendrick; though the two kinds of calculation do not coincide.[4] Nevertheless, cutting the evolution of net value added per man-hour at the points where the graph shows a break, we get the following results:

	average annual rate of growth
from 1850 to 1889	1.0%
from 1889 to 1900	2.5%
from 1900 to 1918	1.0%
from 1919 to 1937	2.5%
from 1947 to 1958	3.0%
from 1958 to 1966	3.2%
from 1966 to 1974	1.6%

The years of the Second World War, as well as those immediately before and after, gave rise to major disturbances with causes specifically linked to the war economy and the problem of reconversion. The period 1889 to 1900 saw a temporary acceleration due to the creation of the foodstuffs complex, which transformed production methods in agriculture and in particular swiftly expanded the circulation space of its

[4] In particular, it is impossible to distinguish between net and gross: Kendrick, National Bureau of Economic Research, *Statistics*.

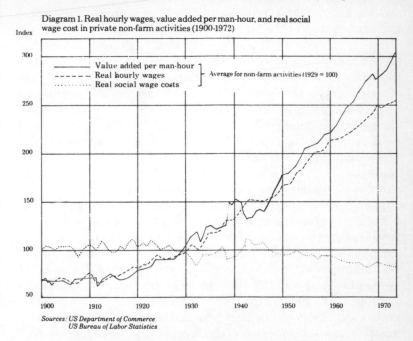

Diagram 1. Real hourly wages, value added per man-hour, and real social wage cost in private non-farm activities (1900-1972)

Sources: *US Department of Commerce*
US Bureau of Labor Statistics

commodities. Setting these periods aside, the essential break in the pace of development is located at the end of the First World War. This witnessed the start of a tendential acceleration continuing up to 1966, the year in which a new change of pace of major significance can be perceived. It should not be surprising that 1919 is the watershed date. This is the beginning of the historical period in which the transformation of the conditions of existence of the wage-earning class got seriously under way.

The tendencies in the evolution of the real social wage cost, moving inversely to relative surplus-value, were as follows:
— very rapid increase during the two World Wars, but without any long-run significance;
— constant between 1900 and 1917;
— moderate decrease in the inter-war years (with sharp fluctuations during the 1930s), at a rate of 0.9% per year;
— more rapid and far more regular decrease in the post-war years through to 1966, at a rate of 1.4% per year;
— constant on average as from this last date.

We can thus discern very significant alterations in the possibilities for extraction of relative surplus-value, which provide a key to the amplitude and limits of successive phases of accumulation.

Before continuing this investigation, it will be instructive to compare the United States with certain other capitalist countries for which there exist estimates of the long-run trends of real social wage costs. This work has been undertaken by E.H. Phelps Brown[5] for the period 1890–99, taking England as his basis. His comparison is based on official inquiries into international differences in cost of living. These were designed to find out what percentage more or less was needed in the money of a particular country, at the official exchange rate, to purchase the same basket of basic articles for the reproduction of labour-power which in England cost £1. The results, combining structural discrepancies in the value of labour-power from those reflected in monetary parities with differences in the parities themselves, which were stable over this period, lead to the definition of average coefficients by which the specific indices for each country have to be multiplied to relate to the corresponding indices for England, taken as equal to 100 over the period 1890–98. For this period, therefore, what we get is strictly the relation between the level of the indicators for each country and the English level.

Comparison of average indices for the period 1890–99 in different countries, assessed in English money and related to the same indices as established for England.

	Index of average hourly real wages	Index of value added per productive worker*	Index of real social wage cost
Germany	0.59	0.66	0.90
Sweden	0.69	0.76	0.87
United States	1.08	1.57	0.68
England	1.00	1.00	1.00

* It was not possible from the data of this period to establish working hours in all the countries under comparison.

[5] 'Levels and Movements of Industrial Productivity and Real Wages Internationally Compared', *The Economic Journal* no. 329, vol. 83, March, 1973. The principal statistical data here are taken from an earlier work, *A Century of Pay*, by E.H. Phelps Brown and M.H. Browne, London, 1968.

The United States already appears as the social formation with by far the highest rate of surplus-value. This comparison in international space is as significant as a comparison in historical time for the purpose of illustrating the theory of accumulation based on relative surplus-value. *A rise in real wages is induced by the processes that raise the rate of surplus-value* thanks to the penetration of capitalist relations of production into the production of the conditions of existence of wage-labour. We shall develop this observation in Chapter 3 by showing how this penetration integrates the reproduction cycle of labour-power into the conditions of production and transforms the social consumption norm. The tendency for real wages to rise is the effect of this dependence. An increase in wages is achieved only to the extent that there are no structural obstacles in the way of relative surplus-value. Once the fall in the real social wage cost slows down, then real wages begin to stagnate or to fall.

Let us now locate this result in the context of the temporal evolution of real social wage costs in the United States, so as to test the law of capital accumulation formalized in the first section of this chapter. What we know of the conditions of development of the productive forces in the United States, summed up above, seems to us a legitimate foundation for the hypothesis that the tendency to decline observed in the social wage cost on the morrow of the First World War, after it had remained constant since the beginning of the century, reflects the historical transition from a regime of predominantly extensive to one of predominantly intensive accumulation. Let us now try to explore this hypothesis by taking into account the principal features of accumulation in the inter-war years and the period after the Second World War.

The decade following the First World War saw a certain prosperity marked by the expansion of Department II, through the creation of effective demand on the basis of the expenditure of a portion of surplus-value as individual income. This gave an impetus to the production of housing, household consumer goods, motor vehicles and associated branches. In connection with the extension of capitalist production in Department II there was a transformation in labour processes characterized by a substantial saving on living labour and an expansion of productive capacity: the systematic introduction of assembly-line work, integrated machine systems and a substantial increase in applied energy. But the disproportion between expansion in Department II and accumulation in Department I rapidly increased, since the forces that were revolutionizing the labour processes were also those reducing effective demand for commodities from Department II. Between 1923 and 1929 the output of producer goods increased by 50%, while industrial production as a whole increased only by 25%. Massive savings on living labour, combined with the crushing defeat of the workers' movement after the First World War, rapidly increased inequality of incomes. According to studies later carried out by the Roosevelt administration's Internal Revenue Service,[6] the share of disposable income appropriated by the top 1% of income recipients rose between 1920 and 1929 from 12% to 18% while the share appropriated by the top 5% rose from 24% to 33.5%. Over the same period, incomes received in the form of industrial profit, interest and rent increased by 45%, while earned income increased by only 13%, this increase resulting chiefly from the development of unproductive work. If we simply take the productive workers in manufacturing industry, i.e. those who suffered the full blast of the radical transform-ation of the labour process, then we see a virtual stagnation of hourly real wages (a rise of 2% between 1920 and 1929). It can thus be estimated, taking due account of the overall data on income distribution and its development, that between 40 and 45% of all households remained outside the market for all consumer goods except the most basic requirements. The aggravation of inequalities attendant on the installation of mass production methods ran strictly counter to the need to expand the markets for Department II.

The evolution of these markets reflected the maturation of this contradiction. Their expansion required the construction of housing and the consumption of durable goods on a scale capable of transforming the conditions of existence of the wage-earning class. Such a transformation multiplies inter-industrial commodity relations; it creates long economic chains uniting the two departments of production, with the result that savings

[6] Quoted by *Fortune* magazine in 'A Remarkable Study of the Great Depression and its Causes', February–March, 1955.

on labour communicate their influence from sector to sector. By 1926, the expansion of the consumption of durable goods had, however, already met its limits:

	Increase from 1920 to 1926	Decrease from 1926 to 1929
Housing construction	215%	37%
Consumption of durable goods	66%	5%

These rigid and brutal barriers were reached because the working class was still largely excluded from these markets and the link between methods of mass production and methods of mass commercialization was still unable to resolve the problem by a renovation of the market. The Great Depression, whose course we shall analyse in our final chapter, was a major crisis of accumulation because the transformation of the labour process itself set up obstacles to valorization. What was ultimately at stake in the crisis was the transformation of the conditions of existence of the working class. This required far-reaching changes in wage formation and work organization. These changes followed two fundamental processes that we shall investigate in Chapter 3: the *development of contractual relations* between capitalist managements and working-class organizations, and the *socialization of one section of the expenses involved in reproducing labour-power* as the necessary condition for the reign of the commodity to flourish. The change in social relations that these processes implied made necessary a major extension and diversification of the economic interventions of the state.

The period following the Second World War presents a far more regular decline in real social wage costs, although one that accelerates in the years 1960–66 and then comes to an end. The last ten years are a phase in which the production of surplus-value encounters serious problems, while direct pressures on real wages make themselves felt amidst heightened social conflicts.

For the post-war period, more comprehensive statistical information is available on the evolution of the various components of unit value added. This variable is defined as the gross annual value added (in dollars) by non-financial enterprises, related to the same aggregate at 1958 prices.

Diagram 2, which summarizes this information, defines indices from the 1958 base of 100 for the costs in current dollars per unit of value added, in order to determine the structural variation of the cost of production and the unit margin. Here we can observe the modification in the value composition of the

Diagram 2. Composition of gross value added per unit produced in non-financial corporations (1948-72)

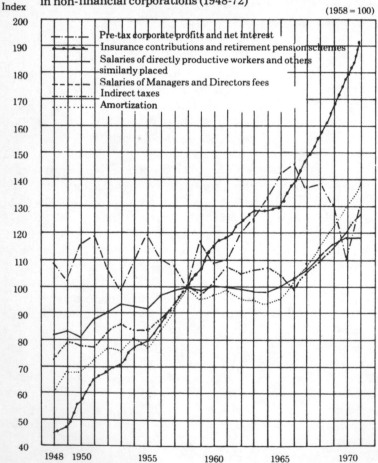

Sources: *US Department of Commerce*
US Bureau of Labor Statistics

average social product that is an inevitable part of the regime of intensive accumulation, and the basis for the successive phases in the contradictory movement of accumulation. The growth in the value composition of capital in the course of this period is reflected in the fact that the growth in the amortization of fixed capital per unit of product is more rapid than that of the wages of productive workers per unit of product. We may also note how spectacularly relative surplus-value developed between 1958 and 1966, confirming the accelerated fall in real social wage costs that was depicted in Diagram 1. Both wage cost and amortization per unit produced declined, thus releasing a very rapidly growing profit per unit produced for the purposes of accumulation. In contrast to this, we have a sudden major break in 1966 in the rhythm of development of labour productivity and in the decline of real social wage costs. This break gave rise to a very severe compression of the unit wage cost for productive workers, which has grown much less quickly than the other components of unit value added, without for all that preventing a decline in unit profit, due to the rapid rise in the value composition of capital.

This modification in the value composition of the social commodity product must now be situated in the context of the investigation we have already made of the conditions of development of the forces of production. We know that the post-war epoch saw the universal extension of capitalist relations of production to the entirety of productive activities and the correlative development of commodity circulation. The fundamental motive force here was the transformation of the conditions of existence of the working class, which enabled methods of relative surplus-value production to be generalized throughout Department II. We have already shown in theory that this dynamic makes possible a certain harmonization of expansion in the two departments of production, by increasing the density of their exchange relations as channels for the transmission of local transformations of the productive forces. This partial neutralization of the tendency to uneven development of Department I was responsible for the approximately regular growth of the social product in the greater part of the post-war years, by contrast with the jerky accumulation characteristic of the predominantly extensive regime that obtained

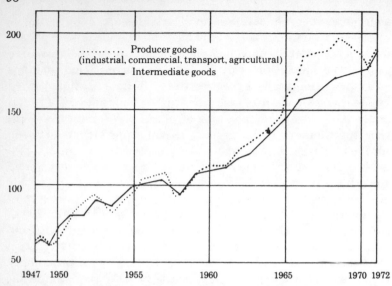

Diagram 3. Industrial production by volume in the department producing producer goods (1957-1959 = 100)

Source: US Department of Commerce

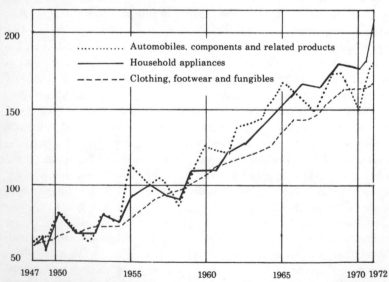

Diagram 4. Industrial production by volume in the department producing consumer goods (1957-1959 = 100)

Source: US Department of Commerce

before this revolutionization of the conditions of existence of the wage-earning class.

Diagrams 3 and 4 illustrate the expansion of the two departments. The period 1947–61 was on the whole one of balanced and intensive accumulation. The two departments expanded at the same average pace (from an index of 70 in 1947 to one of 110 in 1961), the contractions of 1949, 1954 and 1958 correcting disproportions in the internal evolution of each department. This was a period of slow average decline in real social wage costs. The watershed years of 1958–61 saw an acceleration in the fall in social wage costs proceeding from a sudden change in the forms of class struggle to the detriment of the wage-earners, which we shall describe in more detail in Chapter 3. This inaugurated the most intense wave of accumulation in the whole history of American capitalism, which very rapidly broke the dynamic equilibrium of expansion of the two departments. Department I expanded more rapidly than Department II and became more differentiated, the sub-department producing actual means of production experiencing particularly fast growth sustained by the general transformation of production processes. In Department II the proportions obtaining between component branches also broke down. The result was a deeply unbalanced accumulation which was only maintained in so far as the relative surplus-value produced could be accumulated at an accelerated pace. This tempo could itself be maintained only if manufacturing processes were altered more and more quickly to supply the growing demand addressed to the sub-department producing means of production. 1966 saw the impending blockage of this mode of accumulation.

At the point we have now reached, it is possible to formulate certain questions about the trends of the last ten years. According to our analyses so far, this period has been one of a *crisis in the regime of intensive accumulation*. Its originality by comparison with earlier historical precedents can be seen in the novelty of its symptoms, which numerous economists have described and which we shall seek to interpret as our investigation progresses. The present crisis is quite distinct from the Great Depression, where the real issue was the all-round establishment of the regime of intensive accumulation. It is distinct, too, from the transient disturbances that form part of a regime's internal regulation, particularly since intensive accumulation can function correctly only by buffering such disturbances. It seems necessary therefore to pose a deeper question: are there limits to the transformation of the conditions of existence of the wage-earning class in the form of an extension of commodity relations? Are the intractability and novelty of contemporary social conflicts the sign of the emergence of such limits? It is necessary to reiterate that relative surplus-value sustained by an ever more rapid revolutionization of the conditions of production is necessary for the long-run perpetuation of capitalism once the intensive aspect of accumulation has become dominant.

(b) Trends of capital formation. One essential feature of relative surplus-value is the incorporation of labour-power in the production process as an element of capital subject to the valorization of the means of production. This is why the formation of fixed capital indicates a reinforcement in the material base of the power that the capitalist class exercises over society. The net accumulation of fixed capital can be seen from Diagram 5, which shows the long-run trend of the net stock of fixed capital. The periodization that emerged in our investigation of relative surplus-value, via the indicator of real social wage costs, clearly re-emerges on this graph. We may leave aside the two World Wars, characterized by losses of fixed capital due to over-use of existing stock and insufficient replacement, as well as the reconversion periods after the wars, characterized by enormous net investment. With these exceptional periods left out of account, we can note the following phases:

(1) A slow and irregular growth in capital stock from the beginning of the century up to 1915, a period which we saw was dominated by extensive accumulation.

(2) A rapid growth from 1921 to 1929–30, followed by a massive destruction of capital in the Depression and a stagnation in the second half of the 1930s.

(3) A vigorous impetus from 1950 onwards, slowing down at the end of the decade but accelerating again during the phase of sharp growth in the rate of surplus-value in the first half of the 1960s.

Yet observation of a statistical increase in the value of the stock of fixed capital, taken by itself, only masks the underlying problem of the continuity of cause and effect in the production and circulation of commodities as the reproduction of the conditions of production. In this perspective, the single principle of capitalist accumulation, in other words the expansion of surplus-value, presents itself as a cycle of metamorphoses of value, summed up in the formula $M - C \ldots P \ldots C' - M'$, where the production process is no more than one moment in the purely quantitative increase of abstract labour. This cycle destroys in order to produce and produces in order to destroy, since productive activity does not become such by the useful objects it creates, but rather by the commodities

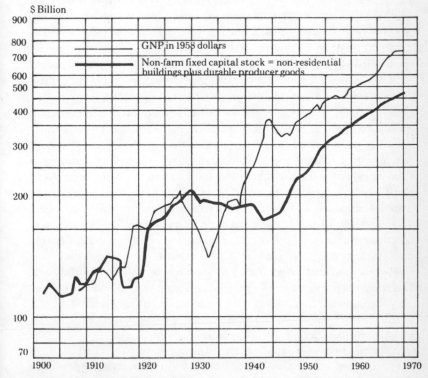

$ Billion

GNP in 1958 dollars

Non-farm fixed capital stock = non-residential buildings plus durable producer goods

Diagram 5. Gross national product and fixed capital stock for private non-farm businesses

Source: Statistical Abstracts

that it puts into circulation. When the metamorphoses of value take place more quickly, then so too does capital accumulation, which means that the products of labour have in turn to be destroyed all the more quickly so that an ever greater amount of social labour can be expended ever more intensely. In this blind and one-dimensional logic, the problem of the replacement of constant capital cannot be separated from that of the conversion of surplus-value into the material elements of productive capital. What best expresses the temporal movement of accumulation is thus the profile of gross fixed capital formation.

In order to interpret observations of this profile theoretically, we need a more precise conception of the effect of the replacement of fixed capital on the law of accumulation. In the cycle of expanded reproduction depicted above, fixed capital is defined as the total value of the material elements of the production process whose use as productive forces extends over several cycles. In accordance with the law of exchange equivalence, or the law of value, the metamorphosis of the value of fixed capital into the value of produced commodities takes place over the total period for which it is in use, with the result that its value is destroyed at the same moment that it becomes obsolete and ceases to be a means of valorization. Fixed capital consequently loses its value gradually with each production cycle. A growing fraction of its total value is found in the monetary form as a financial provision designed later on to purchase commodities that are means of production, replacing those which have become obsolete. In the continuity of capital's overall reproduction, the difference in turnover times for the different elements of constant capital gives rise to a monetary flow which forms part of the profit realized in the course of each cycle. The amount of this amortization fund is determined by the value of the fixed capital and its average turnover time as a multiple of the basic cycle. The sum of the amortization fund and total net profit forms the *total cash flow* or gross profit which the capitalist class has at its disposal.

Now we have shown how capitalist production is founded on the transformation of conditions of production, whose origin is the creation of new means of production and the lowering of the value of those means that replace those that have been consumed. This mutation of productive forces is the material basis of labour productivity as a source of relative surplus-value. But there is no reason why the pace of transformation of the productive forces should be adapted to the pace of replacement of fixed capital which satisfies the conservation of the value of constant capital. We are faced here with a contradiction in the most rigorous sense of this term. This is a real contradiction in the process of accumulation, for which there does not exist any 'synthesis'. On the one hand, as capitalism is a commodity-producing society, the reproduction of the conditions of production implies conservation of the value of all commodities in exchange; on the other hand, as capitalism is based on the antagonism of the wage relation, it cannot reproduce its constitutive relation except by revolutionizing the conditions of production. A contradiction of this kind cannot endure; one of its terms must necessarily destroy the other. It is thus the capitalist relation of production itself which causes the non-conservation of the value of fixed capital. There results a *devalorization of capital*. It is important not to confuse this concept of devalorization with that of capital depreciation, since the former precisely makes it impossible to satisfy fully the latter. Defined as an internal characteristic of capital in general, devalorization of capital is an essential process of modification of the value composition of capital, the importance of which we have seen in the law of accumulation. It is therefore a constitutive process in accumulation. The devalorization of capital means a loss of value. One portion of the labour crystallized in the means of production is not validated in exchange as social labour. It is destroyed, completely annihilated. The growing importance of fixed capital for relative surplus-value makes the devalorization of capital a massive phenomenon with decisive social importance. The condition of its possibility lies in the contradictory character of accumulation as it progresses, in that it increases the dissociation between the gradual transmission of the value of the fixed capital to the product and the conditions of its obsolescence. On the one hand, the amount of value transmitted by depreciation and the time over which it is transmitted tend to increase with the material ramification of manufacturing plant; on the other hand, the consequent rise in the organic composition of capital tends to accelerate the transformation of the productive forces so as to augment the rate of surplus-value, and hence consequently to increase the probability that the means of production invested will become obsolete. The devalorization of capital is therefore the necessary expression of the blind regulation of a mode of production founded on an antagonistic relation, where the social character of labour only appears *a posteriori* in the process of commodity exchange. The more society develops its productive capacity by deepening the division of labour, the more it experiences serious losses of this kind.

Before closing this chapter, in which the concept of devalorization of capital completes the general formulation of the law of accumulation, we have still to examine the manner in which devalorization affects the temporal dynamic of capital formation. This intervenes in a decisive way in the relationships between the two departments of production. That is why the modalities of capital devalorization differ according to the regime of accumulation. These modalities critically determine the way in which the social loss of value is borne and the way this loss is made up in the course of accumulation. They are realized in practice through the metamorphoses of value. From this point of view, the devalorization of capital conforms completely to the law of value. It is realized in practice in money form, and this is how it influences the temporal evolution of gross fixed capital formation.

The essential difference can be summed up as follows.

(1) Inasmuch as the tendency towards the uneven development of Department I is not strongly offset by the general penetration of capitalist production into Department II, then the devalorization of capital is expressed in a recurrent movement formed by successive phases of massive increase in gross fixed capital formation and phases of deep depression. A major cycle of accumulation can be traced in the United States, with a period of some 20 years or so. This large-scale recurrent movement, articulated with minor fluctuations linked to the business cycle which we shall not ignore here, can be observed in Diagram 6, depicting the evolution of gross fixed capital formation from 1890 to 1946.

(2) When the transformation of the conditions of existence of the wage-earning class provokes a powerful counter-tendency

Diagram 6. Gross fixed capital formation in private non-farm activities from 1890 to 1946.
(In billions of dollars at 1929 prices)

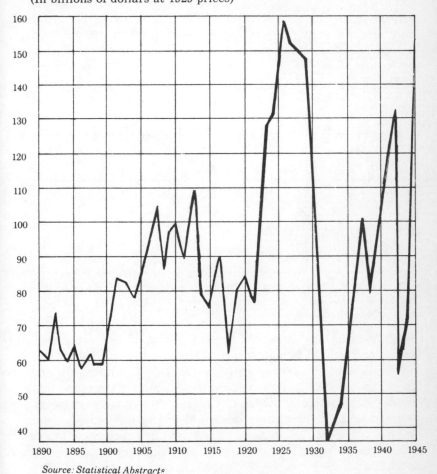

to the uneven development of Department I by way of a rapid expansion of markets for Department II and an increasing density of exchange relations between the two departments, then the devalorization of capital becomes a permanent process, structurally incorporated in the rhythm of capital formation. The temporal evolution of gross fixed capital formation is then profoundly modified, as shown in Diagram 7.

Diagram 7. Gross fixed capital formation from 1929-1970 by category of expenditure (in billions of dollars at 1958 prices)

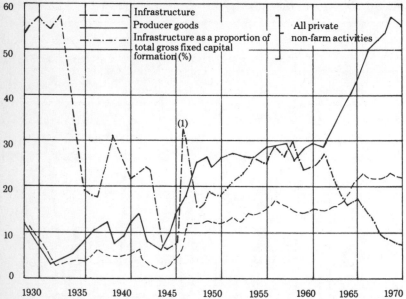

1. Purchase of state-owned factories and replacement of pre-war equipment
Source: Office of Business Economies

Since 1946 there have not been any phases of deep depression in the formation of capital, but rather a phase of slow growth followed by a phase of rapid increase. Yet the profound modification of the long-run cycle of accumulation has not made business cycles disappear. If the latter have been somewhat weaker in amplitude during the long upward phase of intensive accumulation, they have succeeded each other faster than under the regime of predominantly extensive accumulation.

What concretely happens here? Under the regime of predominantly extensive accumulation, Department I develops in successive spurts. Phases of rapid advance in gross fixed capital formation correspond to the creation of new industries undertaking accumulation in Department I. So long as Department I pursues its own development, monetary flows of investment have the upper hand over other monetary flows representing the provisions for replacing existing equipment. They also increase more quickly than overall net profit, because the opening of new investment opportunities by addition of new productive capacity increases the share of profit invested. Yet the massive increase in productive capacity in these very industries of Department I incessantly raises the overall level of exchange needed to realize the sum of gross profit (the combination of net profit and depreciation allowances) corresponding to the depreciation and valorization of the capital invested. Now the uneven development of Department I expresses the discrepancy between the specific dynamic of accumulation as a principle for the overall expansion of value, and the social conditions of the division of labour that permit the extension of capitalist relations of production. This discrepancy is translated into an insufficiency of market outlets to make the capital invested show a profit. When this insufficiency results in a mass of unsold commodities, the consequent non-realization of value provokes a violent contraction in the formation of fixed capital. It simultaneously involves a partial destruction of the fixed capital operative in production. The devalorization of capital thus arises during a crisis of market outlets and reinforces it. The normal depreciation cycle of fixed capital is brutally interrupted. Factories are closed, clusters of productive forces abandoned, while means of production are destroyed on a massive scale right across society. This form of capital devalorization is therefore an essential component of a deep depression in the gross formation of fixed capital. The social losses involved affect the capitalist class by the interruption of depreciation as well as by the sharp contraction of net profits. They affect the wage-earners by mass unemployment and its attendant misery. But the devalorization of capital at the same time represents the escape route from the crisis because it drastically lowers the value composition of capital. This mutation in value relations has as its material substratum a generalized obsolescence within the production process which tends to crystallize during a depression. Accumulation picks up again with a qualitative transformation of the forces of production that initiates a new phase of expansion.

The characteristic movement of the regime of intensive accumulation which became general after the Second World War can be grasped by comparing and contrasting it with the process just described. The contrast is the expression of decisive changes in the regulation of capitalism which have been brought about by the universalization of the wage relation. The fundamental fact is that the qualitative transformation of the forces of production has become a permanent process, instead of being chiefly condensed into one specific phase of the cycle of accumulation. This change is due to the interaction of the two departments of production; each now provides the other with its markets as they combine to lower the value and diversify the commodities of mass consumption. Obsolescence becomes generalized and permanent. This process is the material substratum for the new modalities of capital devalorization. Intimately linked to capital formation, devalorization no longer expresses itself chiefly as a brutal interruption of the course of fixed capital depreciation. It forms part of the metamorphoses of value, and is integrated into the financial provisions for replacing fixed capital. To the extent that obsolescence becomes a perpetual and general process, it can be statistically predicted. This is translated at the monetary level into the formation of an insurance fund out of overall profits. This fund is lumped together with the amortization fund, from which it cannot really be distinguished. It is incorporated *a priori* into cost prices. As a result, *an intensification in the pace of obsolescence is translated into a growth in the share of depreciation allowances in overall cash flow*, and correlatively into a relative decline in net profit.

Diagram 8 depicts this development in the United States after the Second World War. Comparison between this and the profile of gross fixed capital formation given in Diagram 7 provides the indications we need of the new features of the accumulation cycle. We may note that the rapid growth in the share of *depreciation allowances* in overall cash flow coincides with periods in which the gross formation of fixed capital slows down. This means that the intensification of obsolescence is an essential factor in the extraction of relative surplus-value, creating the markets required by the formation of capital when the social conditions of the parallel extension of the two departments are not satisfied. The devalorization of capital in its new modalities thus becomes the force tending to neutralize the uneven development of Department I. We can now under-

Diagram 8. Financing ratios in non-financial corporations (1948-1971)

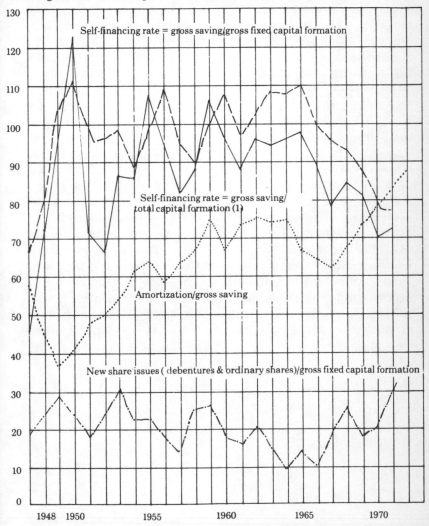

Self-financing rate = gross saving/gross fixed capital formation

Self-financing rate = gross saving/ total capital formation (1)

Amortization/gross saving

New share issues (debentures & ordinary shares)/gross fixed capital formation

Sources: US Department of Commerce 1. Gross fixed capital formation and stocks
Federal Reserve Board

stand the meaning of our earlier assertion that capitalist production produces in order to destroy and destroys in order to produce. The incessant increase in surplus labour imposed on the working class is indissolubly connected with the systematic social waste by means of which serious depressions have been avoided in contemporary capitalism. The question is then how the losses of value involved in the new modality of devalorization are borne. We shall show in Chapter 6 that this modality is at the root of the permanent creeping inflation that is the fundamental feature of the regulation of capitalism since the Second World War. The capitalist class as a whole, by incorporating an *a priori* insurance against obsolescence into the formation of its overall cash flow, itself enforces this generalized obsolescence, while simultaneously shifting the social losses that follow from it onto the wage-earners. This shift is both diffuse and general. It is effected through the loss of value of the purchasing power of wages as a result of monetary inflation. The devalorization of capital thus becomes a devalorization of the rights allocated to the wage-earners. It is this process that enables the capitalist class to continue to appropriate an overall cash flow sufficient to maintain accumulation. We shall thus be in a position to assess the profound significance of the recent crisis, characterized first of all by an acceleration of inflation, then by the first serious contraction in the gross formation of fixed capital for thirty years. The features of this crisis are well and truly such as to jeopardize the mechanisms of regulation specific to intensive accumulation.

2

Transformations in the Labour Process

I. The Mechanization of Labour

Capitalist production is the unity of a labour process and a process of valorization, in which the valorization is dominant. Investigation of this unity involves a further conceptualization of capitalist relations of production. On the one hand, we have defined the wage relation, the appropriation of labour-power as a commodity, as *the* fundamental relation of production. On the other hand, we said that capitalist relations of production present a dual character of antagonism and cooperation. In showing how the labour process is transformed under the impulse of the struggle for surplus-value, we must acquit a task that is essential for the transition from the abstract to the concrete in any theory of accumulation: namely to demonstrate that the transformation of the labour process creates relationships within production that adapt the cooperation of labour-power to the domination of the wage relation. Production thereby constitutes a structure in motion, in other words an organic set of social relations whose evolution is the condition for perpetuating the wage relation.

We must now, therefore, broach an essential element of the theory of capitalist regulation, which will shed light on certain problems that are widely debated at the present time. In effect, when the class struggle becomes intense, it cannot be easily held down to the wage contract, i.e. to the amount of wages in money terms. For it tends to put in question the internal relations of production by challenging the conditions of labour, the classification of jobs and the rules of work organization. The struggle gives rise to a rapid evolution of the labour process, thus creating new social relations. In this struggle the capitalist class stakes its existence – in other words the maintenance of the wage relation. Theoretical analysis of the labour process must thus dispel the illusions spread by bourgeois ideologists in the supposedly liberating character of the new types of work organization. It is obvious enough that these illusions do not deceive the working class, who daily confront the concrete realities of exploitation. But they do have an effect on broad sections of public opinion, which have only a highly abstract conception of the labour process and whose sensitivity to human dignity is easily reassured by an emollient propaganda.

Analysis of the labour process must also dispel a further illusion – that of the liberating character of technology, or of the 'scientific and technical revolution' as it is called nowadays. This illusion finds, of course, formal expression in neoclassical theory, where the forces of production are innocent of any social conditioning. It inspires a whole spectrum of productivist ideologies, not the least of these being that of French planning as popularized by Pierre Massé and other exponents of incomes policies. Let us produce as much as we can, and then everyone can have more, is a simple and persuasive slogan. An even more insidious notion is the idea that the capitalist character of production is dissolved simply by the application of science to it. Hence the odes to automation in which modern prophets depict for us a society in which burdensome work will have disappeared. Ideological amalgamations of the problem of onerous sorts of concrete labour with that of capitalist exploitation are typical of elevated contemporary discourses on manual labour.

The reality, unfortunately, is quite different. The technical division of labour is subject to the social division of labour. Technology is the material substratum of relations internal to the labour process which make collective labour-power a single force producing surplus-value. The technical division of labour progresses in such a way as to fragment living labour and thus render essential only *an output norm for labour-power defined in terms of time*. It is in this way that the collectivization of labour proceeds in conformity with the valorization of capital. It should not be surprising that the United States has been in the vanguard of major transformations of the labour process. These transformations involve changes in the general principles of work organization in all domains of production when the latter becomes capitalist. These principles develop with the deepening of the social division of labour. Their very generality, whatever the concrete fields of their application, is the best proof of the fact that homogenization via abstract labour is now written into the process of production. The major transformations have arisen in the United States first of all because it is there that the wage relation was most quickly universalized. It is these transformations that we must now succinctly survey.

1. Principles of Taylorism

We shall confine our study to those major transformations of the labour process which have taken place in the so-called second industrial revolution, which began in the latter half of the 19th century and has continued through to our own time.[1] This is the period in which the capitalist mode of production has systematically brought into being systems of productive forces able to link absolute and relative surplus-value closely together. Their basis is the *principle of mechanization*, which incorporates in its mode of operation the qualitative characteristics of those concrete labours previously performed by the dexterity of workers. The machine system is a complex of productive forces in which a series of tools is set in motion by a mechanical source of energy, the motor, via an appropriate transmission system. The relationship between workers and means of labour is thus reversed. Instead of wielding tools, the workers become appendages of the machines. By transferring the qualitative characteristics of labour to the machine, mechanization reduces labour to a cycle of repetitive movements that is characterized solely by its duration, the output norm. This is the foundation of the homogenization of labour in production. All modifications in the organization of work represent a further expression of this principle.

The output norm of social labour-power is therefore the pivot

[1] A historical survey may be found in the collective work edited by André Gorz, *The Division of Labour*, Hassocks, 1975, particularly the essay by S. Marglin, 'What Do Bosses Do?'

of any analysis of the labour process. Here it is necessary to take account of the changes that occur in the interaction between the different periods of time that make up the working day. Let us recall that the return on social labour is $e = (t_v - t_n)/t_n$, where t_n is the time necessary for the production of those commodities whose consumption reconstitutes labour-power, and $t_v - t_n$ is the surplus labour-time. The total abstract labour-time t_v is itself located within a working day of duration T. The difference $T - t_v$ expresses the porousness of the working day from the standpoint of abstract labour. With a given degree of mechanization of labour and a given type of work organization, the working day has necessarily to be T so that abstract labour can be t_v. The gaps in the working-day arise from two kinds of time period:

(1) Time periods bound up with the coordination of different segments of the labour process. These are the result of those discontinuities in production practices that prevent the totality of the working day from being made into one single mass of abstract labour. They are periods for shifting material in the course of transformation, for repair and maintenance, periods bound up with changes in the nature of productive tasks (preparation and inauguration of a particular production run, insufficient coordination between successive operations causing a delay, shifting of workers bound up with the spatial configuration of the machine system).

(2) Time periods bound up with the partial reconstitution of labour-power at the workplace (various pauses and breaks due to fatigue).

The term Taylorism might be defined as the sum total of those relations of production internal to the labour process that tend to accelerate the completion of the mechanical cycle of movements on the job[2] and to fill the gaps in the working day. These relations are expressed in general principles of work organization that reduce the workers' degree of autonomy and place them under a permanent surveillance and control in the fulfilment of their output norm. In the United States, Taylorism came into force in the engineering industries at the end of the 19th century. It was a capitalist response to the class struggle in

[2] This involves the intensification of labour, which as we have seen in Chapter 1 can be interpreted as an increase in t_v with T being given.

production in a phase when the labour process was composed of several segments, each organized on mechanical lines internally, yet whose integration still depended on direct relations between different categories of worker. The insufficient mechanical integration of the different segments meant that constraint had to be exercised by way of rules of work fixing the output norm for each job as well as the nature and order of the movements to be performed. A managerial staff was organized for the sole purpose of securing obedience to these rules. A further type of staff, organized as a time and motion department, was charged with devising the rules, experimenting with them, putting them into application and modifying them. The aim of this separation and specialization of functions was to combat the control over working conditions that the relative autonomy of jobs in the old system could leave the workers. Detailed time and motion analysis of jobs, combined with research into the psycho-physiological reactions of individuals subjected to the repetition of different configurations of movement, provided information that enabled specialists to remove this obstacle. This information was the basis for a great simplification of jobs. Each production worker was given a simpler cycle to perform. The inauguration of patterns of this kind led to the conception of new methods of production and new types of machine-tools. 'Technical progress' was completely determined by the intensification of output norms. It sought to alter the content of jobs in such a way as to circumvent the workers' resistance where it was not possible to break it directly. Such changes modified both the work performances to be accomplished with the means of labour and the specification of the articles to be manufactured or assembled (for instance a change in thresholds of tolerance).

Taylorism culminated with the organization of work teams. This form of organization became important when increasingly large work collectivities set in motion a fixed capital of extremely high value. This value was immobilized in productive infra-structures which it was extremely costly to operate and which remained in service for a very long time in comparison with the period of wage payment. Team organization combined every rule designed to reduce the gaps in the working day. By restricting the individual working day, it was possible to fix output norms involving a very high pace of work. By guaranteeing continuity, it was possible to limit the loss of time involved in the starting-up of machines and the preparation of production runs. By making machines function either continuously or semi-continuously (e.g. stopping only at the week-ends), it was possible to reduce the time they were kept in service via a more intense utilization of them. The increased rapidity of capital turnover thus obtained reduced the risk of obsolescence and associated losses through devalorization.

After the Second World War, team organization became general in most industries both in the United States and in Western Europe. This extension represented the assimilation of Taylorist principles by managements, the establishment of time and motion study as an autonomous function in the charge of specialists placed closely under management control, and the creation of a vast reservoir of homogeneous and mobile labour-power, both constrained and resigned to capitalist labour discipline. The migration of large masses of workers, divorced from all socio-cultural ties to their communities of origin, played a major role in the considerable growth of this reservoir. In the United States this involved in particular the movement into industry of the proletarianized black population of the South, from the beginning of the Second World War onwards. In Western Europe it especially involved successive waves of immigration from the Mediterranean and from Africa.

2. Taylorism superseded by Fordism

Fordism is a stage that supersedes Taylorism.[3] It denotes a series of major transformations in the labour process closely linked to those changes in the conditions of existence of the wage-earning class that give rise to the formation of a social consumption norm and tend to institutionalize the economic class struggle in the form of collective bargaining. Fordism is a striking illustration of the Marxist thesis according to which the technical division of labour is determined by the deepening of the social division of labour. It marks a new stage in the regulation of capitalism, the regime of intensive accumulation

[3] See Christian Palloix, 'Le procès de travail. Du fordisme au néofordisme', *La Pensée*, no. 185, February 1976.

in which the capitalist class seeks overall management of the production of wage-labour by the close articulation of relations of production with the commodity relations in which the wage-earners purchase their means of consumption. Fordism is thus the principle of *an articulation between process of production and mode of consumption*, which constitutes the mass production that is the specific content of the universalization of wage-labour. In this chapter, therefore, we shall study only one aspect of Fordism, that which affects the organization of labour and the modalities of wage payment. We shall investigate it in the light of our earlier exposition of the role of the transformation of the conditions of existence of the wage-earning class in the production of surplus-value. In Chapter 3 we shall go on to study more fully both this transformation itself and the forms of wage relation it has created.

The characteristic labour process of Fordism is *semi-automatic assembly-line production*. This particular type of labour process was established in the United States from the 1920s onwards, especially for mass consumer goods produced in long production runs, and was subsequently extended upstream to the production of standardized intermediate components for the manufacture of these means of consumption. The establishment of one and the same type of labour process was a powerful force for the vertical integration of production processes and a material support for the transmission of local mutations in the productive forces between the two departments of production. It is for this reason that the semi-automatic assembly line is the most suitable labour process for relative surplus-value. The organic liaison it establishes between the two departments of production enables value relations to be revolutionized in the direction of a reduction of the unit value of items of mass consumption. Fordism thus generated a tendential fall in the time t_n needed for the reconstitution of social labour-power. But we have already noted in the first chapter that relative and absolute surplus-value are intimately related. This is concretely expressed in the labour process, where Fordism took up the principles of Taylorism and put them more effectively into practice, to obtain an ever greater intensification of labour.

Fordism further developed the mechanization of labour, increased the intensity of work, radicalized the separation between manual and mental labour, rigorously subjected workers to the law of accumulation and turned scientific progress against them as a power serving the uniform expansion of value. The decisive influence of Fordism can be seen in the accumulation of capital in general by the break in the pace of development of the rate of surplus-value after the First World War, which we have already remarked. Fordism deepened Taylorism in the labour process by the application of two complementary principles:

Firstly, the integration of different segments of the labour process by a system of conveyors and handling devices ensuring the movement of the materials to be transformed and their arrival at the appropriate machine tools. This is the system that justifies our reference to a semi-automatic assembly line. It represented a mutation of the forces of production that considerably lowered the time taken for the transfer and manipulation of objects that were often heavy and difficult to move, or else corrosive and dangerous to handle. The system was similarly responsible for a major saving of labour-power and a notable increase in the organic composition of capital. A condition of its success was a revolution in energy which generalized the industrial use of electricity and made possible the construction of high capacity motors which enormously increased the power available in industry. In this way, the labour process could be converted from a dense network of relationships between jobs, with intermediate products passing back and forth, and trial and error in the case of assembly, into a straightforward linear flow of the material under transformation. This conversion was accompanied by a normalization of the specifications of component elements, inducing the upstream penetration of assembly-line work.

The second principle, which was complementary to the integration of segments of the labour process, was the fixing of workers to jobs whose positions were rigorously determined by the configuration of the machine system. The individual worker thus lost all control over his work rhythm. The continuous linear flow prohibited the formation of buffer stocks between jobs and subjected the collective rhythm to the uniform movement of the machine system. In this mode of organization workers are unable to put up any individual resistance to the imposition of the output norm, since job autonomy has been totally abolished. It thus became possible to simplify tasks yet further by fragmenting cycles of motion into mere repetition of a few elementary movements. This simplification, planned in engineering departments which were themselves subject to the division of labour, was pursued through a continuous ameliora-tion of assembly-line performance, modifying machine types, inventing new positions and jobs, altering manufacturing and assembly plans.

Once established, the assembly-line process can be systemati-cally modified in accordance with these two principles to increase the share of surplus labour in the working day. But this process itself has its limits, set on the one hand by the social conditions necessary for the labour process to play its role in valorizing capital and on the other by barriers internal to the labour process itself and by the class struggle that occurs within it.

The first limits are not external and absolute, but rather the effect of the process itself, which is not automatically harmo-nized by the constitutive relationships of the capitalist mode of production. The far-reaching transformations of the technical division of labour that the semi-automatic assembly line per-mits give an enormous boost to productive capacity and consequently demand social conditions specific to the mass circulation of commodities at a rapidly increasing rate. This requirement is all the more urgent in that assembly-line production is subject to a specific constraint: the further the fragmentation of individual tasks and integration of jobs by the machine system have already been taken, the more costly in means of production is subsequent intensification of the output norm. The reason is the great technical rigidity of the machine system. This way of raising labour productivity consequently makes investment propel investment on an ever more colossal scale, while markets must be expanded at whatever cost, with increasing risks of devalorization of the fixed capital thus immobilized.

The internal limits of the labour process itself can be identified by analysis of the time periods making up the working day. When the fragmentation of tasks is pushed to an extreme limit, several elements combine to prevent a further decline in time wasted and even to reverse its direction. The chief factors at work here are:

(1) The increase in the 'balance delay time', i.e. the delays caused by imbalances on the assembly line. This phenomenon derives from the fact that the spatial configuration of the assembly-line plant imposes certain constraints on the disposition of the series of partial tasks, the result of which is that not all workers have a cycle of movements of the same duration. This impossibility of distributing time equally leads to a total time lost equal to the sum of those periods spent waiting by the workers with shorter cycles. This time increases with the further fragmentation of tasks.

(2) The effects of intensification of labour on the mental and physical equilibrium of the workers. The first negative effect here is due to uniformity of rhythm, combined with constantly increased tempo. The idea that productivity depends on a uniform pace of operation throughout the working day is a product of the capitalists' need to reinforce control over the labour-power at their disposal. In no way does it derive from an observation of the ideal psycho-physical conditions for human activity. On the contrary, if one thing is clear, it is that human performance is improved by changes in pace and by the possibility of self-control over the moments and modalities of such changes. Subjection to a uniform but ever increasing pace of work, combined with the curtailment of resting time, immensely increases fatigue and creates new forms of nervous exhaustion from which it is impossible to recover from one day to the next. Symptoms of this modern form of destruction of human capacities have multiplied during the course of the 1960s, especially in the most mechanized industries: a high level of absenteeism, and particularly an irregular level that defies any attempt at prediction; an increase in temporary disabilities precipitated by the accumulation of nervous exhaustion; a rise in accidents on the assembly line; an increase in the proportion of defective products, and consequently in the time devoted to quality control. The irregularity of absenteeism has particularly disastrous effects, since it significantly increases the time needed to build up production teams and consequently also the time taken to get the assembly line going, as well as requiring the employment of excess labour-power devoted to various

ancillary tasks but primarily serving to make up the gaps on the assembly line when needed.

(3) The abolition of any perceptible tie between the collective output of the work force and the expenditure of energy by the individual worker. This follows directly from the collectivization of labour accomplished by the assembly line. It enables capitalist managements to avoid any direct challenge to the output norm. But its drawback is that it makes it difficult to divide the workers against themselves, and induce them to participate in the degradation of their own conditions of labour by means of individual output bonuses. Assembly-line work tends to unify the workers in an overall struggle against their conditions of labour. If the capitalist managements try to re-establish divisions between individuals by differentiating the rewards for jobs which have been rendered substantially uniform by the fragmentation of tasks, then these artificial differences falsify analysis of cost prices, and consequently also of investment criteria. They also upset the balance of the assembly line by impeding the transfer of workers between different machines. If jobs are not individualized, then complicated plans are needed to involve the participation of the workers in apparent productivity gains. The success of such schemes is highly uncertain, yielding the results expected in terms of social stabilization only when they secure trade-union collaboration. We shall see in Chapter 3 what an essential role collective bargaining played in the orientation taken by the technical division of labour in the 1950s and 1960s, as this procedure involved the workers' official abandonment of direct struggle over conditions of labour in favour of various plans to give them an 'interest' in the performance of the enterprise. The violent reactions of workers to certain of these plans in the late 1960s, together with unofficial actions taken outside the framework of the trade unions expressed their growing consciousness of the illusory character of these schemes as against the very real abandonment of their means of struggle.

The considerable slowing down in the fall in real social wage costs that can be observed from the mid 1960s onwards was the expression in the value field of this challenge to Fordism as the general mode of management of wage-labour. In studying the general panorama of capitalist accumulation in the United

States, we started by identifying the contemporary epoch of restraint on the rise in the rate of surplus-value as a crisis of the regime of intensive accumulation. We can now take one step further in our account of its structural determinants and begin to characterize its general features as a *crisis of the reproduction of the wage relation*, which affects methods and goals of production, as well as modes of life. The social conditions which permitted capitalist relations of production to be universalized through the transformation of the way of life of the wage-earning class have now undergone a profound alteration. The class struggles in production today bear the germ of a major new transformation of the labour process – Neo-Fordism.

3. The Problems Posed by Automation in the Labour Process: Neo-Fordism

'Neo-Fordism', a term proposed by Christian Palloix,[4] is an evolution of capitalist relations of production, still in its embryonic stage, that is designed to meet the crisis in such a way as to safeguard the reproduction of the wage relation – in other words, to perpetuate capitalism. It is impossible to tell here whether this evolution will succeed, for it implies not only a major transformation of the labour process, but also a socialization of the mode of life, with forms that are still hard to perceive. Only at the end of this work shall we attempt to make any overall judgement. What we are concerned with in the present chapter are simply those problems which directly bear on obstacles to growth in the output of social labour-power and arise on the semi-automatic assembly line, as well as the manner in which capitalism has sought to overcome them.

Neo-Fordism, like Fordism itself, is based on an organizing principle of the forces of production dictated by the needs of capitalist management of the work collective. The new complex of productive forces is automatic production control or automation; the principle of work organization now in embryo is known as the recomposition of tasks. The combination of these two lines of development has unleashed the most shameless propaganda about the liberation of man in work. It is certainly

---

[4] See Palloix, op. cit.

possible that automation does contain possibilities which will eventually, in the very long run, lead mere operative work in production to disappear. But one thing is sure here and now. These possibilities will have no chance of being realized unless capitalist relations of production are abolished. This abolition will not be accomplished by pondering over possibilities that have not yet been realized by scientific development. Capitalism has shaped automation, just as it shapes every other system of productive forces, so as to make it a material infrastructure for the production of surplus-value, on which the reproduction of capitalist relations of production depends. If automation is a revolution, it is so in the sense that every major transformation of production methods within capitalism provokes a change in the value composition of total social capital that accelerates the devalorization of fixed capital invested and creates conditions favourable to accumulation. The problem is to know whether the change in work organization made possible by the introduction of automatic production control can canalize the class struggle into forms compatible with the law of accumulation.

(a) Automatic production control. In principle automatic production control is qualitatively superior to the coordinated machine complex of 'systems engineering'. We have seen that the latter still involved the direct application of living labour to the flow of productive operations. It was this direct connection that, even while it subjugated labour, created constraints in spatial organization and in temporal rhythm. We have also seen that the technical division of labour under this principle ended by colliding with these constraints. In Fordism, the production process has been completely liberated from any limits imposed by the physical strength of individual human beings. Yet it remains dependent on the reaction times, faculties of perception, concentration and detection of individuals, and on the rapidity with which they can coordinate their movements. When all these faculties are pushed to their limit by the logic of assembly-line work under the spur of relative surplus-value production, we saw that multiple forms of time-wastage appear. These tendencies are reinforced by the diversification of production processes which imposes on one and the same manufacturing unit an output plan made up of distinct and successive

short production runs. The rigidity of the assembly-line process is costly in terms of balance delay time, starting time, as well as of modification of the moving parts, special tooling and skilled labour able to adjust multiple functioning machine tools.

The new principle of work organization is that of a totally integrated system in which production operations properly so called, as well as measurement and handling of information, react upon one another as elements in a single process, conceived in advance and organized in its totality, rather than in successive and separate steps of an empirical process of heterogeneous phases. An organization of this kind is made possible by the systematic application of the principle of feedback to the functioning machine tools. The basis of the entire system is thus the ability to *construct machines that control their own operations.*

This requirement presupposes a considerable development of forces of production, in three respects:

(1) A scientific and no longer merely empirical knowledge of each phase in the production process. This is true above all for continuous flow processes that do not depend merely on mechanical but also on chemical actions. In order for the production process to be capable of controlling itself, a circular flow of information is required on the determinant parameters of the process, so that their variations can give rise to suitable corrective impulses that are instantly transmitted. This requires a rigorous and complete mathematical representation of the material transformations that are to be controlled.

(2) It is one thing to set up automatic control of assembly-line production sequences whose configuration has already long been developing in the direction of a fragmentation and integration of jobs. It is something else again – a far more considerable and risky enterprise – to create an automatic linkage between distinct sequences in a labour process that have formerly been accomplished by different work collectives. This second objective requires a complete reconstruction of the production unit according to entirely new plans for the circulation of products, a complete redefinition of production norms, job positions and changes in both the nature of the responsibilities and the identity of those responsible for the course of production.

(3) These changes in work organization have only been made possible by the dual advances of electronics in the treatment of information and capacity to programme systems on the one hand, and in the production of instruments of measurement and control for diverse production processes on the other. It is this progress that has led to the introduction of *numerically controlled machine-tools*. It is the perfecting of the forms taken by this numerical control that determines more than anything else the contemporary pace of transformation of the labour process. Automatic 'production control introduces a new flexibility. For the same principle can be incorporated in different complexes of productive forces; it is adaptable both to mass production and to production in short or medium runs. In the first case what is involved is direct numerical control in which a series of machine tools operating on a definite segment of the production process is linked to a central computer and programmed to adapt itself to any kind of variation. This combination is known as a transfer machine. The coupling of transfer machines and automatic conveyors, programmed so as to provide reserves of intermediate components as a function of the production rhythm, forms a transfer line. The installation of transfer lines, which is very costly in terms of fixed capital, centralizes production enormously, and only becomes worthwhile from the capitalist point of view if very high levels of output can be regularly maintained. This is why automatic production control has only made its big leap forward very recently, with the introduction of incorporated numerical control. Here each machine tool is equipped with its own mini-computer, of the kind which the miniaturization of integrated electronic circuits has made possible to produce. The functioning of the machine is then completely freed from the motor and sensory limits of the human operator. Precision is improved, production time sharply reduced, and above all, the time taken to prepare the machine system for different conditions of use can be reduced from several hours to a few minutes, while completely eliminating the need for skilled personnel.

The role of the economist is to envisage the effects that the development of these new forces of production have on value relations. The first and most important of these effects is a relative saving of labour-power in production. This saving results from a series of changes affecting the work collective. First of all, there is a de-skilling process that arises from the suppression of complex tasks. As the operatives have only to supervise the machines and test their correct functioning, it is possible for each to supervise several at a time. One section of production jobs is thus eliminated. Since the work of these operatives has no direct effect on output, they can be paid simply by the hour, thus dispensing with all problems related to the determination of output. Finally, since it is no longer necessary to individualize jobs, and since the ending of manual operation of the machines makes tasks objectively homogeneous, it is easy to switch workers around, adding some and taking away others, and in this way reduce to a considerable extent the problems posed by absenteeism. The number of foremen, quality controllers and other supervisory staff is also sharply reduced. The engineering department, on the other hand, is expanded. The complete transfer of production programming decisions to this department creates new jobs for skilled technicians, in a division of mental labour that is ever more rigorous. But the very centralization that is realized by this automatic control means that the creation of new skilled jobs is far from making up for the destruction of old skills resulting from the change in work organization, inasmuch as it makes sense to speak of compensation of this kind, since the skills involved are heterogeneous and thus incommensurable. What is certainly true is that the homogenization effected by exchange absorbs the transformations in the labour process when the general commodity circulation satisfies the monetary constraint – that is to say socially validates the totality of abstract labour. The transformations in the labour process that are based on automation then have an overall effect in the field of value: a reduction in the variable capital required to produce the same amount of value. They thus give rise to a relative surplus-value. But we know that this surplus-value is only effectively realized if the equivalence relationships of exchange evolve in such a way as to counteract the tendency to the uneven development of Department I that follows from the rising organic composition of capital, as the translation into the value field of the relative saving on labour-power.

What then is the effect of automation here? It is scarcely

possible to answer this without analysing the new type of interactions that the extension of this mode of organization is coming to establish between the two departments of production. There is as yet no overall study of this question, inasmuch as we are still at the moment in the midst of the crisis of Fordism, and the new interactions are as yet only little visible. Yet it is possible to make some general points about the perspectives for change that the division of labour based on automatic production control must necessarily induce in the value division of the overall product into quantities of value of different sorts of commodity. Automatic production control divides up the production processes in a new way, linked on the one hand to a centralization that permits direct control of production by long-distance transmission of information, and on the other hand to a rearrangement of the segments of a complex labour process to allow for important savings in transfer time, quality control and the preparation of production programmes. A far more advanced centralization of production becomes compatible with a geographical decentralization of the operative units (manufacture and assembly). A far-reaching modification of relationships between industries develops, replacing electro-mechanical items of high value by electronic items of low value. The capitalist class can benefit from this in two ways. On the one hand, a far greater flexibility in the installation of production units allows it to break up large working-class concentrations and create an environment that minimizes convergence of struggles at the point of production. On the other hand, the development of electronic industries with simple and standardized production methods tends to lower the value of constant capital and consequently to counteract the rise in the organic composition of capital. The capitalist class then has simply to make sure of the essential factor: total domination of programming centres, research methods, and processing of information, and total submission of the highly skilled personnel responsible for them. If such a separation between the work of conception and the work of execution, and such a concentration of effective managerial power over the forces of production can be accomplished, we can foresee a simultaneous long-run pressure on both constant and variable capital. The regime of intensive accumulation could then survive the crisis of Fordism.

(b) The recomposition of tasks. The attempts to alter the organization of labour which have multiplied since the mid 1960s must be seen in the perspective of the development of automatic production control, and the transformation of capitalist relations of production which has just been explained. Their objective is to overcome the crisis in the reproduction of the wage relation inherited from Fordism by transforming the labour process in accordance with the flexibility given by automation. At the present time, no new dominant form of the labour process has yet emerged. All we can do therefore is to elicit the significance of the principles now being experimented from the basic standpoint of the perpetuation of wage-labour.

The analysis of the labour process we have already conducted allows us to assert that there is a change in the general principles of work organization whenever there is a change in the modalities of capitalist management of the labour process. Automation brings with it the possibility of such a major transformation, because it replaces the rigid integration of the mechanical principle with an integration that is both more flexible and more far-reaching, based on overall control by a general information system able to analyse and correct the parameters of production. The hierarchical principle of capitalist control is thus somewhat modified. Control via directives transmitted from a high command is replaced by direct control over the production process. This control is both more abstract and more rigorous. *The workers are no longer subjected to a constraint of personal obedience, but rather to the collective constraint of the production process.*

The various different experiments now being made in the labour process should be assessed by the criterion of whether or not they betoken new relations in production. In this respect, *job rotation* and *job enrichment* are simply the ultimate extensions of the principles of Fordism and Taylorism. They are palliatives for the time imbalances between different jobs which appear on the assembly lines when work is too fragmented. A certain rearrangement of the workers' operating cycles is needed to combat these losses of time and to secure a more effective fit between the number of job positions and the number of distinct tasks. This rearrangement, which may include a certain regrouping of operations, is itself based on a parcelization of work which tends to make the workers indifferent to their jobs. A certain polyvalence on the part of the operatives results, not because they become more skilled, but on the contrary because the division of labour has pushed the process of de-skilling to a maximum, by stripping work of all its specific characteristics. It would be a serious mistake, therefore, to interpret the multiplication of tasks within a single job position as a backward step. On the contrary, it is the collectivization of work in the form of abstract labour that creates the uniformity permitting this multiplication, which is in no way the revival of the kind of qualitative content characteristic of a craft. Widened work is just as empty as before, and as completely reduced to pure duration as was earlier fragmented work.

Job enrichment, leading to the formation of *semi-autonomous groups*, is on the contrary the mode of work organization corresponding to the general principle formulated above, even if it is still in its embryonic stage. It combines operations of component control, preparation and regulation of the machines, with tasks of execution under the responsibility of the same operators. This is because job enrichment is not an enrichment in the literal sense of the term. On the contrary, numerically controlled machines also strip the tasks of preparation and regulation of any qualitative content requiring specialization; the principle of automatic control completely removes the manufacturing process from the workers' vigilance or influence. In conditions of this kind, the interest of capitalist management lies in the suppression of categories of skilled workers, fitters and setters, who are no longer needed, and the devolution of all supervisory operations and simple manipulation of the machines to the operators themselves. At the same time, the division of the production process is modified by automation in a far-reaching way. Semi-autonomous groups emerge, responsible for manufacturing or assembly programmes. Rigorously integrated into the overall information system of the enterprise, and entirely subjected to the programming and controlling centre for the branch in which they are situated, these groups are constrained by a detailed production programme defined for them and by prescribed links between the various groups. Each group, moreover, is collectively responsible for the execution of the production plan, and has charge of the functional services directly bound up with it. It divides up its tasks between its members. Freed from the necessity of making sure that the labour constraint is respected in each individual case, capitalist management can thin out the hierarchical pyramid of command. It thereby hopes to be better able to isolate and attenuate conflicts that arise at the point of production, and to paralyse the functioning of the trade unions, by creating a form of organization for the working class that is alternative to that of the trade-union structures and integrated into the enterprise.

II. The Struggle to Establish a Normal Working Day and the Formation of the Trade-Union Movement

As we have seen, under the regime of extensive accumulation, where absolute surplus-value predominates, the length of the working day is the principal means of extracting surplus labour. This was therefore the main issue of the class struggle in the 19th century. A social norm codified in legislation, and thus guaranteed by the state, was only definitively obtained after three-quarters of a century of class struggle. It was only obtained, moreover, in the context of the development of Taylorism, then of Fordism, which created more effective ways of increasing the output of social labour-power. The problem of the determination of working hours, which poses the question of the role of the trade-union movement, is thus complementary to the study of the labour process.

The specific conditions of the development of capitalism in the United States had a considerable influence on the formation of the wage-earning class, which took an original course. Up till the Civil War, the existence of an open frontier gave wage workers the hope of being able to escape their condition. The formation of stable proletarian organizations, at once permanent and provided with sufficient resources to conduct ongoing struggles on a wide front in the face of extremely powerful adversaries, proved to be an extremely lengthy historical process. In the sixty years up till 1890, the trade unions managed to create a structured national organization only in two short periods, after the Civil War and then again in 1880–85. It was only in the final decade of the 19th century that the American Federation of Labour managed to establish itself as a permanent organization.[5] Up till that time, trade unions were essentially local organizations formed in phases of prosperity, which the employers easily managed to destroy as soon as economic conditions took a turn for the worse. Organized on a craft basis, these unions only managed to organize narrow fringes of the working-class population, generally among the skilled workers. Seeking as they did to obtain and safeguard conditions of labour suitable for their craft, they had no interest in conducting any continuous action for general legislation.

They also had to face political and legal conditions that were highly unfavourable. The federal character of the USA gave each state almost total autonomy in labour legislation, and as in every other field, this prerogative was fiercely defended. A particularist mentality, whose origins went back to the struggle against English colonialism, was particularly virulent in the newer states, which were determined not to fall into political dependence on the rich states of the Northeast. It was thus extremely difficult to enforce any general legislation. Besides, in a country where socio-economic relations secreted an extremely strong individualist ideology, and an identification between the idea of private property and that of the national interest, any mass movement appeared anti-American. There was always a strong tendency, therefore, for those states which had passed a more progressive labour legislation subsequently to regress in order to align themselves with the others. The defence of private property, finally, was interpreted in the law courts in an extremely broad sense, the courts actually becoming the most effective state institutions for combating the workers' movement. Judges repeatedly upheld the unconstitutional character of legislation placing barriers on the exploitation of the workers, as a violation of the freedom of the wage contract; without actual legal opposition to the establishment of trade unions, the courts sought to paralyse their action by

[5] See J.R. Commons and others, *History of Labor in the United States*, New York, 1921–35 (4 vols), J.G. Rayback, *A History of American Labour*, New York, 1966.

interpreting their struggles as interference with free exchange (the right to work being defined in law as individual free exchange between the wage-earner and the employer), and later as a violation of the anti-trust laws. It was only in 1935, in a completely new political climate, that the trade unions were officially recognized at the national level by the National Labor Relations Act (better known as the Wagner Act).

The struggle to reduce the working day was marked by these institutional conditions. The movement for a legal limitation began in New England in the 1840s. This was the most industrialized region, and the most densely endowed with means of communication. In Massachusetts a workers' organization with the explicit aim of obtaining the 10-hour day in law was founded in 1842, and rapidly spread throughout New England. Its demands also included a ban on the employment of children under 12, and the prohibition of night work for women and children. But this movement did not win much in the way of results. Certain city authorities did grant a 10-hour day to public employees, but only rarely was this legislation extended to the private economy. When it was, as in Pennsylvania in 1848 and New Jersey in 1851, legislation restricting the duration of labour was hedged with clauses allowing the law to be evaded if the worker accepted this in his contract of employment. This clause, designed to safeguard the 'freedom of the labour contract', gave employers a convenient and legal escape route. They had in fact a whole arsenal of weapons for dissuading from employment workers who refused to accept this 'free contract'. The employers' action was also greatly facilitated by the weakness of working-class organizations, itself a product of the relative lack of class consciousness in a mobile society where individualism was incited by genuine economic opportunities. Since labour organizations represented above all the interests of those categories of workers who were both skilled and located in the most dynamic branches of the economy, rises in wages that were granted in periods of prosperity were sufficient to weaken the will to struggle for a uniform legislation on working conditions. In periods of crisis, on the other hand, the employers had every interest in dismissing whole sections of their workers and extracting the maximum labour out of the remainder. These two modes of the appropriation of labour-power combined to put pressure on wages and increase absolute surplus-value. The weakness of the unions and the narrowness of their base made it easy for the bosses subsequently to cancel the few gains that were won. If local legislation had been passed, it was either formally repealed or else abandoned in practical application. In every trial, the courts upheld the bosses' case.

Finally, direct violence with its habitual arsenal of black-lists, spying, private repressive forces, campaigns of defamation in the press, the hiring and introduction of a servile labour force recruited clandestinely, lock-outs, were all used on a vast scale.

These features of the American class struggle, marked by the instability of workers' organizations, the intermittence of their objectives, the reinforcement of repression by the bosses, the great sensitivity of the balance of forces to the economic and political conjuncture, the heterogeneity of the working class, incessantly aggravated by the arrival of new strata of immigrants of disparate origins, all left their stamp on the struggle for the social determination of working conditions, right through to the New Deal.

With the degradation of living standards and the concentration of workers in the industrial centres which sprang up under the impulse of a very rapid accumulation of capital, labour conflicts increased in scope, duration and violence. After the sanguinary clashes that punctuated the late 19th century and the first attempts at mass unionization, the struggle for the 8-hour day and the 6-day week culminated in the bloody demonstration in Chicago's Haymarket Square on May 4th, 1886. The Haymarket defeat spelt the end of the hope for a mass movement unifying the working class for fifty years. The trade unionism that grew up on the ruins of earlier struggles, and which took advantage of the serious dissensions that the defeat in Chicago had provoked within the working class, was consciously a corporative unionism intended to defend the interests of workers of specific crafts and trades.

This is not sufficient, however, to explain the political campaigns to reform labour conditions which gained in strength between 1907 and 1917. This movement, however, developed to a great extent outside militant trade unionism. It is evidence of the impact on the United States of the upsurge of socialist ideas and movements in this period as a whole, even if transformed by the particular political structures and ideas of North America. This progressive movement succeeded in getting the state governments to pass a series of ameliorative laws. Nearly every state established a minimum age for wage-labour (12 or 14 years); a certain number prohibited night work for children, as well as certain dangerous or strenuous tasks; forty states fixed maximum working hours for women. But the restriction of working hours for men continued to be blocked by insurmountable obstacles. Among major industries, it was only the railways, after countless accidents and the intervention of the Federal government, which did not want to see the transport system paralysed by a general strike, that adopted the 8-hour day in 1917. It was war production, moreover, by strengthening the position of the workers, that finally enabled the generalization of the 8-hour day and the 44-hour week in all industries except steel, with overtime paid at a higher rate.

The gains won by the working class during the First World War were once again short-lived. Capitalist reaction took advantage of the international political conjuncture created by the deep split in the socialist movement after the October Revolution in Russia. In the United States more easily than elsewhere, the revolutionary fraction of the workers' movement, which had been weak in any case, was isolated and crushed in the propitious conditions of the 1920–21 recession. These events enabled the capitalist class to launch a general anti-union campaign and take the offensive on the political front. A number of craft unions were forced to disband, while the courts paralysed the actions of those that remained. The big corporations organized their own company unions and embarked on the new methods of personnel management characteristic of Fordism. It was this far-reaching transformation of the labour process according to the principles of Fordism that explains why the weakening of the working class was not expressed at this time in an extension of average working hours.

The Great Depression profoundly changed the consciousness of the working class, as well as the attitude to industrial conflicts of a large number of social groups politically attached to the liberal bourgeoisie, especially when these conflicts occurred in branches of industry dominated by the giant corporations. On the one hand a mass movement developed and led to the formation of the Congress for Industrial

Organization (CIO) in 1936. Its positions were far more radical than those of the traditional unions, and found expression in a massive unionization of workers in the key branches of steel and motor vehicles, after the spectacular strikes of autumn 1936 to winter 1937.[6] On the other hand, the political balance of forces had greatly changed when a reformist bloc with a great majority in the industrial states and Congress carried the New Deal administration to power. One of the fundamental principles of this wide-ranging overhaul of the institutions of capitalist society was the codification of the class struggle. This involved official recognition of trade-union organizations with major powers of negotiation vis-à-vis the bosses, and the means to exercise these powers without their legal existence being endangered. It also required negotiations and arbitration procedures to take place within a legislative framework established at the national level. This was the spirit of the Wagner Act of 1935. This time the organized rebellion by employers against the new labour legislation was defeated, thanks to the vast political support won by the struggles of the working class to impose recognition of its trade-union organizations, a support that motivated a change in the Supreme Court's interpretation of the constitutionality of social legislation. This political success was expressed in the Fair Labor Standards Act of 1938. This law, passed by Congress, was applied under the authority of the Federal government. It established a minimum wage and laid down a framework for working conditions. The working week was set at 44 hours, with a clause stipulating its reduction to 40 hours within 3 years. Additional hours had to be paid at time and a half. The employment of children under 16 was forbidden in almost all sectors of industry. This law was genuinely enforced. The 40-hour week was generally established after the Second World War in those industries where the level of unionization was high.

III. Forms of Wage and Labour Process

We broached the problem of wage-determination by defining a nominal reference wage $\bar{s}$. This first approach, however, was far from exhausting the question, since it conceptualized wages in

[6] 'The Industrial War', *Fortune*, 1937.

their most fundamental or most abstract respect. At this degree of abstraction, wages can evidently not be directly equated with the individual worker's pay slip. They are a monetary sum denoting a social relation of distribution by which total revenue is divided.

Theoretical development from abstract to concrete is not only a scientific mode of exposition. It also involves a decisive ideological issue. For the observer uninterested in the overall reproduction of economic relations can readily concern himself simply with the labour market, taking it in isolation as a market where the parties to exchange stand on an equal footing. For such an observer, what exists spontaneously is an individual hourly wage as the price of an hour's concrete labour in such and such a trade, or else a piecework wage which is the price of the 'labour factor' expended in the manufacture of this item. It is therefore labour itself which seems to be paid for. The daily, weekly or monthly wage appears to be simply the product of the unit price of labour and the amount of labour expended. The labour involved in this conception has absolutely nothing to do with abstract labour. For, as we have seen, the latter is a principle of abstraction that permits the construction from economic objects of a space, the set of equivalence classes in exchange, whose mathematical structure is such that a measurement can be defined for it. For the neo-classical school, on the contrary, labour is a 'productive service', in other words a use-value. There are as many productive services as there are different species of labour. These species are heterogeneous, but exchange is deemed to be an immediate quantitative relation between a useful good and a type of labour, which directly determine the price of the labour in terms of the good. The price determinations for different types of labour are written into the general equilibrium, as a configuration of quantitative ratios in which net excess demands are all cancelled, those of different types of labour included. In this conception, it is clear that the existence of a nominal reference wage, which has a strictly social character and forms the pivot for different individual wages, cannot be entertained. Nor can the diversity of forms in which wages are paid, or their historical evolution, be theorized. These are relegated by neo-classical theory to institutional contingency, and therefore excluded from economic thought. The neo-classical claim to grasp the concrete can only convince those fascinated with monetary differences in individual wages, who think these differences are capable of an immediate interpretation without any prior need to investigate what wage-labour actually is.

It remains true nonetheless that differences in individual wages form part of the complex phenomena of the reproduction of wage-labour. They need to be explained, though there is no single principle for explaining them. With this problem, we approach the immense question of the internal stratification of the wage-earning class. The definition of the concept of wages and its position within the theory of value characterize wage-labour as the product of a general and uniform social relation that is the basis of capitalism. The stratification of the wage-earning class forms part of the concrete conditions of reproduction of the wage relation. It is not to be analysed in the field of value, but it is evident in the effects of these conditions on the monetary form of value, in other words here on the wage. Now there are different types of division superimposed on one another within the working class, and these in turn are changeable since they result from the class struggle and are subject to the unifying force of the wage relation itself. But in the homogeneous field of monetary quantities, the effects of these divisions are additive. Hence any immediate rather than critical registration of differences of wages is a mystification, which makes it impossible to analyse either what all wages have in common, or those differentiations that arise from diverse processes of stratification.

The factors of differentiation with which we shall be concerned in the present chapter are the major changes in the labour process. These changes generate qualitative modifications in the concrete forms in which wages are paid, and correlatively in the principles obeyed by the quantitative differences between the individual wages of interchangeable workers.

The superimposition of different types of labour process in different industries does not make it possible to identify a strict historical succession in the modalities of immediate wage payment. Yet the dominant character of the organizational principles of Taylorism, and subsequently of Fordism, can be perceived in the importance assumed by certain forms of wages relative to others for those industries that underwent changes in their labour process. At the present time, moreover, the emergence of Neo-Fordism is engendering debates and experiments tending to loosen or even completely dissolve the relationship between wages and output.

The identification of forms of wages and the demonstration of an irreversible evolution from some forms to others thus has a great historical significance in the study of the development of capitalist relations of production. The United States has not only originated the major transformations of the labour process in the 20th century, but has also created the most modern – in other words, the most collective – form of direct wage determination.

1. Time Wages and the Working Day

The most venerable and classical form of wages in large-scale industry is hourly payment. We may note that the hourly wage actually paid to different individual workers fluctuates around a basic rate which forms the object of general negotiations when the workers' movement is organized on a major scale and its rights are recognized in law. Such negotiations, which go far beyond any individual contract between employers and employed, reveal that wages express an overall relationship between the classes. We can also observe that the determination of the basic hourly wage is indissolubly tied to the overall duration of the labour inscribed in its definition. Thus it is not the duration of labour actually performed, which may well vary from one date to another, which enters into the definition of the basic hourly wage, but rather the duration of labour considered normal by society.

The determination of the basic hourly wage is therefore the product of the general class struggle over the fixing of a typical wage contract and the establishment of the duration of labour by which the basic hourly wage is calculated. What is the relationship between the basic hourly wage and the nominal reference wage? The latter denotes the overall relation of distribution characteristic of capitalism. As we have seen, it is defined by the total wage sum paid to the workers producing commodities divided by the total abstract labour performed by this social labour-power.

A first difference appears between the basic hourly wage and the nominal reference wage when the duration of effective labour is higher than the legal limit. This corresponds to the payment of overtime. It is important to note that the rates paid for overtime work are socially determined. They are products of the class struggle, which thus enters into the formation of the nominal reference wage. If this latter was simply a direct wage, as is the basic hourly rate, then the number of additional hours would be the sole source of divergence. But the nominal reference wage is the monetary form of the reproduction of social labour-power. For reasons which we shall examine in Chapter 3, this includes a purchasing power that is not directly paid to the individual workers but which appears in the form of an indirect wage whose payment depends on different modalities from those of the direct wage. Consequently, if we are speaking of the overall reproduction of the wage-earning class, which is necessary in order to define the nominal reference wage, then the wage total to be taken into account is the sum of direct wages and social benefits paid in the sectors producing commodities. This sum is the monetary form of variable capital. It is necessary to consider it in theory as divided into a quantum of direct wages and a quantum of indirect wages, each ensuring a different aspect of the reproduction of the wage-earning class. The law of this division, even if complex, still involves a series of social rules which fix the amount of indirect wages as a function of the sum of direct wages.

This double distinction between effective and nominal duration on the one hand, and between direct and indirect wages on the other, introduces an important flexibility into the determination of individual wages. Time wages appear as the product of the basic hourly rate multiplied by the duration of effective labour, corrected by social rules governing the payment of overtime, and the formation and receipt of indirect wages. This is what makes up the monetary resources of each worker. Since these resources fluctuate with the duration of labour, it appears to the observer interested simply in the marginal variations that what is paid is the quantity of labour provided, rather than the labour-power. In reality, these marginal fluctuations can in no way account for the general relation of distribution which divides the overall income created by social labour-power *en masse* into a sum of wages and a sum of profits. On the contrary, it is the division that the wage relation inscribes in total abstract labour that determines the nominal reference wage according to the law of transformation established in the first chapter. But the fact that total capital presents itself as a relation of competition between autonomous individual capitals gives rise to a modulation of individual wages. The total wage sum is distributed unevenly to the individual workers by the mechanism of time wages. This variability in the formation of individual wages is an important element of the laws of competition. It enables individual capitals, whose valorization is subject to the jerkiness of a mode of production that finds its unity only in the blind regulation of equivalence relations of exchange, to ensure that this jerkiness is partially absorbed by the labour-power which they employ.

The evolution of the distribution of individual wages in the course of accumulation passes by way of the mechanism of overtime. The rise in effective duration of labour above that of normal labour derives from the increase in the volume of profit that the capitalists seek in the upswing phases of accumulation. The working class bends its effort to seizing a few advantages in the wake of the expansion of capital. The outcome of the conflict is completely dependent on the control of working conditions. In effect, each individual capitalist has the choice, if he wants to increase his profits, between prolonging the working day for the labour he already employs, making it work extra days outside of those normally composing the working week, or recruiting new workers and making them work in additional teams outside of normal hours. But just as each individual capitalist is subject to the overall movement of accumulation, so is labour-power to the law of population that is a function of it. During an upswing, relative surplus population is absorbed, since new capitals are formed and invested in production, while the expansion of existing capitals is accelerated. Competition for workers can act to the detriment of the employers, if the rate of growth of capital formation is sufficiently rapid. In order to attract additional workers, or else to get the existing work force to work longer hours, the capitalists may be forced to concede special advantages. These concessions will be the more inevitable, the more the trade unions have been able to impose a strict definition of the notion of the normal working day on which the basic hourly wage is calculated. This normal duration does not refer simply to the length of the working day, but also to its position in the working week (for example the 8-hour day and the 5-day week), as well as its position in the 24-hour day. It is in relation to this definition that additional hours and hours worked outside the usual limits of the day or week are paid at a higher rate. The nominal daily or weekly wage rises more sharply than the time worked rises above the normal duration. The outcome is then that the apparent hourly wage rises above the basic hourly wage, particularly for individual workers in the upper fringes of overtime.

The opposite is the case when effective working time falls below the normal duration during a downswing in the business cycle. This happens to an uneven degree in different branches and firms, and the payment of workers according to a stipulated basic hourly wage then reduces the decline in profits. In the United States, where the risks of competition are shifted systematically and massively onto the workers, as part of the normal course of events under capitalism, recession brings not only the total unemployment of some workers, but also the partial unemployment of others. The form of time wages is admirably suited to these jolts. Flexibility in the workers' mode of consumption is, of course, essential to this mechanism. But this flexibility has its limits, marked by the existence of a minimum wage compatible with a basic maintenance of labour-power.

Working-class struggles have long sought to gain recognition of the need for a guaranteed minimum wage, however sharply the actual hours worked may fall. In this way they directly reveal that what is at issue in the wage relation, under the guise of the hourly wage, is the division of the working day between the value of labour-power and surplus-value.

2. Piecework and the Stimulation of Output

Piecework is a derivative form of time wages that forms part of the application of the principles of Taylorism. The two forms are generally found together in related labour processes within the same industry. Piecework provides an expression of the basic wage that explicitly takes into account the variations in the intensity of labour. This is why piecework can only be practised in labour processes that are sufficiently mechanized for the cycle of each worker's actions to be simple and repetitive enough to be readily reducible to pure duration, though insufficiently integrated for output still to be measurable individually for each job.

The first theoretical problem raised here is the relationship existing between piecework and the basic hourly wage. Piecework payment is fixed to a job with rigorously specified characteristics. Its foundation is an elementary measurement of output in terms of the time needed to complete a cycle of actions pertaining to a specified job. Knowledge of the output norm for the job makes it possible to determine the number of items it is possible to produce in normal working conditions, in other words by deploying labour-power according to an average intensity for the cycle of actions in question, over a working day of given length. We thus get the following relationship:

Average number of items produced (for a specified job position) = Normal working day/Job output norm

This measurement takes into account those periods of inactivity that cannot be utilized by a labour process whose technical characteristics and overall organization are both already determined. The *basic piecework wage* can then be defined in the following way:

Basic piecework wage = Nominal daily wage for normal working time/Average number of items produced per day

Hence:

Basic piecework wage = Basic hourly wage × job output norm.[7]

By tying the basic wage explicitly to the job, Taylorism created far more opportunities for individual wages to be differentiated, and the capitalists took advantage of these to link remuneration to a stimulation of labour intensity. Payment for overtime at a higher hourly rate is in strict accordance with the prologation of working time. The determination of the basic

---

[7] The output norm being measured in fractions of a working hour.

hourly wage itself is social in nature, and follows from the nature of the wage relation. This is a determination that escapes the individual capitalist.

Yet time wages do not enable a precise calculation of real costs, since they cannot give rise to any measurement of differences in productivity in different jobs. It is only such an attentive and repeated measurement that can provide the motivations and means for a transformation of the technical conditions of production in the direction of an ever greater compression of living labour, and hence a rise in the rate of surplus-value. Now the collectivization of work fragments individual tasks and multiplies their diversity; it makes it necessary to study very precisely both partial movements and their integration. Piecework thus makes it possible both to lower the basic wage to the extent that the productivity of partial tasks increases, and to individualize wages in such a way as to sharpen competition among workers to a maximum. The common interest of all capitalists here appears to coincide with that of individual workers taken in isolation. Piecework has the signal ideological advantage for the capitalist class of inducing the illusion that wages as an economic category are tied to work performed, since individual wages actually are modulated as a function of differences in labour intensity. Once again, marginalist doctrine comes to the aid of capitalism. The nature of the wage relation and the social norm that corresponds to it are completely hidden. All that is visible is a distribution of individual wages that is deemed to represent the natural fit between the categories of 'wages' and 'labour'.

What happens in reality is that those workers endowed with a greater aptitude than that taken into account in the output norm, or else those who themselves force up the pace of their work, produce more items in the working day than the average number on which the norm is based. They receive an addition to their wage for the additional items produced. Those whose skill and intensity are less than the norm do not meet their quotas; they not only receive a wage lower than the basic rate, but also risk being replaced by other workers. On the average, however, these differences in either direction compensate for one another, with the result that the overall group of workers employed on a particular job are paid at the level of the basic piece rate.

This means that social labour-power receives its proper price, the monetary equivalent of the working-class consumption norm. If this is not so, then the antagonism of the wage relation creates the force to modify the content of the job, or more generally the labour process as a whole, in such a way as to bring the wage back to its basic level. If the norm is too easy, then a significant proportion of the workers get an additional reward, and capitalist management uses the engineering department to enforce a refixing of the output norm, either directly or by way of a more severe quality control or stricter regulation, or else by technical modification of the job content. If the norm is too severe, then competition between the workers becomes pointless; the work collective solidarizes and the team disrupts production on the job by a concerted decrease in tempo. The more the labour process is integrated and the workers' solidarity extends to associated operations, the more production is disorganized. The work climate then deteriorates. In the long run, management will have to redefine an output norm close to that which yields the basic wage.

There are however three further aspects to the process of this general reduction to the basic wage:

(1) The distribution of individual wages around the basic rate for a given job does not generate the full distribution curve that might be expected of the workers if they pursued the individualistic behaviour of neo-classical logic. This would in fact predict that each worker, as a provider of services, steered between the unpleasant effort and the pleasant remuneration in complete freedom and independence. Since it is reasonable to consider that ability is allocated among individuals on a curve of normal distribution, it is only logical to expect this to be reflected in the distribution of wages. If the output norm had been properly worked out, then the basic wage would be the mid-point of this distribution, from which it would shift a little to one side or the other. But the investigations of American sociologists have shown that this interpretation is totally false.[8] The wage curve for workers on the same job shows two

[8] For a detailed examination of the problems raised by piecework payment, see W.F. Whyte's remarkable study *Money and Motivation*, New York, 1955 and 1970.

very sharp peaks located one on either side of the basic wage. The existence of these two modes indicates two different types of group behaviour. The group of workers producing above the quota corresponding to the basic wage regulates the production of each of its members in such a way that the output gives each of them an equal additional wage, and one sufficiently substantial to justify the higher intensity of work from the workers' point of view; but effective production is limited so as not to be too high above the quota, thus avoiding the risk of a more demanding output norm being imposed. Experience shows that no incentive gives sufficient motivation for increasing labour intensity unless it promises a wage some 15 to 20% above the basic rate. The alternative response is systematic and concerted restriction of production on jobs reckoned to be rated too low to make it worthwhile to fulfill the quota. It is better then to try and force a refixing of the output norm. The two peaks of the curve are not generally the same in height; their relative height rather indicates that the output norm is either on the loose side or on the tight side. The shape of this curve indicates both the potential for competition between workers and the existence of collective responses among them. This gives rise to complex conflictual relations between groups of workers, management and its executive agency in the engineering department, over the fixing of output norms. While the workers will seek to achieve a united position, the management will try to divide them by changing workers round between jobs and possibly taking advantage of the support of temporary workers or those in minority categories. The management's aim, above all else, will be to prevent the workers from acquiring a collective consciousness of their objective unity in the labour process.

(2) Management's room for manoeuvre increases with the diversity of job positions that results from the deepening of the technical division by the specialization and fragmentation of tasks. The result is that a single labour process with different and independent job positions can have a large number of output norms providing a whole series of basic piecework rates. It is no longer possible to say that each of these basic piecework rates is equivalent to the basic hourly wage. But this equivalence is realized on the average. If this were not the case, then

there would be serious conflicts arising from a permanent structural gap between the wages of workers on piecework and those paid by the hour, whether these groups coexisted within one and the same production unit, or were found in different units of a single enterprise. But the existence of a spectrum of basic piecework rates makes it possible to create a wage hierarchy by marking out some jobs as better paid than others. Managements will attempt to use this hierarchy in order to set up scales of promotion by seniority. The more acute labour conflicts are, the more managements seek to extend these differentiations. Since, however, this band of variations can only be marginal around the basic hourly rate, grades become so compressed that differentiation loses its efficacy in dividing the workers. But it still has the serious inconvenience for the capitalists that it obscures analysis of real costs by introducing norms that do not correspond to socially necessary labour-time. The reduction and simplification of wage scales, if constantly countered by the antagonism of the wage relation that obliges the capitalists to divide the workers, is still imperative for the rationalization of production.

(3) The transformation of the labour process modifies the content of jobs and requires a perpetual refixing of their output norms. In the course of this evolution of the basic piecework rate, the wage of the overall group of workers paid on this basis remains governed by the nominal reference wage. This means that there is no link between the increase in individual earnings and the increase in productive efficiency of a worker in a particular job position. If the number of items produced in the working day doubles, then the basic piecework rate is divided by two; the daily reference wage is unchanged. But this reduction is not enforced instantaneously. In order to weaken the workers' resistance to job modifications which may call into question traditional patterns of seniority, management can fix a loose norm when a technical change is introduced, presenting it as a trial. It can then later move to a stricter determination, when the new job has become a well organized routine position. Since such modifications are incessant, the existence of jobs in this trial phase gives rise to an additional reason for variation in individual wages.

3. The Influence of the Collectivization of Work on Forms of Wages

The major transformations of the labour process denoted by the terms Fordism and Neo-Fordism engender changes in the forms of wages. These changes express an ever growing rigidity in the wage distribution and represent the contractual relations by which the growing unification of the wage-earning class is expressed in the fixing of individual wages. At any point in time, the distribution of wages among the workers is the resultant of the modes of work organization that coexist in production. The temporal evolution of this distribution is chiefly influenced by the type of labour process that becomes socially dominant in the conditions of production.

(a) Collective output bonuses. These bonuses establish the specific correspondence between basic hourly wage and the nominal reference wage which is characteristic of Fordism. Collective plans for stimulating output were developed in the course of the Second World War and particularly in the 1950s, the period in which Fordism became the dominant form of work organization in the United States.[9] We know that in this type of labour process individual jobs lose their autonomy and independence. Henceforward the inability of the workers to exert any influence on the pace of work breaks the link between wages and output at the individual level. Output can be determined only for a work collective defined by a series of organically linked tasks. The collective output bonus replaces piecework as a modulation of the basic hourly wage. Collective output bonuses are devices to induce collectives of workers to renounce any challenge to working conditions in exchange for a general monetary compensation. In order for these plans to succeed, the trade-union organizations must closely collaborate in their operation in the context of collective wage negotiations.

Unlike the basic wage, the collective output bonus does not have the character of a sum of money advanced by contract. It is only paid when sales figures are higher than those correspond-

[9] The most celebrated scheme, which served as a model for several industries in the early 1950s, was known as the Scanlon plan.

ing to the level of production that brings a normal rate of profit in the industry to which the firm in question belongs. The collective output bonus is thus subject to all the vicissitudes of capitalist production, from bad planning to fluctuations in market conditions. The capitalist does not take any risk here. If he has forced up the intensity of the labour process, and the additional product cannot be sold at a price that will realize a monetary surplus over and above the normal sale, then the additional work performed is pure loss and is not paid. It is not the capitalist who bears the costs of it, but the workers. Since the output bonus is an addition to a wage that corresponds to normal production conditions, an output norm must be fixed just as it is with piecework. But here the norm is defined for the collective worker, either the overall group of hourly paid workers, or even the totality of non-managerial employees. The norm thus forms part of the total production cost, and is measured in monetary terms. It is the *wage cost per dollar of sales* for a labour process with given characteristics when the workers are paid the basic hourly wage. The transition from this normal wage cost to the overall wage cost is made by multiplying it by the volume of sales corresponding to a normal activity of the workforce (in duration and intensity), and setting a reference price for these sales. The wage cost per dollar of sales is then compared month by month with the relation between the effective overall wage cost and the exchange-value of sales effectively realized. A planned correction can be made so as to take account of variations in the sales price. If the ratio between total real wage costs and the exchange-value of sales is lower than the normal wage cost per dollar of sales, then there is an output bonus. The total bonus is determined by the formula:

Collective bonus = [(Normal wage cost − Actual overall wage cost)/Exchange value of sales] × Exchange value of sales.

This bonus is then divided among the workers according to forms that can vary as decided (equal division, division proportional to working hours or wages received). In certain cases one section of the overall bonus is not immediately distributed, but forms a reserve fund to compensate for periods in which working hours fall below the normal level.

Finally, just as modifications in the content of a particular job lead to the refixing of the output norm on which the basic piecework rate is calculated, so too do transformations of an integrated labour process require the refixing of the normal wage cost per dollar of sales on which the overall output bonus is based. Just as the price of labour-power is not affected by individual changes in productivity for a particular job, since the basic piecework rate falls in the same proportion as that in which productivity rises, so the price of labour-power is not affected by local changes in the productivity of a labour process, since the normal wage cost is modified in such a way that the output bonus remains unchanged. The collective output bonus is thus a complex form of wage that derives from the complexity of the labour process engendered by the socialization of the productive forces. But like those we analysed earlier, this form does not change the nature of the wage as the expression of the value of labour-power in commodity relations.

(b) The guaranteed monthly wage and the wage fund. The forms of wage involved here do not represent a return to the individual mechanism of time wages. They are on the contrary forms that push the logic of Fordism to its limit, and begin to become socially significant with the recent development of Neo-Fordism. These forms can make their appearance only when the collectivization of labour has reached so high a degree that productive efficiency becomes a social power entirely de-termined by the integrated system of the productive forces. The emergence of Neo-Fordism marks the onset of a historical tendency in the development of the forces of production that Marx already indicated as a possibility on the horizon of capitalism: the evolution of productivity towards an ever greater independence from the expenditure of living labour, where productive power essentially resides in the growing capacity of modern forces of production to realize an organic integration of productive processes. This organic integration is a different and more advanced form of socialization of labour than equivalence relations of exchange. It can play a part in replacing the blind regulation of the law of value by the possibility of a collective control of production. To the extent that it develops within commodity production, it can weaken the relationship between individual wages, or even the wages of

a group of workers, and output, to the point of non-existence. It thus acts as a powerful force of homogenization in the determination of wages for workers on fragmented jobs. Individual wages lose their flexibility and tend to approximate ever more to the nominal reference wage. The most recent forms of wages, therefore, express more and more clearly the overall relation of distribution imposed on the wage-earners by the capitalist appropriation of the forces of production.

The guaranteed monthly wage evinces rigid differences between industries and regions that derive from the social stratification within the working class. On the average, however, it expresses the nominal reference wage paid on a monthly basis. It protects the reconstitution of labour-power from the consequences of a reduction in working hours below the normal level. It directly appears, therefore, as the monetary counterpart of the social consumption norm. The guaranteed wage may also present itself in form as a time wage, since it is equal to the basic hourly wage multiplied by the number of hours of work, when working hours are equal to the normal duration on which the basic wage is defined.

The wage fund is a guaranteed wage allocated not to each worker separately but rather to a work collective. Individual modulations can lose their capitalist character when they are defined in ways determined by the work collective itself, for example by a semi-autonomous work group.

3

The Transformation of the Wage-Earners' Conditions of Life

I. The Capitalist Production of the Mode of Consumption

The object of this chapter is to investigate the reproduction of social labour-power. It will therefore not deal with individual consumer behaviour, but rather with the formation and transformation of the conditions of existence of the working class – in other words, with the very foundation of capitalist accumulation, the material content of the generalization of the wage relation. We will thereby deepen our theory of wages by identifying those forces whose interaction leads to the fixing of the nominal reference wage, a problem to which we gave an exclusively formal solution in the first section of Chapter 1. We shall also be dealing with the social stratification of the wage-earning class and the way in which capitalism aggravates it. Finally, we shall analyse the creation by the class struggle of new social relations organized into institutions which yield the procedures of collective bargaining, and assess the effect of these procedures on the long-run evolution of the average wage.

In the space of social activities, the reproduction of the wage relation involves a maintenance cycle of social labour-power that is depicted in Diagram 9. Two phenomena at once stand out. On the one hand, the maintenance cycle of social labour-power is a cycle of metamorphoses of value which includes the consumption process, such that the latter is dominated by commodity relations. On the other hand, the cycle has a transverse relationship to the expanded reproduction of capital, via the connection between the two departments of production which we studied in Chapter 1. This relationship of the maintenance cycle of social labour-power to the cycles of accumulation in the two departments of production shows that commodity circulation under capitalism is organized according to a general pattern. For such a general pattern to exist, generating an expansion of commodity circulation as a closed circuit containing the necessary links between the two departments of production, the collective worker shaped by capitalist relations of production must also be structured by those social relations determining the practices of consumption. The separation of workers from the means of production that is the origin of the wage relation brings about a destruction of the various modes of traditional consumption and leads to the creation of a mode of consumption specific to capitalism. A *social norm of working-class consumption* is formed, which becomes an essential determinant of the extension of the wage relation, as a fundamental modality of relative surplus-value. Through the social consumption norm, the mode of consumption is integrated into the conditions of production. The mutations in the productive forces engendered in Department I take effect in Department II by way of a reduction in the value of labour-power and a correlative increase in the rate of surplus-value. Analysis of this integration is an essential aspect of the theory of accumulation.

1. The Formation and Evolution of a Norm of Social Consumption

There are multiple connections between production and consumption in the maintenance cycle of social labour-power. We have seen that the capitalist labour process is governed by the mechanization of labour. Deprived of any craft content, work loses any qualitatively differentiated character that could have an influence on the working-class mode of life. Because labour-power becomes a commodity, it is incorporated into a productive system whose alpha and omega is surplus-value; the fragmentation of tasks and their reduction to pure temporal duration are the internal principles of its evolution. The transformation of relations of production creates a mass production of commodities which tends by the logic of the equivalence relations of exchange to destroy non-capitalist forms of

Diagram 9. The 'Double Reel' of the Reproduction of Capitalist Relations of Production: reproduction of the total capital in each of the two departments of production, and reproduction of the social labour-power.

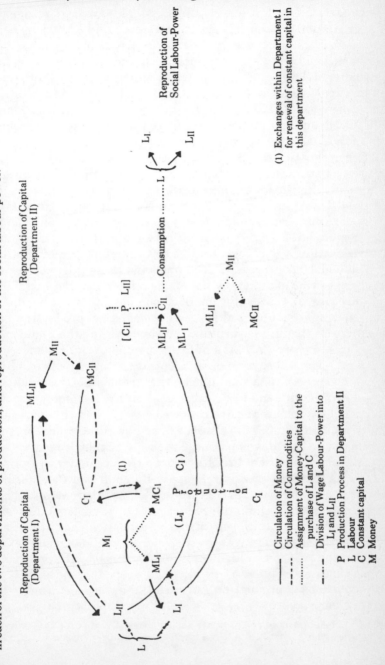

Reproduction of Capital (Department I)

Reproduction of Capital (Department II)

Reproduction of Social Labour-Power

——— Circulation of Money
‑ ‑ ‑ Circulation of Commodities
·········· Assignment of Money-Capital to the purchase of L and C
‑ ·· ‑ Division of Wage Labour-Power into L_I and L_{II}
P Production Process in Department II
L Labour
C Constant capital
M Money

(1) Exchanges within Department I for renewal of constant capital in this department

production to the extent that a single space of commodity circulation is formed. If the workers are rendered homogeneous in the first instance by the capitalist labour process, this homogeneity is decisively reinforced when they are cut off from individual ties of family, or bonds of neighbourhood proximity or supplementary activity that still link them to a non-capitalist environment. Classified as fragments of a single social labour-power, but simultaneously isolated by the wage contract as individual labour-powers in mutual competition, workers are inevitably tied to capitalism by the individual consumption of the commodities provided by mass production. This uniform mode of consumption of simplified products is a *mass consumption*. This is an essential condition of capitalist accumulation, for it counteracts the tendency to the uneven development of Department I. The connections between the two departments of production it forges generalize certain major transformations in the labour process. On the one hand these raise the organic composition of capital, while on the other hand they counteract this rise in the evolution of constant capital over time by reducing the unit value of the means of production, and increase the rate of surplus-value by lowering the social value of labour-power (t_n in the notation used above). This is why the developmental rhythm of mass consumption is at once induced by the preceding accumulation that transforms the conditions of production, and forms a base for future accumulation. The need for a comprehensive linkage between the two departments of production, and the absence of any automatic mechanism to balance their development, has been acknowledged in non-Marxist theoretical literature since Keynes under the guise of the problem of effective demand. But non-Marxist literature never saw the origin of this problem in the inherent antagonism of capitalist relations of production. Keynes opened the way to a far-reaching criticism of the neo-classical adjustments by showing that there was no such thing as a labour market and that the level of employment was determined by the prospective incomes distributed by firms, when account was taken of the conditions of production in which these were operating.[1] This dynamic approach was generally not followed by post-

[1] For an extended analysis of effective demand and post-Keynesian deviations, see B. Schmitt, *L'Analyse macro-économique des revenus*, Paris, 1971.

Keynesian writers like Kaldor, Pasinetti[2] and Sweezy, who reduced the problem of effective demand, in Harrod's perspective, to the question of the effect of rigidity in the distribution of incomes on paths of balanced growth. In the Marxist tradition, the problem of effective demand is an aspect of the production of surplus-value. It is linked to the way in which the class struggle either succeeds or does not succeed in revolutionizing the conditions of production and exchange, and consequently in calling forth an expansion in the mass of commodities produced. We have seen, for example, how in the mid 1920s the semi-automatic production process created an internal barrier to its own development by further weakening the workers' movement after the blows it had already suffered in the wake of the First World War. If in the first phase this weakening led to a rapid divergence in the distribution of incomes, thus inaugurating new consumer markets, the very narrow social base of these markets was incapable of neutralizing for very long the uneven development of Department I, which was considerably accelerated by the new productive forces. Fordism, in other words the entire set of social conditions of the regime of intensive accumulation, had to proceed by way of considerable changes in the modalities of class struggle, in order to establish itself.

(a) The characteristic mode of consumption of Fordism. In order to understand how the transformations of the relations of production within the labour process create impulses that play a primordial role in the formation of a mode of consumption, it is necessary not to view consumption empirically as a sum of expenditure functions, nor in terms of the theory of the individual consumer as the source of an axiomatic set of well-organized and stable choices, given certain resources and market conditions. The praxiological conception of the theory of the individual consumer forms part of a definition of the object of economic science as a logic of individual choices subject to the constraint of scarcity and the rule of a universal principle of rationality (principle of optimization), which is

---

[2] In his more recent work, however, Pasinetti tends once again to give effective demand a broader theoretical status within the dynamic of disequilibrium. See 'The Economics of Effective Demand', in *Growth and Income Distribution; Essays in Economic Theory*, Cambridge, 1970.

radically foreign to the conception on which we base ourselves here – that is, a science of the social laws governing the production and distribution of the means of existence by men and women in organized collectivities. Empirical observation of expenditure functions has a completely different status. It is the statistical expression of the subjection of consumption to commodity relations. It is indispensable in order to grasp how an already established mode of consumption evolves over time, because of its location at the point of contact between exchange and consumption proper. What we need here, however, is something more basic – a theory of those practices that make consumption a socially conditioned *activity*, subject to contrary forces of homogenization and differentiation that modify it in a manner favourable to the generalization of wage-labour. We cannot develop this approach in a book devoted primarily to a general theory of capitalist accumulation; in any case, it is dealt with in several recent studies and controversies.[3] Basing our argument on certain of these studies, we shall confine ourselves to linking the concepts which concern the effect of the transformation of capitalist relations of production on the mode of consumption, to the law of accumulation.

Our point of departure will be a definition of consumption as an activity or more accurately a process, that is, an organized set of activities, which – while predominantly private – are subject to a general logic of the reconstitution of energies expended in social practices and the preservation of abilities and attitudes implied by the social relations of which their subjects are supports. This definition calls for several remarks. First of all, since consumption is a material process, it is located in space; it has a specific geography and object-network. It is also a set of operations in time, an employment of time in the literal sense. The nature of the consumption process and its place in the maintenance cycle of social labour-power are thus strongly conditioned by the importance of labour-time, its intensity as an expenditure of human energy, and the other temporal constraints directly connected with it. Consumption, moreover, is a predominantly private process; its concrete

[3] See in particular 'Besoins et consommation', special number of *La Pensée*, April, 1975; M. Guillaume, *Le capital et son double*, Paris, 1975; J. Baudrillard, *Le système des objets*, Paris, 1968.

practices take place principally within the household, a site where individuality is protected. They are not directly under the sway of the relations of production. This is why they can give rise to varying ideologies and are susceptible to differenti- ation. This differentiation is not contingent, for consumption is also the conservation of abilities and attitudes. This aspect of consumption should not be seen in a principally functional sense. It concerns the position of the individuals concerned in social relations, and the representation of this position within the group of individuals who share it, as well as vis-à-vis other social groups with whom they maintain relations. The basis of this representation is evidently the exercise of real abilities, not intrinsic to the individual, but inherent in the place occupied in social relations, i.e. the *role* required by society. But this representation is effected in the form of a recognition which involves the perception of definite cultural attitudes. This recognition maintains social relations of an ideological nature, although these possess just as 'material' an existence as economic relations. Such relations, which issue from social stratification and require specific reproduction, actively dif- ferentiate the process of consumption. They can be referred to as *status* relations. The concept of status is not merely needed to interpret social differentiations in consumption; it is equally necessary to understand their renewal over time, and the conditions of their stability or distortion which make it possible to speak scientifically of a social process of consumption, or even a mode of consumption. The effect of status on the consumption process is expressed in acquired habits which stabilize the maintenance cycle of labour-power into a routine. These habits are transmitted from one generation to the next. The learning of cultural status codes and the principles of behaviour that follow from them is one of the essential functions of the family; it accompanies the learning of the roles to which families aspire in their inter-generational choices. New individuals thus enter the labour market seeking positions with a status whose ideological features they have already internalized. Only the forces unleashed by capitalist accumu- lation can dissolve these habits, by generalizing mobility and insecurity of employment.

Given these very summary indications, how should we view

the formation and reproduction of the specific mode of consumption of Fordism, which is an essential aspect of the regime of intensive accumulation? For the first time in history, Fordism created a norm of working-class consumption in which individual ownership of commodities governed the concrete practices of consumption. This involved a reversal both of traditional ways of life and of the initial experience of the working class in an epoch of extreme poverty and total insecurity, which provided no basis for any stabilization of consumption habits. In these circumstances, the consumption process was either totally destructured or else organized in the context of the extended family, with a strict division of domestic labour and a great expenditure of domestic labour-time. With Fordism, on the contrary, the generalization of commodity relations extended to their domination of practices of consumption. This was a mode of consumption restructured by capitalism, because the time devoted to consumption witnessed an increasing density in individual use of commodities and a notable impoverishment of non-commodity interpersonal relations. Once the social conditions that enabled this mode of consumption to be reproduced were established, its consumption norm evolved dynamically because its commodity content was directly inscribed in the generalization of the mechanized labour process with semi-automatic control. These conditions were multiple in character and implied so great a change in social practices that it is in no way astonishing that the expansion of Fordism after the Second World War was preceded by a long period of crises and intense class struggles, whose outcome was the establishment of social controls to guarantee the formation of the working-class norm of consumption and to regularize its evolution.

The most immediate of these conditions relate to the influence of transformations of the labour process on the maintenance cycle of labour-power. We have seen how Taylorism, and later Fordism, adapted to the restriction of the working day by sharply increasing the intensity of labour and systematically compressing wasted time. The result was the disappearance of any time for recuperation at the workplace itself. The increased exhaustion of labour-power in the labour process had to be entirely repaired outside the workplace, respecting the new time constraint of a strict separation between working and non-working hours. Since this was overlaid by the further constraint of separation and increased distance between workplace and residence, transport time was considerably prolonged, with the result that the time constraint imposed by labour did not fall despite the limitation of working hours. Individual commodity consumption is the form of consumption that permits the most effective recuperation from physical and nervous fatigue in a compact space of time within the day, and at a single place, the home.

The structure of the consumption norm thus coincides with its conditioning by capitalist relations of production. It is governed by two commodities: the *standardized housing* that is the privileged site of individual consumption; and the *automobile* as the means of transport compatible with the separation of home and workplace. Whilst remaining commodities for private use, these are durable goods whose acquisition goes far beyond the purchasing power of current wages. The formation of the working-class norm of consumption therefore presupposed a vast socialization of finance, and correlatively a very strict control over workers' resources and expenditures. It was important for the process of individual consumption to be organized and stable, while remaining compatible with the apparently individual and free relationships of commodity exchange. This was achieved by the generalization in the working class of the social structure that was the condition for its cultural integration into the nation, i.e. the small family unit and household. Here the working class received a statute that functioned as the regulator of its norm of consumption, through the formation of its expenditure habits. But it still remained essential to limit the consequences of capitalist insecurity on employment and on the formation of individual wages, so as not to break the continuity of the consumption process, and in order to enable the workers to meet the financial commitments contracted with the acquisition of their consumer goods. This implied legislative arrangements, a homogenization and socialization of wages, and the establishment of social insurance funds against the temporary loss of direct wages. All these will be explored later.

When the wage relation had been transformed in such a way

as to permit the socialization of the conditions for purchasing standardized housing and automobile transport, the production of these complex commodities itself became the central process in the development of the mode of consumption. The production of standardized housing of a chiefly suburban kind had multiple effects. Constructed according to certain basic standards, the new housing put an end to unhygenic and unsafe interiors, and permitted the installation of household appliances that saved domestic labour. Standardized housing is also a symbol of status, once it can be bought rather than simply rented. Its mass production by techniques of prefabrication reduced its costs to a point where, stretched over the overall term of payment, it was less of a burden on the working-class wage of the 1950s than were the rents extorted by the landlords of the inter-war years for the unhygenic housing of that time. So far as the automobile was concerned, its mass production coincided with the establishment of the semi-automatic assembly line, in other words the creation of that model of work organization that was later to be extended to the long production runs of means of mass consumption. The general introduction of the assembly line revealed the intimate relationship between the labour process and the mode of consumption that it shapes. For the two basic commodities of the mass consumption process created complementarities which effected a gigantic expansion of commodities, supported by a systematic diversification of use-values. This diversification was inscribed in the very logic of the social norm of consumption, whose evolution was governed by the replacement of direct activity at home by time-saving equipment. It was also sustained by the quest for a status adequate to this norm. But in order for this logic of consumption to be compatible with a labour process oriented towards relative surplus-value, the total of use-values had to be adapted to capitalist mass production.[4] This meant the creation of a *functional aesthetic* ('design'), which acquired fundamental social importance.[5] This aesthetic had firstly to respect the constraints of engineering, and consequently conceive use-

[4] On this essential point, see A. Granou, *Capitalisme et mode de vie*, Paris, 1972.

[5] Lapidus and Hoffenberg, *La société du design*, Paris, 1976.

values as an assembly of standardized components capable of long production runs. It also had to introduce planned obsolescence, and establish a functional link between use-values to create the need for their complementarity. In this way, consumption activity could be rendered uniform and fully subjected to the constraints of its items of equipment. Finally, this functional aesthetic duplicated the real relationship between individuals and objects with an imaginary relationship. Not content to create a space of objects of daily life, as supports of a capitalist commodity universe, it provided an image of this space by advertising techniques. This image was presented as an objectification of consumption status which individuals could perceive outside themselves. The process of social recognition was externalized and fetishized. Individuals were not initially interpellated as subjects by one another, in accordance with their social position: they were interpellated by an external power, diffusing a robot portrait of the 'consumer'. Consumption habits were thus already calculated and controlled socially. Yet it cannot be stressed too greatly that the role of the image in consumption, which many sociologists have made into a fundamental explanatory principle of capitalist development, is strictly subordinate to the material and social conditions that we have discussed.

In so far as Fordism increased the rate of surplus-value by developing an overall set of social relations that closely combined the labour process with the social consumption norm, the department producing means of consumption appeared to be endowed with a dynamic arising from consumption itself. Since accumulation managed to preserve a relatively regular rhythm thanks to a certain harmonization of development between the two departments, at the price of a planned obsolescence and a permanent devalorization of capital, the problem of effective demand was not too serious. The 'consumer society' appeared to have definitively resolved the contradictions of capitalism and abolished its crises. Such was the pattern of the two decades after the Second World War, which we indicated in summary form in Chapter 1: a relatively regular rise in real wages, made possible by a continuing fall in real social wage costs that reflected a rise in the rate of surplus-value.

(b) The crisis of Fordism and the perspectives of Neo-Fordism.
The ideologists of the consumer society were harshly awakened
to the realities of capitalism by the deep crisis that began to
intensify in the latter half of the 1960s. As we showed in Chapter
2, the crisis of Fordism is first of all the crisis of a mode of labour
organization. It is expressed above all in the intensification of
class struggles at the point of production. By challenging
conditions of work bound up with the fragmentation of tasks
and intensification of effort, these struggles showed the limits to
the increase in the rate of surplus-value that were inherent in
the relations of production organized in this type of labour
process. This was the root of the crisis. It can be seen in the halt
to the fall in real social wage costs that occurred simultaneously with the outbreak of sporadic conflicts and endemic
confrontations challenging work disciplines of the kind
Fordism had established. But it is clear enough that the crisis
extends to the sum total of relations of production and exchange, and is upsetting the regime of intensive accumulation.
It is possible to speak of an organic crisis of capitalism without
implying its inevitable disappearance. Let us examine the
problem more closely. The impasse of relative surplus-value
that originates in the labour process brakes the expansion of
exchange relations between the two departments of production.
The development of the department producing means of production encounters a constraint, since it no longer gives rise to
technical mutations leading to a further mechanization of
labour, capable of generating a sufficient saving in direct labour
time to compensate for the increase in the organic composition
of capital. It is not surprising, therefore, that the replacement of
the semi-automatic assembly line by the system of transfer lines,
establishing automatic control over mass production, has so far
found only limited application. Certainly this form of automatic
production control saves direct living labour, but it does so only
by extending and pushing to its ultimate limits the form of work
organization and the working-class consumption norm characteristic of Fordism. It cannot therefore offer any solution to the
mounting class struggle in production. This has been shown by
the introduction of transfer lines in the automobile industry.
The new factories established on this basis have been marked by

the strongest working-class challenge to labour discipline.[6]

The difficulties encountered by accumulation in Department I lead to an upsurge of unemployment and growing job insecurity. At the same time, the exhaustion of the possibilities for increased productivity in mechanized assembly-line work forces capitalist management to a frontal attack on the purchasing power of the direct wage. Two essential conditions for the development of the working-class consumption norm are thus affected. The result has been a falling proportion of those able to buy their own homes in the younger age groups, and the stagnation of automobile production. The buoyancy of the social consumption norm is thus structurally threatened by those commodities that are the very foundation of mass consumption under the conditions of Fordism. It is menaced even more seriously by the deterioration in its social pre-conditions. We have seen, in effect, how the consumption norm geared to private commodities can only develop if there exist social modalities of finance, procedures by which society assumes responsibility for the risks and expenditures of a collective infrastructure. The production of this environment of private consumption enters into the reproduction value of social labour-power. Its cost forms part of the nominal reference wage as defined in the broad sense, where it includes both a direct and an indirect component. Now the exclusive nature of the tie that Fordism establishes between a mechanized labour process and a strictly private consumption of commodities generates a rapid increase in the cost of so-called collective consumption as the consumption norm develops. This phenomenon counteracts a rise in relative surplus-value to the point of reversing its developmental trend, once the crisis of Fordism is expressed in a challenge to this particular form of work organization. This is why we have seen such a literal explosion of what are known as social costs of growth from the mid 1960s onwards.

The rapid increase in this component of the value of social labour-power can be seen in Diagram 2 (p. 96 above). While it is the direct wage cost per overall unit of value added that has increased least since the Second World War, the unit cost of

[6] 'Blue-Collar Blues on the Assembly Line', *Fortune*, June 1970.

Diagram 10. Distribution of national income by category of income (1929-71)

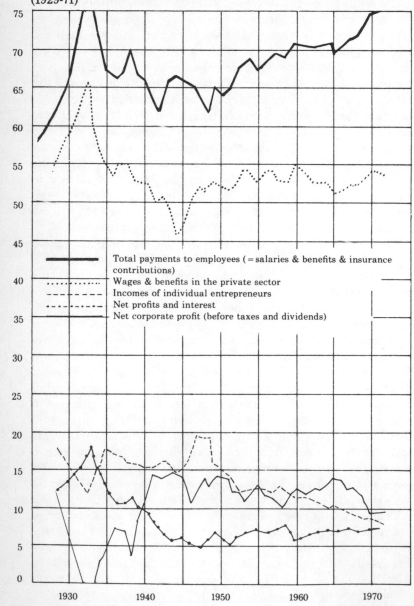

%

Total payments to employees (= salaries & benefits & insurance contributions)
Wages & benefits in the private sector
Incomes of individual entrepreneurs
Net profits and interest
Net corporate profit (before taxes and dividends)

indirect wages has increased far more than anything else, with a real explosion in its growth since 1965. This observation is confirmed by Diagram 10, which shows the long-term trend in national income distribution. This clearly shows that the overall aggregate of wages plus social benefits was stable only agerial, technical and commercial personnel) has been held steady since the Second World War, whereas the share in the overall aggregate of wages plus social benefits was only stable in the period of very swift expansion from 1960 to 1965, and began to increase very rapidly after that date.

We have now reached a fundamental point in our understanding of Fordism as a regime of intensive accumulation, and of its present crisis. We started with the hypothesis that the latter was essentially a crisis in the reproduction of the wage relation. If that is in fact the case, then it is justifiable to see it as an organic crisis of capitalism. We have already explored this hypothesis by showing how this crisis is rooted in the organization of the labour process. We can now consolidate this demonstration by showing that the social consumption norm characteristic of Fordism could regulate the evolution of private working-class consumption only by reinforcing the antagonism of the wage relation and generalizing this to the conditions guaranteeing the continuity of the maintenance cycle of labour-power: provision for the unemployed and the sick, covering of family expenses and the means of existence of retired people. The universalization of the wage relation under the impulse of the collectivization of labour in accordance with the principle of mechanization means that the general conditions of the mode of consumption must be guaranteed at the overall social level. The *socialization of consumption* becomes a decisive terrain and battle-ground of the class struggle. For this socialization is ever more necessary as precapitalist forms of everyday life are destroyed together with the social structures in which these could develop. When the wage relation is extended to the whole of society, so too must be the social means of consumption, either to be purchased as commodities or to be provided by public authorities. It is impossible to encompass the distribution between the two in any general law, since it varies considerably from one capitalist country to another. In the United States, capitalist production is very widespread indeed.

It covers, for example, the major part of health services, and a good part of education. This should not be surprising, since there are no use-values which are commodities by nature, nor others which are not. The commodity is a social relation of exchange, and its use-value only the support of this exchange. It can well happen, therefore, that certain use-values that are not commodities under certain types of labour process and certain evolutionary logics of the mode of consumption become so at other periods in capitalist development.

What is a general law, on the other hand, is as follows. In the context of Fordism, collective consumption declines and its costs rapidly increase, until they eventually cancel the general tendency towards a rise in the rate of surplus-value. The labour process of Fordism, in fact, pushes to the limit the mechanical principle of work collectivization. This principle only proves effective in the repetitive long production runs of standardized commodities. It is totally inadequate for the production of collective services. Either these services are produced by capitalists with undeveloped methods, and their cost grows astronomically as the social demand for them rises. This is the case with health services. Their cost must then necessarily be translated into a rapid rise in indirect wages. Alternatively, these services are produced by public bodies. They then absorb labour that is unproductive from the point of view of surplus-value. Far from being complementary to labour that does produce surplus-value, this unproductive labour is from the capitalist standpoint antagonistic to it when it absorbs a share of social labour that grows more quickly than the total sum of surplus-value. The social cost of reproducing labour-power then rises, with various financial consequences. There are several ways in which such financing can impose a burden on capitalist accumulation. Either it inflates direct wages, and the increase is taken back in the form of income tax. Or else it is levied on profit in various different forms. In either case, there is a restriction on relative surplus-value and consequently an obstacle to the law of accumulation. As long as major trans-formations in the production of standardized commodities and a corresponding upsurge in the mode of consumption were predominant, the collective costs of the reproduction of wage-labour could be held steady and a rising rate of surplus-value could still be imposed. But these very forces themselves generate a more and more rapid increase in collective costs, at the same time as they exhaust the potentialities contained in the mechanization of labour. It is not surprising, therefore, that the crisis of Fordist work organization should at the same time have been the occasion for a general drive of the capitalist class to curtail social expenditures, and have ushered in a period of retrenchment in public finances. All these phenomena are integral manifestations of the crisis in the reproduction of the wage relation.

We can now define more clearly the overall socio-economic conditions for a capitalist resolution of the crisis of Fordism in the United States. The only avenue of escape from the crisis is one in accordance with the law of accumulation that is the kernel of the capitalist mode of production. For this to be successful, the system must engender new conditions of production and exchange capable of accomplishing a lasting and massive rise in the rate of surplus-value. This can only be done if the labour process is revolutionized in such a way as to render it capable of radically transforming the conditions of production of the means of collective consumption. In order to pursue its development, capitalism must therefore push to its limit the transformation of the conditions of existence of the wage-earners. This is what Fordism cannot do. The conditions of production must be modified in such a way that the value of the social reproduction of labour-power is lowered in the context of a process that facilitates the development of collective consumption. Such a process may be in course of preparation already, with the emergence of the labour process we have called Neo-Fordism. This involves a major revolutionization of the labour process that tends to replace the mechanical principle of fragmented labour disciplined by hierarchical direction with the *informational principle* of work organized in semi-autonomous groups, disciplined by the direct constraint of production itself. It is evident that this principle is founded on a complex of productive forces centred on the automatic control of the means of production by an integrated system of measurement and treatment of information, analysis of data and elaboration of programmes that formalize the productive process, and transmission of instructions inherent in these programmes. Pilot studies conducted in hospitals, in the educational system, in pollution control, in the organization of public transport, have confirmed that this is a principle of work organization capable of effecting a considerable saving of labour-power in the production of means of collective consumption, while also transforming their mode of use in a far-reaching way.

The development of Neo-Fordism in commodity production in general, on the other hand, confers a new and notable flexibility on the labour process, which may be divided up into semi-autonomous units. This flexibility may be the condition for a profound reshaping of the urban environment which would deploy new methods of production of collective services. The increasing socialization of consumption would be an essential support for accumulation in Department I and the development of further productive forces. A new regime of intensive accumulation, Neo-Fordism, would arise from the crisis, articulating the progress of capitalist accumulation to the transformation of the totality of conditions of existence of the wage-earning class – whereas Fordism was geared simply to the transformation of the private consumption norm, the social costs of mass consumption continuing to be met on the margins of the capitalist mode of production. The fact that this transformation of the foundations of the regime of intensive accumulation is the sole durable solution to the crisis does not in itself mean that it is possible under capitalism. What it implies is rather such a modification of the conditions and modalities of the class struggle, of the internal stratification of each of the two polar classes defined by the wage relation, that it would be extremely presumptuous to make any judgement on this question at the present stage of our analysis. The development of our theory of accumulation, however, will enable us gradually to discern what precisely is at stake here.

It is essential to note that the problem to which we are led by the development of the law of accumulation has nothing in common with what is known as 'redeployment'. The latter is still enclosed in the theoretical field of the profitability of individual capitals, and based on the concept of industrial sector. According to this perspective, it would be sufficient for capitals to shift into new and expanding sectors – whose presence is taken for granted in a problematic for which capital alone exists and therefore the essential question is merely a rearrangement of the space for its valorization.

Our investigation of the law of accumulation leads us to a different point of view, because we conceive capital not as an immanent entity but as the development of the wage relation. Every major crisis of accumulation is a crisis of the present conditions of reproduction of this relation. Its outcome requires that obstacles to the transformation of these conditions be broken. In the United States, where the wage-earning class makes up more than 90% of the economically active population and where Fordism has been pushed to its ultimate conclusion, the social conditions for a new and lasting upsurge of accumulation can only be created by an internal reallocation of the wage-earning class which would involve a massive transformation of unproductive labour into labour productive of surplus-value. A transformation of this kind cannot be analysed starting from the concept of sector, but only from that of department of production. It is not intelligible in the abstract logic of profitability, but only in the emergence of a new interaction between the organization of work and the conditions of existence of the wage-earning class.

3. The Factors that Differentiate the Wage-Earning Class

The wage-earning class is not stratified according to a single or simple principle of division. Processes of division of different nature are superimposed on each other, though these are all derived from the fundamental tendencies that we have studied either in the perspective of the formation and transformation of capitalist relations of production in the labour process, or else of the evolution of the social consumption norm. This is because the most general law affecting the evolution of the working class is that of relative surplus-value, which predominantly tends towards the unification of the proletariat. The achievement of an ever higher rate of surplus-value, however, passes by way of practices that create factors of differentiation within the wage-earning class. It is essential to assess the due order of importance, stability and distortion of these factors. Two distinct problems must be examined here: the internal stratification of the proletariat and the problem of managerial staff.

(a) The stratification of the proletariat. The basis of this stratification is the organization of labour. In its systematic application of the principle of mechanization, Fordism largely destroyed all skilled crafts and dissolved the status that was founded on them. In this way it created the conditions for the trade-union organization of the working class on an industrial basis. This organization bears witness to the progressive unification of the working class. To the extent that mechanization has taken hold of non-industrial activities, the workers in these activities too have experienced a fragmentation of tasks making them into interchangeable elements of a collective labour-power, i.e. proletarianizing them. The existence of their old employment status typically contributed to maintaining certain differentiations in wages for a longer or shorter period, but the ever more pressing need to reduce wage costs generated an irresistible pressure to align these categories of workers with the standard working-class consumption norm. When American sociologists used to celebrate the enlargement of the 'middle class', what they were really observing was the superimposition of two different phenomena: on the one hand the extension of the proletariat, in other words of the fragmented, interchangeable and unskilled worker; on the other hand the rapid growth in the consumption norm to which all these workers were adapted. These were two complementary aspects of Fordism.

This fundamental tendency is qualified by certain secondary differentiations whose modalities we have already come across in studying the forms of wages. These differentiations tend to acquire a certain stability inasmuch as they are compromises in the class struggle which are then codified by collective bargaining. In enshrining the principle of seniority and certain limited opportunities of promotion, these differentiations play a double role. On the one hand they form part of the methods of discipline used by managements, which seek to stifle the consciousness of proletarian solidarity in their labour-force by playing up individual 'merit'. On the other hand they serve the purposes of bureaucratized trade unions which are in no way prepared to face a democratic challenge to their routine methods and objectives of struggle in collective bargaining. It may happen, however, that neo-Fordism will threaten these differentiations if capitalist managements can make use of semi-autonomous work groups as a weapon against trade-union organizations. The latter will then be forced to update their methods of action under threat of otherwise becoming the involuntary instruments of a major and lasting setback in the economic class struggle.

But there exist factors stratifying the proletariat that are far more powerful and active than these in weakening the workers' movement, by provoking a deep and lasting division within the class. They represent the effects of political and ideological relations on the maintenance cycle of certain categories of labour-power. These relations involve a status degradation in the sense that the norm of social consumption is not recognized in the wages of the workers affected. They take several different forms, of which the most important are the two following:

(1) Certain categories of labour-power are oppressed ethnic minorities subject to a systematic discrimination in all conditions of work and life;

(2) The organization of the consumption process within the family household assigns certain categories of labour-power (women and young workers) a reduced wage.

These politico-ideological relations show how the reproduction of class society is a single totality in which superstructural forms can exert a considerable influence on the law of capital accumulation. So far as the phenomena we are presently examining are concerned, these relations exert a general pressure on the nominal reference wage and raise the rate of surplus-value. They also play a large role in capitalist competition. We shall see in particular how the stratification of the proletariat assists the centralization of capital organized into subcontracting networks.

The most powerful weapon used by American capitalism to create exceptional conditions of exploitation derives from the permanence of ideological relations inherited from slavery, in other words *racism*. Like a cancer in the social formation, racism has spread from the South to the United States as a whole, and from the black population to all those who are not white in the strict sense. Capitalism has made far more effective use of racism than the slave form of production ever could, by transforming slaves into wage-workers who were refused all possibility of integration into the working-class mode of consumption. Once racism was deeply implanted in social consciousness, and reproduced by the regular functioning of politico-ideological institutions, a segmentation of the labour market could be introduced even into large-scale industry. The same simple labour-power, employed at the same type of fragmented activities, was paid differently according to race, since one section of the working class was ceded lesser rights of reconstitution than the other by society. For this to be so, it was evidently necessary for racism to have taken deep hold on the working class itself, to a point where trade-union organizations only took account of the interests of white workers. Progressive currents had also to be nipped in the bud, by conceding formal political rights to minorities and by trumpeting the promotion of a black bourgeoisie in the liberal professions (medicine, entertainment, law).[7]

A further powerful force creating a permanent differentiation of wages is the structure of the consumption process within the family cell formed by the couple and its young children. It is the reconstitution of labour-power in this social unit, which engenders an elementary form of cooperation in housework, that fixes the working-class norm of consumption. Housework in the nuclear family cell supplies the expenditure of labour needed for the process of consumption. It is thus possible to speak of a domestic form of production. This form of production assigns a special place in society to the female population. Women provide labour that is entirely encompassed in the process of reconstituting wage-labour, and thus cannot be considered as directly producing commodities. The simple cooperation of housework indirectly provides the capitalist mode of production with unpaid labour.

[7] For the role and development of racism in the formation of a black subproletariat, and the limited effects of the civil-rights movement, see in particular P. Baran and P. Sweezy, *Monopoly Capitalism*, New York, 1965. There are also more recent works by radical economists. Various articles in *Radical Perspectives on the Economic Crisis of Monopoly Capitalism*, URPE, 1975, deal with the effects of the crisis on women, young people and minorities.

The combination of this social organization and the individual perception of the wage permits the capitalist mode of production to set women to work for a *supplementary wage*. So long as the nuclear family remains dominant, even the wage of unskilled women workers, whether married or single, is determined by the role of women in housework. Modern capitalist urban development makes the consumption norm ever more rigid and ever more dependent on capitalist production, by suppressing the social fabric within which housework can be effectively extended. Capitalist urbanization tends to throw the female population into wage-labour. Women's wages are then determined by the price of those commodities required to assure the consumption process with reduced housework. The capitalist mode of production benefits from a transfer of labour with low productivity (the domestic labour from which it profits indirectly) towards labour with high productivity (wage-labour, from which it profits directly), while still paying for female labour-power as a function of the domestic labour it saves. This is also why women move in and out of wage-labour according to the economic climate. Women have to choose between wage-labour and domestic labour according to whether economic conditions are more or less favourable to one or the other.

The superimposition of racism and sexism assured the permanent hierarchy of wages to be observed in the United States throughout the period of Fordism: white male worker/black male worker/white female worker/black female worker. This was a hierarchy within the same simple labour-power. It was an effect of the overall structure of US class society.

Will this stratification be maintained in the perspective of a possible development of Neo-Fordism? It is still rather early to make any definitive judgements on this point. The socialization of consumption implied by Neo-Fordism will make absolutely necessary and unavoidable new types of social control for regularizing a consumption norm very different from that which prevailed after the Second World War and is now in crisis. Neo-Fordism, however, can only become the future principle of intensive accumulation if it bears with it qualitatively new productive forces. Such productive forces imply a far greater degree of unification of the proletariat. The material conditions of the maintenance cycle of labour-power will probably have to be embodied in an urban development that is no longer compatible with the maintenance of the ghettos. An increase in relative surplus-value by a revolutionization of the production processes of means of collective consumption seems possible without massive unemployment only by a significant shift in the frontier between working time and leisure time, in the direction of a reduction of working hours. The development of collective consumption would remove every objective basis from the discrimination against woman's work. It is clear that all these forces point in the direction of a gathering threat to capitalism as a whole. This is why the wage relation, the very principle of class domination, can probably only be maintained by way of an ever more totalitarian system of ideological controls and mechanisms of repression. The events of the last few years in the United States, as well as the disturbing developments in West Germany, indicate that such processes are indeed at work. Whether they will succeed in merging into a single system of social control is a question to which we are today still far from being able to give an answer. But the important point here is to see clearly that a very considerable renewal of social controls forms part of a capitalist solution to the crisis, because a transformation of the conditions of production and exchange permitting a new and lasting upsurge in relative surplus-value seems to work in the direction of a unification of the proletariat.

*(b) Managerial staff.** The position of managerial staff in the wage-earning class has always been notoriously ambiguous. This ambiguity obviously derives from the relation of their position in the capitalist organization of labour to the basic cleavage which defines the capitalist class and the proletariat. Managers appear as an intermediate social category. The term social category can only be justified by a position in social relations betokening a preponderant homogeneity amidst a diversity of situations. Now this homogeneity certainly has no functional basis. The social division of labour does allocate

* Translator's note: the French term *cadres* is here rendered as 'managerial staff', in the absence of any exact equivalent. It should be taken, therefore, as including technicians and engineers.

managerial staff skilled – i.e. diverse, complex and mobile – activities. These involve the practices of management, supervision and control that are necessary to valorize the capital deployed by a firm. But this functional organization is the support of an administrative hierarchy. The latter cannot be reduced to the former, since the valorization of the individual capital, apparently independent in each separate enterprise, forms part of the overall reproduction of capitalist relations of production, in other words of class society. If the managerial staff thus act within a technostructure, this latter still does not acquire a life of its own. Its existence and operation are determined by the accumulation of capital in general. It is in the nature of this technostructure, therefore, to be a perpetual field of tensions assigning managerial staff a position in social relations that makes them into a social category sometimes referred to as the salaried petty bourgeoisie.[8] Managerial staff belong to the wage-earning class inasmuch as they are parties to the wage contract. But they do not belong to the proletariat, and do not tend to dissolve into it as a category, because the social division of labour always renews control over the proletariat, even if its forms change. The individual fate of certain managers, who may become proletarianized in periods of large-scale change, when old hierarchical functions disappear, should not be confused with the social category itself. The latter is the agent of capitalism in the organization of labour under the legal form of the wage contract. The internal stratification of the proletariat, based on a diversity of concrete conditions of exploitation subjected to a movement of unification, should not be confused with the distinction between the proletariat and the social category of managerial staff, which is an unchangeable feature of the capitalist organization of labour.

Since the social category of managerial staff is the agent of capital, yet is subject to the wage-contract, status becomes very important for its autonomy. Such status involves not only differential norms of consumption, but also a series of relations that are constitutive of the social category itself – not merely

---

[8] See the detailed analyses by C. Baudelot, R. Establet and J. Malemort, *La petite bourgeoisie*, Paris, 1973.

secondary factors of internal differentiation of a social group whose cohesion is determined by a more fundamental cleavage. They homogenize the social category despite the heterogeneity of its functions, and they stabilize it by absorbing the multiple tensions that erupt within it, due to its ambiguous relation to the fundamental antagonism inherent in capitalist relations of production. The status of managerial staff is determined by their *qualifications* and by *career* structures. These distinctive features, which differentiate them from all other groups, make competition the principle of their internal relations – a competition incited by the hierarchy of titles and salaries that forms part of the personnel policy of any capitalist enterprise. If status homogenizes the social group of managerial staff, then the elements that determine status are controlled by the capitalist class, and form part of its global power over society.

It is absurd, therefore, to consider the salaries of managerial staff as determined by the reproduction value of a complex labour-power, or to seek to identify the elements of this complexity by a functional analysis and impute specific costs to it. Fascination with 'human capital' and justification of the wage hierarchy have unfortunately infected several economists outside the neo-classical school.[9] These errors derive from a serious confusion between complex labour and labour-power. Complex labour denotes those specific activities that are organically determined by the collective worker and homogenized by the social process of exchange. The phenomenon of complex labour forms part of the analysis of commodity prices within the laws of capitalist competition. It has nothing to do with the salaries paid to members of the category of managerial staff. What is true, however, is that the latter are tied to their employers by the wage contract. They therefore cash their qualifications as an exchange-value. In a relatively stable state of the social division of labour that determines a certain permanence of forms for the administrative hierarchy, a price tends to be established for each category of qualification, resulting from the competition among managerial staff. These prices do not appear as such; they are expressed in the hierarchy

[9] For an extended critique of 'human capital', see S. Bowles and H. Gintis, 'The Problem with Human Capital. A Marxian Critique', *American Economic Review*, May, 1975.

of salaries paid to managerial staff from the beginning of their career. In periods of rapid transformation of the organization of labour, on the other hand, with correlative changes in the structure of the enterprise, the exchange-value of certain qualifications can be seriously threatened. The hierarchy may alter, certain specialized qualifications become worthless, other new ones appear, so that only the most general managerial skills and legal expertise retain their position at the head of the hierarchy.

But qualifications are not the only way in which the wage hierarchy is modulated. Career structures also play a major role. It is the career system that subjects managerial staff so closely to the capitalist class and reinforces the differentiation of this group in society, as well as the mutual competition within it. For this to be so, there must exist opportunities for monetary success. These arise from the complexity of the structure of the enterprise, which includes a large number of hierarchical levels and a multiplicity of functions. To ensure that career competition, an inevitable source of tension, does not jeopardize the social climate of the firm and make managers into a social group hostile to the bosses, the principles of personnel policy have to be rigorously applied: a strict definition of individual responsibilities, a great objectivity of performance criteria, and intense mobility of individuals within the structure. It is these principles that make the giant American corporation so remarkably adapted to the valorization of capital, and at the same time so effective an instrument of social stability. The US pattern is notably distinct from the congealed structures typical of France, where rational principles of organization are largely unknown and careers are petrified by formal qualifications, and above all by nepotism and personal connections.

The sum total of the relations that assign managerial staff their place in society is strongly internalized in the specific ideology of this social group, which reinforces capitalism by adapting them to their roles in the social division of labour. Its two complementary poles are *respect for authority* and *individualism*.

Respect for authority is determined by the severe constraints specific to the structure of the enterprise, the performances required for promotion, the meagreness of the fragmented knowledge of the great majority of managerial staff and the commodity character that it assumes under capitalism. Managerial staff thus typically and uncritically obey the combination of promotion and sanction that marks their careers. Respect for authority is also reinforced by very significant cultural attitudes – the relations of protocol between superiors and inferiors in the hierarchy, the effacement of personality behind function, the most absolute conformism in outward expressions of character, and the suppression of any independent opinions.

The individualism of managerial staff conforms completely with bourgeois ideology. It has only one dimension, that of monetary gain, which is the alpha and omega of the career system. It is expressed by the almost total absence of trade-union organization among them. It stamps all inter-personal relations within this social group, in which each is judged and assessed in terms of his success in the incessant pursuit of monetary gain and the lifestyle that follows from this. This mode of life makes differences completely external. The one-dimensional reduction of personality leads to the reappearance of differentiation in the possession of commodities, this in turn being a further incitement to the intensified quest for monetary gain. Competition between individuals thus invades every aspect of life.

Yet this insidious ideology, composed of unconscious norms that govern everyday life, has recently experienced certain reverses. Three distinct phenomena can be noted here.

The first is related to the emergence of certain political themes to which managerial staff are not insensitive, questioning the goals of the giant corporation of the Fordist type in the midst of the mounting problems arising from increases in social inequalities, deterioration of the environment and falling standards of collective consumption. Political reflection on these themes will not go so far as to yield an understanding of the nature of capitalist relations of production. But problems of consumption, of the environment, of social inequalities and discriminations are awakening managerial personnel to the responsibility of the giant corporations, and diffusing the conviction that their concentration of colossal productive resources imposes certain social duties on them as much as on the state.

The second phenomenon is the emergence of discontent within middle-ranking administrative staff due to the changes in the structure of the enterprise caused by the introduction of automatic control systems, which destroy the rank attached to certain hierarchical functions. These form part of the reorganization within the category induced by the rise of Neo-Fordism.

The third phenomenon is the dissatisfaction of technical staff at the regimentation of research. The increasing fragmentation of the labour process, corresponding to the principle of mechanization, obliged the employers to divide up applied research into separate departments. The resultant rigidity, and the straitjacket of detailed performance criteria, have harmed cooperation between different fields of research in a domain where results are always difficult to foresee. Research is a particularly favourable arena for the establishment of semi-autonomous groups, as a result of a transformation of the labour process by automatic production control.

The tensions that have disturbed managerial staff as Fordism has entered into crisis do not seem seriously to threaten their cohesion, nor to modify significantly their situation vis-à-vis the capitalist class on the one hand and the proletariat on the other. It would appear, on the contrary, that they are in the process of absorbing and assimilating the social transformations that characterize the transition between two modalities of the regime of intensive accumulation, Fordism and Neo-Fordism.

II. The Effects of the Socialization of Consumption on Changing Forms of Wages

As we have already argued, the reproduction of social labour-power involves more than simply its physical reconstitution from one production cycle to another. There is also the renewal of the working class from generation to generation. The costs of this reproduction thus include the expenditure for the maintenance and education of the children who are to replace the existing labour force. They also include the maintenance of former workers during the short interval, as it is on average, that separates retirement and death. Finally, they include insurance costs against sickness, which puts labour-power out of service for a shorter or longer portion of its total activity. The integration of these needs into the working-class norm of consumption, in other words their management by the capitalist mode of production, got under way during the Great Depression. Since the end of the Second World War, they have developed spectacularly, at an ever accelerating pace. These needs are induced by the transformation of the conditions of existence of the wage-earning class. They form part of the socialization of the general conditions of production. In all these cases, the covering of these needs enters into the value of *social* labour-power. But the flows of income and the institutional mechanisms by which these needs are met vary greatly from one social formation to another. Differences arise according to whether taxes and other charges are more or less socialized, i.e. brought within an institutional mechanism for balancing out the risks and costs of collective expenditures. The differences between the direct wages paid to simple labour-power in different countries are linked in part to divergences in the ways in which these needs are covered.

The structural forms of the wage relation which developed in the United States – during the phase of its generalization under Fordism – to ensure the coverage of expenditures considered as constraints induced by the rise of mass consumption were the system of public *assistance* and the *insurance* system. Each functioned through a range of institutions. Assistance was financed from the budgets of the public authorities, and administered by a special apparatus; it was highly selective and uncertain from the claimants' point of view. The right to assistance was always in jeopardy, both in scope and in the degree of its coverage, as the assistance system was directly in the hands of bourgeois political organs.[10] Popular movements could exercise only an external pressure on it. Insurance is a more codified system than assistance, since it relates contri-

---

[10] See F.F. Piven and R.A. Cloward, *Regulating the Poor*, London, 1972.

butions to benefits, and to a greater or lesser extent socializes the financing of certain risks within the wage-earning class. Insurance enters into the agenda of collective bargaining procedure and forms part of the compromises of the class struggle. In certain cases, workers' organizations have won the right to examine the operation of the institutions of social insurance. But in every case insurance, like assistance, enters into the social value of labour-power and is thus entirely subject to the constraints of the law of accumulation. The monetary flows to which these systems give rise do not grow in any regular way, as far as their actual purchasing power is concerned. Still less are direct wages compensated for by indirect wages. When the rate of surplus-value is prevented from rising, then so too is the norm of social consumption, as much by the stagnation of real wages as by the deterioration in the financial equilibrium of the systems for coping with risks, at the very moment when all risks are increased by the growing insecurity of employment. In point of fact, the threat to relative surplus-value raises the level of unemployment by slowing down the overall rate of accumulation, and by encouraging methods of production that save on labour-power. Now the social security systems can only absorb these risks if the labour-power that is actually operative can pay for the labour-power that is not. This is the indispensable condition for these systems to guarantee the continuity of the process of social consumption, without which the regime of intensive accumulation would totally collapse. This can be fulfilled only if the nominal direct wages of those workers with jobs remain constant, as it is to this wage level that the whole system of contributions and benefits is indexed. The constancy of the nominal wage is what enables a consumption process dominated by articles of mass production to continue. This continuity limits unemployment by counteracting the decline in the rate of accumulation. The limitation of unemployment gives the unemployed relative security by maintaining a flow of contributions sufficient to prevent the insurance funds from being exhausted. The benefits from these funds create expenditure flows that consolidate the level of employment. The *constancy of the nominal reference wage*, therefore, which can be historically observed throughout the period of Fordism, *is the keystone of that socialization of consumption which prevents a*

cumulative shortfall in effective demand when the conditions of
surplus-value production deteriorate. This is the fundamental
lesson that Keynes opposed to the conception of an automatic
equilibrium between the supply and demand for labour, allegedly defined independently of one another, accomplished by the
flexibility of an 'equilibrium price of labour'.

In the United States, where the ideology of individualism is
particularly strong and belief in a link between work performed and remuneration is peculiarly persistent, the establishment of private insurance funds on the whole prevailed over the
principle of social solidarity in meeting risks. In studying the
American insurance system, therefore, it is preferable to speak
of deferred wages rather than indirect wages. These take the
form of insurance funds set up by workers privately, principally
for medical and surgical expenses, and pension funds for
retirement. Private insurance schemes far outweigh the public
system of social security. These funds subordinate the meeting
of social needs to the exigencies of capitalization. They are the
principal forms of a very rapid development of contractual
saving. This development has been the source of a gigantic
financial centralization.

The most rapid mode of financial centralization has derived
from the expansion of pension funds. The establishment of these
private pension funds slowly developed from the early 20th
century onwards, for certain particular categories of skilled
workers (particularly in building) who were shielded from the
fragmentation of tasks and concomitant reduction to simple
labour-power by their very position in forms of the labour
process that were relatively backward. These workers,
moreover, were organized in powerful trade unions which could
bargain with the employers over plans for the establishment of
pension funds. But it was only in the Great Depression that the
social scale of the problem was revealed, when the unemployment of millions of active workers left the retired in a situation
of indescribable poverty. The Roosevelt Administration prevailed on Congress to pass a social security plan financed by the
Federal budget, funded half by deductions from wages, and half
by the employers. This very modest plan provided only an
absolutely minimal benefit, but it did combine individual
insurance with a modest redistribution of income. Administered

by the Federal government, the scheme was gradually extended to a greater number of beneficiaries, but benefits remained minimal. Only in 1973, in a situation of accelerating inflation, and under pressure from social forces that had secured a broad consensus, did Congress raise the minimum benefits considerably, add a clause indexing these benefits to the cost of living, and significantly increase contributions. The social security system, therefore, which up till then had been intended to establish simply a minimum standard for pensioners, leaving each individual to supplement this from his or her own private insurance scheme, now began to be qualitatively transformed into a national pensions scheme eventually planned to encompass all private arrangements and weld them into a single system in which social distribution of risks and provision for pensioners would replace individual insurance.

A social conflict of major importance is involved here, for private pension funds form very significant reservoirs of capital. They are bitterly defended by industrialists and financiers alike. Yet the defects in the operation of these schemes are so immense that dissatisfaction with them has been steadily increasing. These private pension funds are a grotesque example of the antagonism between social needs and the exigencies of accumulation. The average American worker, after contributing all his active life to a private pension fund, obtains less than 25% of his terminal wage as a pension on retirement. In Europe the percentage ranges between 50% and 70%, with payments guaranteed by the state.

Let us examine briefly the particular operation of these schemes. Private pension funds developed rapidly with the establishment of collective bargaining in the late 1930s. The rate of growth of their assets averaged 15% from 1950 onwards. The total financial assets accumulated in this way stood at 2.5 billion dollars in 1940, 12 billion in 1950, 52 billion in 1960 and 136 billion in 1970. This growth accelerated under the pressure of separate but convergent forces: the rapid increase in nominal incomes, the lowering of the retirement age, the need to reduce the difference between the incomes of pensioners and the incomes of the economically active. But the forces pressing to accelerate the growth in these funds were also those pressing to abolish the private system of capitalization. In a system of social insurance, in fact, the benefits paid derive from present and accumulated receipts, either drawn from taxation on the incomes of the whole population, or directly from the overall exchange-value of commodities by social contributions. In private pension funds, the benefits obtained by all individuals at the end of their lives are a function of the contractual savings schedule. But these benefits are in no way guaranteed. The ownership of the assets involved, in fact, does not lie with the wage-earners but rather with the capitalist class. The funds are set up in the framework of the corporation, in a scheme codified by collective bargaining. They include a contribution from wages, and a contribution from the employer which is seen as a kind of participation by the wage-earners in profits, whose proceeds are deferred into the future. In actual fact, the employers' contribution is not actually paid, or is so only to a small degree. Corporations transfer funds to the accounts of trusts centralized by the more powerful commercial banks, who invest them. The corporations thus expect the nominal value of the funds to grow as foreseen by the scheme, from the return on the investments made simply with the employees' contributions. Since this return arises from the surplus-value produced by the working class as a whole, the circular process of exploitation and accumulation takes care of itself. The more the wage-earners pay, the more the capitalists accumulate, and the more the funds rise in value, the less the capitalists actually contribute to the financing of pensions. The remarkable result is achieved that the sum of retirement pensions that will be paid in the future to a wage-earner who has made contributions throughout his life depends on the increase in the nominal stock-market value of the shares in which bankers have invested his contributions.

The dynamic effect of these funds for the accumulation of capital is thus readily understandable. It derives from the fact that they are neither guaranteed nor regulated, leading them to be considered by the corporation as current expenditures that form an integral part of wages, while also possessing the ideal attributes of long-term financial investments (total tax exemption, constant new injections, liquidity needs plannable in advance). We can also understand, however, how the contradictions of this type of financial investment are now becoming ever more acute. For decent retirement pensions to be paid in a period of inflation, ever higher returns have to be obtained on ever greater investments; and this becomes impossible, as the big banks cannot invest everything in those sectors with a high growth rate without the return on share capital eventually coming to appear artificially high in relation to real profitability. Up till about 1965, the establishment of new funds and the relatively recent character of these pensions schemes kept the ratio of benefits to the value of the funds low – all the more so because the nominal value of shares on the stock-markets had grown steadily and far more rapidly than the rise in prices since 1950. All these conditions were reversed from 1966 onwards. The average ratio of annual payments to accumulated assets, which had risen from 3.3% in 1950 to 3.5% in 1960, climbed to 4.8% in 1970. This tendency was thereafter strongly accelerated by the more rapid rise in prices, and by the persistent stagnation on Wall Street as the production of relative surplus-value reached its limits. But what the rise in this ratio does not reveal is the sharp increase in cases of non-payment of pensions, either total, or at levels below those for which the workers contributed. This crisis in the private pension fund system erupted at a time when, as we have seen, the forces pressing for a generalization of the pension system and a rise in the pensions paid had become stronger than before. The problem thus became a political issue. The integration of pension schemes into a single national scheme, operated according to the principle of a balance between contributions and benefits under the responsibility of the Federal state, regulating the use of the funds and guaranteeing the stability of payments from them, is the only possible solution in the long-run.

In several capitalist countries, the insufficient socialization of consumption that is one aspect of the crisis of Fordism has found expression in a deterioration of the financial position of insurance systems. This deterioration provokes a pressure on benefits which aggravates the crisis. In the United States, the heteroclite mosaic of private schemes, in which the employer's commitment is only conditional, has brought about a particularly severe crisis. In the period when mass consumption was rising, the managements of the big corporations themselves favoured the negotiation of pension schemes in return for trade-union abandonment of resistance to the transformation of work organization so as to strengthen labour discipline. This weakening of the working class's means of action played a major role in the accelerated pace of accumulation that marked the first half of the 1960s. By the capitalization of its contractual savings, the working class gave a massive long-term credit to the capitalist class. With its trade-union leaders placing their faith in indefinite economic growth, it was not only robbed to a large extent of the real value of its assets by inflation, but very often even of their nominal value, since the pension schemes did not offer the guarantees that any creditor is normally granted. There could be no more striking expression of the fact that the wage relation is not an exchange relation, even at the point of the wage contract. The two antagonistic classes are not social partners, as is complacently maintained. They are not players subject to the same rules, one simply being stronger than the other. The wage relation determines qualitatively different class positions. The two 'players' are not playing the same game, they do not have the same goals, and they are not subject to the same rules.[11]

III. The Effects of the Socialization of Consumption on the Long-Run Movement of Wages

The conclusions of our analysis of the wage relation suggest the need to take a further step forward in the interchange between historical analysis and conceptual elaboration. We must now deepen and apply the concept of *form* to give the theory of wages its full range. We have already met this concept of form in the theory of exchange. The concept owes the position that it occupies in economic science to its mediation between the homogeneous field of value, whose identification founds that science as such, and the concrete and heterogeneous space of production, distribution and consumption of use-values. This concrete space cannot be conceptualized. It denotes the content

[11] For an interpretation of the wage relation in terms of games theory see G. Maarek, *Introduction au Capital de K. Marx*, Paris, 1975.

of economic acts, the description of the specific processes by which human individuals transform resources in accordance with particular projects, and create artefacts through which they enter into social interaction. The concrete space of activities refers therefore to the general determination of labour. But this concrete space is in no way sufficient to characterize a society. What gives a human grouping the cohesion that enables us to speak of a society is a *mode of distribution of tasks* that does not derive from their content but which is imposed on this content. A particular mode of distribution of tasks is articulated to a specific and exclusively social determination of labour. We know that the commodity economy is a mode of distribution of tasks characterized by the existence of independent processes of private labour. Social cohesion is obtained by a particular procedure of social valid-ation of these private labours, effected *ex post* on the products of labour, which become commodities. In this case, the mode of distribution of tasks can be conceptualized as a homogeneous abstract space, the space of value. The constitutive relation of this space is the social relation of exchange, and the specific determination of labour is abstract labour.

The fundamental epistemological problem is that there is no possibility of immediately conceiving the unity of the abstract social space and the concrete space of activities, the specific and the general determinations of labour. To relate these two spaces requires the construction of an intermediary theoretical space, that of *social forms*. This space has a topological and not a metric structure. Its elements are relations, social interactions, endowed with a law of reproduction. We know that in a commodity economy the archetypical form of morphology is the metamorphosis of the commodity $C - M - C'$. The developed morphology is the general circulation of commodities. The law of reproduction is exchange equivalence. This space of social forms exercises a very real mediation. The concrete space of activities and use-values is a *support* space for the meta-morphoses of commodities. The space of social forms, finally, is related to the homogeneous space of value in the sense that the principle of exchange equivalence imposes an application of the latter on the former, i.e. a transformed measurement of value which is the monetary expression.

We can thus see why it is necessary for economic science to construct the space of social forms, in a two-way movement between observation of this teeming support space of activities and analysis of the measurable magnitudes that are impressed on the homogeneous space of value. This two-way process is of great importance in the study of capitalism, where the wage relation is governed by a law of reproduction that is much more complex than the principle of equivalence. We know that this is so because the wage relation is a relation of appropriation and expropriation. The division it defines is subject to the principles of qualitative difference and unequal influence. The reason we have undertaken an analysis of the transformations of work organization and the conditions of existence of the wage-earning class is so as to study more concretely the nature of the wage relation, and its relationships in turn with the support space of activities. We know now that this is not just a simple exchange relation, even though it presents itself as such in the form of the free contract. Nor is it an abstract balance of forces, even though it gives rise to a division in the homogeneous field of value. The wage relation contains these different patterns within it under the predominant determination of a relation of production, in other words an appropriation by one part of society of the resources needed to produce the conditions of existence for society as a whole. This is why study of the reproduction of the wage relation requires before all else an analysis of the material transformations that are the basis of capitalist appropriation. This analysis has enabled us to identify the basic social forms created by the development of the wage relation.

It is now necessary to go further, and study the overall morphology of the wage relation. Since the wage relation is complex and the diverse forms in which it presents itself are qualitatively different and dynamic, the law of reproduction of the wage relation in the space of social forms is the principle of the organic unity of all these basic forms. We shall call such a unity a *structural form*. A structural form, then, is a mode of cohesion of basic social forms arising from the development of one and the same basic social relation.

In accordance with the above theoretical elaboration, we

shall now pursue the investigation of the wage relation in the following directions:

(1) Structural forms evolve with the material transformations of the mode of production. This capacity for evolution is precisely what ensures social cohesion under the domination of an antagonistic relation of production. As a new stage of capitalism bound by the quest for relative surplus-value to the predominance of a regime of intensive accumulation, Fordism unifies the different partial forms of existence of the wage relation and constitutes a structural form involving a major legal codification, *collective bargaining*.

The massive development of collective bargaining in the United States was indissolubly connected with the rise of Fordism. It remains one of the most essential structural forms for the regulation of contemporary capitalism. In studying this structural form, we shall be able to understand the modalities in which the class struggle has developed.

(2) The formation and operation of structural forms are the theoretical site of the articulation of social relations – economic, politico-legal and ideological. To develop a theory of collective bargaining as a structural form means to conceive this articulation as a unity of the social practices necessary for the reproduction of the wage relation. The theory of structural forms is thus a way of laying the foundations for a theory of the capitalist state.[12]

(3) The laws of reproduction of social forms give rise to transformations in the homogeneous field of value. The structural form in which the wage relation is reproduced affects the transformation of the value of labour-power into wages. Investigation of collective bargaining will enable us to complete the determination of the nominal reference wage. We shall then show how the establishment of collective bargaining has led tó a change in the long-run quantitative development of wages, and in their regulation in the different phases of the accumulation cycle.

---

[12] For different Marxist views on this question, see N. Poulantzas, *Political Power and Social Classes*, London, NLB, 1974; P. Herzog, *Politique économique et planification en régime capitaliste*, Paris, 1971; S. de Brunhoff, *État et Capital*, Paris, 1976.

1. The Canalization of Economic Class Struggle by Collective Bargaining

It would be impossible in the present book to describe in detail the processes of American collective bargaining, on which there already exists an abundant literature.[13] Our task will rather be to show, in terms of the concept of structural form, why and how this overall procedure is linked to the regime of intensive accumulation, as a regularization of the interaction between work organization and the social consumption norm which is the foundation of the general conditions of accumulation specific to Fordism.

(a) The tendencies in the trade-union movement after the Second World War. The immediate post-war period was decisive for the later development of the workers' movement. Massive strikes inspired by grievances over wages and working conditions that had built up during the war brought the working class a series of economic victories. But this was the last such occasion for a long time, since in the same conjuncture the labour movement was to lose a decisive battle on the political front.

The New Deal had seen a significant weakening of the conservative bloc in the United States, ejected from power in the disarray provoked by the economic collapse of the Great Depression. But this situation was short-lived. The war economy enabled the industrial and financial community to establish close ties with the Federal government and to obtain strong positions in the administration. The same period saw the beginning of a major anti-working-class ideological campaign, which enlisted the full range of means of communication. The ultimate aim of this campaign was to obtain a complete revision of the Wagner Act of 1935, so as to break the new power of the unions that had been recognized in law. The anti-labour campaign reached a new height at the time of the 1946 strikes, taking advantage of the scarcities of the reconversion period. Even during the war, various states in the South, West and

[13] Two systematic works are D.C. Bok and J.T. Dunlop, *Labor and the American Community*, 1970; and L. Litwack, *The American Labor Movement*, Englewood Cliffs, 1962.

Midwest had passed legislation prohibiting the closed shop. The 1946 elections, however, returning a strong conservative majority, were to give this ideological campaign a national juridical force. In 1947 Congress passed the Taft-Hartley Act, which met the employers' demands in almost every detail. This law obliterated the progressive provisions of the Wagner Act and became the new charter for settling social conflicts.

In its preamble, the Taft-Hartley Act asserts the need to restrain trade-union action in so far as it imperils 'the freedom of exchange'. The chief provisions of this basic law can be analysed as follows:

(1) The workers' right freely to choose their trade-union representatives is confirmed. When a majority union organization has been chosen by election in a production unit, it alone is empowered to bargain collectively in the name of the workforce as a whole. The procedures of union formation, the renewal of union mandates, and their legal recognition, are controlled by the National Labor Relations Board.

(2) This control empowers the N.L.R.B. to prohibit any employer from obstructing the legal formation of a trade union. The N.L.R.B. must then apply the following restrictions on the freedom of union action: prohibition of the closed shop, and of any strike seeking to establish this, as well as any pressure seeking to force an employer to recognize a union not certified by the N.L.R.B., or any refusal of collective bargaining.

(3) The act attempts to define those problems which should or should not form part of the content of collective bargaining, and the forms in which this bargaining should be pursued. Trade unions can be prosecuted for breach of contract, refusal to apply a contract, or a strike aimed against the terms of an agreement before that agreement has expired. Strikes against the unilateral transformation of working conditions by the employers are forbidden. This provision is decisive. It leaves the workers disarmed in the face of constant restructuration of jobs, intensification of output norms, and deskilling under cover of technical progress.

(4) The act prohibits unions from financially supporting any organizations except in times of national elections. It deprives employees of the Federal government of the right to strike.

(5) Finally, the act explicitly confers on the Federal govern-

ment the power to intervene in social conflicts which 'endanger
the national economy'. The definition of the scope of this power
reflects the ambiguity of the employers' position. On the one
hand, the employers were anxious to have at their disposal the
institutionalized force of repression of the Federal state, to
break large-scale strikes. On the other hand, they were unwil-
ling to compromise their own freedom of action by recourse to
administrative intervention that might replace their own
powers of decision. This attitude was inspired by their aware-
ness that wages and working conditions were closely tied to
major decisions of the corporations over prices and investments. The Taft-Hartley Act gives the Federal government a
whole arsenal of weapons which fall short of imposing compulsory arbitration. These include the setting up of fact-finding
commissions to make recommendations which then become the
starting point of negotiations, the summoning of White House
conferences under Presidential authority, the possibility of
issuing an injunction to force the suspension of a strike for 80
days, and the power to seize production units affected by a
dispute and operate them under the management of Federal
functionaries acting in place of the private owners.

The trade-union movement's attempt to get the Taft-Hartley
Act repealed soon petered out. The political climate quickly
deteriorated after Truman solemnly launched the doctrine of
the Cold War. The anti-working-class ideological campaign
took an anti-communist turn and escalated in virulence. It
culminated with the Korean War, in a climate of generalized
fear and delation. The massive expulsion of Communist mil-
itants from the CIO-affiliated unions decisively weakened the
labour movement and brought the CIO into close alignment
with the AFL in the same narrowly corporatist attitude, with
very limited objectives. This corporatism progressively im-
poverished the content of collective bargaining itself, and cut
off working-class trade unionism from the political forces of the
liberal petty bourgeoisie. The result was that the organized
labour movement was absent or tailist when the political
struggles of the 1960s got under way, from the campaign for the
civil rights of minorities, to the fight against economic discrimination, through to the battle to extend the social security
system and the mass revolt against the war in Vietnam.

The political climate of the Cold War and the restrictions imposed by the Taft-Hartley Act were of enormous importance for the stagnation of the trade-union movement after the Second World War. No substantial progress in membership was achieved after 1950, and the proportion of union members even fell from 36% of the active non-farm population in 1945 to 28% in 1970. Moreover, the constraint involved in collective bargaining, once it was institutionalized, did much to petrify the labour movement. Procedural rules imposed a new rigidity on the trade-unions, qualitatively reducing their objectives, absorbing the energies of their officials in problems of management, and limiting the horizon of social conflicts. The Taft-Hartley Act codified a corporative unionism, formerly practised only by craft workers, by creating the politico-legal relations to adapt it to the mass trade unionism brought into being by the social transformations of Fordism. This adaptation was consolidated by the merger between the old corporative union centre of the AFL and the new centre resulting from the class struggles of the 1930s, the CIO, in 1954–55.

(b) General features of collective bargaining procedure. During the war, the direct intervention of trade unions alongside factory managements in settling problems of work organization had been warmly encouraged. In those industries where the level of unionization was high, there resulted a series of rules that shaped collective bargaining over working conditions. These rules often included restrictions imposed on the employers' powers of dismissal. These could no longer be discriminatory; sub-contracting and the employment of temporary staff were strictly limited in periods when the employment of the firm's permanent staff was in danger. In periods of reduced activity, systems for sharing work among the regular employees were jointly operated by management and trade-unions; dismissals could only be made after tasks had been reallocated over a reduced working week. Trade-union officials often forced employers to notify plans for lay-offs in advance, as well as the reasons for these and the procedure that they intended to follow, so that the workers could be consulted and be able to make counter-proposals. Lay-offs were not to be used for a major shifting of workers between jobs unilaterally

imposed by the management to raise output norms. Rights of seniority were in all circumstances to be protected. The unions also sought to win rights over the allocation of workers to jobs by introducing promotion procedures into collective bargaining. They tried to obtain precise job descriptions in the collective contracts, with clauses forbidding the management to change these unilaterally during the period for which the contract was in force. Finally, they sought to establish a concerted regulation of work schedules and overtime.

Collective bargaining can thus have a very rich content, and foster an active trade-union life, when it is applied to the organization of the labour process. It is then a weapon for the workers in their struggle for security and the improvement of their working conditions. But the entire drift of the class struggle in the United States since the war has been to transform collective bargaining into a battering-ram of the employers. It was the recession of 1953–54, with its surplus production capacities, financial difficulties aggravated by the new Eisenhower administration's abandonment of the cheap credit policies of the New Deal, and fall in the rate of profit, that showed the employers how great a transformation of production conditions was needed in order to relaunch the accumulation of capital in a sustained fashion. Their reaction was to unleash a general assault to reduce direct wage costs, which is the only meaning of a rise in productivity within capitalist relations of production. This objective required the rapid generalization of those transformations of the technical division of labour that had matured in the 1930s and the Second World War; in other words the installation of assembly-line work, the introduction of multi-operational machine tools making the labour process more flexible, the modification of the patterning and interconnection of productive operations, and their segmentation and localization to utilize new collective means of production and new forms of energy (oil and electricity). The capitalists were well aware that such a mutation in the technical division of labour, whose aim was to increase the rate of surplus-value, could in no way be the product of a common effort. For them the imperative necessity was to eliminate the regulations governing work organization that had been imposed by collective bargaining. To attain this objective, profound changes were

needed in the managerial practices and administrative organization of firms, which implied the need for a confrontation with
the unions over the content of collective bargaining. The
following were the directions in which the employers sought to
obtain these transformations.

(1) The formulation of overall wage policies of long duration
so as to deal with the unions at the highest level possible or
compatible with the degree of centralization of capital.

(2) The development of procedures of managerial control,
fixing levels of responsibility and forming a framework in which
overall wage policy could be strictly applied in all units of the
industrial complex affected.

(3) The exclusion from collective bargaining of working
conditions, and the imposition of new rules governing them by
the employers; the strictest possible circumscription, in keeping
with the Taft-Hartly Act, of trade-union rights to examine those
processes vital for the production of surplus-value; the elaboration of various procedures of disciplinary sanction and the
multiplication of supervisory staff charged with their
application.

(4) The compensatory development within the framework of
collective bargaining of incentive and profit-sharing schemes,
insurance funds against the immediate financial consequences
of dismissal, and pension funds for retirement.

These objectives were imposed by the employers after very
acute conflicts, but they could take advantage of the politico-
ideological development of the trade-union leaderships con-
sumated in the fusion of the AFL and CIO in 1954–55. *The
content of collective bargaining thus shifted from working conditions to monetary gains from capitalist production, and the form
of collective bargaining from a decentralized pattern of decision to
an ever more centralized pattern.*

This development, without which the regime of intensive
accumulation specific to Fordism would be incomprehensible,
was imposed in a series of major struggles culminating in the
years 1958–61, which took the form of test conflicts ending in the
signature of pilot contracts which were then rapidly
generalized.

The role of 'government arbitration' was decisive for the
outcome of these test conflicts. The Taft-Hartley Act gave the

Federal government a whole spectrum of means of intervention in social conflicts, while leaving it a broad latitude in the exercise of its arbitration. Naturally this was arbitration only in the purely formal sense of the literal procedure adopted. Effectively, state intervention meant support for the employers, if only because it broke the trade unions' principle weapon of action at the most decisive moment in negotiations. During the period of the rise of Fordism, there was no need for constant state intervention. It was sufficient for the government to choose exemplary conflicts whose outcome could not but set the model for major sectors of the economy.[14] In the 1960s, however, the Democratic administrations then in power began to use the Taft-Hartley Act in a dual direction. On the one hand, they instituted compulsory arbitration in certain industries, amounting to a *de facto* suppression of the right to strike. On the other hand, they sought to establish a national wage policy by fixing general norms of average wage increases (wage guidelines).

(c) The role of collective bargaining in the development of wages.
Collective bargaining still kept the appearance of decentralization. According to Federal figures, 150,000 wage contracts were made in 1961 (1 for every 100 unionized workers). In actual fact, however, these contracts were dependent on models fixed by keynote negotiations, which then spread through the industries in question. Some 8.3 million workers were covered by only 1733 contracts, and 1.9 million by the 9 most important contracts.

Whatever the level of negotiation establishing the model contract, this then becomes a norm for the entire industry; it may be more or less favourable to the capitalists, but competition between them ensures its generalization. This model and the norm it contains only cover the basic wage and the major schemes for collective bonuses and pension funds.

At the same time as it became centralized in form and altered in content, collective bargaining underwent a further change that contributed to the inflexibility of the nominal wage which, as we have seen, was a characteristic feature of Fordism. Not

---

[14] These included interventions into conflicts in mining, steel, armaments, telecommunications, docks and meat processing, during the fierce period of 1958–60.

only did wage contracts become more and more uniform and all-embracing, they were also extended to periods sufficiently long to conform with the planning horizon of the big corporations. The sum total of collective bargaining procedures thus tended to make it an instrument for planning the development of the working-class norm of consumption, adjusting the basic wage automatically at certain fixed dates. By divorcing wage adjustments from the business cycle, collective contracts extending for several years made the expanded reproduction of capital less sensitive to the instability of the equivalence relationships of exchange resulting from the transformation of production conditions. Now that they could incorporate into capital advanced a future wage movement known with a high degree of probability, the corporations systematically introduced and extended the semi-automatic labour process applied to long and standardized production runs. Hence the accelerated fall in real social wage costs in the first half of the 1960s, and the most powerful wave of investment in the whole history of capitalism. Hence also the low sensitivity of capital formation to short-term fluctuations in output and the reciprocal role of capital formation in the evening out of these fluctuations.

From the point of view of the proletariat, these long-term contracts were extremely powerful instruments of exploitation. They left the field free for a ferocious intensification of capitalist labour discipline in production. In fixing the nominal basic wage, the long-term contract lagged its indexation to the cost of living, so that real wages deteriorated the more inflation accelerated. Finally, the spread of schemes for higher deferred wages, designed to compress direct wage increases, meant – as we have seen – that workers were often literally robbed in the payment of pensions.

It is not surprising, then, that the crisis of the collective bargaining procedures engendered by Fordism coincided with a blockage of relative surplus-value. Collective bargaining as a structural form now contained the class struggle within a framework where the capitalists could take advantage of all the possibilities of exploitation inherent in an organization of the labour process centred on the mass production of standardized commodities. But there its usefulness for capital accumulation came to an end. It was not in its power to remedy the deficiencies of this type of labour process and its inability to increase direct exploitation in production any further. On the contrary, the growing crisis of work organization actually threatens collective bargaining and promotes further state intervention in the fixing of wages. From 1966 onwards, workers came increasingly to reject the contracts negotiated. This rejection was accompanied by spontaneous actions which grew more frequent towards the end of the decade, particularly in those industries where collective bargaining procedures had seemed most harmonious and sophisticated (automobiles, steel, and electrical construction). These sporadic struggles were concerned with issues which collective bargaining had neglected.

The far-reaching transformations in work organization introduced by Neo-Fordism inevitably generated a modification in collective bargaining. The new flexibility in the organization of the labour process can make working conditions once again an object of decentralized negotiation by semi-autonomous groups, without thereby blocking the further development of a more advanced work organization. The typical response of the capitalist class to the crisis of Fordism, however, has been direct pressure on wages by state intervention. The fact that this authoritarian determination of wages was imposed in the United States by a Republican administration which arrived in office intending to abandon the directives of its Democratic predecessor, only confirms the depth of the crisis. The Nixon Administration set up a national office charged with fixing norms for the growth of the nominal reference wage. Such an office had previously existed only in time of war.

2. The Determination of the Nominal Reference Wage in the United States and the Long-Run Movement of Wages

We showed in Chapter 1 how the nominal reference wage is formally expressed as a transformed monetary value of the rate of surplus-value, via the equation: $\bar{s}_t = \overline{m}_t / 1 + e_t$. This relationship is the effect on the field of exchange relations of the unity of the different aspects of the wage relation. The negative influence of the rate of exploitation, synthesizing prevailing social conditions of production, is an expression of the fact that the nominal reference wage derives from the capitalist relation of appropriation. As far as the function $\overline{m}_t$ is concerned, we have seen that this is a function of the past magnitudes of the monetary expression of a working hour, a function that itself changes over time. We can therefore write:

$\overline{m}_t = \mu(m_{t-t'}, m_{t-t''}, \ldots)$, where the intervals t', t'', ... form part of the definition of the function μ.

What is the significance of this expression? It shows that the nominal reference wage, in the guise of an exchange relation, is the object of a procedure of formation, in other words it is derived from a structural form. Let us take a closer look at the situation. The function μ represents the procedure itself. Its values show the effect of changes over time in the monetary expression of a working hour. These changes denote the variability of the general equivalent when the transformation of the conditions of production radically changes the whole set of equivalence classes in exchange. The series of temporal intervals defines the way in which the variability of the monetary expression of a working hour affects the wage contract. This series depends on the bargaining procedure and consequently on the whole set of determinants of this structural form.

The law by which the nominal reference wage is formed shows that the evolution of this variable may be legitimately described by an econometric relationship, but first and foremost it underlines the conditions of stability for this relationship. It is stable only if wage formation is effected according to a determinate procedure of collective bargaining with clauses fixing the series of intervals and a sufficiently rapid diffusion of model contracts. The econometric relations that describe the evolution of the nominal reference wage are given a direction only by phases of the accumulation process that are identified and characterized by historical analysis.[15]

The substance of the econometric relationship can be made more precise. In effect, the variation in the monetary expression of the working hour between two dates t and t' is estimated in the following way, as we already saw in Chapter 1: $m_{t'}^t = \pi_{t'}^t \cdot P_{t'}^t$, where π and P are indices of the average change in labour

---

[15] I have attempted to apply such a procedure to France in my article 'L'évolution des salaires en France au cours des vingt dernières années', *Revue économique*, January, 1971.

productivity and in the general price level between the two dates. The variation in the rate of surplus-value, moreover, is given by the inverse of the variation in real social wage costs, which involve nominal wages, prices and productivity. We are then led to envisage a relationship in which the variation in the nominal reference wage is a function of the staggered delays in the variation of the general level of prices and average productivity. It is also possible to envisage an auto-regressive relationship, with a delayed growth in the average productivity of labour as the independent variable.

In the long run, relationships such as these would be illusory and scientifically incorrect. A pertinent interpretation of quantitative movements must be far more modest in its numerical precision. But its theoretical importance is much greater. Since we have shown that the reproduction of the wage relation is the kernel of the law of capital accumulation, the different historical regimes of accumulation that we identified, either predominantly extensive or predominantly intensive, are characterized by the expression of the wage relation in different structural forms. The evolution of the nominal wage and its real purchasing power, as functions of the rhythm of accumulation, are necessarily very different in epochs when the working-class mode of consumption is not stabilized and in epochs when the norm of social consumption is rising, when accumulation cycles are pronounced and when accumulation is continuous with permanent obsolescence, when the working class is in process of formation and when collective bargaining is already codified. It is possible to contrast the regulation of wages under the law of accumulation that preceded the First World War and in the expansionary phase of Fordism after the Second World War. The inter-war period is more ambiguous in this respect, as a transitional phase between two regimes of accumulation.

(a) The development of nominal wages and real wages before the Second World War. Observations conducted on the basis of a long-run series of nominal wage rates[16] permit the conclusion that relatively protracted phases of rise or fall in nominal wages match almost perfectly the phases of the cyclical movement of

---

[16] E.H. Phelps Brown and M.H. Browne, *A Century of Pay*, loc. cit.

accumulation expressed by the gross formation of fixed capital, for the whole period between 1860 and 1914. But this temporal simultaneity in no way implies that the two rhythms were one and the same. In the years leading up to 1914, the phase of decline in the cycle of nominal wages became less and less visible. Instead there was simply stagnation or a slower rate of growth. After the First World War there was a definite discrepancy between the two. Gross fixed capital formation reached a peak in 1926, nominal wages in 1929.

We can also observe over the whole of this period an inverse relationship between the nominal wage rate and the rate of unemployment. In a l regime of predominantly extensive accumulation, the rate of unemployment is closely tied to the evolution of variable capital, which fluctuates as a function of the rate of accumulation and the evolution of the organic composition of capital, in accordance with the relationship established in our first chapter. So long as capitalism has not restructured the mode of consumption, in effect, there is very little room for unproductive labour. The rate of unemployment varies as a direct result of the growth or decline in the industrial reserve army. Falls in nominal wages combined with sharp contractions in employment were the ways in which the division between profits and wages was re-established. The more brutal the falls in nominal wages, the shorter were the phases in which accumulation was blocked, and the more far-reaching the transformations of the conditions of production that redressed the balance between profits and wages and consequently provided the foundations for a new phase of accumulation. In its wake, this phase in turn led to a rise in nominal wages which permitted an extension of consumption. The position of the workers in wage negotiations thus varied very greatly according to the phase of the accumulation cycle, to a point where their trade-union organizations themselves were ephemeral. The nominal wage was consequently a very unstable derivative of the value of labour-power (the function μ fluctuating a great deal), which expressed the basic conditions of reproduction of the wage-earning class. In this way, even though relative surplus-value was not the motor of capital formation under the regime of predominantly extensive accumulation, the division between wages and profit still fluctuated sharply while real social wage costs grew only very slowly.

Changes in the value of labour-power were linked in particular to the transformation of production conditions in agriculture and in those industries such as textiles and leather that were among the first to benefit from the mechanization of labour that followed the Civil War. The prices of means of consumption underwent a long decline through to 1896, then turning and rising slowly up to 1914. The long-run movement of these prices depended very little on the rhythm of accumulation by which heavy industry was built up in successive waves. This is why the real wage rate, unlike the nominal rate, had little connection with the rhythm of accumulation. Its long-term tendency depended essentially on that of the prices of consumer goods.

The following data trace the annual rate of growth of real wages:

Phase of long-term fall in prices (1865–96): 1.3%

Phase of long-term rise in prices (1896–1915): 0.8%

Within these long-run tendencies there was certainly a modulation in the real wage rate with the rhythm of accumulation, since the nominal rate fluctuated closely together with it. But the modulation in the real wage rate was greatly reduced due to the fall in market prices below the long-run trend of prices when the rate of accumulation dipped, and the rise above this trend when the rate accelerated. In practice the real wage rate increased throughout, but more so in phases of low accumulation than in those of high accumulation. The paradox here is only apparent. The situation of the workers might appear to improve when the regular functioning of the capitalist mode of production is jammed. But this illusion is dispelled when we remember that the wage relation affects the entire labour force of society. The rise in unemployment produced by sharp contractions in accumulation largely cancelled out the small improvement in the purchasing power of those actually employed, all the more so since the temporary decline in working hours could itself more than offset the increase in purchasing power of the basic hourly wage. In the Great Depression, for example, the purchasing power of the hourly wage increased by an average of 2% per year. But working hours fell at an annual rate of 4%. Thus the purchasing power of total wages fell by 35% in 4 years under the crushing effect of the decline in industrial employment.

(b) The trends in nominal and real wages since the Second World War. After the Second World War, the relationships we have just outlined between nominal wages, real wages, prices, and the long-term rate of accumulation underwent far-reaching changes. These changes undoubtedly reveal new tendencies in the modalities of the overall regulation of the system.

During the zenith of Fordism, before the crisis of work organization seriously disrupted the overall accumulation process, the following pattern obtained:

| Average annual growth rate (%) | *Relative direction of the movement of accumulation* | | | |
	1951 *decline*	*1961* *acceleration*	*1966*	*1970* *decline*
Basic nominal hourly wage	3.6	3.9		4.6
Index of consumer prices	2.0	1.6		4.6
Real weekly wage	2.2	3.5		− 1.5

The configuration of the previous epoch was now completely reversed. The evolution of the nominal wage rate no longer reflected in any way the changing rhythms of accumulation. Consumer prices, which had previously oscillated around the long-run tendency of the rate of accumulation, now moved in an opposite direction. Real wages, formerly inflexible and prone to rise in phases when accumulation dipped, now moved in the same direction as accumulation. Their absolute fall in the second half of the 1960s was a symptom of the onset of the organic crisis of Fordism which henceforward threatened the historically established norm of social consumption.

All these phenomena express the predominance of relative surplus-value. We showed in Chapter 1 how a decline in real social wage costs was central to the regime of predominantly intensive accumulation. Changing trends in real social wage costs now become the essential determinant of the ups and downs of accumulation. When extensive accumulation was predominant, real social wage costs were more stable. The active role in the changing pace of accumulation was rather played by the fluctuations in the industrial reserve army. The fundamental pattern in Fordism seems to be that the breaks in the rhythm of accumulation are not governed chiefly by the fluctuations in the nominal wage rate and the rate of unemployment, but rather by those in the general price level, or more basically by the conditions of formation of the general equivalent, in other words the evolution over time of the monetary expression of the working hour. Given a general tendency for the value of money to fall, *modern capitalism exhibits an accelerated rise in prices in those phases in which real social wage costs are stabilized, i.e. in phases in which accumulation relatively declines.*

Under the regime of intensive accumulation, the radical changes in the conditions of production rooted in the transformation of the means of production and consequently in relationships internal to Department I are subsequently oriented towards the production of means of consumption. We have seen that the basic interaction between the two departments was effected by the generalization of a labour process which on the one hand fragmented individual tasks and created a collective worker, while on the other hand it correlatively gave rise to the formation and development of a norm of social consumption structured by the mass production of standardized commodities. This interaction is therefore governed by relative surplus-value. A permanent revolutionization of the productive forces in Department I is the condition for lowering the value of labour-power. This decrease must be sufficiently rapid, and consequently the mode of consumption must be transformed sufficiently quickly in the direction of a diversified range of standardized commodities structured by the consumption process, for accumulation in Department I to be able to sustain such a transformation of the forces of production.

These infrastructural processes operate under the constraint of capitalist appropriation, and betoken the extension and reinforcement of the constraint of accumulation itself. They operate therefore in production processes rendered autonomous from each other by capitalist ownership, whose interaction is effected only *a posteriori* by the general circulation of commodities. As we have seen, this series of exchanges is ordered by the maintenance cycle of social labour-power. It is thus composed of relations between the two departments that are the more densely woven, the more the wage-earning class is extended and unified, and the more irreversible is the norm of social consumption. The latter must consist of a mass of exchange-value in money growing with the greatest possible regularity, and possess a content of use-values rapidly developing in such a way that the production of individual commodities in Department II incorporates the new productive forces created in Department I, and thereby precipitates a fall in real social wage costs.

The inherent unevenness in the development of the two departments thus assumes a form that is characteristic of the regime of intensive accumulation. The revolutionization of the conditions of production creates a permanent instability in the equivalence relations of exchange through which links are established between the component parts of social capital. But this instability operates under the continuity of an overall growth in the norm of social consumption, in other words *under the constraint of the inflexibility of the nominal reference wage.* From now on, the contradictory forces that both promote the uneven development of Department I and counter this development interact in such a way that the overall value relations defined in Chapter 1 develop in an unambiguous direction over time. The general characteristics of this process are as follows:

(1) The obsolescence of fixed capital investments becomes generalized and permanent, as we have shown in Chapter 1. Renewal of fixed capital is the basis for transformations of the production process. Integrated into investment plans as now a modality of capitalist accumulation, obsolescence is still sanctioned by the law of exchange equivalence as a loss in value. But since a permanent devalorization of capital can be predicted probabilistically, it is incorporated into the total gross profit in the form of a provision for the renewal of the conditions of production. The more that an anterior obsolescence in Department I takes effect in Department II and precipitates a rise in the norm of consumption there, the more it must be intensified so that the rate of increase in relative surplus-value makes up for the accelerated social loss of value. In this interconnection, the uneven development of Department I is

manifested in an increase in the devalorization of capital that is more rapid than the rise in relative surplus-value. The result is a rate of growth of provisions for amortization in gross profits that accelerates while the fall in social wage costs slows down.[17] The value composition of capital thus tends to develop in the direction of a relative expansion of constant capital. These phenomena are produced as soon as the transformations of the labour process which stimulate obsolescence but are nonetheless pursued according to the same organizational plan become incapable of preventing the rising class struggle in production.

(2) The devalorization of capital expresses the instability of equivalence relations in exchange. If it were experienced by individual capitals in their cycles of expanded reproduction, it would take the form of unsold commodities. The monetary constraint of exchange would be expressed in a sharp fall in prices, which would lead to the contraction of accumulation in Department I, then to massive unemployment and a fall in nominal wages in Department II. This is the process that can be observed under the regime of extensive accumulation. But when the devalorization of capital is incorporated into the value composition of the total capital as a permanent modality of accumulation, commodities are actually sold. There seems not to be any monetary sanction for the loss of value. We are thus faced with the following contradiction: exchange takes place, so equivalence relationships are respected; yet capital is permanently devalorized, so there is necessarily a non-equivalence, a social loss of value. There is only one way of escaping from this contradiction, and this is *by the general equivalent itself losing value*. This is entirely possible, moreover, because the general equivalent, as we indicated in Chapter 1 and will demonstrate in Chapter 6, is formed in the social process of the circulation of capital $M - C - M'$. It is involved in every system of equivalence relationships, but it is constantly reconstituted over time as the system evolves. The modality of capital devalorization inherent in the regime of intensive accumulation leads to a mode of formation of the general equivalent which is expressed in a *weakening of commodity*

[17] For a detailed examination of its developments in the decade 1965–75, see M. Aglietta, 'Monnaie et inflation', in *Économie et Statistique*, April 1976.

circulation.[18] This happens because money absorbs and diffuses the loss in value. The more the devalorization of capital accelerates, as the consequence of a deterioration in the conditions of intensive accumulation, the greater the acceleration in the loss of monetary value that is necessary for exchange to continue, which in turn induces an accelerated growth in the monetary expression of the working hour. This weakening of commodity circulation reveals a more general crisis, although one induced by the crisis in the reproduction of the wage relation; a crisis of commodity equivalence as the form of social unity of all productive activities. It is in no way surprising, therefore, that inflation leads to a general disarray in private economic calculation, since this calculation is based on the social validity of compatible values, in other words on the rigour of the monetary sanction.

(3) At this point we can grasp the organic unity of modern capitalism. In order for accumulation to continue despite the deterioration in its conditions, it is necessary for the general effect of the devalorization of capital on the declining value of money to recur spontaneously. Here the inflexibility of the nominal reference wage implied by the maintenance of the norm of social consumption plays a decisive role. We have seen that this inflexibility is assured by the structural form of collective bargaining. The accelerated growth in the monetary expression of the working hour reacts on the rise in monetary wages in a process that may take the form of a lagged, sliding scale of payments. Monetary wages grow sufficiently quickly to prevent a shortfall in effective demand, but sufficiently slowly for their rate of growth to remain less than that of the provisions for amortization incorporated in overall gross profits. The preservation of the gross division between profits and wages can thus sustain obsolescence and accelerate the whole process. Capital formation does not collapse, therefore, it simply slows down. The rise in nominal wages accelerates, but that of the general price level accelerates more quickly, with the result that real wages grow more and more slowly and eventually decline, as the above table has shown.

[18] See S. de Brunhoff, *Etat et Capital*, loc. cit.

We are now on the threshold of an analysis of the process of inflation. But there is a further task ahead that has first to be acquitted. To study this process in concrete detail and determine its limits, it is essential to understand the precise characteristics of the monetary system that give such a flexibility to the reproduction of the general equivalent at the price of actually weakening commodity circulation. This is only possible by a careful study of credit and the financing of capitalist accumulation on the basis of the general laws and structural conditions presented in this first part of the book. The second part will therefore be devoted to this study.

Part Two

The Transformations of Inter-capitalist Relations: The Laws of Competition

This part of the book will deal with the laws of competition. Up till now we have studied the general law of capital accumulation by developing an analysis of the conditions of reproduction of the wage relation. By gathering together the threads of this analysis, we have already arrived at certain overall results illuminating the causes of the organic crisis of contemporary capitalism and the structural conditions of inflation.

We now need to advance much further in our concrete conceptualization of these phenomena. To do so, we must take into account a dimension of capitalism which did not appear in our theoretical analysis of the wage relation. This is the fact that capital is partitioned by its very nature into distinct and separate capitals that are centres of individual decision, autonomous from the standpoint of their valorization. The second part of our work will therefore be concerned with the transformation of inter-capitalist relations. In no way, however, can this analysis be simply juxtaposed to that of the wage relation. Relations between autonomous capitals, in fact, are relations of competition, whose concept we now have to construct. But we can say right away that autonomous capitals are in competition because they all have the attributes of capital in general, i.e. they are all constituted by the wage relation. It is correct therefore to say that it is by way of competition that these capitals experience the constraint of the law of accumulation. Conversely, this latter is expressed through the laws of competition. This is why study of the laws of competition is the most concrete aspect of a general theory of capitalist regulation. We shall pursue this study in the following manner.

Chapter 4 investigates the concentration of capital, in other words the mode of reorganization of capitals in competition. It analyses the objective conditions of stratification within the capitalist class. The analysis comprises two aspects. On the one hand we intend to investigate how capital accumulation in general gives rise to a tendency towards centralization within the autonomous individual capitals – a tendency which is in no way regular or homogeneous, but operates rather through violent jerks that rearrange the links between capitals. On the other hand, we shall study the nature of these links themselves. Just as the wage relation develops by way of the creation of structural forms that expand into collective bargaining, so the centralization of capital creates structural forms by which coalitions of capitals are formed. These are the giant corporation and the financial group. Insight into the functioning of these structural forms will allow us to grasp concretely the nature of capitalist control of property.

Chapter 5 studies the competition of capitals as a process. Our first task will be an exposition of the manner in which the general constraint of capital accumulation bears on individual capitals. This will lead us to define the concept of the general rate of profit. The next task will be to show how fragmented individual capitals are valorized under the constraint of the general rate of profit. This problem demands the introduction of the concept of industrial branch, and leads to the laws of price formation. On the basis of these results, we shall then be able to ask how the refashioning of the links between capitals subjected to capitalist centralization interferes with the laws of price formation. This analysis will open the way to an understanding of the actual price systems that obtain in the United States, on which we shall venture a few remarks.

The developments of Chapters 4 and 5 will enable us to establish the conditions for the financing of capitalist accumulation. It will then be possible to return in Chapter 6 to the basic problem which we were only able to treat in a very abstract way in the first part of the book: the law of money formation. We shall investigate the dynamic of credit on the basis of the conditions for the financing of capitalist accumulation. Thereafter we shall proceed to explore the link between money and credit, and to demonstrate that the dematerialization of money involves a structural form necessary for the preservation of the unity of the national currency: a centralized monetary system under the constraint of a state-enforced parity. We shall then be prepared to confront the key concluding problem of our study. We shall seek to show how the contradictions of the law of capital accumulation identified in the first part of this book and embodied in the structural conditions of inflation condense and explode in the form of financial crises. This final step will enable us to explain the phenomenon of inflation and to emphasize the originality of contemporary inflation as an expression of the organic crisis of Fordism.

4

The Concentration and Centralization of Capital

I. The Definition of Concentration and its Determinants

The individualization of capitals is already implicitly contained in the definition of capital in general, or social capital. To say that there are individual capitals means that the production of surplus-value takes place at points that are distinct and separate from the standpoint of appropriation, i.e. of the ability to control the forces of production and to dispose of the products of social labour. This is the case when the products of labour are sold as commodities. For then, in effect, the forces of production are fragmented and production processes are not coordinated, with the result that the social character of the products is expressed only *ex posteriori*, in the relations of exchange. It follows from this that the individual capitals are characterized by the absence of a common plan for valorization, that they stand in mutual opposition inasmuch as each seeks to affirm the social character of the labour under its control, on which its own valorization thus depends, at the expense of the others, and that they are only connected together by their insertion into the general circulation of commodities.

This definition of the individualization of the social capital has the advantage of being relative to the conditions of development of the forces of production. It has nothing in common with the 'atomicity' of the theory of general equilibrium. The law of capital accumulation stamps the individualization of autonomous capitals with a general tendency towards concentration. The configuration of autonomous capitals changes historically according to a general law. To study this it is necessary to proceed step by step. The first step is to analyse the essential determinants of concentration by studying the link between the individualization of capitals and the major transformations of the labour process and conditions of existence of the wage-earning class which form the content of capital accumulation. The next step, on the basis of the valorization of autonomous capitals, is to demonstrate the decisive influence of the financing of accumulation on the process of concentration itself.

1. The Concentration and Centralization of Industrial Capital

Study of the concentration of capital is made more difficult by the frequent confusion over the concept of autonomous or individual capital. An individual capital is neither a thing, nor possession of a thing. Since any individual capital is under the determination of the social capital and derives from the wage relation, it follows that it is a centre of disposal over a circulation flow whose form is that of a circular process of changes in the form of value.

True, this process embraces production in the strict sense. But the integrity of the individual capital presupposes effective control of all those functions which make valorization a permanent process. This is why the phenomenon of concentration involves more than the partial statistics devised to measure it. *Concentration is the expansion of ownership over a process of valorization.*

If this theoretical starting point is forgotten, then it is impossible to interpret the statistical data coherently. On the contrary, these will then conflict with one another. If only the labour process is taken into account, then emphasis will fall on the increase in size of factories at certain times and in certain industries. But the transformations of the labour process themselves experience a dual movement of segmentation and integration. At a different moment in the development of the productive forces, the same individual capital may be able to increase the scale of its valorization relative to others while organizing its labour process in a series of dispersed units, with the result that the size of its factories declines in relation to those of its competitors. Has concentration then increased or decreased? In the same way, when attention is drawn to another phase of the circulation process, emphasis often falls on the shares of the market controlled by different firms. Once again, it is highly dangerous to draw conclusions from this one aspect. It assumes that markets and therefore commodities can be divided up in terms of use-values. Now the valorization of an individual capital in no way implies anything about the use-values which support value proper. It may happen that the conditions of production and exchange develop in a way that favours a rapid diversification of use-values. In this case, it might well be possible to establish a decline in the indices of concentration as calculated by taking the market shares for each type of use-value in isolation, even though the total number of firms in the market as a whole has dropped and the volume of turnover and number of workers controlled by each of these has greatly increased. Has there not then been an increase in the power of autonomous centres to dispose of social labour? We may note that valorization of capital in its most general sense is the expansion of homogeneous value. This is why it is the monetary form of value that gives the flow over which there is a power of disposal its closed and cyclical form. It is the predominance of this monetary form that enables one and the same individual capital to direct several production processes and to sell commodities on several markets, while appearing as a single centre of production. Now the redeployment of the money destined to be employed as capital is effected by financial agencies. Can we infer from this that these agencies are the true centres of power and that the concentration of capital can be identified with the financial connections established between these agencies and legally autonomous firms?[1]

In our view, some order must be established in this profusion of partial approaches if serious intellectual confusion is to be avoided. This can only be done by proceeding concept by concept on the basis of the theory of accumulation outlined in the first part of this work. Only on this condition can the very bulky statistical data on the question of concentration lead to genuine knowledge, or current typologies (horizontal concent-

[1] This state of mind is very widespread among Marxist economists. See for example F. Morin, *La structure financière du capitalisme français*, Paris, 1974.

ration, vertical concentration, concentration by diversification, or conglomeration) really enrich our understanding of
the phenomenon. In the present work we shall confine ourselves
to theoretical analysis of the essential aspects necessary to
render the laws of competition intelligible.

The first step is to distinguish between *simple concentration*
and *centralization* of capital. Simple concentration is the
immediate effect on the fragmentation of capitals of the uneven
development whose origin we have seen in the way that labour
productivity increases. Each individual capital is a focus of
concentration in that it combines the means of valorization on
an increasing scale. Since this valorization is subject to the law
of accumulation, it inevitably involves a quest for relative
saving on living labour. It tends, therefore, in the direction of a
technical modification of the composition of the means of
production that raises the value mass of the capital needed to
control production and consequently to run through the full
cycle of valorization. Simple concentration is therefore a derivative phenomenon of accumulation, its importance varying
according to industry and period. As a corollary of uneven
development, this phenomenon is intrinsically not operative to
a uniform extent over the whole field of commodity production.
When the concrete development of different systems of productive forces is taken into account, it is possible for certain
domains of industrial production to be foci of concentration
(e.g. steel and oil at the turn of the century, automobiles in the
inter-war period, rubber or packaging after the Second World
War), while others are at the same time just emerging or are
rapidly developing, and hence propitious to the formation of a
large number of new capitals (such as the production of
electrical household goods in the 1920s, or the electronic
components industry after the Second World War).

If simple concentration is a diffuse phenomenon at the overall
social level, permanently present but differing in importance
according to the different zones of commodity production,
centralization of capital takes a quite different form. While
simple concentration is a quantitative fact of uneven accumulation in the field of value, and preserves the autonomy of
separate capitals, *centralization* is a qualitative change that
refashions the autonomy of capitals and *establishes new relation-*

ships of competition. It is a process that is discontinuous in time, related to successive phases of capital formation in the sequential process of global accumulation explained at the end of Chapter 1 (see Diagrams 6 and 7), simultaneous in its impact on the economy as a whole, and irreversible in its effects. In the course of centralization, a whole host of individual capitals disappear, absorbed by others, while yet others fuse together by merger or consolidation. The centralization of capital is therefore a violent form of competition. It may happen that centralization is ushered in by a merciless struggle between capitals in a particular domain of industrial production. In that case it puts a final end to a period in which simple concentration in this domain was intense. But the centralization of capital has a more general significance than that. It is the *effect on the fragmentation of capitals of the general process of devalorization* by which the movement of overall accumulation finds new conditions for its future advance. That is why the centralization of capital is not limited to particular fields. We shall see below how mergers between capitals occur in waves, with a precise location in the overall movement of capital formation. They occur at the end of the ascendant phase, when the rate of surplus-value begins to dip and the struggle against this decline gives rise to an intensification of obsolescence. They also occur at the end of the phase of depression, when centralization sets in to reorganize an industrial system that has been revolutionized by massive destructions of capital. In the depression itself, the destruction of capital far prevails over the formation of new capital. Centralization is essentially effected by the elimination of businesses. Thus capital centralization does not stop with a reduction in the number of autonomous capitals and an increase in their size. It establishes new relations of competition, because the destruction of one section of industrial capital reduces the total mass of capital involved in production and gives all capitals new possibilities of valorization. We have seen how under the regime of intensive accumulation, devalorizations of capital tend to become continuous and form part of the articulation between the two departments of production. The establishment of new relations of competition between centralized capitals is the mediation that organizes these devalorizations, and enables a continuous transformation of the conditions of production by reducing the deleterious consequences of brutal eliminations of capital.

The centralization of capital regroups under a single power of disposal and control cycles of valorization that may remain distinct from one another from the standpoint of the production and realization of commodities. Such a centralized power of disposal can only be established by the creation of new structural forms. These are chiefly the giant corporation and the financial group, which we shall investigate at the end of the present chapter. But the centralized organization of capital also extends to the network of *sub-contracting*, in which firms that are legally autonomous and are not controlled by financial holdings still do not form autonomous capitals from the standpoint of the valorization cycle. These capitals make segments of valorization function in an integrated series. Their dependence is set by technico-economic norms over which they have no influence. Their clients are imposed on them. They do not produce commodities properly speaking, but rather inter-mediate products within a broader production process creating complex commodities. The quantities produced and the prices at which they are marketed are similarly imposed on them. The latter are not market prices but simply transfer prices. Yet these sub-contracting firms play an essential role in the stratifi-cation of the proletariat. We have seen that this stratification is an important form for obtaining higher rates of surplus-value under conditions of Fordism. The socio-economic conditions that perpetuate it include a segmentation of the labour market. The establishment of sub-contracting networks enables centra-lized capitals to organize this segmentation while dispersing and isolating their work-force.

2. The Influence of Financial Conditions: Waves of Mergers

The preponderance of centralization in the movement of con-centration of capital, and the way it is tied to the law of accumulation, give great importance to financial conditions.

The operations by which centralization is effected are chang-es in ownership which involve significant portions of mo-netary capital. In the flow of the circulation fund that goes through the various phases of the valorization cycle, the ability to dispose of free and uncommitted monetary resources by simply letting the cycle continue is the decisive weapon for maintaining an autonomous capitalist centre, able both to defend itself against any attempt to take it over, and to pursue an aggressive accumulation strategy of its own. Such an ability must be based on an overall gross profit previously accumulated, which can rapidly be mobilized – what one might call the margin of manoeuvre yielded by cash flow not tied by the need to finance productive capital. Now this cash flow is itself engendered to a large extent by the provisions for obsolescence incorporated into ordinary running costs. As a result, not only is centralization induced by the devalorization of capital in its modern form, which throws the cost back onto society, but it is itself a powerful factor of this devalorization. In phases when the movement of centralization intensifies, the cash flow engendered in the valorization cycle is extracted from it to fuel a *financial circulation* whose effect is to reshuffle control over property. Breaking loose from its role in financing the renewal of the conditions of production, gross profit becomes an instrument of social waste, expended in the overt or hidden struggles unleashed by capitalist competition. The more that capitalist control is centralized, and the more it can deploy a cash flow accruing from several different valorization cycles, the more formidable its competitive ability to extend its power of disposal over property.

Since what is at stake in the centralization of capital is actual ownership of the means of production, it is not surprising that this centralization cannot be explained in terms of technical and commercial considerations. These latter sustain centralization, but in no way cause it. Nor is it surprising that centralization occurs chiefly in periods of financial crisis, where the disorders of financial circulation, fed by speculation, favour major redistributions of disposable monetary funds. The most correct indicator to assess the concentration of capital is therefore the distribution of the accumulated mass of uncommitted cash flow between autonomous capitalist centres. This would give a dynamic picture of the struggle between capitals. But information of this kind is not available. We have therefore to be satisfied with the distribution of the total assets that firms control. In the United States this information is supplied by the Federal Trade Commission,[2] which is responsible for applying regulations governing competition. The following table shows the developing concentration of assets from 1925 to 1968.

Year	Percentage of Total Assets held by	
	the 100 biggest firms	the 200 biggest firms
1925	34.5	——————
1929	38.2	45.8
1933	42.5	49.5
1939	41.9	48.7
1947	37.5	45.0
1954	41.9	50.4
1958	46.0	55.2
1962	45.5	55.1
1965	45.9	55.9
1968	48.4	60.4

Comparison between these figures and Diagrams 1 and 8 shows that the centralization of capital advances in periods when relative surplus-value declines (as attested by a deceleration or halt in the fall of real social wage costs), and in periods when capital is being strongly devalorized (attested after the Second World War by the rapid increase in the share of provisions for depreciation in cash flow). It remains equal, on the other hand, or falls only slightly, during the upswings of an approximately regular accumulation.

The characteristic features of capital centralization are confirmed in a striking manner by examining the waves of mergers shown in Diagram 11. The extreme irregularity of the phenomenon is immediately apparent. There are three major waves: at the turn of the century, in the late 1920s, and in the late 1960s. Each major wave is preceded by.one or more minor waves. By extending our earlier analyses, we can explain the position of these merger waves in the trajectory of capital formation and establish the following propositions.

[2] *Report to the Congress on the Hearings of the Sub-Committee on Anti-Trust and Monopoly* (91st Congress, 1969–70).

Diagram 11. Corporate mergers (1888-1972)

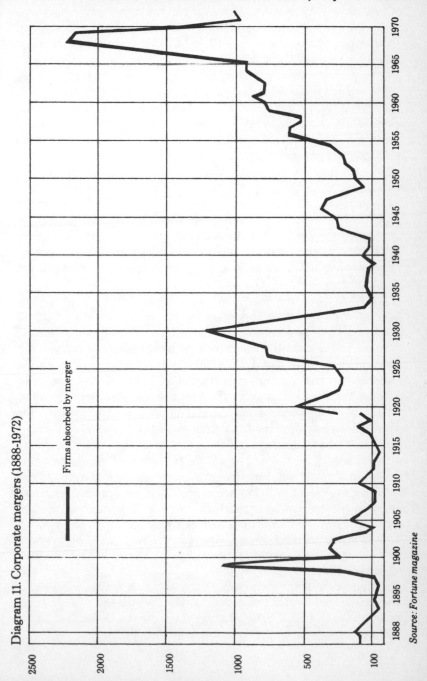

Firms absorbed by merger

Source: Fortune magazine

Waves of mergers occur in two circumstances:

(1) At the end of a phase of stagnation or reduction in capital formation, and at the start of the following phase of upswing, when the destruction of capital and changes in the labour processes and new interbranch connections engendered by them reduce the total value of productive capital, or slow down its growth relative to that of total relative surplus-value, raising the rate of surplus-value again, and thus setting in motion a growth in the overall rate of return on productive capital. The centralization of capital then leads to a reorganization of the division of labour, reinforcing developments already under way in operations of valorization, by giving full play to economies of scale. Those production units that function at a cost higher than the social average at prevailing methods of production are eliminated; markets that were previously restricted are opened up; productive forces are shifted towards those economic branches where a growth potential is beginning to show.

(2) At the end of a long phase of increased capital formation, when the rate of growth begins to dip or when the movement even begins to go into reverse (e.g. 1926 and 1967), as a result of the fall in the overall rate of return on productive capital. We have seen in Chapter 1 that this fall occurs as soon as the increase in the rate of surplus-value is checked or stopped altogether, given the rise in the organic composition of capital. These overall processes are manifested in a disproportionate growth in the different departments of production, disturbing the flows of exchange-value between them that are needed for the expanded reproduction of the elements of capital's value composition. In this situation, those capitals that are well situated seek to strengthen their positions, and profit from their high rate of return to extend their space for valorization. The upshot is a wave of mergers proceeding chiefly via the absorption of some firms by others, whereas the wave that puts a final end to the depression phase proceeds rather by way of consolidation.

This theoretical interpretation of waves of mergers would be incomplete if the financial conditions that directly made them possible, and which have already been mentioned above, were left out of account. There are two such conditions.

(1) *An upswing of financial circulation.* Such circulation is induced by the financing of capital accumulation, in other words by the practices of financial agencies, either locked into the circuit of payments or linked to holders of unused liquid resources, which capture money already created and transform it into *money capital.* Yet this transformation, as well as the investment of money capital in the financing of production, are neither exclusively nor even chiefly technical operations. They are *transfers of ownership.* The basic nature of money, a general and permanent purchasing power as the representative of abstract labour, evidently remains when money becomes money capital. An expression of the abstract wealth of society, money capital as a homogeneous mass does not purchase individual commodities, but it acquires disposal over the means of production in proportion to its quantitative importance and the forms in which it is invested. This is why transfers of ownership take the form of purchases and sales of various kinds of titles to property which stipulate the conditions on which the capitalist, i.e. the holder of money employed as capital, agrees to part with his assets, and the rights he acquires in return. Financial circulation is the circulation space of money capital, whose basic elements are the buying and selling of shares. It is at once diversified by the nature of the titles that are issued and negotiable, yet at the same time the source of a formidable centralization of ownership in that it enables a single capitalist, or a coalition of capitalists, to accumulate assets of the same kind whose mere number indicates the expansion of ownership involved. In the United States, the principal form of financial circulation has been the stock market, which registered a major surge upwards in the last decade of the 19th century. Essentially a reorganization of capitalist ownership, the centralization of capital operates by way of massive transfers in the sphere of financial circulation. The latter must be sufficiently active, i.e. sufficiently attractive to money capital by virtue of the diversity of stocks obtainable, the intensity of transactions, and the nominal profits feasible, to enable vast transfer operations to be realized. This is the reason why, in a country where the stock market is the predominant form of financial circulation, it always witnesses an intense speculative fever during the high point of a wave of mergers. Such a fever is unleashed

when the upswing of capital formation peters out, yet the flow of monetary facilities remains abundant while the return on their productive employment becomes uncertain. Large amounts of money capital are then thrown into financial circulation. The subsequent wave of excitement on the stock market is highly propitious to large-scale manoeuvres conducted behind the scenes by the financial oligarchy.

(2) *An abundant cash flow that is not tied up in the firm.* This exists in times of centralization of capital. When a phase of massive destruction of capital or stagnation in capital formation comes to an end, there is on the one hand a recovery of profits, on the other hand a delay in the material renovation of means of production compared with the theoretical renovation that would ensue in the average situation, given the productive life of different categories of materials and the usual perspectives of obsolescence. The gaps that intervene in the renewal of fixed capital give rise to a quickened pulsation in the use of cash flow, and consequently also in the formation of monetary resources that can separate off from the circulatory flow of valorization. Once capital formation starts to recover, effective renovation occurs at a more rapid pace than theoretical renovation. It then rises above the theoretical level and stays there throughout the period of regular accumulation. At the end of the upswing effective renovation decelerates to a slower pace than theoretical renovation, then declines absolutely.[3] It falls below the theoretical level with the onset of a recession. The alternation between a tumescence and detumescence of free cash flow in monetary form fixes certain maximum limits for the cash flow available in times of merger waves. In the post-war period, the correspondence between the pattern of merger waves and the growth in the share of amortization provisions in overall profit can be strikingly seen from Diagram 8. The periods when mergers leapt forward (1954–55, 1959, 1967–68) were three periods of rapid growth in accelerated amortization. The period 1960–66, in which mergers were stable, was one of great upsurge in relative surplus-value. This took place in the

[3] The gap between the actual replacement of fixed capital and the theoretical replacement which should follow from conditions of use and accounting for obsolescence in a schema of regular growth has been estimated for the American energy industries over the 1948–61 period. See *Fortune*, 'The Crucial Capital Goods Market', October and December 1962.

context of a sharp growth in capital formation, with a rapid increase in the share of net profit in value added and a dip in the share of the cash flow set aside for depreciation allowances. There was certainly regular formation of an abundant cash flow, but money capital was directly committed to a productive function, and the relations of competition between autonomous capitals were stabilized.

II. The Foundations of Financial Centralization

In developing the concept of the centralization of capital, we established an essential aspect of the way relations of competition between individual capitals are determined by the law of capital accumulation in general. We have shown, in effect, the importance of the formation of money capital under the constraint of the financing of capital accumulation. We can now go on to link the laws of competition to the law of capital accumulation, by identifying the general processes through which financial centralization, as the mode of formation of money capital, is decisively influenced by the structural conditions of accumulation.

The scale of financial centralization is expressed in two tendencies:

(1) On the one hand an *accumulation of money capital that is more rapid than that of the value of the material elements of productive capital*, the latter itself being more rapid than that of the overall value of the flow of marketed goods and services. Between 1945 and 1965, the characteristic indicators of these different elements of capitalist accumulation showed the following increases:

Gross National Product	190%
Industrial production	200%
Capital expenditures on the installation of factories and the purchase of plant	470%
Bank credit	480%
Capital assembled by financial intermediaries[4] or seeking direct investment on financial markets[5]	750%

[4] Excluding bank credits, but including the banks' trust departments.
[5] Excluding capital from abroad.

(2) On the other hand, *an ever greater predominance of financial intermediaries in the funding of capital accumulation.* This predominance is the basis for the truly financial pole required for the formation of financial groups. According to Goldsmith,[6] total financial assets managed by the financial institutions multiplied 40 times between 1900 and 1955, while other types of assets multiplied by only 18. The ever more crushing preponderance acquired by the financial intermediaries in the advance of money capital can equally be observed in the proportion of savings earmarked for investments of all kinds that were not directly provided by non-financial agents, but which passed by way of financial institutions. This percentage has undergone the following changes:[7]

1901–12	46%	1946–49	62%
1913–22	38%	1954–56	78%
1923–29	51%	1961–64	83%
1934–39	59%	1965–70	85%

These overall tendencies, so massive and uncontestable, show that in the long run the accumulation of capital itself creates the system of financing that is indispensable for it.

1. Financial Centralization through the Financing of Fixed Capital

The forms for financing gross fixed capital formation have developed considerably in the 20th century. This is evident if we compare two major periods, the first (1920–29) preceding the transformation of the proletarian mode of consumption, the second (1945–70) witnessing the mass production of means of consumption. The first period fell largely under a regime of predominantly extensive accumulation, the second was the great period of boom under the regime of predominantly intensive accumulation. These two historical epochs were dominated by long phases of capital formation separated by relatively short phases of decline (1915–21 in the first period,

[6] R. W. Goldsmith, *Financial Intermediaries in the American Economy Since 1900*, Princeton, 1958.

[7] Sources: up till 1950, R. W. Goldsmith and others, *A Study of Savings in the U.S.*, Princeton, 1955–6 (three vols.); for later periods, *Federal Reserve Bulletin*, 'The Role of Financial Intermediaries in U.S. Capital Markets' (January 1967, extended since then on the basis of periodic Federal Reserve statistics).

1957–61 in the second). At the end of Chapter 1 we pointed out the theoretical distinction, from the standpoint of fixed capital formation, that separates the regimes of accumulation on which these two periods depend: regular succession of capital formation and destruction under the predominantly extensive regime, and permanent obsolescence incorporated into capital formation itself under the predominantly intensive regime.

The change at this level gives rise to a change in the forms by which capital formation is financed. The regime of intensive accumulation allocates a less major role to the stock market in the mobilization of money capital intended for direct use in the financing of fixed capital formation, and establishes ever closer ties between the big industrial corporations and the big collectors of savings. The regime of intensive accumulation gives predominance to funds directly engendered by the corporation in the form of cash flow and to direct indebtedness in the form of loan capital as opposed to the issue of shares. The result is the decline universally noted in the role of the stock market in absorbing savings destined for productive investments, and a strengthening of the financial intermediaries and particularly the banking system. Private financial relationships consequently replace the public supply of capital to an ever greater extent.

This development has immense consequences. Hurled into the competition for investment by the need to bend the pace and content of the obsolescence of production processes to their own advantage, the centres of industrial capital seek to plan their fixed capital formation in such a way that it will be least affected by the net return on capital already invested productively. This is why financing gives ever greater room for the incorporation into current operating costs of various write-off provisions and for indebtedness in the form of bank credit or new forms of high-risk credit that are supported and guaranteed by the banks. *The financing of fixed capital formation thus becomes a decisive link in the transition from the structural conditions of inflation to the process of inflation proper.*

The predominance of the big commercial banks in the collection of savings, in other words in the transformation of temporarily idle liquid resources into money capital, is a striking expression of the far-reaching change in the forms of financing. It can be illustrated by the distribution of the assets held by financial intermediaries, as between the two different categories of institution, for the two types of circuit by which savings are absorbed. The following table gives this distribution for the year 1968:[8]

Deposit savings

Commercial banks (Banking departments)	34.4%
Mutual savings banks	5.9%
Other savings and loan institutions	12.9%
Total deposits	53.2%

Contractual savings

Commercial banks (Trust departments)	24.0%
Life insurance companies	15.6%
Other insurance companies	3.8%
Investment companies (Mutual funds)	3.4%
Total contractual savings	46.8%

The predominance of the banks in both types of network gives them great flexibility in their choice of financing instruments, and in access to alternative sources of refinancing by the mediation of financial circulation. The overall importance of the banking system, moreover, conceals a far-reaching heterogeneity. The American banking system is superficially very decentralized, as a result of the stringent legal restriction on the geographical area in which the banks were and still are authorized to open offices and establish branches. A very uneven development has resulted from this, due to the nature of their customers and the proximity or otherwise of the banks' field of action to industrial centres, and especially to the financing of international trade. A very small number of financial centres can thus polarize the absorption of savings via a dense network of inter-bank relationships. This polarization was considerably increased after the bank collapses of the Great Depression and with the rise of financial intermediaries after the Second World War. In the 1950s banking centralization crossed a new threshold due to the mergers between giant

[8] Source: Committee on Banking and Currency, House of Representatives (90th Congress, 2nd session).

banks, particularly those of New York, which tremendously accelerated the concentration of savings, contractual savings in particular. By 1968, twelve New York banks held 75 per cent of all pension fund assets, these being the fastest growing of all savings funds. In the 1960s, the banks diversified their financing activities by setting up holding companies that could free themselves from the restrictions of bank regulation and create branch networks. At the present time, the giant banks are organized into banking groups, which besides the traditional operations of providing finance for productive capital, intervene in housing construction, control household finance subsidiaries, offer various financial services (leasing, factoring, insurance), and manage trading and service companies.

2. Financial Centralization through the Transformation of the Mode of Consumption

The formation of a norm of social consumption has had a substantial effect on financial centralization. The structuring of this norm by the acquisition of consumer durables has led to the development of both hire purchase and savings out of wages. The financing of consumer durables has to bridge a double gap, between the exchange-value of these goods and current money income on the one hand, and between direct wages and current consumption expenditure on the other. On top of this, the socialization of risks and the collective expenditures necessary to stabilize the private consumption of individual commodities have led to the formation of an indirect wage which is itself at the root of a double flow: on the one hand a flow of contributions levied on the nominal reference wage, on the other hand a flow of benefits which accrue to the wage-earners in forms independent of the current maintenance cycle of labour-power. Let us briefly examine the influence of this dual character of the norm of social consumption on financial centralization.

(a) Domestic credit and savings deposits. Domestic credit takes on the form of housing loans and loans for the purchase on instalment of automobiles and consumer durables. The overall long-run trend of loans for housing construction (farmers excluded), and the share of them provided by financial intermediaries, is summed up in the following table.

Year	Amount in billions of dollars	Proportion financed by financial intermediaries (per cent)
1900	3	50
1912	6	68
1922	12	63
1929	30	63
1939	26	69
1945	31	70
1949	50	79
1952	82	89
1968	370	90
1974	480	92

Hire purchase credit only developed after 1945, but it then experienced astronomic growth. From an outstanding credit of 6 billion dollars in 1946, the total grew to 43 billion in 1960, 113 billion in 1968 and 155 billion in 1974.

Whilst being essential to the development of the consumption norm, and consequently an indirect instrument for the financing of accumulation, this credit remains completely distinct from credit between capitalists. Domestic credit is not an advance on production, but a way of spending income that absorbs the divergence between the rhythm at which income is received and the rhythm at which it is spent, given the lumpiness of durable goods. It is an extremely burdensome form, weighing heavily on the wage-earners' incomes, and can only develop given sufficient regularity and security. *The inflexibility of the nominal reference wage is an essential condition of stability for this entire construction.* Wage income has to be a sufficiently regular flow, and sufficiently above total current expenditure, to be able to form the monetary reserves needed to meet earlier bills as increased by the interest charged, and to offer a sufficient perspective of solvency to obtain further credit. This is why the transformation of the mode of consumption in the direction of consumer durables is the source of a more rapid increase in monetary deposits than in wages, so long as the overall exchange-value of the mass of consumer durables purchased by wage-earners' households increases in relation to the flow of current expenditures. As this tendency has been continuous ever since the Second World War, becoming especially pronounced in the 1960s, which saw the rapid creation of new households as a result of the earlier rise in the birth rate, the growth in liquid deposits has been sharp. On top of this, as the money thus deposited was not all intended to serve immediately as the means of purchase, the average duration of its absence from circulation made it possible to form long-term deposits. The financial institutions, and especially the commercial banks, created different types of savings account, each bearing a slightly different rate of interest and offering different conditions of withdrawal, so as to match as far as possible the characteristics of the discontinuous flows of expenditure that are tied to the households' management of their stock of durable goods.

(b) Contractual savings. A further major gap between the social value of the reproduction of labour-power and current expenditure on consumption follows from the establishment and very rapid extension of deferred wages. This is the factor that generates contractual savings, which have been the chief form of financial accumulation since the Second World War. Together with the growth in long-term deposits, these have been the essential tools in the decisive control acquired by the financial intermediaries over the advance of money capital. We have seen how in the United States the institutional mechanisms for balancing risks remain highly restricted, forcing wage-earners to resort to private insurance schemes, which form the basis for a centralization of the major institutions that collect contractual savings (mutual funds, life insurance companies, trust departments of the major commercial banks). We have seen how among these funds, retirement pension funds have a major dynamic significance for capital accumulation in that they are as a rule unguaranteed. Though taken out of wages, they are the property of the capitalist class, acting through the 'trustee' system. All that the wage-earners have is a right, not guaranteed, to the payment of a deferred wage deriving from the income obtained from the investment of these savings funds which were originally deducted from the formation of wages. These funds are therefore *current expenditures for firms which have all the attributes of an ideal form of savings for long-term*

financial investments. They make the financial system into the principal agency in the acquisition of share titles and in the operation of financial circulation.

The long-run change has been a radical one. In the 1920s, more than half of the annual net growth in domestic financial assets was made up of shares purchased directly on the financial markets. The greater part of the shares purchased through financial institutions were actually purchased on behalf of the personal trusts of capitalist families, who used this procedure to avoid the dispersal and weakening of their power of control by the method of pooling monetary resources. At this date the financial agencies really did play a strictly intermediary role, that of executors. In the mid 1950s, however, the proportion of asset growth that can be imputed to the direct purchase of shares had fallen to less than 20% of the total, and was down to 2.5% in 1962–65. This drastic change took place even though the rate of 'free' personal saving (as a proportion of disposable income) was around the same level in the two periods (averaging 10% in 1922–29, and 11% in 1962–65). Thus it is centralization of the contractual savings of the mass of the wage-earning population that has radically transformed both the modalities of investment and the role of the financial intermediaries. We shall go on to show that the importance assumed by the financial institutions in the formation and investment of money capital has brought far-reaching changes in the forms of control of corporate ownership, by creating the phenomenon of the financial group.

The accelerated development of contractual savings characteristic of the mid 1950s was due to the change in the content of collective bargaining. The table below sums up the most dynamic elements of these savings (in billions of dollars):

	1954	1967
Private pension funds (not guaranteed, managed by the 'trust departments' of the big commercial banks	13	70
Collective pension funds (guaranteed, managed by the big life insurance companies)	10	28
Pension schemes organized by public agencies	10	35

The funds of the public pension 'schemes are also managed by the big banks, though these latter are here only financial executors. The assets are invested in the purchase of stocks with a low rate of return issued by public bodies and regulated corporations (airlines, telecommunications companies, electricity supply, etc.). The pension funds managed by the insurance companies are dominated by the imperative of security, and pursue the classical strategy of diversified portfolios, preserving a stable proportion between debentures, preference shares in industrial companies, and mortgages. The non-guaranteed private pension funds, on the other hand, managed by the big New York banks, are the spearhead in changing the structure of financial control over industry.

The concentrated assignment of these savings deriving from pension funds into stocks whose returns depend directly on the activity of business enterprises leads the banks irrevocably into direct participation in determining the general strategy of accumulation. Yet contractual saving no more makes the wage-earners into capitalists than does deposit saving. It is the massive centralization of these funds that forms money capital. Control over the formation and investment of these capitals, and the concomitant power of disposal over industrial decisions, are completely beyond the influence of the wage-earners themselves. The complexity of the financial mechanisms only reinforces the radical separation of the workers from possession of the means of social production.

3. Financial Centralization through Public Expenditure

The third major force that has determined the tendencies of financial centralization is *government debt* and *forced saving of a fiscal kind*, deriving from the Federal budget plus the budgets of the different states. Public expenditure has risen sharply ever since the New Deal, under the impulse of different forces. In every historical period, budgetary expenditure serves to finance those activities, either economic or non-economic, that form the general overheads of capitalist production. The management of these by the state is not basically related to the content of the activities in question, at least as far as the economic activities of production are concerned, but rather to the general conditions for the extension of capitalist relations of production, to the degree of fragmentation of capitals and the forms of their competition, as well as the scope of the financial centralization undertaken by the private financial intermediaries and the sophistication of the instruments of financial circulation. It is important to note, therefore, that there is no inherent distinction between the public sector and the private sector as absolute and universal categories. Allowing for the basic transformations of the forces of production and the conditions of existence of the wage-earning class, however, the law of accumulation functions in every historic period to extend commodity production, while at the same time giving rise to social overheads which in the given conditions cannot be covered on the basis of this commodity production. These overheads lie on the margins of the capitalist mode of production, yet are nonetheless indispensable to its development.

This results in a profound ambiguity in the economic relation of public expenditure to the law of capital accumulation. In the conditions of Fordism, for instance, we have seen that the development of the norm of social consumption implied the development of collective services, while the production of these means of collective consumption was not suited to the labour process based on mechanization. The continuous technological advances inherent in the regime of intensive accumulation, moreover, call for an organization of scientific research which must fall largely in the public sector if it is not to be seriously damaged by relations of competition, and which for reasons bearing on the position of American capitalism in the class struggle on a world scale, is inextricably interwoven with gigantic military spending.

These two types of expenditure, even though violently opposed to one another, form the major part of the public budget, and are the essential premises for the continuous increase in public spending. They form part of the organic unity of Fordism, but they are nonetheless obstacles to capital formation. The result is that these expenditures are financed either by an increase in the public debt or by a fiscal levy on incomes (direct taxation) or on commodity expenditure (indirect taxation). In itself an increase in the public debt is no more than the acquisition of rights on future fiscal levies. In no way is it the formation of a money capital able to finance accumulation. The swelling of the public debt from scarcely 1 billion dollars before 1917 to 10 billion in 1930, 250 billion in 1948 and 400 billion in 1972 is necessarily bound up with the rise in fiscal exactions. The latter may be a levy on wages; in that case taxation increases the cost of the social reproduction of labour-power, for the nominal reference wage must stand at a level permitting the satisfaction of the norm of social consumption while paying taxes as well. If this is not the case, and taxation is too heavy to allow wages to rise, the increase in expenditure on consumption is threatened, and with it the balanced development of the two departments of production. When taxation is a levy on overall profits, it can still take different forms according to the manner in which the profit is divided between different parties (interest, dividends, managerial salaries, fees for various spurious services and emoluments, industrial profit). As long as it remains moderate, taxation on incomes from capitalist appropriation need have hardly any influence on the formation of capital, for it can simply affect income which would otherwise have been wasted on luxury consumption. But this taxation is nonetheless an obstacle to the capitalist class's free power of disposal over total profits. If it becomes too heavy, it can impede the formation of money capital and stifle financial circulation. The state then risks a polarization of financial centralization and a profound alteration in the dynamic of accumulation.[9]

Capital accumulation is still not imperilled for all that; the war economy is a good example. But a sharp increase in public expenditure cannot but make a far-reaching difference to the relations of competition between capitals. Accumulation continues, but *the expansion of public expenditure is a powerful factor in the centralization of capital in industry and finance.*

To take industry first of all, it acts by selective and concentrated public contracts (an overall contract with a principal firm which organizes its own sub-contracting, this giving rise to chains of sub-contracting relationships) and by research and development programmes in the most advanced technological fields. In this way public expenditure has sustained the chief

[9] For a detailed analysis of the contradictory aspects of public financing, see P. Mattick, *Marx and Keynes*, London, 1969.

centres of accumulation and centralization of capital since the
Second World War. This was the economic basis of the 'military-
industrial complex'. Through the effects it generates via exchange relations between different industries, public expenditure extends its influence far beyond the immediate results of
these contracts. Those capitals that are best placed for obtaining public contracts have been able to make use of the flows of
surplus profit and the technico-economic positions thus acquired to set in motion a strategy of integration and diversification that further accentuates centralization to their own
advantage. The ensuing increase in the tax burden was highly
selective in its impact, and greatly contributed to the changing
forms of saving. Taxation acted to discourage individual saving
and the direct attempt to make remunerative investments, and
to encourage the formation of pools of capital in different
institutional forms (trusts, foundations, holding companies).
Finally, the very size of the Federal public debt has itself
involved the entire financial system in its management. This
was the chief factor in the reconstitution of the financial system
during the New Deal, and in the monetary accumulation during
the Second World War. It then became an instrument of the
banks in their interventions on the money market and in their
pressure on the Federal Reserve Bank to obtain liquidity as
cheaply as possible. As far as the stocks issued by other public
bodies are concerned, they are distributed privately and benefit
from an extremely favourable regime of tax exemption, which
makes them much appreciated as outlets for investment by the
agencies that centralize great amounts of contractual savings.

The steep increase in public expenditure since the Second
World War has thus given rise to forms of ownership that
increasingly evade the catchment of the tax system, at least in
relative terms, while the latter has impinged on the incomes of
wage-earners more and more heavily. Between 1945 and 1971,
the share of Federal taxation paid out of property incomes fell
from 61% to 37%.[10]

As long as real social wage costs continued to fall, the
increase in taxation could be absorbed without any damaging

[10] Taxes on the incomes of physical persons drawn from property + direct
taxes on companies + taxes on land + nominal gains from dealings in securities.

consequence for the advance of real wages. As a result, coherence was maintained between the development of private consumption and the socialized services acquitted by the budget. But these different processes were subjected to the unity of the regime of intensive accumulation, in other words to a rising rate of surplus-value. From the mid 1960s onwards, the ever more rapid advances in the socialized dimensions of consumption tended to raise the cost of the social reproduction of labour-power, at the same time as a crisis erupted in labour organization itself. In the second half of the 1960s budget expenditure leaped ahead while real weekly wages, after tax, remained stagnant and profits began to diminish. While budget expenditure had only risen from 75 to 125 billion dollars between 1955 and 1965, it climbed from 125 billion to 200 billion between the fourth quarter of 1965 and the first quarter of 1969. This increase resulted both from the military expenditure occasioned by the American war in Vietnam, and from a growth in social expenditure and outlays on the administrative services required by Lyndon Johnson's project of the 'Great Society'.

More important than this change in the actual rate of growth was the new inflexibility of the increased expenditure on welfare programmes and the financing of public services. The acute social needs that these expenditures were designed to meet continued to worsen in the 1970s. The rigidity of these new budget expenditures came above all from the very rapid growth in their costs, particularly in the fields of health and urban services.

In these new conditions the capacity of the trade cycle to modulate public expenditure lost some of its controlled flexibility, all the more so since the slowing down in the growth of productivity and the hardening of the struggle over the division between wages and profits began to make future taxation an explosive political issue. These phenomena greatly contributed to the predominance that monetary policy began to assume over budgetary policy in the 1970s.

The present decade has thus seen the eruption of a crisis of public finance. Public expenditure has continued to accelerate, at the state and local authority level as well as that of the Federal government. The increase in Federal expenditure from

18 to 23% of GNP between 1965 and 1976 was functionally
distributed as follows.

Functional Distribution of Federal Expenditure
(by financial year, and in billions of dollars)

Functions	1945	1950	1955	1960	1965	1970	1975	1976
Defence and International Affairs	84.6	17.7	43.0	48.9	54.7	82.8	90.9	95.1
Income Security	1.0	4.5	8.8	18.3	25.7	43.1	108.6	127.4
Debt Interest	3.7	5.8	6.4	9.3	11.4	18.3	31.0	34.6
Health	—	—	—	0.8	1.7	13.1	27.6	33.4
Education	—	—	—	0.9	2.3	7.9	15.2	18.2
Total Federal Expenditure	92.7	42.6	68.5	92.2	118.4	196.6	324.6	373.5

We can note immediately that the 1970s have seen a rapid
decline in the relative importance of military and associated
expenditures. This decline has been under way for more than 20
years, but since 1970 it has assumed an accelerated pace, as
shown in the following table.

Share of Military Expenditure in Total Federal Expenditure (%)

1945	1950	1955	1960	1965	1970	1975	1976
84.5	36.9	64.6	47.6	40.8	39.0	25.6	23.1

It would certainly be wrong to expect this decline to continue,
in a situation of renewed international tension marked by the
multiplication of centres of local war, a characteristic sign of
the generalization of the system of states throughout the globe.
Yet the reduction in the relative share of military outlays has
had an influence on intensive accumulation, since these outlays
have long provided the major directions of scientific research in
the United States. Though the mediations involved are complex, the ceiling placed on military expenditure and the
reduction in research programmes financed by the Federal
government are closely connected. The crisis of research is now
so acute that the White House has sought to bring together all
the interests concerned in a special commission, entrusted with
summarizing the methods and results obtained over the past 30

years or so, and putting forward new procedures. The commission's task will be a hard one, as the deterioration of American positions in vast areas of technological development is a sure sign of the crisis of the regime of intensive accumulation in its present form. Concentrated as it is on advanced technologies stimulated by military requirements, American scientific research promotes centralized power of disposal over technical innovations. By guaranteeing regular contracts to a limited number of giant corporations, and absorbing all excess costs in the Federal budget, the US system has rendered these corporations somewhat passive so far as the commercial risks of technical innovation are concerned. It would not be possible otherwise to explain how corporations capable of mobilizing the most advanced productive forces in the world have abandoned without a struggle entire areas of electronics and electrical engineering to their German and Japanese competitors. These relations of competition express the commercial sanction of completely different structural forms. German research and development is far more widely diffused: the state provides indirect support by nurturing initiatives undertaken by firms of moderate size, but the active role is played by technological institutes run by the professions themselves. In Japan the directions of technical development are far more systematically organized; priorities are set by commercial firms on the basis of information that they centralize and prospective studies that they make of tendencies on the world market.

The militarism that has been so deeply implanted in American society since the Second World War and was initially a determining factor in Atlantic integration and the restoration of monetary and financial multilateralism is now one reason for the exhaustion of the dynamic of accumulation in the United States that has set in since the mid 1960s. Yet it is the explosion of the social costs of the mode of consumption that has very largely come to dominate the irrepressible increase in public expenditure, and which is at the core of the crisis of Fordism. As Hirsch has shown in a recent book on the social limits to the regime of intensive accumulation pursued after the Second World War, [11] the mass production of consumer durab-

[11] F. Hirsch, *Social Limits to Growth*, London, 1976.

les gives rise to a deterioration in the quality of these goods and an incessant pursuit of purely quantitative differentiations of social status. The same process of relative surplus-value which systematically improves the conditions of commodity production by its logic of social division and stratification, creates generalized external social effects which the law of value does not take into account. As we have seen, these are expressed in the proliferation of state institutions for the standardization of economic activity. But this standardization is ever more costly, to the extent that the prescriptive models of social custom involve a deterioration in the conditions of appropriation of space and time. The massive phenomena of urban congestion, and the merciless struggle for a rung on the hierarchy of consumption, give rise to a gigantic social waste, which mounts ever more rapidly with the rise in industrial productivity. The *relative* progress of wage incomes is decreasingly relevant when a rigid scale of social positions is inscribed in bureaucratic structures that have been adopted in all large organizations of capitalism in which a power of decision over wage-labour is exercised. This permanent pressure on nominal incomes fuels an inflation in which the losers are more numerous than the winners, as the increase in average incomes is accompanied by a more rapid deterioration in social solidarity, a palpable increase in insecurity, and a degradation of the environment on which the quality of the inter-individual activities and relationships that constitute use-values depends.

This impoverishment of use-values caught in the network of functional norms indispensable to the mass production of commodities has been particularly pronounced in the United States. It is particularly evident in the exclusion from the wage-earning class of a large number of individuals unable to find a place in the wage hierarchy by virtue of their age, sex or race. The extent of this discrimination in the great wave of accumulation of the first half of the 1960s gave birth to a political movement for the furtherance of civil rights. This process was a revealing response to the development of the state as the product of contradictions inherent in the generalization of the wage-earning class. The struggle for civil rights was an acknowledgement of the disintegration of civil society. Institutional guarantees were now rushed forward to meet this threat to social cohesion. This was the meaning of the 'Great Society'. An institutional machinery was established to absorb the political expression of conflicts that were formerly diffuse and spontaneous, by creating new social groups as the recipients of public assistance. The state itself conferred institutional existence on collections of scattered individuals who would not otherwise have formed social groups, but only constitute such in the context of welfare programmes of one kind or another. The project of a 'Great Society' saw the development of the classificatory and identificatory logic of the state with an ever more complex and differentiated system.

The irresistible growth of public expenditure, despite all the warnings and incantations of reactionary politicians, is merely the economic effect of this institutionalization of social relations. It is simply the blossoming out of the wage system. The suppression of a given social programme now tends to amount to the annihilation of the social group created by this programme. In exorcizing its political threat, the process of institutionalization has transformed the civil rights movement into a mosaic of interests attached to the defence of one or other programme. Since the state has reinserted the individuals involved into social groups, these must participate in the general progress of money incomes needed to maintain their existence. The accelerating monetary cost of these programmes in a context of inflation is inherent in their indexation to wages or consumer prices, managed by an ever more complex administration, and fed by an expanding number of claimants as the inability of capitalist accumulation to internalize the costs of the socialization specific to Fordism becomes ever more manifest. The number of those entitled to social security grew from 20 million in 1965 to 34 million in 1977, while the average monthly benefit paid increased from 84 dollars to 260 dollars. In the same period, welfare programmes expanded from a coverage of 4 million to 11 million people, and their average annual benefit from 621 to 948 dollars.

Welfare programmes themselves involve a wide spectrum of inequality between one state and another. This inequality is a direct result of the autonomy of local and regional political power in the United States, and the fragmentation of struggles which have had differential success according to different political situations. But the risks involved to claimants in programmes with insufficient resources, coupled with the threats hanging over non-guaranteed pension funds, are leading the Federal state to intervention on an ever increasing scale. This tendency was accentuated by the worsening of the economic crisis from 1973 onward, and by the total failure of the 'revenue sharing' project undertaken by the Republican Administration in 1971. The Federal government's transfer to the local authorities of a portion of income tax revenue was supposed to lead to a greater involvement by the local authorities in welfare programmes and a gradual withdrawal of the Federal government. But this did not in fact take place. As the local authorities are in general very closely tied to financial and property interests, they used these funds to replace local taxation, which was reduced or held constant. Less than a tenth of the funds transferred from the Federal budget were used for the purpose of public assistance.

The Federal government's social budget has thus continued to increase despite everything, and at an ever more rapid rate. This is particularly evident in the case of unemployment benefits. In so far as these fall within the competence of the different states, there are very wide disparities from one state to another, in the level of payments, the length of time for which they are paid, and the conditions of eligibility for them. The growing number of unemployed who are ineligible on grounds of not having held the same job for the requisite period of time (e.g. women, young people, unskilled workers who have suffered forced mobility), and the exhaustion of available funds in certain states, led to Federal government intervention in 1974 and 1975. Congress now allocated Federal funds to guarantee the payment of benefits for six additional months at times when 4% of the population of a state have been out of work for three months or more. It also extended unemployment insurance to workers who had not previously been covered, and authorized the granting of interest-free Federal loans to states whose funds had been exhausted. Federal assistance was also extended to social security, in an attempt to meet the explosive rise in costs of collective consumption. The diversity of systems of retirement and sickness benefit (only five states had legislation making such insurance obligatory) led to a recasting of the

OASDI. This system, set up in the 1930s, financed old age and disability pensions for employees out of contributions levied on wages. The benefits paid rose from 16 billion dollars in 1965 to 29 billion in 1970 and 69 billion in 1975. The Medicare programme, for instance, inaugurated in 1965, finances medical care for old people and those in need, while the Medicaid programme provides the different states with subsidies for people already receiving assistance.

This analysis confirms our conclusion that only the transformation of the regime of intensive accumulation into what we have called Neo-Fordism, and James O'Connor[12] terms a socio-industrial complex, could avoid an intensification of the crisis of public finance. It would be quite illusory to believe that recourse to market mystique and private initiative could magically limit the takeover by the state of the social costs engendered by the expansion of commodity relations. We are now in a position to define the chief characteristics of the crisis of public finance and its connections with the general crisis of Fordism.

(a) The accumulation of deficits and the burden of public debt. The Federal budget has been in deficit for seventeen of the past eighteen years. No improvement in this situation is envisaged, in fact quite the reverse. If it continues on its present course, as extrapolated by the most likely forecasts for the end of the decade, the Federal debt will have increased more in the 1970s than in the entire previous history of the Republic. From less than 400 billion dollars in 1970, it will reach at least 850 billion by the end of the 1979 financial year. Even during the upswing of the trade cycle, the average Federal deficit was some 50 billion per year. The fact that the Federal government is bearing ever more of the weight of the social costs of capitalism is attested by the average annual surplus of 30 billion dollars in the budgets of the local and state authorities. The enormous Federal debt disturbs financial circulation in several ways. In the first place, the pressure exerted by the issue and renewal of government bonds keeps long-term interest rates at very high levels, so powerfully contributing to inflation. Secondly, some of this

[12] James O'Connor, *The Fiscal Crisis of the State*, New York, 1973.

pressure on national savings is offset by the key position enjoyed by New York in international finance. At the present moment, foreign institutions and private individuals hold more than 20% of the Federal debt over the whole range of bonds. These foreign-held portfolios are, however, always liable to redeployment. The liquidation of even 10% of the approximately 120 billion dollars of debt now held abroad (against only 10 billion dollars ten years ago) would unleash severe tension across the whole range of interest rates and precipitate a major fall of the dollar on exchange markets. Thirdly, the continuous rise in public debt has substantially increased the burden of interest. From 18 billion dollars in 1970, this has now reached 50 billion (1978); more than 10% of the total is now paid to foreign creditors, which aggravates the deficit in the current balance of payments.

The contribution of the Federal debt to the very high and permanent credit pyramid of the American economy, whose effects we shall study in Chapter 6, has no chance of being reduced or even stablized in the near future. Not only would it be impossible to halt the rapid increase in social expenditure, but the very weak tolerance of taxation that American society exhibits deprives the Federal government of any room for manoeuvre. The recent referendum on Proposition 13 in California, even if it only affects local taxation, indicates the *fiscal barrier* that is imposed by the present mentality of many strata of wage-earners, to which competing politicians are keenly attuned. Yet the tax pressure in the United States is very light when compared to the levels that the Social-Democratic governments of Northern Europe have managed to achieve. In the USA, Congress has passed a whole series of measures designed to attenuate the movement of a growing number of tax-payers into the higher fiscal brackets. On top of this, the multiple occasions for tax relief provided by the thicket of an over-complex legislation gives rise to considerable losses of fiscal receipts. This is why the combination in the last five years of political pressure for a reduction of taxes and for the extension of social rights has constantly frustrated the experts in their forecasts of a balanced full-employment budget, which has now become a real myth. On top of the deficit due to the severe recession of 1974–75, there is a structural deficit that is far more serious for the regime of intensive accumulation.

(b) Public expenditure and the stifling of private investment. A comparative macro-economic analysis of the increase in public expenditure, or more precisely the social costs of Fordism, has been undertaken for the three major Anglo-Saxon countries (United States, United Kingdom, Canada) by Bacon and Eltis.[13] This analysis uses a terminology other than our own, but it is governed by the same perspective. In the logic of the capitalist economy, only what is produced as a commodity can be the object of an autonomous process of valorization. Every other social activity, whether public or private, must be financed by a deduction from the monetary surplus deriving from the excess of the sale price of the commodity products over their costs of production. This deduction reduces the funds available to finance the expansion of commodity relations by accumulation. In the conceptual framework we have adopted here, this magnitude appears as *accumulable surplus-value.* Bacon and Eltis argue the same case. They show that the capitalist dynamic is not rigorously dependent on the proportion of the private sector vis-à-vis the public sector, or of industry vis-à-vis services. The pertinent theoretical distinction is that between the monetary expression of the commodity product and the rights of purchase that are acquired over this commodity product by the fraction of the total income that results from non-marketed activities. An increase in this share may result from public expenditures, but it can also result from property speculation or from a disproportionate growth in commercial and financial intermediaries. All these reduce the fraction of income that marketed activities can keep for their own expansion, i.e. accumulable surplus-value.

In the United States, according to Bacon and Eltis's calculations, the rate of growth in the per capita commodity product available for accumulation was only 0.3% in the period 1965–74, as against 2.0% in the preceding decade. This decline in the American economy's capacity to engender an accumulable

[13] R. Bacon and W. Eltis, *Britain's Economic Problem: Too Few Producers*, London, 1978.

surplus-value in the way that it did in the past is the result of the combination that we have already examined of a significant reduction in the rate of increase in productivity and the increasing rate of unproductive deductions (i.e. unproductive of future surplus-value). The direct result has been a quasi-stagnation of private per capita consumption of commodities in the same period 1965–74 (a growth rate of 0.4% as against 2.0% in the period 1955–65), which is compatible with our earlier observations on the stagnation of real post-tax wage incomes. Contrary to the case in the United Kingdom, the United States has not experienced a collapse in the rate of productive investment, but rather a parallel slowing down in the growth rates for commodity production, private consumption of the net commodity product, and productive investment. Between 1955 and 1975 the proportion of public purchases has grown from 23.8% of the gross product to 34.2%. But as we have already noted, the importance of local and state finances relative to the Federal budget (until recently some 40% of the total) has led to an extreme regional inequality in both public expenditure and tax burden. The result has been an adaptive capacity within American capitalism which is not available to other countries. There was an intense migration of productive activities (investment and skilled workers) into regions with low social costs and a reverse migration of the marginal population in search of public assistance to regions of high social costs. It was the mobility of US capital, therefore, expressed in a geographical redistribution of commodity production, that made possible a relative maintenance of accumulation. But this forced mobility involved a terrible social waste. The process of destabilizing migration led to a new form of social malady, the *urban crisis*.

(c) The urban crisis: an acute form of the antagonism between rising social costs and capitalist accumulation. The civil rights movement of the early 1960s found an institutional expression most easily in the large industrial cities where Democratic administrations were solidly established. Political coalitions were formed to extend public assistance, to remedy the deteriorating quality and inadequate quantity of collective facilities, to improve wages and working conditions for employees in the public services. Municipal authorities had to

meet a very rapid increase in the operating costs of these services, and in social benefits. In the euphoric atmosphere produced by the rapid growth of that period, they elected to combine compliance with the demand for an improvement in public services, considered as the realization of the 'Great Society', with accommodation to the pressure of landlords, manufacturers and financiers – to restrict the growth in taxation. The immediate solution to the financial problem was therefore unlimited debt.

This solution, designed to avoid the establishment of the political priorities essential for genuine urban planning, enabled many cities to handle contradictory interests for a decade or so. Others, however – of which the most famous example is, of course, New York – were propelled into structural changes that made the debt burden intolerable. The rapid growth of suburbs after the Second World War brought about major changes in the distribution of population. The hierarchy of social position assumed the topological form of a social segregation of urban space. Discrimination here is economic, operating through the price of land. As always, however, this economic relationship is simply the guise assumed by a social relation in the arena of landed property. Legislation that was extremely favourable to real-estate owners, the political influence of the latter on local authorities, and the participation of major financial institutions in the construction industry, combined to make the great American cities a veritable paradise for property speculation. The result was a constant process of urban upheaval which lacked any planned direction and was far more far-reaching and rapid than anything that has been seen in Europe.

The better-off groups abandoned the urban centres on a massive scale, followed later by the middle-income groups. More and more, the population left in the big cities was made up of unskilled workers or unemployed, as well as ethnic minorities excluded from the wage system. The indigence of tenants, and the spread of rent strikes, led landlords to abandon the upkeep of dwellings, seeking either to claim insurance for damage, or else expecting to profit from a possible renovation financed out of municipal funds. A chain reaction then set in: degradation of housing in very widespread urban zones, deterioration of collective facilities, breakdown of social control, endemic delinquency and violence, and finally appearance of lasting budgetary deficits.

When the situation had reached a high degree of social waste, the financial communities who made up the chief creditors of municipalities obtained the capitulation of political leaders and imposed austerity plans of extreme brutality. The case of New York is exemplary in this regard. In the 1960s the city lost 20% of its industrial jobs and saw ever more welfare claimants arrive. A powerful popular movement succeeded in obtaining the highest level of social benefits in the whole United States, the most widespread network of public hospitals and the only major free university. Municipal officials won salaries and conditions of work which absorbed the gains in productivity derived from the efforts to rationalize the public services. Municipal expenditure underwent a staggering acceleration, from 1.8 billion dollars in 1955 to 2.3 in 1960, 4.0 billion in 1965, 8.1 billion in 1970, and 12.6 billllion in 1975. During the 1960s, the banks and other financial institutions saw it in their interest to subscribe to tax-free municipal bonds. But with the general rise in indebtedness, the scarcity of capital and the subsequent increase in interest rates, they ceased to subscribe to these and imposed a short-term debt structure. Henceforward the city of New York was in their hands.

From 1974 onwards, the cost of further credit increased significantly. In spring 1975 the banks unleashed a financial crisis. Rejecting the issue of new municipal bonds, they imposed a new increase in short-term debt while the Federal government refused to grant any exceptional aid. In June 1975 the Municipal Assistance Corporation was created with the task of consolidating this debt and restructuring the city budget. An austerity programme of extreme severity was inflicted on the population. Power passed completely from the elected authorities to the representatives of the financial groups. Municipal employees, tax-payers with modest resources and users of public services were all affected together: closure of municipal hospitals and fire stations, reduction of university activities, cutbacks in urban transport, increase in taxes, suppression of some tens of thousands of municipal jobs, forced subscription to municipal bonds by the trade unions under threat of new dismissals. The New York financial crisis, imposed with the positive support of the Federal government, has an exemplary significance for the forms now taken by class struggle in the United States.

III. The Forms of Centralization of Capital: The Giant Corporation and the Financial Group

As we have seen, the integrity of an individual capital is dependent on the renewal of a valorization cycle. This does not just ensue spontaneously. The inter-connection and coordination between the different phases in the metamorphoses of value require specific practices of management. The organization of these practices forms a dense network of economic relations, which takes the structural form of the *enterprise*. The existence of this structure makes it possible to effect a certain partition in the field of economic relations. The interweaving of valorization cycles is not equivalent to an undifferentiated whole. Through the unity it provides, the enterprise protects those practices that are vital for the integrity of the capitalist power of disposal within its boundaries. This is why relations of competition are expressed as external relations between enterprises. All the illusions symbolized in the hypothesis of pure and perfect competition derive from this. The existence of the enterprise, readily apparent to all, is idealized into a subject, an atomic unit without any significant metabolism of its own. This subject is equipped with certain *ad hoc* behavioural orientations, so that relations of competition can be expressed as an anonymous coordination of decentralized decisions generating a universal harmony. Thereby the real significance of competition is fundamentally obscured, since the relations between enterprises are only scientifically intelligible on the basis of the determinants of their internal functioning: the struggle of capitals for valorization under the constraint of the law of accumulation, deriving from the overall antagonism inherent in the wage relation.

By the profound change it effects in the relations of competition, the centralization of capital also modifies the structural form in which these are expressed. The enterprise is transformed into the *giant corporation*. The giant corporation is a coherent, autonomous and dynamic structure interiorizing part of the social constraints involved in the valorization of capital. Analysis of this structure must be undertaken from a double standpoint:

(1) The *organization* that is the structure's characteristic mode of articulation, in other words the unifying principle of the managerial practices inherent in the valorization of productive capital. This organization should not be posited in an *a priori* fashion, which would only lead to the abstract and purely logical analysis of its internal relations dear to organizational theorists. It must be understood as the product of constraints determined by the relations of production and exchange, which obviously include first and foremost the antagonism of the wage relation. It is also a response to constraints in the sense of a resolution of contradictions and the search for a coherent set of economic practices. Organization is therefore a structure in motion, on which the transformation of the social conditions of production stamps a law of development.

(2) The *planning* and *control* that represent the principle by which the structure functions, and explain how the stability of its organization is ensured, in other words how it is reproduced, and how capitalist ownership is secured. It is necessary to distinguish clearly between *managerial control* and *proprietary control*, if we are to understand the relationship between the two. It is the confusion between these two types of control, combined with an analysis in terms of behaviour, that has led to the ideology of the disappearance of capitalist ownership and the advent of the era of the 'managers', in which the technostructure is a substitute for property.

In order to dispel these illusions, we must study how the different aspects of the centralization of capital are articulated. We have shown how it is control over property itself that is ultimately at issue in this centralization. This is why financial centralization is the dominant characteristic of capital centralization. When the valorization of productive capital in industrial enterprises can no longer occur without the formation of vast associations that hold money capital and convert wage-earners' savings into money capital, ownership is formally partitioned into rights represented by share titles, and its unity takes the legal form of the joint-stock company. This is why the question of the capitalist power of disposal over production takes the form of the control over property exercised in the enterprise by coalitions of capitalists who wield the weapon of financial centralization to their own advantage. The name *finance capital*[14] is properly given to the mediation by which coalitions of capitalists exercise proprietary control over the structural forms necessary for the continuing cycles of valorization of productive capital, thanks to the centralized money capital at their disposal. Finance capital is no abstraction. It takes concrete form in *financial groups*, which are systems of interrelation effecting the cohesion of finance capital. Study of proprietary control is then the study of the modes in which the financial groups are articulated to the structural form of the giant corporation in such a way as to fix its strategy and direct its operations.

1. The Evolution of Modes of Corporate Organization

The historical succession of the predominant forms of corporate organization in the United States was engendered by changes in the regime of accumulation. These periods of change had far-reaching effects on proprietary control, by giving rise to major waves of mergers. The changes in organization were thus accomplished by way of crises that involved acute conflicts of ownership.[15]

(a) The emergence of constraints on valorization. The first great wave essentially consisted of the horizontal and vertical type of merger. It saw the development of the corporation with several distinct plants, combining under one single authority units which collaborated in the production of one and the same category of commodities. A purely formal centralization of ownership was unable to ensure effective exercise of this single

[14] R. Hilferding, *Finance Capital.* For a critique of Hilferding's concept of finance capital as the criterion of a new stage reached by capitalism, see for example S. de Brunhoff, *La Politique monétaire,* Paris, 1973.

[15] A synoptic presentation, based on abundant historical documentation and studies of exemplary cases, is provided by A. J. Chandler, *Strategy and Structure,* M.I.T., 1962.

authority. The formerly independent capitalists who remained in charge of the various units continued to act independently in decisions of day-to-day management. Changes in personnel, even if necessary, were not in themselves sufficient. In order for the new groups of centralized capitals to be integrated for the concrete operations of valorization, the component units had to be constrained to act as links in a single whole, by the organization of new relations internal to the corporation. This requirement was satisfied by the creation of a *centralized functional structure* with the following governing principles:

(1) Creation of *functional departments*. Each major function of management became the responsibility of a central organ, with local executive organs tied to it in strictly hierarchical dependence. The result was a production department for each category of commodity. If an enterprise involves several types of production process, then the functional structure cuts across it. The functional production department is the organizational structure for a vertical integration of labour processes. The central organ of the functional department lays down a production norm for each integrated process, defines the criteria of performance for the different units in relation to this norm, notes divergences, analyses their causes and specifies the corrections needed. The information exchanged within the department, therefore, as well as its hierarchical relations and respective competences, are strictly specified by the vertical functional structure. This makes it possible to specialize plants, abolish their autonomy and coordinate their activities.

(2) The *separation of production and sales* into distinct functional departments. In actual fact, once the production units are specialized as segments of an integrated process, they become incapable of realizing the value of their output by sale. A functional sales department, organized vertically into sales units and a centre for the coordination and control of these units, manages those operations that adapt the enterprise to the constraint of realizing value. The sales units receive directives that set the prices of different commodities, methods of promotion and sales quotas for them. There is no horizontal communication between local production and sales units, only between the central organs of these departments. The centralized functional structure thus involves a circulation of inform-

ation that uses fixed channels, stabilizing and reinforcing it.

(3) The creation of a *head office* that effects the coordination of functional departments and subjects their management to the single goal of the accumulation of centralized capital. To break the rivalries over the control of property engendered by the centralization of capital, *a strict separation must be maintained between routine managerial activities*, as pursued in the functional departments, and *the activities of the enterprise as a whole.* The latter involve the formulation of strategic goals, the assessment of performances from the standpoint of the valorization of capital (the criterion of the rate of profit), and long-term planning of future activities. The head office takes sole charge of the activity of the enterprise as a whole, and in order to coordinate the vertical functional departments it sets up departments with a horizontal competence, of which the main are: *personnel*, responsible for collective bargaining, dealing with conflicts and organizing the managerial career structure; and *financial*, responsible for accounts and reserves, as well as the preparation and application of financial policies. The head office itself, which may be organized into executive and financial boards, decides on the use of liquid assets and authorizes expenditures as the sole centre of power in the enterprise.

(b) The emergence of the financial constraint. The establishment of the regime of intensive accumulation gave rise to very serious disturbances in the relations of competition, to which the centralized functional structure was incapable of responding. A gigantic organizational crisis prevailed for more than a decade, punctuated by the wave of mergers of the First World War, preceding the big wave that culminated in 1929, and then by the shocks of the Great Depression. Intensive accumulation forced the centralization of capital to change its nature; it took the new direction of a *diversification* of production. With this diversification, capitalist managements encountered an entirely new constraint. The need now was to subject capital to an overall objective of valorization, in various fields of commodity production in which completely different conditions of production and exchange prevailed. This problem exerted insurmountable tensions on the centralized functional structure and burst it apart. The result was a new divisional structure.

This structural transformation took more time or less according to the particular case, unleashing internal conflicts that were more or less acute, under the control of groups that often changed. This was so because the structure of the giant corporation is the outcome of the constraint of competition, i.e. of power relations within the capitalist class. Diversification brought about insurmountable tensions in all phases of the cycle of productive capital: inability to foresee very differentiated conditions of sale and to adapt to these, inability to analyse costs and separate production norms, inability to select investment projects. Coordination between departments was completely blocked, and the head office submerged in the flood of tactical decisions of a routine nature. This reflected the incapacity of the structure to master the intersections of different functions and economic lines.* Performance indicators for the different departments confused different problems and no longer gave any clear information. The coordination of exchange flows between the functional departments was thus completely disrupted. Overcapacity in certain fields went together with undercapacity in others, since neither production norms nor variations from them could be registered any longer. In such conditions, activity by the enterprise as a whole became impossible. In every case in which the problems thus encountered were effectively analysed, it was discovered that each economic line within a functional department was managed efficiently, but what was lacking was cooperation between the functional departments to assure continuity of valorization in these lines. The lack of separation between the conditions of production and exchange in the different economic lines meant that it was impossible to know which was profitable and which was not, where corrective action should be taken, and how its impact should be measured. It was the sales departments on which the most acute inter-departmental tensions weighed directly. New products were created, but the social demand for them was entirely unknown; the sales departments had to deal with very different types of customer and market reaction according to the commodity involved. The problem was less the

---

* *Filière economique*, translated henceforward as 'economic line' is a technically-integrated system of industries.

lack of market research than the lack of any adequate structure to transmit impulses from it to all the operations of valorization. The fundamental principle on which the solution rested was to make the commodity rather than the function the basis of the organization. The new sub-grouping of the structure became the division, created by combining the conditions of production and exchange corresponding to a category of commodity. It follows from this that divisions are *centres of profit*. The division must be considered as a sub-enterprise, autonomous in terms of day-to-day management. Each division is organized internally according to the principle of centralized functional structure. But any two divisions correspond to distinct spaces of valorization. In this sense, the structure is decentralized, flexible and open-ended. The enterprise can expand into new spaces of valorization by adding on new divisions, without the structure being called into question.

The unity of the enterprise is effected by the transformation of the head office into a *general office*, responsible for the planning and control of the enterprise as a whole. The profitability of the divisions is the criterion for judging their management. The dominance of the general office over the divisions rests on the centralization of the cash flow engendered by the divisions and its allocation according to their profitability and the objectives of overall finance policy.

(c) Perspectives of change in the organization: the corporation as a global system. At the present time corporations are in the process of undergoing an organizational transformation just as radical, if not more so, as that from the centralized functional structure to the decentralized divisional structure. This transformation leads back in the direction of centralization, but on a completely new principle. We have seen how the principle behind centralization on a functional basis was vertical hierarchical dependence. The new centralization rests on the principle of information. We have already seen how this enables constraint by directive to be replaced by the direct constraint of production. The same principle extends from the control of production departments to the control of the sum total of managerial practices.

Centralization on the basis of a self-monitoring managerial structure involves the entire corporation in a single system on which even the higher levels of responsibility are dependent. Instead of the coordination of functions being a groping process of hierarchical relations, it becomes a planned process conceived in advance and organized as a whole. This mode of organization has a single nerve centre in the shape of the *central coordinating and planning organ*, towards which all information converges. This organ integrates all functions of the corporation and transmits the necessary directives on routine management and its control. If the divisional structure topped by a general office had the form of a pyramid, the new managerial structure takes the form of a star. The centre is occupied by the central coordinating and programming organ. One part of its branches is concerned with operational functions of every kind; the others are charged with the elaboration of methods and norms. Integration is effected from the start, with each element of the enterprise interacting with all others.

This structure corresponds to the new mode of organization of labour that we have termed Neo-Fordism. It generalizes the division of labour into semi-autonomous groups at the level of the sum total of managerial practices. This generalization constitutes participatory management controlled by a common objective. The programming of the connections between each unit makes it possible to do more than simply give each operational agent an executive autonomy. These agents can intervene in the overall managerial process on the basis of the information with which they provide the central organ. By bringing into full play the observation and initiative of local agents, the firm can greatly improve its sensitivity to its environment. The structure is conceived so as to react to a modification of competition by a transformation of norms. It becomes in its totality the weapon of finance capital in its attempt to plan the rhythm of transformation of the conditions of production.

The possibility for firms to evolve towards this mode of organization rests on two developments. On the one hand a more rigorous and systematic conception of management has been developing for at least a decade. This involves the progressive mechanization of all routine managerial tasks (assembly of quantitative information, calculations, presentation of accounts and performance indices, etc.), the refinement of planning and budgeting methods, their representation by sequences of operations that are precisely definable and logically linked, the improvement of techniques of prediction and control. On the other hand, there has also been a more recent movement towards automatic production control and connected operations. The establishment of automatic systems of management comes from the union of these two tendencies. It bears within it a radical separation between the tasks of conception and of execution in all economic practices, not merely in production itself. It tends to suppress the intermediate levels of the bureaucratic hierarchy. It has been estimated that within a further ten years or so, some 80% of the decisions that are now the province of intermediate staff will be taken automatically. A large number of hierarchical levels will be abolished, and those that remain will be far less posts from which orders are transmitted than posts of conception that require abilities of general knowledge and synthesis of the firm's activities. A higher portion of work will be devoted to analysis of the corporation's economic activity. But the material infrastructure of management will also become considerably heavier. The system can only be established if the saving arising from the suppression of the intermediate hierarchy more than makes up for these new expenses.

2. Planning and Managerial Control

Planning is a process integrating the structure's practices of management from the top down, and is therefore the structure's principle of functioning. It is a prescriptive process guiding the numerous decisions that have to be made daily for capital to be valorized. This process seeks to arrange practices hierarchically and to fix the succession of decisions. As a prospective act, it has to prepare the structure to react to unforeseen changes in external constraints and take into account the interdependences between functional units and divisions.

But planning does not determine the goals of the capitalist enterprise; it simply arranges the deployment of the means to them. The goals result from the constraint of competition as an on-going process. This constraint fashions the strategy of the corporation and leads to the evolution of its organization. Such strategy will lie in anticipating the transformation of the conditions of production and exchange the better to adapt it. To the extent that this is achieved, the corporation is that much less blind in the competitive process. The norms of planning are the basis on which the functioning of the organization unifies managerial practices. It establishes priorities for reallocating resources as a function of the anticipated development of conditions of production and exchange. The more numerous the elements that can be programmed, the less investment plans are sensitive to short-term disturbances, and the more regular is the long-term growth of the firm. It is in this sense that the unity of the giant corporation's structure and strategy is effected by planning and forms part of the regulation of the capitalist mode of production.

(a) The general strategy of valorization is imposed on planning in the strict sense. The general strategy of valorization concerns the corporation as a whole. It is elaborated within the general office and approved by the agencies of proprietary control (board of directors, shareholders' meeting). This strategy involves three orders of decision: the choice of fields in which to invest productive capital, the division of the overall profit from exploitation and speculation, and the definition of general directives for collective bargaining and the principles of personnel policy.

Planning translates the general strategy of the enterprise into norms to be pursued and maintained according to a procedure involving: the prediction of the enterprise's environment, the establishment of objectives in terms of performance indicators, the insertion of these elements into a calculable framework and the interconnection in time of three types of projections (long-term planning incorporating the choices of future economic lines and other prospective decisions, short-term planning oriented to objectives of divisional profitability, and expenditure budgets for the lower-level functional units).

The most general measurement of the economic performances of those units that are centres of profit is the contribution they make to the overall return on the productive capital invested by the firm. This contribution gives the managerial boards a very important set of data for their control. Short-term targets of profit, i.e. the norms of profitability from one year to the next, are fixed by the general office for the enterprise as a whole. They form the principal directive for fixing profitability norms by division. Defined as a rate of return on the productive capital invested, this indicator provides a summary measure of performance. But the overall rate of return must be closely linked to the firm's financial policy. For the capitalist, the sole aim of a firm is to make sure that money brings money back to its owners. The true objective is net earnings per share. It is the evolution of this variable that principally determines the market value of the firm by directly influencing the price-earnings ratio, and which therefore conditions its entire financial policy. But the net earnings figure depends on the overall cycle of productive capital for the firm as a whole. It gives rise, therefore, to a directive as to the rate of return on its productive capital.

(b) Planning is a procedure involving all levels of the organization. Extending from the first overall estimates to the finalized objectives and their expression in an annual budget, planning procedures are more or less protracted to and fro processes. They start with a prospective long-term scheme proposed by the planning department within the general office, which integrates the reallocation of spheres of investment envisaged in the strategy of the firm.

The divisional heads receive this overall projection, together with strategic directives for the relative development of different economic lines. They themselves have a summary projection prepared of the elements required for an estimation of the rate of profit in their division that seems compatible with the overall choices of the firm, and analyse the possibility of attaining this norm and the corrections they deem necessary in capital expenditures.

The planning department centralizes and synthesizes the divisional results. A coordinating committee, headed by the managing director and involving the central planning office, the financial director and other members of the finance department, and the heads of divisions or groups, organizes this procedure. The revised directives become the basis for revised budgets predicted by the divisions. These budgets are collated by the central planning office, which prepares a balance-sheet for the following year (and possibly also for later years). This system of projections involves norms of profitability that the company sets itself as objectives. A financial expression of the objectives of valorization, it becomes, after approval by the management boards and finally the board of directors, the overall plan for the company at all levels, determining all functional performance indicators. The prospective elaboration of these operational practices and criteria of performance forms the detailed preparation of the plan, as pursued in each division.

The overall plan is a process enabling the entire structure to be subordinated to a single set of objectives, by overriding the contradictory projects and interests of horizontally placed functionaries. Each division makes its contribution to the plan in the form of its own prospective budget, associated with a norm of profitability in terms of the rate of profit anticipated from the productive capital invested in the division. The prospective divisional budget generally involves a prediction of sales, current expenditures, capital expenditures, profits and liquid assets.

The detailed preparation of the plan on the basis of the predicted divisional budgets determines the operations to be effected and the indicators by which control is maintained during the plan's execution. An accurate sales prediction is crucial, if plausible objectives of profitability are to be defined. The link between sales and profits reacts on the fixing of prices. It demands a close collaboration between the sales department and the production department, in order to achieve both an exact analysis of costs and particularly an assessment of their variability as a function of the volume of sales. A periodic revision of the detailed performance indicators within the year is generally necessary.

(c) The choice of investments in the planning process. The planning of investments involves the construction and transformation of systems of productive forces capable of producing commodities for the projected volume of sales in the various

markets. It is therefore a component of the enterprise's general planning, and not simply a particular process. This is quite clear from those investments that ensue directly from the strategic decisions of the top management and involve the creation of something entirely new. The investment project is then initiated at the highest level, and forms part of long-term planning. This could not be otherwise, since it involves major decisions in the transformation of the conditions of production and exchange, designed to shift the constraints of competition significantly rather than merely to adapt to them – decisions liable to determine far-reaching changes in the relative contributions that the different divisions make to the firm's overall profit. These major projects form the link between decisions to change fields of production within the economic division of labour, or to open markets in new geographical areas, and financial policies. The flow of new expenditure over several years necessitated by these development decisions requires centralized disposal over a cash flow that is not tied up in the reproduction and consolidation of economic lines yielding current and foreseeable profit. It thus usually presupposes a change in financial policy. Accelerated amortization in the traditional lines is the condition for generating an untied cash flow; while at the same time it accelerates the demise of these lines.

In this case, the development decision is not only integrated into planning, but itself structures the long-term plan. Its implementation over time depends on the one hand on the specific characteristics of the development project, on the other hand on the regularity and progression of the flows of profit yielded by the economic lines in operation. Planning of these two elements makes it possible to plan debt management and recourse to increases in capital.

Investments in *development* of this kind cannot be accomodated in the traditional theory of investment choices, which assumes it is possible to identify distinct projects separated from one another, and to calculate in advance the expenditures they require and the subsequent receipts they will yield. The real world is not divided into rational slices of this kind. The chief source of the profit yielded from a strategic investment of productive capital comes from its reinforcement of the integration between the different modalities of valorization bearing on related activities. This is why a full analysis of the inter-connections of company activities is a binding imperative in all investment planning.

Routine investments in existing economic lines do not escape this imperative either, even though these are different in kind from development investments. The latter open up new fields of valorization and change the structure of the firm. Routine investments, on the other hand, merely adapt the enterprise to the evolution of the prevailing conditions of production and exchange. They arise in current managerial practice from the tension engendered by the difficulty in reaching the indicators of efficiency that are programmed into the budget. They involve the use of the tied part of cash flow. The main tensions that generate these routine investment projects are: a rise in costs above the norms laid down or a fall in the prices asked by competitors, the stratification of a particular category of commodity into different varieties whose range does not cor-respond with market needs, or the prediction of an excess of sales beyond production capacities. The means for detecting and analysing deviations from the projected norms bring into play the plasticity of the structure of the firm, the density of its communications network and the precision of its assignment of internal responsibilities; it is these which render it capable of reacting and responding at the appropriate levels with the shortest possible delay.

(d) Managerial control. Managerial control is an essential process in the execution of the budget. We have just seen how it is in this process that routine investment projects arise, hence one of the elements for preparing the following budget. There is therefore an indispensable chain of continuous planning. The overall results of managerial control for the profitability of the firm, moreover, influence and modify its strategy. The quality of this control depends entirely on the pertinence of the norms laid down in the budget. The exercise of strict control on the basis of inadequate norms leads irrevocably to a disorganization of the labour process, a deterioration in its atmosphere, vexatious frustrations and bitter rivalries among managerial staff, and a

general scepticism as to the top management's capacity for
overall direction.

Budgetary control is the form of control best adapted to a
divisional structure, by virtue of its flexibility, its capacity for
integration, and its ability to include detailed norms matching
the practices of the functional units within the divisions. It can
also very well accommodate more precise controls for those
very specialized units that do not have sufficient autonomy to
provide elements of the budget.

The processes that make up managerial control are the
observation and recording of real performances, systematic
comparison at appropriate levels of competence between planned norms and real results, the selection of those deviations
that need corrective action because they are not simply fortuit-
ous in character, the determination and execution of the
corrective action required, and the observation of its results. If
the results are not satisfactory, then the cycle of administrative
practices that has just been described is embarked on again and
becomes a recurrent process.

The form in which the flow of information circulates, its
periodicity, and its content at each hierarchical level are all of
primordial importance for efficient managerial control.

Overall supervision of the establishment, transmission and
analysis of reports, is carried out by the financial control office,
for the company as a whole. The importance of this office is that
it assures the smooth operation of the control process. To this
end, it assists the responsible managers in the preparation and
utilization of reports, by giving advice as to accounting procedures, methods of consolidation, definitions of results and
problems of their interpretation. It sees to it that the detailed
system of norms is such that control is applied at each level of
the organization to those variables which really are effectively
controllable at that level. Nothing is more destructive for the
control process as a whole than a poor definition of performance
indicators which renders a manager responsible for a divergence outside his range of control.

If a rigorous correspondence between norms and levels of
responsibility is strictly respected, then effective and prompt
corrective action can be taken. Corrective action is a key link in

the self-regulation of the structure. In these practices the structure selects those problems that are raised at the overall level and require the top management either to redefine its planning objectives, or to reallocate financial resources between the divisions.

3. The Predominance of Proprietary Control: Financial Groups

In the course of development of the capitalist mode of production, the centralization of capital alters the form of ownership at the same time as it effects far-reaching changes in the way that the process of valorization is organized and controlled. The key phenomenon here is financial centralization, which leads to the formation of a new mode of association between capitalists, finance capital, as defined above. *Finance capital is the ultimate mode of capital centralization.* It makes possible a centralization freed from the obstacles posed by the heterogeneity of the material conditions of production. To this end, it prompts the mutation of the structure of the giant corporation into an integrated global system. But finance capital is still far from having pushed the logic of this centralization of ownership to its limit, at least in the United States. This centralization is in some respects the counterpart of the unification of the wage-earning class.

We must now study how the financial groups, as structural forms into which finance capital is partitioned, are articulated to the giant corporations. To tackle this problem in a concrete way, we have to ask the two following questions:

(1) Given that ownership titles are nominally distributed to a large number of share-holders, who really controls property? Who lays down financial policy and controls its execution? A proper response to this question requires investigation of the structure of ownership in the company, and the demonstration of the existence of a *controlling group*. This controlling group is the effect of the dominant presence, in the capital ownership of the enterprise, of a financial group or an alliance of financial groups.

(2) The valorization of finance capital requires that of the total capital productively invested in firms. The controlling

group which defines financial policy must utilize and modify the structure of the company to ensure that it is managed in accordance with its own objectives. Complex as they might be, economic relations within the company must be reduced, by their subordination to the controllers of property, to a one-dimensional and purely quantitative objective: the self-valorization of money.

1933 saw the publication of Berle and Means' famous work.[16] While the whole world was stunned by the recent financial collapse in the USA, and dumbfounded by the pyramid of interests that this had revealed, Berle and Means explained that the divorce between capital and corporate activity had already been completed. In the greater number of cases, industrial firms were in the hands of 'managers' exercising an *internal control*. The owners, very numerous and each wielding only infinitesimal fractions of share capital, played no active role and were content simply to receive their dividends. A trenchant refutation of this thesis was produced by the Temporary National Economic Committee (TNEC),[17] which the Roosevelt Administration had charged with a far-reaching investigation into the ownership of the 200 largest industrial firms. Out of a total of 7 million shares with voting rights at that time, an average of some 35,000 shares for each company, the average distribution took the following form: 20 very large shareholders held 32% of the voting rights, 980 major sharehol-ders held 18%, and 34,000 small shareholders divided the remaining 50% between them. This degree of inequality in the composition of ownership disclosed the existence of controlling groups, which in certain circumstances can become antagonis-tic, and of alliances and splits as financial groups restructure their investments in industry, seeking to reconcile controlling power and immediate requirements of profitability. The conclu-sions of the TNEC study showed that eight financial groups played a dominant role in controlling the 200 leading industrial corporations. It is clear that in conditions such as these the great bulk of shareholders serve simply as a reserve for

[16] A. A. Berle and G. C. Means, *The Modern Corporation and Private Property*, New York, 1933.
[17] TNEC, *The Distribution of Ownership in the 200 Largest Non-Financial Corporations*, Monograph no. 29, 1940.

manipulation, not by the 'managers', but rather by centralized financial capital.

More recently, J.M. Chevalier has scrutinized financial interconnections in an attempt to update the TNEC study.[18] In the same work, he has put forward a theory of proprietary control which is directly linked to the theory of a centralization of capital dominated by financial centralization. Four groups of shareholders are identified here:

(1) The group represented by the board of directors, in whole or in part (group I); this the controlling group.

(2) A group potentially hostile to the directors, unrepresented on the board (group II), whose behaviour may be either active, if it has a chance of seizing control, or passive and available to a tacit alliance with the controlling group.

(3) The institutional investors, in so far as these are not instruments of either of the two preceding groups (group III). These investors wield large blocks of shares, but they generally vote together with the controlling group, except when they consider the corporation's performance inadequate, in which case they sell their shares.

(4) The other individual shareholders (group IV) are passive and ill-informed. Their inertia leads them to vote largely in favour of the established board.

On this basis, the threshold of control is a variable defining a limit below which the controlling group risks losing its position. It depends on the percentages of share capital P_I, P_{II}, P_{III}, P_{IV} held by each of the groups, and on the behavioural coefficients expressing the probability that each of these groups will vote in favour of the board of directors, C_I, C_{II}, C_{III}, C_{IV}.

Proprietary control is defined here as the ability to obtain the absolute majority of votes in the shareholders' meeting. The threshold of control is the share that group I must hold in order to obtain such an absolute majority with the aid of those other shareholders who will vote in its favour. The absolute majority is equal to $(50 + h)$ per cent. To obtain this, group I must hold a share P_I such that:

$$P_I = (50 + h) - (P_{II} \cdot C_{II} + P_{III} \cdot C_{III} + P_{IV} \cdot C_{IV});$$

since it can be assumed that $C_I = 1$.

18 J. M. Chevalier, *La structure financière de l'industrie américaine*, Paris, 1970.

If we view group II as a financial group with a strategy opposed to that of the controlling group, then $C_{II} = 0$.

$$P_I = (50 + h) - (P_{III} \cdot C_{III} + P_{IV} \cdot C_{IV}).$$

The controlling group can stay in power even with a weak shareholding (which may fall to some 1% of the share capital) as long as groups III and IV hold the bulk of the shares and the conditions of valorization make possible a financial policy that yields the institutional investors a satisfactory return. Even so, in these conditions the controlling group might be very vulnerable to the action of a financial group that sought not so much directly to evict the existing board of directors as to have the firm taken over by another firm already under its control. This is how the institutional investors have played a role in the last major wave of conglomerate mergers. The very rapid growth in the funds at their disposal, and the need for higher profitability on which their own profits depend, force the institutional investors to turn their funds over rapidly. Since they wield great blocks of shares and can pursue concentrated policies of purchase and sale, and since these funds are managed by professionals with a good knowledge of the stock market, these institutional investors are sensitive to the financial gains ensuing from mergers. We may thus conclude that the weakening of group IV and the strengthening of group III as a result of financial centralization, itself furthered by the predominance of contractual over individual savings, are phenomena with an important effect on the competition between financial groups for the control of sites of valorization. The institutional investors play both a passive role, since they are not themselves potential controlling groups, and an active one, in that the increased mobility which they inject into financial circulation provides easier and more frequent occasions for financial groups to change their constellations. In this perspective, the purely conglomerate mergers of the late 1960s can be seen in part as the attempt to create new financial groups which could free themselves from the grip of the dominant groups and pursue an independent strategy.

It remains to be seen how the controlling group fits into the structure of the corporation, and how it exercises its power over planning and routine management.

Study of proprietary control in the 200 largest American

corporations shows two chief ways in which the controlling group inserts itself into the corporate structure. The actual existence of one or the other type in such a corporation often depends on historical factors. But at all events it is the composition of the controlling group that determines that of the board of directors and its subordinate authorities.

(1) When the controlling group is homogeneous, as a single group enjoying a majority in the general shareholders' meeting that is very much above the threshold of control, the board of directors is itself very homogeneous in its recruitment and closely knit around the controlling group (the 'inside board'). This close connection can be effected in two ways. Either the financial group, which may be merely a single family and is the real owner of the enterprise, itself heads the board of directors and the main committees under it. Those executive personnel that it lacks it finds among the managerial staff. This is the case for example with the chemical enterprise E.I. Du Pont de Nemours, which is closely controlled by the Du Pont family; it is also the case with the Mellon group, which enjoys almost sole control of Alcoa (Aluminium Company of America) and has placed several top administrators of the Mellon bank in the corporation's leading positions. Alternatively, the financial group that holds control of the enterprise does not have a major presence on the board of directors; in this case it favours the perpetuation of a homogeneous directing group that buys up shares in favourable conditions by way of option schemes. A close and almost unbreakable alliance is formed between the financial group which is the true owner of the corporation and the group of directors who are internal to the firm. This alliance forms a solid controlling group dominated by the financial group. It is in this way that the Rockefeller group managed to maintain its oil empire even while itself withdrawing from the boards of the oil companies.

(2) When the distribution of ownership between several financial groups is such as to require a consensus on the principles of financial policy (increases in capital and external financing, bonuses and option share schemes, amortization rules and formation of reserves, ratios of dividends, acquisition of new firms and tax evasion, etc.), then the controlling group appears as a more or less fragile community of interests. A

situation of this kind generally arises after the group which originally owned the company sold off its investments, either voluntarily or otherwise. The reorganization of the company then depends on a coalition of banks and other financial agencies, forming a network of intertwined financial groups. In this case, the board of directors and its subordinate agencies must be carefully mixed in composition (an 'outside board'). This is what happened with the consolidation of U.S. Steel, for example, and with the reorganization of General Electric at the instigation of the Morgan group. The composition of the board of directors reflects the commercial, financial and political connections which the corporation requires. This is why we can see the recruitment by the controlling groups of political or intellectual figures, high functionaries invited to sit on the board to give this a broader base of support.

The controlling group inserts itself into the structure of the corporation by dominating the general office. The tools of management, the methods of personnel policy, the hierarchical relationships and centres of profit are means for the controlling group to unify the practices needed for the valorization of capital that is its *raison d'être* and the sole source of its position in society. Within the corporation, the controlling group must make sure of a total hegemony over the work force. It consequently utilizes the structure of the company and the principles of management, promotion, propaganda and psychological pressure, as tools for pre-empting and partitioning contradictions, to avoid any critical reflection by the personnel on the goals it pursues. Through its power of disposal over centralized cash flow, the controlling group can ensure that the distribution of profit is highly unequal. To this end it can exploit its connections with allied groups within financial circulation, and information drawn from its 'insider' positions in a whole series of firms. The sources of surplus profits that the financial groups can garner thanks to their proprietary control come chiefly from two major types of operations:

(1) Flows of profit that the financial groups canalize in the form of overheads into service or financial companies set up for this purpose. If there is one heading in the balance sheet that is growing with meteoric speed, it is that of 'services to the corporation'. This directly expresses the grip of finance capital.

Costs of legal counsel, auditing, advertising and tax advice are transferred to specially set up companies which charge very high rates for their services. These companies, generally having only a very limited personnel, are no more than facades for concealing relay-stations in the circulation of profit. On top of this are the directors' fees, commissions, bonuses, share options, representation and travel allowances, which are so many means for the members of the group that decides on financial policy and holds power of control over the overall cash flow generated by the company to drain off surplus-value.

(2) The second type of operation for capturing surplus profits comes from the financial activity of groups exploiting their controlling positions in groups of firms that are linked. Here we cannot list in any detail these forms of financial circulation. The following items, however, can be mentioned: free acquisition of large amounts of shares as promotion benefits when new companies are founded, and when mergers and consolidations take place; enlargements in capital base; duplication and transfer of shares; speculation in industrial land, mines and other sites bought cheaply by property and development companies belonging to the financial groups and sold off at high prices to the industrial firms they control; share transactions making use of the opportunity to buy stocks at rates lower than the official market price and exploiting inside information to sell them at higher rates; possibilities for influencing share prices by the impact on the stock market of finance policy decisions.

5

General Rate of Profit and Competition Among Capitals

I. The Conditions of Existence of a General Rate of Profit

The aim of this chapter is to provide a conceptual framework for the concrete forms taken by the social link between autonomous capitals. We shall therefore have to establish step by step, starting from the conclusions reached so far, the concepts that will enable us to show how the laws of competition derive rigorously from the law of accumulation. The sum total of these laws constitutes the metabolism of the social formations subjected to the capitalist mode of production.

To attain this objective, we shall firstly proceed to deepen our analysis of the articulation between the production and circulation of commodities under capitalism. This is not a new theoretical problem. From the beginning of Chapter 1, in fact, we have defined the homogeneous space of value as the space of equivalence classes determined by a social relation, exchange, which effects the social validation of private labours that are independent from the standpoint of production. This point of departure has enabled us to show that money as the support of the social relation of exchange is intrinsically different from any individual commodity. This difference makes every act of exchange into a polarized relationship that realizes the value of commodities, i.e. socializes the private labour expended to produce them. Money is the pivot of those exchanges that are organized into general commodity circulation, because it is the expression of abstract labour, i.e. the homogeneous total labour of society. On this basis we have been able to account for the formation of monetary sums within the law of accumulation itself. The transformation of abstract labour and the concepts linked to it, the value of labour-power and surplus-value, into monetary sums, total social income and its division into wages and profits, is not a problem in which two different theoretical fields are counterposed. It is rather the articulation of capitalist production and circulation. The two concepts that enable us to conceive this articulation are the monetary expression of the working hour and the nominal reference wage. We have held over a study of the concrete formation of the first of these to Chapter 6, as it can only be undertaken on the basis of the relationships between money and credit under capitalism. But in the final section of Chapter 3 we have already studied the second in detail and summed up the transformation of the value of labour-power into wages. The laws by which total income and wages are formed enable us to understand why total profit, issuing from the surplus-value produced by social labour-power, is, even as a homogeneous monetary sum, the expression of a relation of distribution, a levy on total social revenue.

It is total profit, whose amount is determined according to relationships established in the first part of this book, depending on the set of conditions of production and exchange, that is the strategic variable in the relations of competition between autonomous capitals. The total profit that the capitalist class as a whole can capture always expresses the constraint imposed by the law of accumulation of social capital. In deepening our analysis of the articulation of capitalist production and circulation, we come back to an investigation of the form in which this constraint is expressed. We shall embark on this investigation in two stages. Firstly, we shall put forward a more precise concept of prices under capitalism; secondly, we shall demonstrate the exact form that general commodity circulation takes under capitalism. This investigation will lead us to an important conclusion, that the constraint imposed by the law of accumulation is expressed in the relations of competition as the formation of a general rate of profit. Once this essential result is established, the laws of competition follow easily from it.

It is important to note the difference between this procedure and that of the classical doctrine. This difference will have its effects on our interpretation of competition and on the characteristics of the price system as it is conceived by the two distinct approaches.

In the Marxist procedure that we have formalized, the determination of the total volume of profit logically precedes that of the rate of profit. In the classical doctrine, on the contrary, profit is grasped only by way of its rate. The uniformity of the rate of profit here forms the very definition of profit. This definition however is simply a conceptualization of inter-capitalist relations. This is because the classical writers, as also those modern writers who lay claim to the classical tradition, take capital as an absolute premise of the economic system, thus in no way considering its existence as a problem.

The Marxist procedure, on the other hand, poses a dual problem: that of the commodity economy as conceptualized by abstract labour, and that of the wage relation as conceptualized by the partition of abstract labour into the value of labour-power and surplus-value. We have sought a solution to this dual problem by developing a theory of the forms of social relations and studying the transformations brought about by the effect of these social forms on the homogeneous space of value. This has led us to pose and develop the concepts of the monetary expression of the abstract working hour and the nominal reference wage, in order to account for the formation of total income and its macro-economic distribution. This is why total profit appears as the economic form of the capitalist relation of production. It is a concept linked to that of capital in general, i.e. logically prior to the division of this capital into fractions.

These divergences over the object of economic science find expression in far-reaching differences over the theoretical status of the rate of profit. In the dominant conception of classical economics, the uniformity of the rate of profit is what defines the concept of price. Firstly there is a surplus product in use-values. The uniform rate of profit is the distributive rule governing the price of the surplus product, which enables the price system to be determined. The formation of the price system is the valorization of the economy. It guarantees the reproduction of the surplus product, incorporating the modality of its distribution. The rate of profit for the classical writers is thus the representation of capitalism as a natural economic order. This is why they employ a very abstract conception of time. The fact that the surplus product is given in use-values presupposes that the conditions of production have an exclusively technical character and are independent from the rule of distribution. Reproduction is then the affirmation of the eternal character of this rule. It is no longer possible to distinguish between the unit period of production and perpetuity. This is expressed in the formal possibility of reducing the price system to amounts of labour with definite dates, in such a way that each price appears as an infinite series of labour quantities, each compounded by the rate of profit.[1]

In the Marxist conception, abstract labour refers to present time. It is the homogeneous working day of a society. Its basis is the actual social conditions of production, forming an indissoluble unity of technical relationships and relations of production within the organization of labour. The priority of the concept of profit over that of the rate of profit follows on the one hand from the fact that capital is not seen as a natural entity but as issuing from the wage relation, and on the other hand from the fact that only the present conditions of production count for the social validation of private labours. As a result, the general rate of profit is not a constitutive concept of value, but rather a concept derived from the accumulation of capital; it is first necessary to understand this latter. We shall see in the present chapter that a general rate of profit is a condition of the regular functioning of the regime of accumulation. This condition may or may not be realized. Accordingly, the general rate of profit may not in fact exist, whereas the wage relation always does define capitalism. The formation of the general rate of profit is the result of a conflict involving two different dimensions of time: on the one hand the homogeneous social time that defines the space of value, on the other hand the time of valorization of capital, which seeks a unity between the past labour crystallized in the means of production and current social labour. The classical writers considered only this second dimension, since they saw capital as an immanent entity filling the entire social space. Marx asserted the predominance of the first dimension, since it defines capital as an antagonistic social relation. He conceived the relationship between the two temporal dimen-

[1] See P. Sraffa, *The Production of Commodities by Commodities*, Cambridge, 1960.

sions as a conflict whose solution was the devalorization of capital. The question then is to study the role of the formation of the general rate of profit in this conflict as a force unifying the capitalist class, despite those forces that tend to disrupt it by threatening the valorization of past labour.

1. The Theoretical Status of Prices

At the start of Chapter 1 we examined the exchange equation that represents the relationship of equivalence. We saw that contrary to appearances, this equation is not an equalization of two values but rather a polar relationship expressing the value of a commodity in relation to an equivalent, i.e. a representative of society's homogeneous total labour. It follows from this that exchange is only thinkable as monetary exchange. Once the neo-classical thesis that every economic act is an exchange is abandoned, production is acknowledged as an original act of value creation, and the problem of the liaison between production and exchange is posed, it is no longer possible to consider the sale of a commodity in order to buy another as a direct act $C - C'$ with only two terms. It is now necessarily an act $C - M - C'$, involving three terms, in which the sale and the purchase are separated and follow one another. This is not for some contigent reason due to the practical inconveniences of barter. It is due rather to the very nature of the commodity economy. Production creates use-values while simultaneously forming a social purchasing power over the sum total of these use-values. But the fact that the use-values are the products of independent private labours gives them the character of commodities. Social purchasing power is borne by monetary revenues; but it is not yet realized, only potential. The products of private labours are not use-values for their producers; all that matters for them is the realization of the social value of which their products are as yet only conditional counterparts. Thus commodity production forms social value. But it can only do so in a manner that decomposes it. The realization of value is the unity of the elements dissociated when determinate fractions of monetary income purchase quantities of products. The expenditure of monetary income is both the realization of value and its annihilation. When commodities have finished their metamorphoses, they actually do become use-values and are consumed, either productively or otherwise. Their destruction simultaneously abolishes the value, which however is created anew by the continuity of the act of production. When the sum total of the products of private labours accomplishes its metamorphoses through exchange, total income is realized. But there is nothing automatic about this realization. Each autonomous centre of production creates particular varieties of commodity and forms a fraction of total monetary income by participating in the general labour of the society. But the social purchasing power borne by money as representative of this general labour is by definition capable of purchasing any commodity whatsoever. There is no *a priori* reason why total monetary income should facilitate the exact purchase of all commodities of all kinds. The general commodity circulation may be interrupted by a break in the interconnection of acts of purchase and sale; certain commodities do not become use-values, because they remain unsold. Thus there is always a problem of the social validation of private labours, which makes itself felt in the form of a monetary constraint.

This conception of monetary exchange has important implications for the theoretical status of prices.

(1) Formally, prices are the exchange-values of commodities as expressed in money. They are realized by the effective sale of the commodities, in other words their exchange against determinate sums of money. All prices are therefore necessarily monetary prices. Relative prices are simply results of the sum total of monetary exchanges, and in no way can they be determined directly.

(2) In exchange, particular quantities of commodities confront determinate sums of money. In this confrontation, the prices posted are either realized or not. The manner in which the realization is effected is what causes prices to move. Social market prices are therefore first of all, from the conceptual standpoint, sums of money denoting the division of total exchange-value by *social demand*, i.e. by monetary sums bearing on the different varieties of commodity. Unit prices are simply the quotients obtained when the social prices of these different varieties of commodity are divided by the quantities sold. Since prices are given in unit terms, what impresses itself

on the obserber is the relative stability of the posted price by contrast with the incessant movement of purchases and sales. It is easy to believe, therefore, that in practice the unit prices are intrinsically determined by an equilibrium between supply and demand, and that the total sales and purchases are the products of these unit prices multiplied by the quantities sold. This actually is the way in which the social constraint is experienced by individuals involved in exchange. But in order to grasp the movement of prices as a whole, it is necessary to investigate the determinants of this constraint, i.e. the formation of social demand on the basis of the division of total income, and the flows of exchange induced by the renewal of the social conditions of production, including of course the reconstitution of social labour-power.[2]

The characteristics we have just described affect every commodity economy. Under capitalism, the division of total income and the renewal of the conditions of production obey the law of accumulation. We know that a formal characteristic of this law is the reversal of simple commodity circulation $C - M - C'$ into capitalist circulation $M - C - M'$. The monetary flow moves in a circle, with money figuring at both start and finish of the metamorphoses of value. We also know that the form taken by capitalist circulation is an effect of the wage relation. Each individual capitalist absorbs labour-power in return for a wage expressed as a sum of money, and begins a production process which is a valorization of the monetary advance. The realization of the sum total of commodities involves the realization of the surplus-value which accrues to the capitalist class as its total profit. The manner in which each individual capitalist experiences the monetary constraint follows from this. All that appears in the sphere of circulation is the relation between two monetary magnitudes, one of these being the total capital advanced and the other exceeding the former by a difference which is profit, a fraction of total profit. This is why the monetary constraint imposes itself on the individual capitalist as the need to realize a certain *rate of profit*

[2] The formation of effective demand is a characteristic problem of capitalism as a generalized commodity economy. Absent as it generally was from the dominant classical conception, though perceived to some extent by Malthus and Sismondi, it establishes a certain link between Marx and Keynes.

on the capital advanced. The formation of prices in the capitalist mode of production is indissolubly bound up with the realization of the rate of profit. By specifying this constraint more precisely, we shall demonstrate the nature of those external relations of competition between autonomous capitals that follow from the law of accumulation.

2. The Expanded Reproduction of Social Capital

Individual capitals stand in a relation of competition because they have the characteristics of capital in general. These characteristics are stamped on them by their subjection to the law of accumulation, which forces them to realize a certain rate of profit. What rate of profit does this involve? It cannot be deduced from the individual rates. If it were nothing more than an average of the individual rates weighted by the sums of capital advanced as expressed in money terms, it would form no constraint on the valorization of these capitals. The constraint of competition requires a social law proceeding from the nature of capital as a social relation, which operates as the law of formation of a *general rate of profit* by which the valorization of individual capitals is forcibly governed. If this is the case, then the general rate of profit is the basis of competition. We are thus led to investigate why and how the law of accumulation gives rise to the formation of a general rate of profit.

The solution of this problem is given by a combination of two results already established. On the one hand we have shown that accumulation, i.e. the expanded reproduction of the wage relation, requires determinate exchanges of value between the two departments of production. On the other hand, we have seen that in every commodity economy exchange is effected in the form of purchases of determinate amounts of the products of labour by determinate fractions of total monetary income, and that under capitalism these exchanges have the form $M - C - M'$, implying the realization of a rate of profit. The conjunction of these two properties defines a general schema for the reproduction of the social capital which we have already given diagrammatically in Chapter 3 (Diagram 9). The task now is to analyse this schema algebraically so as to establish the formal conditions of existence of the general rate of profit.

To avoid any logical ambiguity and to guard ourselves against the objection of conceptual circularity, we remind the reader that our definition of the departments of production and the relationships obtaining between them owes nothing to the fragmentation of capital into autonomous units. These are rather concepts directly deduced from the wage relation and the formation of surplus-value as a continuous process. In order to express the formal conditions for the existence of the general rate of profit, it is necessary to assume that relationships between the two departments of production are inscribed within a capitalist commodity circulation in which total income is realized and where surplus-value consequently flows back to the capitalist class in the form of total profit.

(a) The general rate of profit and the realization of total exchange-value. Let us express the exchange-value composition of the departments producing means of production (Department I) and means of consumption (Department II) as follows:

$$G_1 + S_1 + P_1 = VE_1$$
$$G_2 + S_2 + P_2 = VE_2$$

The total amount of wages S then $= S_I + S_{II}$; the total profit $P = P_I + P_{II}$, and the total income $VP = S + P$.

We know that VP is transformed into abstract labour VA by the realization of the total exchange-value, in accordance with the relationship $m = VP/VA$, where m is the monetary expression of the working hour. The mass of wages is transformed from abstract labour on the basis of the formation of the nominal reference wage:

$$\frac{S}{VA} = w = \frac{\overline{m}}{1+e}, \text{ where } e \text{ is the rate of surplus-value.}$$

From this it follows that

$$\frac{P}{S} = \frac{VP - S}{S} = \frac{m}{\overline{m}}(1+e) - 1$$

The amount of wages and the total income are divided between the two departments of production in accordance with the division of society's homogeneous labour: $VA = VA_1 + VA_2$.

We may note that in this general schema there is no need to

introduce directly the operations of the state. w is in fact the nominal reference wage, i.e. the expression in money of the social cost of the reproduction of labour-power. P is the total profit, as defined prior to its division between the different parties involved. There is thus no need to add in the operations of the state; they are taken into account in the categories here defined. In a more detailed examination of the schema, it would be necessary to amplify these basic magnitudes. We must lastly note that the schema as written here applies to a single turnover time for the capitals in the two departments.

If there is a general rate of profit, it is defined by:

$$r = \frac{P_1}{G_1 + S_1} = \frac{P_2}{G_2 + S_2}$$

Let us now define $k'_1 = G_1/S_1$ and $k'_2 = G_2/S_2$; we then have $P_1/S_1 = (1 + k'_1)r$, and $P_2/S_2 = (1 + k'_2)r$; k'_1 and k'_2 are transformed functions of the organic compositions of capital in the two departments of production, functions therefore of r.

We can call the allocation of the social labour VA between the two departments of production the *macrostructure of production*. This is defined by the relation VA_1/VA_2. The formal condition for the existence of the general rate of profit involves two steps: we first express the link between the macrostructure of production, the determinants of the formation and the distribution of total income, and the internal characteristics of the capital advanced in the two departments. We then write the condition for the full realization of the total exchange-value, thanks to which the value formed according to the macrostructure VA_1/VA_2 is effectively realized by the social demand borne by the fractions of overall monetary income.

First step

$$\frac{P}{S} = \frac{P_1 + P_2}{S_1 + S_2} = \frac{\dfrac{P_2}{S_2} + \dfrac{P_1}{S_1} \cdot \dfrac{S_1}{S_2}}{1 + \dfrac{S_1}{S_2}} = \frac{(1 + k'_2)r + (1 + k'_1)r\ \dfrac{VA_1}{VA_2}}{1 + \dfrac{VA_1}{VA_2}}$$

$$\therefore \frac{VA_1}{VA_2} = -\frac{\dfrac{P}{S} - (1 + k'_2)r}{\dfrac{P}{S} - (1 + k'_1)r} = -\frac{\dfrac{m}{\overline{m}}(1 + e) - 1 - (1 + k'_2)r}{\dfrac{m}{\overline{m}}(1 + e) - 1 - (1 + k'_1)r}$$

Second step. In order for the total exchange-value to be realized in such a way as to renew the conditions of production and expand accumulation, it is necessary for a determinate fraction of the income formed in Department I to purchase a determinate fraction of the exchange-value of the product of Department II. In actual fact, S_2 and the share of profit P_2 that is either consumed or earmarked for the expansion of the labour-power employed in Department II directly purchase the corresponding portion of the exchange-value of the means of consumption produced in this department. The fraction G_I of the exchange-value of Department I, moreover, renews by its purchases within Department I the means of production for this department which have been consumed during the period in question. In order for the total social labour to be realized in the general exchange of commodities, it is necessary that the incomes formed in Department I and not spent in this department, i.e. not spent on the renewal of the means of production consumed or in purchasing additional means of production, should exactly purchase the exchange-value of the means of consumption not otherwise assigned within Department II. This enables Department II to renew its own means of production and to purchase from Department I the additional means enabling it to extend its accumulation. The formal condition for full realization is thus expressed as follows:

$$S_1 + P_1 - \Delta G_1 = G_2 + \Delta G_2$$

$$\therefore \quad \frac{S_1}{S_2} + \frac{P_1}{S_1}\frac{S_1}{S_2} - \frac{\Delta G_1}{G_1} \cdot k'_1 \cdot \frac{S_1}{S_2} = k'_2(1 + \frac{\Delta G_2}{G_2})$$

or

$$\frac{VA_1}{VA_2} = \frac{k'_2(1 + \frac{\Delta G_2}{G_2})}{1 + (1 + k'_1)r - k'_1\frac{\Delta G_1}{G_1}}$$

Bringing together the two expressions of VA_1/VA_2, we obtain the condition for the formation of the general rate of profit. Its significance is clear enough. By expressing the fact that the realization of the total exchange-value must be compatible with the macrostructure of production, this condition makes explicit the exchanges of value between the two departments of production which neutralize the tendency to uneven development. The formation of the general rate of profit thus certainly derives from the law of capital accumulation.

(b) The general rate of profit and the contradictions of accumulation. The general condition expressed above is a synchronic one. It would be tempting to extend it by additional conditions which would lead to the construction of one of those models of balanced growth so dear to the economists. One would only need add that the share of profit invested is divided within each department of production into ΔG and ΔS, in such a way that the coefficients k'_1 and k'_2 are constant, and to add a constraint for the balanced allocation of social labour between the two departments by requiring the relation VA_1/VA_2 to remain constant. In this way we would obtain a regime of balanced growth in which the general rate of profit would be constant and the rate of growth of total capital formation would be determined by the relationship $\Delta(G+S)/G+S = a \cdot r$, where a is the share of the total profit that is accumulated. On the basis of this intellectual construction, we could devote ourselves to the methodical analysis of the coefficients and their relationships, so as to investigate whether there really does exist an equilibrium rate of profit. This would be a sure way of running into a dead end.

In actual fact, the condition for the full realization of total exchange-value is an effective social constraint related to the cohesion of the regime of accumulation. It may either be respected or transgressed. If it is transgressed, then the result is an uneven development leading to a crisis of accumulation from which new conditions of production arise after a massive devalorization of capital. But if this condition is a real one, it is not the same with the supplementary conditions that it might be tempting to add. These latter are purely imaginary. They would be borrowings from the theory of balanced growth, which generally conceives economic relationships of growth only with all proportions in the economy held constant. The Marxist procedure, however, has no need to impose this yoke on itself, since it has rigorously constructed from the outset an economic space in which a real measurement can be defined: the homogeneous space of value. The definition of this space in no way requires any artificial equilibrium condition.

Yet the constraint of the full realization of exchange-value does express a certain concept of equilibrium. It defines a balance of forces that may or may not be broken. If it is broken, however, economic phenomena do not thereby become less intelligible. This remark enables us to give a more precise definition of what it is we mean by the uneven development of the two departments. We have seen in studying the law of accumulation that relative surplus-value is created only by a far-reaching transformation of the conditions of production. This transformation alters the characteristic proportions of social capital, whatever may be the macrostructure of production or the determinants of the division of total income. As a consequence, to say that development is not uneven is not to say that the two departments of production grow at the same rate, which would be absurd. It means rather that the transformations in the conditions of production, which are inherent to the antagonism of the wage relation, are interconnected in such a way that developments in the macrostructure of production and the division of total income are compatible. This compatibility is expressed in the social constraint of the full realization of total exchange-value. This is the profound significance of the formation of a general rate of profit.

As a result, a rupture in the cohesion of the regime of accumulation is an overall phenomenon which has nothing to do with the flexibility or rigidity of market adjustments. It takes the form of uneven development in the strict sense in which we have understood this, and puts in question the formation of a general rate of profit. We have seen that a mutation in the forces of production necessarily has its origins in the department producing means of production. When it occurs within a particular type of labour process without a major transformation of this process, then it does so by a deepening of the principle of mechanization that induces a rise in the organic composition of capital as the counterpart of the saving on labour-power. Relative surplus-value increases thanks to an ever more intensive renewal of the means of production. Department I consequently grows at an ever more rapid rate.

Now in the case in which the transformation of the conditions of production takes place by a saving of labour-power without a saving of constant capital, corresponding therefore to a rise in the organic composition of capital, the social productivity of labour can increase only if wage costs fall more quickly than the proportion of constant capital in total exchange-value rises. If this is not the case, then the total costs of production increase, and the rate of accumulation slows down until a major transformation of the labour process devalorizes a portion of constant capital and brings about a technical revolution that economizes means of production. If total costs of production fall, the result is an increase in the general rate of profit and an acceleration in the rate of accumulation. But this process can be impaired by diverging forces. On the one hand, the internal development of Department I runs too far ahead, since the social demand for means of production must be ever greater to sustain a sufficient saving of labour-power to permit the fall in the costs of production to continue. On the other hand, the exchange-value of wages distributed undergoes a relative decline, whilst profits build up more and more, particularly in Department I. A moment is necessarily reached when the rate of profit in Department I increases relative to the capital advanced, by virtue of the accelerated development of this department, whereas accumulation in Department II is restrained by the restriction of the social demand for means of consumption. The proportion of income assigned to purchase the exchange-value of Department II grows far less quickly than the proportion of income assigned to purchase means of production, with the result that Department II can no longer purchase the means of production at the rate required to continue the growth in social productivity. There is then an inevitable difference between the rate of profit in Department I and that in Department II. The result is that Department II becomes unable to purchase sufficient means of production to match the rate of growth in Department I, since the distribution of income develops in a way that does not enable the formation of sufficient social demand for means of consumption. In these conditions, the constraint of full realization of exchange-value is transgressed. The difference in rates of profit leads to an overproduction of means of production. The result is a relative contraction of accumulation in Department I, and a restraint on social productivity that blocks any rise in the rate of surplus-value.

We can now complete our synoptic analysis of the organic crisis of the regime of intensive accumulation whose origin we situated in the mid 1960s and which we illustrated by a whole series of diagrams in the second half of Chapter 1.

Diagram 12 presents the movement of the net pre-tax rate of profit, along with various different indicators of the development of total profit as related to fixed capital. The variations in this indicator may be taken as a reasonable estimate of the variations in the general rate of profit. In the context of a long-run tendency to fall, bound up with the slow but steady rise in the organic composition of capital since the Second World War, it is possible to observe the scope of the turn experienced in the second half of the 1960s. We have seen that the first half of this decade was the period of a formidable acceleration in capital formation, permitting a rapid fall in real social wage costs.

Diagram 12. Profitability Indicators (1948-1971)

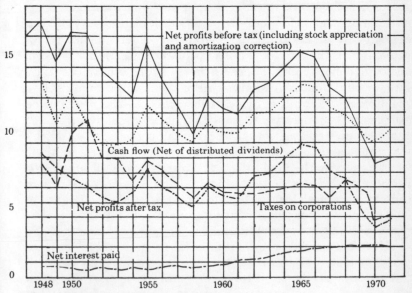

Each variable is related to net fixed capital stock
in non-financial corporations (%)
Net profits = cash flow + distributed dividends
--Depreciation allowances

These conditions of accumulation brought about a spectacular rise in the general rate of profit at the same time as they fostered those tendencies to uneven development whose roots are to be found in the crises of the reproduction of the wage relation.

II. The Competition of Individual Capitals on the Basis of the General Rate of Profit

The formation of the general rate of profit unites the relations of capitalist production and distribution by way of the realization of total exchange-value. This is a social law founded at the macro-economic level. The schema of the expanded reproduction of the social capital embraces all the determinants of the formation and division of total income; it forms the theoretical basis for national accounting and should make possible a rigorous retheorization of its principles. This social law owes nothing to the behaviour of individual capitalists. On the contrary, it determines this behaviour. There is no microeconomics as the praxiology of a rational subject detached from all social conditioning. There are laws of competition that take into account, under the constraint of the law of accumulation, the diversity of forms of competition and the diversity of price systems that follow from them. In studying these laws we shall proceed one step at a time. The first task is to demonstrate the ways in which individual capitals are constrained in their valorization by the general rate of profit. This will lead us to introduce new concepts to elucidate the social link between individual capitals, and will yield an interpretation of what are generally known as prices of production very different from that of classical economics. We shall then take into account the effects of the centralization of capital for a study of the concrete price systems obtaining in the United States. The detailed analysis of these systems, however, cannot form part of a work whose aim is to develop a general theory of capitalist regulation.

1. The Modalities of the Division of Capital into Fractions

The division of capital into independent capitals derives from the fact that capitalism is a commodity economy in which social labour is not the result of a collective organization of production but rather of a confrontation between independent private labours. This confrontation takes the form of a process of competition in which the independent capitals seeking to realize a rate of profit for their valorization are constrained to adjust themselves to the general rate of profit. The process through which capitals oppose one another is thus the same as that in which they express their solidarity vis-à-vis the wage-earning class, since it tends to reduce them to the status of 'equivalent capitals', simple fractions of a social capital that appropriates a total profit and divides it up among its constitutive elements in proportion to their respective sizes. Defined in this way, *competition is a process of unification of the capitalist class*. But it is not enough in itself to accomplish this unification, which is closely dependent on the creation of structural forms, particularly that of the company, in which the vital practices of valorization are internalized and protected. We have also seen that the centralization of capital is a process of unification in its remodelling of proprietary control itself. We must thus be more precise. We are now going to investigate competition as an *external* economic link between capitals that already enjoy autonomy and are organized into companies with independent proprietary controls. We can call this distribution of capitalist ownership *full competition*. Only after having established the laws of full competition will we be able to deal in the last section of this chapter with the complications arising from the forms of competition engendered by the centralization of capital.

The external relations between individual capitals can be defined on the basis of the concept of industrial *branch*. This concept designates a division in general commodity circulation. Between industrial branches there are markets on which different categories of commodity circulate. As the commodity is the fundamental principle behind the individualization of capitals, the industrial branch is a common arena of capitals which, while remaining individual, produce the same category of commodity and consequently are valorized under the constraint of those conditions of production that are socially dominant. The appropriateness of the concept of branch for the investigation of relations of competition between autonomous capitals is confirmed by the structural forms created in this economic space. The procedures of collective bargaining over wages, in effect, occur within these branches, and it is at this level that firms organize into the typical institutions of class struggle that are employers' associations. This point is a fundamental one. It clearly shows how competition involves a capitalist solidarity induced by the wage relation. The fact that all enterprises in an industrial branch can count on identical rules as far as the formation and evolution of the basic wage is concerned is an essential element in the formation of the socially dominant conditions of production. But the organization of firms into an industrial branch in no way implies total similarity in the concrete processes of production. From this standpoint, a branch may well present itself simply as a diverse variety of lines of production. This should in no way be surprising. The homogenization of production conditions takes place exclusively in terms of value. If, over time, old production processes disappear and new ones are created, this is a process entirely determined by the evolution of the homogeneous relations of value.

We can now define the way in which the constraint of competition is imposed via the division into branches, thereby formulating at the same time the socially dominant conditions of production. Let us recall that we are discussing a situation of full competition. Our definition, then, is that the exchange-value of the sum total of commodities is divided between the different branches in such a way that the total capital invested in each branch yields a rate of profit equal to the general rate. There then exists a system of exchange relations that is evidently stable only in so far as the division of labour remains unchanged. There is an instantaneous system of *norms of production and exchange* that is not exactly respected by the valorization of individual capitals, but to which these are constrained to refer, and which governs the distribution of total profit. This system of norms implies that total income is divided in such a way that a monetary social demand purchases a determinate amount of each category of commodity, so that the rates of profit realized on average in each branch approximate the general rate of profit. Given the unambiguous determination of this social demand, each industrial branch operates on average in conditions of production that are socially and *actually* dominant. Everything happens as if a single social capital were valorized by dividing up into a set of qualitatively different commodities. The unit price that follows from the norm of production and exchange in each branch is known as the *price of production*. In the purely illustrative case in which the turnover period is the same for capitals in each different branch, the definition of the price of production is simple, since it is expressed as a mark up on the theoretical cost of production that reflects the socially dominant conditions of production:

Theoretical cost of production $x(1 + r) =$ price of production, where r is the general rate of profit, determined in advance together with wage costs. This system is not homogeneous; it determines the monetary prices.

Given an exact understanding of the significance of the norms of production and exchange, we can give a synthetic definition of the industrial branch. *The branch is the economic space formed by capitals subject to the same norm of production and exchange.*

Certain results can already be drawn from this preliminary elucidation of the laws of capitalist competition. The formation of prices of production is a procedure specific to capitalism. It specifies exchange-values by imposing a constraint on the field of value. This constraint forms part of the laws of regulation, since it signifies that capitalism has an overall unity despite the fragmentation that commodity production implies. It is the only commodity-producing mode of production in all history that has such a unity. But the formation of these prices of production signifies nothing more than the universal dictatorship of the law of accumulation, which grows as the wage relation is generalized. A procedure that is internal to a particular mode of production can in no way claim to be a universal rule of social efficiency. Its rationality is entirely contained within the formation of the general rate of profit, in which social labour-power is reduced to the position of an ingredient of capital. Prices of production are indissolubly linked to the existence of wage-labour. Those who believe that this rationality can be used to regulate a socialist mode of production are victims of a serious illusion, commodity fetishism. Under this illusion, they conceive socialism as optimal control over a planned market. In reality, however, the advancement of the working class demands collective mastery of social labour, the end of wage-labour and with it of the blind logic of prices of production. It is at the overall level of the formation of incomes and the coherence of the two departments of production that the means for a socially mastered regulation are located. Social mastery of newly created value abolishes the law of accumulation. The conditions in which the local agents of economic activity operate are then necessarily transformed. The constraints that they experience can in no case be expressed as the formation of a system of prices of production.

2. The Struggle Between Capitals in the Transformation of Norms of Production and Exchange

The concepts we have just developed will enable us to analyse the process of competition itself. The socially dominant conditions of production in each industrial branch are transformed by the sum total of forces intervening in relative surplus-value, as we have studied these in the first part of this book. These conditions are always changing, and this is why the system of norms of production and exchange develops over time. This development goes as far as to put in question the partition of total exchange-value into categories of commodity. A radical quantitative change in the forces of production, in effect, gives rise to the disappearance of certain branches and the creation of new ones. There is a displacement of the constraint of competition in the homogeneous field of value, and thus an instability of relations of exchange equivalence over time. It is none the less true that the reconstitution of the general equivalent guarantees that prices permanently preserve the theoretical status demonstrated at the beginning of this chapter, and that they are always determinate. The evolution of the system of norms of production and exchange is therefore the evolution in time of a system of relations of equivalence which are always defined in the same abstract homogeneous space. Competition consequently only takes on any meaning in the concrete process that transforms the social conditions of production. Such a transformation is initiated by those individual capitals that find themselves in a position to create conditions of production that are exceptionally favourable in relation to those that are socially dominant. They set in motion a labour which is exceptionally productive, at the local level, in relation to that embodied in the formation of the social price presently prevailing for the variety of commodity in question. The spur here is the quest for the highest possible rate of profit, which mobilizes the sum total of those practices of company management that we studied in Chapter 4. If the price of production was immediately governed by these marginal conditions of production, i.e. those of exceptional productivity, then the unit price of these commodities would be lower than the social price. The latter would immediately disappear, and the most efficient firm would govern the social price. But this is not what takes place. The norm of production and exchange follows from the division of total exchange-value by the social demand, expressed in money terms, that purchases the mass of commodities in this category. The social unit price is consequently an average, and necessarily endowed with a certain inertia. Relations of commodity exchange sanction the social price, and inasmuch as the new conditions of production remain the exception, then the previously formed price still prevails. During a period of transition everything happens as if the labour of exceptional productivity counted as a complex labour that conferred on the capitalists who dispose of it the advantage of selling their particular commodities above their individual price. These capitals receive a rate of profit higher than the general rate. They appropriate a *surplus* profit in the total distribution.

However, the struggle between capitals that forms the stimulus for this exceptional productivity creates a force that tends to cancel out its exceptional character. The situation which enabled the difference between the virtual individual price and the social price to arise disappears as competition forces more and more capitalists to adopt the new conditions of production. In order to benefit from these, the most efficient capitalists, who become more and more numerous, reduce their prices below the former social price. To the extent that the new conditions of production become general, an ever greater portion of social demand purchases commodities produced in the new way. The social price changes to the extent that a greater portion of the mass of commodities are produced in the new conditions. When these latter become socially dominant, the new price of production is established, and enables the capitals operating in accordance with it to receive a rate of profit equal to the general rate. The continuity of the price system is respected in the course of the transformation, which may be more or less rapid according to the concrete situation of competition. The cohesion of exchange relations is maintained even though the relations of equivalence evolve. But since the transformation of the conditions of production is permanent, the social market price is constantly influenced by new forces, so that the price of production is in perpetual flux. The norms of production and exchange that are in course of transformation, however, make competition intelligible for what it is, a process and not a static state of equilibrium. In this sense, statistical observations of the prices of production must be conceived as an average over a period of time in which, in a situation of full competition, the rate of profit for the industrial branch in question tends to fall into line with the general rate of profit.

In the originating movement of these new conditions of production, there are always individual capitals unable to follow the transformation. They make profits below the general rate, or even experience losses. This means that the labour expended under their direction cannot fully count as socially necessary labour. This disability may lead to their elimination. The only solution then available to them is to interrupt their current process of valorization and go into massive debts to acquire the new and very expensive means of production required for the new methods. They can do this only by a more or less brutal devalorization of a portion of their capital presently immobilized in productive functions. The most drastic form of devalorization is the dismantling of plant and the closing of production units. In certain cases, an attenuated devalorization is possible by a running down of the old production units.

We can thus grasp the meaning of devalorization from the

standpoint of the competition between individual capitals. This is a process of expulsion by which norms of production and exchange are imposed, and the unification of the capitalist mode of production consequently accomplished. It is the necessary complement of the struggle between capitals constantly in search of new advantages. The capitals left behind are threatened with disappearance as autonomous centres of appropriation of social labour. They can only reinsert themselves into social capital at the cost of a far-reaching reorganization of their practices of valorization. In all cases, though, there is always the sanction of lack of social validation for private labours.

3. Production Prices and Fluctuations in Market Prices

At the point we have now reached, the general principle of capitalist competition has already been established. All prices are exchange values. Prices of production are prices regulating the transformation of the conditions of production. This interpretation of prices directly permits a concrete analysis, because it is linked to a conceptualization of historical time. This is why it is radically different from the definition of the classic price systems as systems related to a logical time. This difference is a function of the point of departure, i.e. the conception of the commodity itself. Through the notion of general equivalent, the Marxist procedure is able to found an objective measurement that is prior to the determination of the price system. Once the general conditions of commensurability are established, this procedure does not have to impose any artificial conditions on prices to render economic magnitudes measurable.

It is incorrect therefore to oppose production prices to market prices. We have seen, however, that the norms of production and exchange are progressively transformed over time. Now historical time does not just have one single dimension. It is rather a complex temporality in which several rhythms of transformation are superimposed. It is quite possible for phenomena to arise which act on the momentary exchange relations without involving the transformation of the conditions of production. As a result, fluctuations in market price may exist independent of the process of transformation of the norms of production and exchange we described above. Two types of phenomenon must be carefully distinguished here.

The first kind is only local in scope. It derives from the fact that the different portions of capital that a firm invests in production do not have the same turnover time. The transformation of the conditions of production involves planning by companies which anticipate future exceptional conditions of production before creating them. In fact, this transformation generally requires the operation of new durable means of production, and even the installation of new production units. Organization of such projects presupposes that a long-term social demand in the branch in question has been anticipated, making it possible to profit from new investments of productive capital. These are the strategic investments analysed in Chapter 4. The function of production prices is to express in the homogeneous space of value those socially dominant conditions of production whose evolution is commanded by the rhythm of structural changes. But the circulating capital whose turnover is the concern of the day-to-day management of the firm, is bound up with anticipations of effective demand in the flows of circulation, whose periodicity is generally much shorter. These flows may be affected by all kinds of disturbances and errors of prediction, which generally cancel out and correct themselves in the course of structural changes. But they nevertheless have their effect on the flows of receipts and expenditures for the firms in question, affecting their gross profits in the short term. Price fluctuations are far from absorbing all of these disturbances. They are absorbed rather by buffer flows which are relatively flexible within the cycle of metamorphoses that forms the valorization of the individual capital. These buffer flows involve increases and decreases in stocks of finished commodities and supplies, fluctuations in credit which enable stocks to be financed and expenditures on a new production cycle to be initiated without having to wait for proceeds from the previous cycle, and greater or lesser recourse to liquid reserves that are not set aside for any immediate purpose. Even so, these buffer flows can themselves amplify the disturbances in demand, if a large enough number of companies create a sudden demand for stock in addition to the current effective demand. Such amplification is the root of speculative behaviour, and of precautionary measures against the risk of a valorization cycle being endangered by shortages. Shortages in turn are caused by the combination of precautionary purchases themselves. Such unstable situations give rise to violent price fluctuations which have nothing to do with the evolution of production prices, and have no serious effect in the long run.

The second kind of phenomenon relates to a far more important and general instability. We know that the formation of prices of production is a function of relations of competition that are bound up with the general rate of profit. But we also know that accumulation as a whole is subject to antagonistic forces which may give rise to general crises, initially through the uneven development of the two departments of production, but prolonged by the non-realization of total exchange-value. In situations of this kind, the conditions for the existence of a general rate of profit do not obtain. The regulation of prices thus breaks down, and relations of competition are then radically modified. From external relations of conflict on the market, waged by capitals whose autonomy is still preserved, they become a force restructuring property in an open struggle for control, through waves of mergers in which available monetary resources are mobilized. In these periods, typically cautious behaviour in all markets gives way to a generalized overproduction of commodities and a massive devalorization of capital. The general price level first rises and then falls, accompanied by major distortions in the relative evolution of prices for particular categories of goods. Relations of competition can only be reorganized once general transformations of the wage relation create a new overall cohesion for the regime of accumulation, by opening a new phase of long-term rise in the rate of surplus-value. The general crises of accumulation are the most striking manifestation of the fact that competition and market relations are subordinate to the class struggle.

III. The Formation of Prices in the Movement of Centralization of Capital

We have put forward a theory of the formation of prices of production in a situation of full competition. This is why the norms of production and exchange involve a rule of distribution of the overall profit which unambiguously determines a normal profit for each branch. This normal profit is such as to give a rate of profit in line with the general rate, when related to the productive capital invested in the prevailing social conditions of production. The evolution of the norms of production and exchange under the influence of the transformation of the conditions of production in the economic system as a whole implies that these norms function as forces giving competition its bearings over time. They are dynamic constraints which reflect the social interdependence between capitals and tend to reduce local differences in the conditions of valorization that are constantly recreated anew under the impulse of the antagonism of the wage relation, which forces each autonomous centre of direction of the productive forces to seek out its optimum conditions of exploitation. As a result, the effective equality of rates of profit on the individual capitals is not actually realized at any given point in time. The general equalization of rates of profit must be understood as an average over time in a double sense. On the one hand, the spectrum of rates of profit within a single branch has a range that fluctuates as a function of the intensity of the structural transformations taking place there, and the different enterprises do not always occupy the same position in this spectrum. On the other hand, taking all branches together, prices of production may be considered as tendencies governing prices behind possible transient disturbances, in historical periods when the general conditions of accumulation make possible the formation of a general rate of profit.

It is clear enough that the concept of norm of production and exchange does not depend on the application that is made of it to particular external relations between individual capitals, relations of full competition. This concept enables us to give a theoretical interpretation of the division of total exchange-value that is effected in capitalist commodity circulation. Its significance as an expression of the socially prevailing conditions of production remains intact when the centralization of capital creates new relations of competition. The norms of production and exchange still define certain constraints on the homogeneous field of value, but these constraints are no longer expressed in the form of a general equalization of rates of profit. Competition still forms prices of production, i.e. prices regulating the valorization of capitals in periods of structural change. But the norms of production and exchange embody relationships of asymmetrical influence deriving from the centralization of capital. Price systems are created which match the different forms of competition, are compatible with a structural and permanent differentiation of rates of profit, and tend towards a permanently uneven distribution of total profit. The condition for price systems of this kind to become solidly established is evidently that the social demand for different categories of commodity is congruent with the asymmetrical relationships of competition. This is why the hierarchical stratification of incomes based on the differentiations within the wage-earning class is an indispensable component of what we can call *monopolistic competition*, as opposed to full competition.[3] It is also why direct action on the formation of social demand becomes a means of competition, through the various practices that seek to manufacture consumer statuses for different income groups and different social positions.

1. The Role of Surplus Profit under Full and Monopolistic Competition

In order to distinguish monopolistic competition from full competition theoretically, before surveying the concrete forms that govern market behaviour, it is necessary first of all to show how these two types of relationship between capitals are distinguished as ways of realizing relative surplus-value through the transformation of the conditions of production. This analysis is of considerable theoretical interest, since it makes it possible to define more precisely what the competition of separate capitals involves. A demonstration of how two types of competition are constitutive modalities of two types of regulation supposes that it is possible to define competition conceptually as a structural form of capitalism, in close relation with the general concepts used to analyse the wage relation.

---

[3] The concept of monopolistic competition introduced here is obviously very different from that customarily defined by reference to general equilibrium in opposition to pure and perfect competition. For this latter, see E. H. Chamberlain, *The Theory of Monopolistic Competition*, Cambridge, Mass., 1935, and J. Robinson, *The Economics of Imperfect Competition*, London, 1959.

This is necessary in particular to dispel the illusions held by many Marxists about the 'power of the monopolies', and to avoid making inter-capitalist relationships into the chief domain of the transformations of contemporary capitalism. We have begun this theoretical analysis of competition by defining the unity of separate capitals as a system of norms of production and exchange. It is now necessary to show in greater detail the precise ways in which the continuous transformation of these norms is possible without the separate economic units being deprived of any social reference for regulating their behaviour. The elements of this problem are, as we have seen, the monetary form of price and surplus profit. The question now is to disclose their theoretical significance. We should note that this problem cannot be raised in either classical or neo-classical orthodoxy. Even though the price system assumes a very different sense for each of these schools, it always possesses the characteristic that it can only be defined in relative terms and depends on the exogenous variable of the conditions of production and exchange. Transition from one set of conditions to another is totally unintelligible here. Only the Marshallian school has sought to tackle this problem with a typology of equilibria over time. But for want of any support in an adequate theory of value, this empirical approach cannot analyse the real historical process of irreversible transformations of the conditions of production. Only a theory of value for which the monetary form of price is not a disguise, but rather the exclusive modality of homogenization of production activities and the conditions of existence for exchange relations, can go beyond the notion of a coherent system of relative prices. The permanence over time of monetary prices makes it possible to understand the incoherence over time of the price system as the characteristic of any real dynamic – in other words, one that is irreversible and radically uncertain for the individual economic agents caught up in it. Surplus profits and monetary losses reveal these incoherences vis-à-vis any underlying system of norms of production and exchange, and are at the same time the immediate forces for the transition from one system to another.

To comprehend more precisely the significance of this process, we shall take a simple schematic example that can be treated numerically. Consider the situation of a branch producing a commodity of which all units are homogeneous and whose unit exchange-value is expressed as follows, as a function of the actual conditions of production:

$$VE = C + V + SV$$
$$\$2 = 1 + 0.8 + 0.2$$

This is the monetary expression of the norm of production and exchange presently obtaining in the branch in question. Let us now consider the introduction of a new production procedure that makes it possible to double the apparent productivity of living labour in the branch. For the sake of simplification, we can assume that the constant capital consumed per item remains the same, as this in no way affects the nature of the problem we are studying here.

To analyse the manner in which the new production method is generalized, we can follow first Marx's own argument, which relates to the situation under full competition. We can draw a general conclusion from this, and will then indicate how it should be applied to the case of monopolistic competition.

The new production process is characterized in our hypothesis by an individual exchange value:

$$VE' = C + VA$$
$$\$1.5 = 1 + 0.5.$$

This applies to a particular and still virtual exchange-value, since the new conditions of production remain exceptional in the branch. The prevailing exchange-value, i.e. the social market value, is still determined by the former production conditions. Since the social norm remains unchanged, the innovating capitalists can in principle sell their commodities at any point in the range between the particular value and the social value, realizing a greater or lesser surplus profit. If they are to realize the maximum surplus profit, they must be able to sell twice the number of units represented by their current share of the market in prevalent selling conditions. To the extent that the social demand for this category of commodity is unchanged – a hypothesis retained by Marx, which assumes that effective monetary demand remains constant – then the sale of the innovating capitalists' output requires an expansion of their share of the market by a reduction of their market price below the social value, but still above the individual value. The fixing of this market price (say $1.8, for example) is a strategic decision that cannot be represented by any functional relationship. It determines the surplus profit that will actually be obtained. The redivision of market shares is the coercive force that pushes the other capitalists to adopt the new manufacturing process or else abandon the branch in question. This is why the market price is gradually reduced to $1.5, which becomes the new social market value. The proof that the new production norm has really been established is the disappearance of surplus profits, which coincides with a new distribution of market shares.

This process as a whole has the following theoretical significance. *Transitory surplus profit is the expression of a measurement in the space of existing social values* (the norms of production and exchange in force) *of conditions of production that do not pertain to this system of values.* When surplus profit disappears, this is the sign that these conditions now do so pertain; but the old conditions of production will then have been destroyed and the capital still fixed in them devalorized. The repercussion of the new social market value in the branch in question on the norm of consumption is the process of *conversion of surplus profit into relative surplus-value.* It attests to the fact that the local transformation of the productive forces is socially necessary from the standpoint of the logic of development of the wage relation. This ability of the monetary determination of prices to give an objective economic representation to local changes in the division of labour beyond the coherence of a system of production prices can be called the *pivoting of value.* It is the continuous evolution of nominal market prices that maintains over time the social link between individual capitals, despite the heterogeneity of the conditions of production. The pivoting of value is thus the homogenization by the monetary exchange $C-M$ through which the value generated in a particular productive operation is measured within the current system of norms of production and exchange. The superiority of the productive labour performed in conditions of production that are still exceptional is socially confirmed in the form of a greater right of appropriation over social surplus-value. Surplus profit is the diffracted measurement of value produced in this production process.

In the above presentation, the fact that the reduction in surplus profit takes the form of a decrease in market price is due to the assumption that the effective demand addressed to the sum total of producers in the branch in question is invariable for each of them at a given price. The restructuring of competitive positions which enables the new conditions of production to penetrate can only be achieved, therefore, by the exclusion from the market of those capitalists who persist in using the old production methods. This exclusion is effected by a reduction in profits, or even the incurrence of losses. Effective demand ends up by increasing *ex post*, but only as a result of the fall in market price. Yet we must still distinguish the theoretical notion of the pivoting of value from the concrete modalities by which this pivoting is effected. To understand this distinction properly, it is necessary to note that in a capitalist economy moved by permanent transformation of production conditions, the social value in each branch is not determined by marginal conditions, which are always evanescent and obtain only for a small number of producers with negligible influence. In actual practice, the distribution of production conditions is not continuous but discrete. Social market value is a means of distributing individual values corresponding to the different production processes that coexist in the branch, as weighted by the shares of the market that these processes supply. The weighting coefficients, therefore, do not depend solely on the spectrum of technical conditions, but also on the total effective monetary demand that can be tendentially satisfied, i.e. without a temporary increase or decrease in stocks, and without abnormal over- or under-utilization of productive capacity. Variations in stocks and in the utilization of productive capacity are the elements of flexibility that make momentary market prices diverge from social market values. The result is that the concrete formation of relative surplus-value through the pivoting of value involves in principle a double process: variation of the distribution of individual values for the producers, and variation in effective demand between the different branches. This double process governs the dynamic reallocation of social labour. In the form of regulation of competition that we have described only one of these two processes comes into play. Since effective demand is assumed not to have any generative force independent of price, the fall in market price is the mechanism that sets the pivoting of value in motion. It redistributes market shares and makes possible the emergence of a new social value.

But there is no reason to believe that competition can be reduced to this partial process. We can be quite certain, in fact, that this is not the case once capitalism has entered the historical phase of generalization of the wage relation. The formation of the social norm of consumption that is associated with procedures of collective wage bargaining, and with the socialization of risks, gives the deployment of effective demand over the different branches an autonomous force. The centraliz-ation of capital, moreover, has given rise to organizational forms which link production, commerce and finance closely together. Thus the size and means of action of innovating firms are now in many fields such as to allow them to plan the tendencies of effective demand in advance by incorporating into their calculations the probable effects of new structural forms. The result is that these firms no longer have to take the demand for the branch as a constant, once prices are given. They may on the contrary consider that an output increased by new and more efficient methods can be sold at a market price equal to the former social value. A new modality of pivoting of value then becomes possible. It denotes a new form of competition inserted within a monopolistic regulation. There is still the formation of a surplus profit, but the conversion of the surplus profit into relative surplus-value follows a different course. We shall demonstrate this by returning to the example introduced above.

The pivoting of value is necessarily accomplished by a modification of market shares. When the effective demand for the branch does not have a dynamic of its own, then the total size of the market is given. This is why the reallocation of market shares in favour of the innovating capitalists takes place to the detriment of the *volume* of sales made by the other capitalists. Price wars derive from this situation. If, on the contrary, a regular growth in effective demand is the effect of a set of procedures of social regulation, then the innovating capitalists will be able to improve their market shares by capturing the *increase* in demand at a given price. The other capitalists then maintain their level of sales. The conditions of competition make possible an introduction of technical progress which can be planned in advance and is far less beset with obstacles. There is no need at all to invent any 'monopoly power', as the majority of economists do, to reach this result. It arises from the combination of structural forms involved in the development of the wage relation and issuing from the centralization of capital. 'Monopoly power' is in reality simply the effect of the sum total of social structures on economic adjustments. We can better denote this effect by the term *monopolistic regulation*. The illusion of a 'monopoly power' is related to the fact that if the branch is considered in isolation instead of being seen as an element in a system of norms of production and exchange, then everything happens as if the innovating firms created their own market.

The pivoting of value may then take place without a fall in price. In the same example, the former social market value of 2 dollars remains the basis from which the introduction of exceptional production conditions departs. The surplus profit is far larger than in the context of full competition. It gives the innovators a cash flow which they can use to expand their productive capacities. The strategic decision is the one that enables them to choose the optimal rate of increase in sales. This involves an increase in wage costs deriving both from a partial redistribution of surplus profits to the wage-earners by way of compensation for their acceptance of technical changes, and from an increase in the commercial overheads necessary to sell the increased output. The unified formation of wages in the branch, whether this is direct by collective bargaining procedures, or indirect through a diffusion resulting from the mobility of labour-power, gives rise to a generalization of the wage increase. Two essential effects follow from this. Within the branch, other firms have to match the increased wages that ensue from the initiative of the innovators. If they cling to the old conditions of production, then they experience a reduction in their profits. In order to react, they are obliged either to introduce the new techniques themselves, or else to leave the branch altogether. So far as the position of the branch in the social division of labour is concerned, the wage rise contributes to maintaining the general process of regular increase in monetary incomes. Thus *the increase in monetary wages plays* the role in the pivoting of value that fell previously to the decrease in prices. The asymmetrical movement of wages, resistant to a fall and pulled upward by the changes in production conditions, becomes an essential aspect of the valorization of capital, by permitting the social validation of investments that transform production methods.

Assuming that daily output under former conditions of production was 10 units, we could construct the following table to describe the full effects of the pivoting of value:

	Old situation	*New situation*
Daily Output	10 units	20 units
Unit Social Value	2 dollars	2 dollars
Daily Wage	8 dollars	12 dollars
Total Cost Price	18 dollars	32 dollars
Total Sale Price	20 dollars	40 dollars

Here it is the rise in wages from 8 to 12 dollars that is the strategic decision of the innovators. Let us then assume that under the former conditions the production of one unit of a commodity required 2 hours of labour (1 hour direct labour in the branch and 1 hour embodied labour). Since what is involved, under our hypothesis, is labour time performed according to the norm of production and exchange prevailing before the technical innovation, the product of one hour's abstract labour is validated by the market at 1 dollar. In the new situation, the unit of the commodity is always sold at 2 dollars, but its production now requires only $1\frac{1}{2}$ hours (1 hour's embodied labour plus $\frac{1}{2}$ hour direct labour, given that productivity is doubled). The product of 1 hour's abstract labour is therefore now valued at $1\frac{1}{3}$ dollars. Our conclusion is that *a complete pivoting of value is effected through a rise in the monetary expression of an hour's abstract labour.* The 1 dollar which formerly represented 1 hour's abstract labour (as validated by the market on sale) now represents only $\frac{3}{4}$ hour. The consequence of this is quite fundamental for the nature of competition under monopolistic regulation. The conversion of surplus profit into relative surplus-value combines into a single process the rise in nominal wages and the fall in the value of money. This is the fundamental principle of *creeping inflation*, which is a regulation of the regime of intensive accumulation that makes possible the continuous social validation of a permanent transformation in the conditions of production. The characteristics of the monetary institution that in turn make creeping inflation possible will be studied in the following chapter. Let us note for the moment that the theoretical definition of inflation has nothing to do with the rise in an empirical index of prices. In the schematic example studied here, creeping inflation takes the form of a stability of nominal price in the presence of a doubling of the apparent productivity of living labour. This result is paradoxical only for fanatical defenders of the quantity theory of money. It is entirely logical in the real economy, which is monetary through and through and is in no way the juxtaposition of an exogenous monetary mass with a system of relative equilibrium prices determined independently of any monetary condition.

2. The Factors that Differentiate Rates of Profit

In order to study monopolistic competition, though we can only deal with its basic principles here, it is necessary first of all to return to the concept of industrial branch. We have seen how branches divide up markets by differentiating between categories of commodity. Now the structural determinants of the centralization of capital alter the very existence of these branches, by processes of integration and diversification of production. We shall therefore examine the consequences of the centralization of capital on the stability of the division into branches, before proceeding to analyse the relations between the giant corporations.

(a) Integration of branches and transformation of commodities.
The specialization of production processes, the creation of zones of integration in the division of labour, and the diversification and transformation of use-values are infrastructural processes of the development of norms of production and exchange under the regime of intensive accumulation that we have labelled Fordism. Specialization and vertical integration of production destroy branches that previously existed

without involving the disappearance of the corresponding labour processes. These branches become technico-economic lines in a larger and reorganized branch. The products that leave these lines are no more than pseudo-commodities, entering into the production of complex commodities as intermediate products. They are pseudo-commodities in the sense that they are not products of labour that have directly to seek social validation in general circulation. The labour spent on their production becomes the object of coordination within a general plan for the integrated enterprise. When the relations between enterprises take the form of sub-contracting, then economic dependence in ways other than the external relations of competition is readily apparent. But this dependence exists even where there is no sub-contracting in the strict sense. There are generally a swarm of small-scale firms operating on intermediate segments of valorization in integrated economic lines, and supplying their products to a small number of giant corporations who hold that link in the chain towards which everything upstream must necessarily converge, and on which everything downstream must be exclusively dependent. This is why these small firms can control the technical characteristics of their labour process independently without having that economic autonomy which would make it legitimate to speak of centres of capitalist appropriation. For them, capital is not abstract (hence essentially mobile) value. These firms are tied to particular technical conditions and have no way of transferring their activities to a different field of commodity production, even one immediately adjacent. This is the essential criterion of the pseudo-commodity and technico-economic dependence. In this case, the norm of production and exchange is established for the integrated economic line as a whole. It imposes on partial segments of valorization certain technico-economic norms that determine *transfer prices* for these pseudo-commodities. There can be no general rule for the distribution of profit within the integrated line. Investigations must be made case by case. The rates of profit for the captive firms are not necessarily low in periods of normal activity, if these firms manage to benefit from the super-exploitation of a sub-proletariat made up of categories of disadvantaged wage-earners trapped in secluded reservoirs of labour. But these firms operate in a situation of total economic insecurity, without any possibility of reacting to deleterious changes in general economic conditions.

Just as there exist zones of integration in commodity production, so there exist zones of diversification, where the obsolescence of use-values is very pronounced and the norms of production and exchange do not stabilize sufficiently for distinct industrial branches to separate out, encompassing different groups of firms. Competition between capitals here becomes a strategic combat for the elimination of adversaries.[4] The objective of each capital is not simply to make sure of a dominant position in a particular economic line, as a bastion of valorization with a particular variety of commodity as its support. It is to control the means and rhythm of diversification itself. As long as this struggle continues, the relations of competition are those of absorption, merger, and association of firms. The importance of strategic investments, the time they take to mature, the great variation in local conditions of valorization, all make it impossible to speak of a competition governed by an immanent social norm. But the outcome of the strategic struggle is always the emergence of a new branch or group of branches in which norms of production and exchange are established. At the same time, a few giant corporations consolidate their positions and stabilize their external relations by interconnecting their investments in the different economic lines within the field of diversification. The resulting form of competition is that of *stratified oligopoly*. This form is characteristic of the regime of intensive accumulation. It extends to all categories of commodities included in the social norm of consumption, once these have reached the stage of maturity. The formation of this type of competition is closely bound up with the development of the social norm of consumption. The latter is organized according to functional processes that form the supports of dense complexes of commodities. The complementarities indicated in Chapter 3, and the need to overcome the financial problems involved in the acquisition of consumer durables for the broad mass of the wage-earning class, mean that the expansion of commodity production conquers the

---

[4] See A. Cotta, *Les choix économiques de la grande entreprise*, Paris, 1970.

spheres of consumption one by one. When a new sphere is annexed, it is the base for a new zone of diversification, in which the processes described above come into play, while the increase in effective demand responds to the phenomena of diffusion that are studied at length by the theorists of consumption. When the new sphere has come fully into mass consumption, and the social demand for it is stabilized and largely a response to the need for replacements, then competition between capitals in this field becomes more rigid and more predictable. This is the period of stratified oligopoly, corresponding to stable external relations between centralized capitals.

(b) Competition between firms in stratified oligopoly. The relations of competition that are characteristic of stratified oligopoly can be summed up under the concept of *barriers to entry.* Barriers exist to entry into a field of commodity production if capitals outside this field that try to invest in it and establish a new valorization cycle experience conditions that set them at a persistent disadvantage in relation to capitals already established. This disadvantage may depend on various different structural elements, such as the protection of manufacturing secrets, control over supplies, crystallization of a variety of markets in which positions of competition are rendered rigid by a brand hierarchy, major economies of scale in production, etc.

In order to define more precisely the influence of these barriers to entry on the formation of prices, it is useful to refer to the price of production under full competition as previously analysed, which follows by definition from the constraint of competition where there are no barriers to entry. Let us investigate whether a price of production for monopolistic competition can exist, and if so in what relationship it stands to the price of production under full competition.

We may take a branch in which a norm of production and exchange is already established. Let Q_n be the quantity of commodities of a particular variety produced in the branch in a given period of time, independent of any short-term disturbances. The establishment of the production price under full competition can then be determined as follows.

Let K be the sum of fixed costs transferred in the period for which normal production is Q_n. K depends on the relative size of the fixed capital, its age structure, average turnover and those structural costs related to the management of production.

Let V be the total direct cost of production for each of the units produced: the cost in circulating constant capital, in variable capital, and sales cost. It is understood that all these costs are determined on the basis of a valorization of their elements at prices of production under the prevailing system of norms. These are therefore monetary magnitudes.

The total cost of production per unit produced (i.e. the theoretical long-term cost of production) in the social conditions of production of the time is: $K/Q_n + V$.

If we call p the price of production in full competition for the branch in question, and r the general rate of profit, then p is determined as follows:

$$p = (\frac{K}{Q_n} + V)(1 + r)$$

The existence of barriers to entry is expressed in the fact that $(K/Q_n + V)_e$ is structurally greater for new capitals seeking to establish themselves in the branch than the $(K/Q_n + V)_f$ for capitals already operating. What is involved here, therefore, is not just a simple distribution of individual costs of production around the norm. In the conditions under investigation, in fact, the very movement of capital is fundamentally affected, since none of the capitals seeking entry is able to realize the general rate of profit at the price under full competition. The upshot is that they do not invest in this branch. But if this is the case, then the same production Q_n can be realized at a price higher than that under full competition, and can yield a rate of profit higher than the general rate, up to the establishment of a *limit price*:

$$p_1 = (\frac{K}{Q_n} + V)_f(1 + r_1)$$

such that capitals newly entering exactly realize the general rate of profit:

$$p_1 = (\frac{K}{Q_n} + V)_e(1 + r)$$

The limit price p_1 is a price of production of monopolistic competition. It embodies a surplus profit that is cornered by the branch as a whole and divided among the giant corporations in a stratified oligopoly. The rate of this surplus profit is equal to:

$$r_1 - r = \frac{p_1 - p}{(\frac{K}{Q_n} + V)_f}$$

It can be taken for granted that this limit price involves a restriction on the volume of output, since the same effective demand on money terms is satisfied at a higher unit price. This price can be formed and maintained so long as the objective determinants of the barriers to entry subsist. It genuinely is a price of production of monopolistic competition, since it does not result from some 'imperfection' in exchange, but is actually founded in the local conditions of production.

The stability of this price is the stability of the barriers to entry. This stability is not a mechanical one, but involves the persistence of a metastable state that may be of long duration, in which the formation of stratified oligopoly is already the resultant of the consolidation of competition in a zone of diversification.[5]

There is therefore a general alteration in the development of the norms of production and exchange as described in the situation of full competition. In place of a transformation of norms assuring a continuous evolution of production prices, we have the stabilization of oligopolistic domains characterized by very rigid production prices of monopolistic competition, and by zones of destruction of former oligopolistic fields as the result of a radical transformation in the conditions of production or the formation of new complexes of commodities in the wake of the development of the social norm of consumption. These zones are highly unstable. They are characterized by price wars, and by restructuration of capitalist proprietary control. There is a kind of *explosion of the forms of competition* that considerably modifies the social link between capitals. The further the distance from the regulatory forms of full com-

[5] Sylos Labini, *Oligopoly and Technical Progress*, Harvard, 1962.

petition, the more the structural forms by which centralized proprietary control operates acquire importance, and the more the hidden powers of finance capital impose themselves, thanks to their disposal over more and more colossal masses of money capital.

3. New Modalities of Devalorization: Planned Obsolescence and Accelerated Amortization

The effect of these new general modalities of devalorization on the laws of competition is only intelligible if we bear in mind the specific mode of cohesion of the regime of intensive accumulation. This regime can only develop by creating the structural forms needed to confront the new guise in which the contradictions of the law of accumulation present themselves. The centralization of capital, chiefly in its financial aspect, and the transition from full competition to monopolistic competition are the conditions for these new modalities of devalorization to arise. At the local level of the firm, these modalities are characterized by the fact that devalorization is anticipated and compensated by a financial flow which is incorporated *a priori* into the cost of production entering into the formation of the price of production under monopolistic competition. This is the classic case of a transgression of the sanction of monetary exchange, since a flow of gross profit is produced in conditions which should not permit a complete valorization of the capital invested. Certainly, the macro-economic significance of this procedure is not perceived by the firm involved, for which it merely represents a financial insurance against the risks of the investment. But there is no automatic guarantee of an adequate insurance in conditions of competition, so the social constraint is reintroduced in a new form.

For firms to protect themselves individually from the risks of devalorization, they must be able to predict its scope and tempo. They can only do this by a strategy of diversification in which the economic life of the means of production invested in each economic line is adapted to the life expectancy on the market of the commodities produced. It is necessary, therefore, to be able to plan the pace of renewal of these processes across the entire space of diversification. If this fundamental condition is satisfied, then the giant corporations can generate their own financial safeguards by manipulating the laws of amortization and the time-scale over which the means of production are amortized, which can be purely fictitious. The generalized obsolescence that follows is evidently not imposed by any technological necessity. It is the outcome of the interaction of financial strategies which is the very principle of monopolistic competition. The result is a gigantic waste of social resources, which is completely disguised in accounting values, since it does not appear as a loss. The loss of substance is not borne by the firms involved, but by society as a whole, in the form of the erosion of money value and the distortions this produces.

But there are limits to the 'effectiveness' of these private financial strategies. The type of planning described above is possible only if the relations of competition are stablized under the form of stratified oligopoly. If this stability is to be produced right across the economy, with the exception of new zones of diversification in the process of formation, it is necessary for the conditions of capital accumulation in general to be favourable. Whether the situation is one of full competition or monopolistic competition, all that the individual capitals have to share between them is the total profit resulting from the exploitation of social labour-power. Competition is peaceful only if the formation of the general rate of profit is not threatened by the uneven development generated by the incompatibility between the evolution of the macrostructure of production and the distribution of total income. But the modalities of monopolistic competition feed certain forces that tend to generate such uneven development.

In order to create in all circumstances those depreciation allowances that are the principal component of a rapidly growing cash flow, the giant corporations must be able to count on an extremely rapid amortization. The support for this amortization is an age-structure of the capital in question that is distorted to give ever more weight to recent fixed investments. The result is that the depreciation allowances do not stop with compensation for losses on past investments; they can only become a regular flow fuelling a growing profit if they precipitate a tempo of future investment that is ever more rapid. The procedures set under way by each giant firm so as to protect itself from local risks of devalorization thus create an ever stronger demand for investments that favours the development of the department producing means of production. Besides, by incorporating depreciation allowances at current sale prices, and shifting the effects onto monetary erosion, the corporations tend to increase the share of total income that they appropriate, since monetary erosion devalorizes the monetary rights given by wages. The result is a restraint on the growth of effective demand for means of consumption. The procedures of monopolistic competition thus actually operate to provoke a dissociation in the development of the two departments of production. The social constraint of the law of accumulation cannot be lifted, it is simply displaced and deferred in time at the cost of an intensification in disequilibria. Seeking to disengage themselves from the local devalorization of capital inherent in private commodity production, the giant corporations precipitate the necessity of a general devalorization which monetary erosion can no longer continue to absorb. This is the root of the process of inflation and its contradictions. We shall need only to develop this analysis in Chapter 6, with the aid of a theory of the relations between money and credit, to understand the divergent trend of the process and the financial limit that the temporal deferment of the monetary constraint finally encounters.

4. Administered Prices in the United States

Administered prices may be understood from two points of view. First of all there are those private practices that emerge in the content of stratified oligopolies with a relative stability. These can be seen as concerted practices which neither necessarily nor chiefly involve explicit collusion and agreement. This is particularly true in the United States, where a very elaborate anti-trust legislation exists, under the aegis of the Federal Trade Commission and the Department of Justice, though the operations of these two agencies are more or less separate from one another. The concerted practices of the giant corporations are determined by the logic of monopolistic competition itself. Administered prices are also matters of public ruling in specific fields of commodity production. Our objective here is not to make a precise descriptive investigation of the different practices concretely employed. A study of this kind should certainly form part of any description of the forms of capitalist regulation. However, it alone would require two comprehensive treatises, one on monopoly agreements, the other on price control. Happily, there is a very widespread literature on these questions in the United States,[6] thanks to the presence of permanent agencies charged with enforcing the anti-trust laws, and of public regulation.* Basing ourselves on this vast material, our task is to seek the significance of these administered prices in the context of the laws of competition investigated above. It is quite indispensable here to distinguish between the concerted practices of private firms and public regulations.

(a) Concerted policies of price stabilization. The objective of concerted practices by an oligopoly is a two-fold stabilization: on the one hand a consolidation of the barriers to entry whose 'height' is defined by the gap between the price of production under monopolistic competition (or the limit price) and the price of production under full competition; on the other hand an immunization of prices against short-term fluctuations that may arise in the conditions of exchange. These two objectives are closely linked. In fact, although the barriers to entry are determined by structural conditions, they have the character of a metastable state vis-à-vis the forces of competition. Contingent disturbances in the level of effective demand can modify the distribution of surplus profits among the firms that share in the oligopoly, in such a way that certain of these may be tempted to react by slightly altering their prices, i.e. fixing an individual price that is slightly different from the price under monopolistic competition. This action may not have any lasting

---

[6] Among the works covering the whole field of administered prices or regulated prices, we may mention E. Kefauver, *In a Few Hands*, Pelican, 1965; P. W. MacAvoy ed., *The Crisis of the Regulatory Commissions*, New York, 1970; U.S. Senate Subcommittee on Antitrust and Monopoly of the Committee on the Judiciary, *Administrated Prices, Compendium on Public Policy*, 88th Congress, 2nd session, 1963.

* Translator's note: 'regulation' here is used in the official administrative sense, as opposed to its theoretical meaning in Aglietta's sense – in French, *réglementation* as opposed to *régulation*.

influence, and be reabsorbed with the ending of the disturbance that gave rise to it. But it may also be that the maintenance of the barriers to entry requires the neutralization of strong competitive tensions, with the result that contingent disturbances have the effect of destroying the metastable state. A unilateral alteration of price by certain firms then unleashes a price war which is followed by a transformation in the conditions of production. The barriers to entry melt away. After a transitional period of disequilibrium, a new norm of production and exchange is formed. The latter may either involve a situation of full competition, or it may form a further oligopoly. But at all events it is the result of a qualitative break with the initial situation.

In order to avoid a process of this kind, the giant oligopolist firms have to operate controls over price changes. The price of production of monopolistic competition certainly does not have any absolute rigidity. It evolves according to general laws of competition, along with the relations of exchange in general. But this change, although not discretionary, must be concerted so as to avoid the risk of destroying the barriers to entry. An essential aim of these concerted practices is to *make prices insensitive to contingent disturbances of demand*. The giant corporations must therefore absorb short-term fluctuations by varying the degree of utilization of their production capacities and their commodity stocks. This is why they must normally have at their disposal a certain excess production capacity, which will vary considerably in the course of the business cycle. It is also why they must pay great attention to the current management of their stocks, each of whose economic lines is crucially dependent on the ability of the sales department to register fluctuations in effective demand.

Assuming that market disturbances are absorbed by quantities sold, how then is the concerted market price fixed? Is it necessarily below the limit price, or can it be equal to it? In a situation of full competition, we have seen that the price of production is concretely realized over time as an average of momentary market prices. In a situation of monopolistic competition, we know that the barriers to entry can only be stabilized if the concerted price falls in the band separating the production price under full competition from the production price under monopolistic competition. The concerted price may be equal to the latter or below it, but it does not stand to it in the relation of a temporal variable to its average.

Let us then consider an example which will elucidate the concrete practices of monopolistic competition. Let us assume that the oligopoly is not stratified but homogeneous. It is established in a branch where only a single homogeneous commodity is produced.[7] We shall also assume that all firms in this branch, protected as they are by the barriers to entry, have the same long-term costs of production. In this case, the firms in the oligopoly all have a common interest in maximizing the total surplus profit by fixing the concerted price as near as possible to the limit price without thereby attracting new capitals. They can do so because the homogeneity of product and costs means that the maximization of the total surplus profit is compatible with a division of the market in proportion to the size of the productive capitals. The division of the market means the division of the surplus profit in such a way that each firm involved in the oligopoly receives a rate of profit equal to the average rate of profit in the branch. In this case, the price of production of monopolistic competition can be unambiguously achieved. Concerted practice involving the division of a homogeneous market is a simple matter. Its solidity is dependent simply on that of the barriers to entry.

This example will enable us to understand *a contrario* the difficulties involved in establishing stable relations of monopolistic competition. When the individual production costs for firms in the oligopoly are different, there can no longer be a concerted procedure that respects the managerial autonomy of the firms involved, permitting a maximization of total surplus profit while yielding each autonomous capital its due share. Oligopoly can now only be achieved by way of rigid cartels with a common sales agency and production quotas assigned to the

[7] An approximation to this case can be found in the majority of branches involved in the transformation of non-ferrous metals into pure metals and industrial alloys. The methods of production in these branches vary only little; upstream vertical integration creates strong barriers to entry and the market is well known and formed by a small number of customers. These branches constitute very stable oligopolies in which the firms involved maintain close mutual relations.

different firms in accordance with their costs, to redistribute the total surplus profit of the branch. Complex cartels of this kind, while forbidden in the United States under the Interstate Commerce Act of 1888 and the Sherman Act of 1890, existed in Europe in the early part of this century and became the general rule in heavy industry during the Great Depression. But such cartels are incompatible with the transformation of the conditions of production inherent to intensive accumulation. They can only survive in particular branches of industry or in exceptional situations: for example, limitations of natural resources or general blocking of accumulation, stability and limited complexity of techniques, immobility of producers, small number of sellers and buyers linked by long-standing ties.

Excluding these extreme cases, or transient responses to short-term situations (crisis cartels), the existence of differences in the long-run production costs of existing firms makes it impossible for any practice of tacit collusion to achieve a maximization of total surplus profit. What the situation then demands is rather a series of empirical practices. The determination of the monopoly price in the interval set by the structural conditions of competition between capitals is such that the worst placed firm in the oligopoly realizes at the very least the normal profit under full competition. If this is not possible, it means that the spread of production costs between firms is larger than the difference between the average production cost for the existing firms and the cost for firms seeking entry. If that is the case, then the conditions of production will certainly be refashioned, and it is impossible for the barriers to entry to survive. If the condition described above is realized, then the monopoly price can vary within certain limits, even if relatively restricted ones. The effective fixing of the price is then such that the division of the market is approximately stable within the oligopoly.

It is now that the stratification of the market plays a major role in moving the concerted price towards the limiting price. We have already seen how this stratification was essential to the constitution of the oligopoly as a whole, by contributing to the formation of an effective demand adequate to the maintenance of its barriers to entry. This stratification is equally necessary to the stability of relations of competition within the oligopoly. For if this stability is threatened by too great a difference in individual costs within a particular economic line, then this difference can be compensated by the interpenetration of the giant firms over the sum total of processes of a zone of diversification. This interpenetration guarantees an attitude of mutual responsibility of each firm towards its competitors. An unfavourable position in one line can be offset by a favourable position in another. Each firm seeks a range of products such that there will still be an equitable distribution of the profit realized in the sum total of lines. It is the zone of diversification, then, which constitutes the industrial branch. This produces a complex commodity whose different use-values are varieties issuing from each component economic line. This illustrates very well the theoretical remark made at the beginning of this book that the commodity has a use-value as its support yet is not defined by use-value, but rather by exchange-value. The development of forms of competition dissociates these two aspects concretely. The stratification into varieties is essential to the formation of prices of monopolistic competition. But the relationships between varieties are not relationships of different commodities, for they share in the delimitation of a single branch. This confirms that the concept of branch and the division of the space of commodities is not a function of technology, but matches the forms of competition.

Thanks to these complex relations of monopolistic competition, empirical practices fix concerted prices approximately in line with the limit prices, by controlling the development of market shares for firms in the different processes. One practice current in American industry is that of *price leadership*. The problem of knowing who leads and who follows is not very important, since the latitude in fixing prices is generally not very great: the aim of the practice is approximate stability of market shares in a restricted interval of price fixing, such that – taking account of the spectrum of production costs within a line and the distribution of market shares in the overall set of lines – the cohesion of the oligopoly is assured. It thus seems logical to adopt a procedure in which price is fixed within the available interval by that firm whose cost of production is lowest, at a level to maximize its own surplus profit. The other firms then conform to this price and accept surplus profits that depend on the level of their production costs at a given share of the market. In those industries where methods of production remain largely unchanged, costs are sufficiently inflexible for it to matter little which firm sets the price. The custom is for the largest firm to do so, as in the well-known case of steel.

The example of steel enables us to note a particular type of market stratification. This is geographical stratification according to transport costs. In the steel industry, for example, the technical concentration of means of production is gigantic, with a new works taking years to set up, and remaining in place while the sources of raw materials, and especially of supplies, change. Fixed costs are enormous and absolutely rigid, with the result that the break-even point, or the degree of utilization of production capacity that just covers them, is an essential datum for the valorization of productive capital. Each tonne produced over and above this limit yields additional profit, whatever the distance to which it has to be delivered, since the direct variable cost of an additional tonne is insignificant. This is why the tendency is for each steel-works to sell at as great a distance as possible so as to expand its production capacity. Flows of commodities cut across one another, with the consumers bearing the expense by absorbing the transport costs. There is a consequent risk, therefore, that competition between firms to expand their respective shares in the market will return under the guise of differentiated costs of production, with certain firms being able to absorb a portion of transport costs and thus conduct an embryonic price war. The primordial necessity of selling above the break-even point makes the motive behind this highly comprehensible. In such conditions, price leadership is endangered, or at all events must be further specified. The solution adopted after 1911, once formal and total cartelization became impossible due to the new anti-trust law, was the system of base-point prices. One or more base points are fixed for different geographical zones. Within each zone, the concerted price of monopolistic competition is fixed at the base point. The customer pays the base-point price supplemented by the cost of transport between the base point and his own destination, irrespective of the location of the works from which the goods are supplied. The economic absurdity of this system lies in the fact that the customers pay fictitious transport costs. Suppliers have an interest in selling as far as possible from the base point so as to maximize these fictitious transport costs and thus surplus profits. The cohesion of the oligopoly leads to a maximum of social waste by producing cross-cutting flows of goods and completely blocking any advantage that might result from changes in plant location. The exorbitant character of such practices of private collusion leads in extreme cases to their codification by the state, which may make it compulsory to redefine and increase the number of base points as changes occur in the sites of steel-works, sources of supplies, and means of transport.

(b) Regulated prices. Here we shall not investigate the control practices of the Federal Trade Commission. These essentially confer social validation on private practices of monopolistic competition when stable oligopolies are formed, while seeking to restrict the social waste to which they lead. In its role, the Commission is backed by a long history of litigation which has pragmatically filled out the very general legal framework of anti-trust legislation. Investigations made by the Commission for its own dossiers provide material for a concrete analysis of relations of competition, from which it is possible to develop a theory of monopolistic competition within the general laws of competition.

To complete our survey of price systems under monopolistic competition, we must mention the case in which the public authority intervenes in price formation. The regulation of prices by public agencies obtains in such sectors of the economy as land and water transport, airlines, gas and electricity supply and telecommunications. In these industries, the conditions of production have given rise to a formidable concentration which has led to irreversible situations of structural monopoly. The decisive importance of external economies or diseconomies in the functioning of these sectors, and the advance or blockage of the forces of production that may ensue, have led historically to a direct public regulation of the valorization of capital. The giant corporations that function in these fields are often referred to as public utilities. The creation of regulatory commissions was not easy. Discriminatory practices and devastating dislocations generated by monopolistic competition in fields with a pervasive influence on the entire system of production and social life unleashed political struggles leading to the creation of these commissions. But in no way have the commissions weakened the monopoly power of the capitalists who control these giant firms. On the contrary, the latter have found in the regulatory commissions the means for strengthening and giving official sanction to irreversible monopoly structures. This is why at one of the Congressional hearings that has investigated the actions of the regulatory commissions without being able to modify them in any way, Professor W. Adams could declare: 'The regulatory commissions do not protect society against the power and monopoly of the industries they regulate; they protect these industries against the contractual power of society'.

The public utilities occupy a curious position in capitalist competition. The rates of profit that they realize are guaranteed by the government, so that they seem to escape the law of value that imposes the social validation of private labours by the mediation of monetary exchange, with the possible sanction of devalorization. Yet these firms have proved very vulnerable to the acceleration of inflation in recent years. They have got far deeper into debt than any others, and the quotation of their shares on the stock market has sometimes actually fallen below the value of their assets.

The principle behind the regulation of these public utilities was defined and fixed *ne varietur* in the first decade of the 20th century. Every commission that was subsequently created to regulate a new field of public services was organized along the same lines. This principle is simple enough. It consists in fixing the maximum tariffs in such a way that the rate of net profit on the productive capital invested in plant and equipment does not rise above the average rate of profit current in industry. At first sight, this rule involves an approximate alignment to the general rate of profit. In reality, however, it gives social sanction to the maintenance of existing production conditions. We have seen, in effect, that the formation of the general rate of profit and the laws of competition based on it proceed from the quest for relative surplus-value. This social constraint is the definitive determinant of the valorization of capital. But it requires the transformation of the conditions of production and revolutionizes the relations of exchange. The devalorization of capital is thus the necessary corollary of the valorization of individual capitals. We have shown that under the regime of predominantly intensive accumulation this process assumes new forms through the planned obsolescence of the conditions of production. The public utilities, on the other hand, with their rate of profit administratively guaranteed, seem to have achieved in the state a substitute for the law of value. But this is only possible by *a regulation devoted entirely to preserving past labour*. The devalorization of capital is thus blocked; the result is to hold back technological progress and discourage the replacement of technically outmoded equipment.

What exactly takes place here? The fixing of tariffs is conducted on the basis of net fixed assets, expressed at their historic cost with the aid of uniform rules stipulating the useful life of plant and equipment without taking into account technical obsolescence, and a linear amortization rule. In practice, the tariff is arrived at by applying a given coefficient to the net fixed capital, valorized as indicated above, in such a way that the rate of apparent profit, related to the nominal value of net fixed assets, is not lower than the average rate of profit in industry. The cohesion of the collective capital is ensured by preventing relations of competition within each sector of public utilities. But this is achieved at the price of a regulation which is totally in conflict with the general logic of intensive accumulation. By contrast with firms that have to generate a cash flow by procedures that constrain them to lay the greatest possible emphasis on new investments and to minimize fixed assets, the public utilities have an interest in increasing the value of their fixed capital as much as possible. The result is to encourage suppliers to inflate their prices by incorporating the greatest possible amount of surplus profit in them, and to minimize amortization. The replacement of equipment is heavily discouraged. It is a long while since the transistor replaced electromechanical switchgear in computers and other calculating machines. But according to the planning of American Telephone and Telegraph, which has a quasi-monopoly in this sector, it will be a further quarter of a century until systems of electronic switching systems completely replace older equipment in the telephone service.

As long as accumulation progresses at a regular rate in the economy as a whole, the contradiction between public regulation and the logic of the law of accumulation remains latent. But when difficulties in accumulation reinforce competition and accelerate an inflation that matches the devalorization of capital diffused throughout the economy, the contradiction suddenly becomes explosive. The rapid rise in the prices of their suppliers has a multiplier effect on the public utilities due to the procedure by which their fixed assets are valorized. The increases in tariffs necessary to maintain their rate of profit become intolerable, while the quality of the services they provide deteriorates swiftly. The regulatory commissions thus have to restrain increases in tariffs and induce firms to undertake enormous loans that strain the financial markets. But since their profitability is declining despite the government guarantees they enjoy, prospective lenders are reticent and their debt burden becomes heavier. These phenomena clearly reflect the impasse that has resulted from the pseudo-social validation of the valorization of capital, by a public regulation designed to safeguard the stability of the oligopolies.

This regulation does not even prevent the distortions that arise from competition within the regulated sectors. The example of transport is a case in point.

The regulation of transport places all transport of goods by land and inland waterways under the authority of the Interstate Commerce Commission.[8] The Commission's administration of tariffs is designed to achieve the following goals: to prevent the formation of individual surplus profits when a monopoly situation exists; to subsidize certain types of transport in the public interest; to prevent any individual discrimination favouring certain sellers or buyers at the expense of others, and to prevent price wars from disorganizing the transport system. In actual fact these objectives are not all attained to the same degree, since they are not entirely compatible. The overall effect of the administration of tariffs is to suppress all competition within a particular form of transport and maintain a collective monopoly profit by fixing minimum and maximum tariffs. It also introduces a competition between forms of transport on prem-

[8] R. Fellmeth, *The Interstate Commerce Commission*, New York, 1970.

ises that are vitiated by the preferences that the tariffs grant to certain types of transport within each form. The result is that the allocation of productive resources between forms of transport cannot be based on the intrinsic advantages of each in terms of distance and the characteristics of the goods transported.

In order to demonstrate these propositions, it is necessary to look somewhat more deeply into the logic behind tariff fixing. The regulation of transport, starting with the Interstate Commerce Act of 1888, came into being historically as a form of collective organization for capital in railways, where competition between companies was having disastrous effects on the whole economy. This regulation was born as a defence of the collective interests of the railway companies in a period in which their only rivals, once all internal competition had been eliminated, were the inland waterway companies. Since water transport was highly competitive for the transport of heavy goods with a low unit value, the railway companies set out to eliminate these rivals by obtaining a regulation that reflected in its price structure the monopolistic character of the organization of rail transport. This structure consisted in a very high tariff on industrial commodities with a high unit value so as to be able to practise dumping for goods with a low unit value and thus capture traffic from the waterways. It thereby maximized the profits of the railway companies. It was accepted because of the support it received at this time from major political forces.

We can say then that the tariff regulation was dominated by the organized group of railway companies, who established themselves solidly in the key positions within the Interstate Commerce Commission. The next step leading to the present situation came in the inter-war period and continued after the Second World War. Having captured a major share of the transport of bulky goods, the railway companies proceeded to raise the minimum tariffs for these products. The same epoch saw the development of road transport. During the inter-war period it was all the easier for this new form, still unregulated, to encroach upon the traffic of the railway companies, because of the very costly tariffs the latter charged on goods with a high unit value. Now the inflexibility of these tariffs was conditioned by the monopoly structure, with its allocation of traffic between the companies. The structural advantages inherent in road transport as compared with rail were proved by investigations of costs made at the time on short-distance transport (up to 200 miles) of products that were either fragile or had a high unit value. The tariff system in force did not permit traffic to be allocated in a way that reflected the movement of costs. Road transport thus captured a far larger share of the total traffic than its intrinsic advantages would have authorized. This eruption of road transport into a frozen monopoly structure did not break up this structure but unleashed the vicious circle characteristic of monopoly situations when the nature of the branch in question does not make it possible to eliminate them: a fall in volume, a rise in tariffs to offset it, surplus production capacity, stagnation in technical progress and a deterioration in the quality of services.

When road transport was brought into the system of price administration, the Interstate Commerce Commission, now reflecting contradictory interests, could do little more after the Second World War than freeze the status quo. The price system thus became more and more rigid, as its monopoly structure was extended to road transport. This certainly did not improve the position of the railways, threatened by surplus capacity, ossified management and an ever greater burden of debt. The tariff system ended by approximately stabilizing the share of the market held by each mode of transport, independently of the evolution of their costs. Here we can see the role of monopoly prices, maintained by the sanction of the state, as a brake on the progress of productive forces (both in road and rail transport), and as an agent of distortion in the allocation of resources in the economy as a whole.

6

Monetary System, Credit and Crises

I. The Development of Credit and the Organization of the Monetary System

We have insisted throughout this book that capitalism is a commodity economy given specific features by the wage relation. The dependence of capitalism on commodity circulation is expressed in the equivalence relationships of exchange. In defining the theoretical status of prices, we have shown that we are dealing with relationships not of symmetry but of polarity by which value is 'realized'. This means that exchange is a social act which effectively moves commodities, and that this act is not simply a technical extension of production. It does not form part of the conditions of production. It is rather a socialization of private labours that are originally independent from one another. This socialization is a general process of metamorphoses of value, whose pivot is money, a commodity essentially different from all others. That is why the realization of commodities in exchange takes the form of a *monetary constraint*.

A formidable theoretical problem is thereby posed, to which we have so far given only an abstract and formal solution, that we must now try to make more concrete. Since money is the general equivalent in exchange relations which are polar, it does not itself confront any equivalent. It is impossible, without begging the question, to define its value relative to that of any other commodity. Yet in order to enter into a relationship of equivalence, money must possess the fundamental character of a commodity, that of being a sum of abstract labour. Now if commodities are sums of this kind in any specific state of the conditions of production and exchange, they still change incessantly with these conditions. The result is that even though money is the pivot of equivalence relationships, it can in no way be invariant. The monetary constraint, accordingly, is not a permanent and absolute reference as is, for example, length in Euclidean space. It depends on the way in which the general equivalent is formed.

The abstract solution that we gave to this nexus of logical requirements was to introduce the concept of the *monetary system*, at the beginning of Chapter 1. We argued that the formation of the general equivalent, and consequently also its reproduction in time, has a certain autonomy in relation to the sum total of conditions of production and exchange. It is in this autonomy that the secret of the commodity economy resides. This economy can only be analysed scientifically on the basis of an objective measurement, abstract labour, that defines a homogeneous social space. But this social space involves the following real contradiction: the production and circulation of commodities are separate and independent economic acts, otherwise there would not be a *commodity* economy; but these acts still have a certain unity, otherwise there would not be a commodity *economy*, i.e. a social organization based on commodity production which can perpetuate itself in historical time. The solution to this contradiction lies in the autonomy of the monetary system. The formation of the general equivalent makes possible a *refraction* of the homogeneous space of value that evolves over time. This refraction is summed up in the *monetary expression of the working hour*. On the basis of this logical solution, we were able to link the formation and division of total income to the fundamental concepts that define value and capitalist relations of production. We have also been able to define the theoretical status of prices and the conditions for the overall realization of value, as the formation of a general rate of profit. The laws of competition follow from this.

The role of the monetary system in commodity economies, and consequently under capitalism, which gives commodity relations their greatest extension, is absolutely decisive. We cannot rest content, therefore, with the formal solution repeated above, still less so in that the monetary system gives rise to all kinds of 'monetarist' illusions. The classical and subsequently neo-classical traditions conceived this autonomy in terms of a dichotomy. In this conception there exists firstly a 'real' economy that determines a system of relative equilibrium prices totally independent of money. Juxtaposed to this real economy, but external to it, the monetary system subject to the discretionary power of the state then fixes the quantity of money. The overall exchange equation, according to Fisher, or the circulation equation of money in relation to total income, according to the monetary formula of the Cambridge school, is seen as determining the general price level. The value of money is identified as the inverse of the general price level. It derives from the quantity of money. This purely quantitative conception of money is the necessary counterpart of the subjective theory of value. It is not modified by those modern theorists who try to gloss over certain particularly extreme features of the dichotomy between real economy and monetary system by resort to the argument that these are the effect of real money stocks.[1] This is a subterfuge because the dichotomy re-emerges when the functions of money break apart.[2] In these conceptions, money is not something that intervenes in exchange; it is not integrated into the economy as a flow. The standard of price is some good that is chosen simply by convention as *numéraire*. The function of a means of exchange is non-existent or has no economic significance. These axioms are necessary to preserve the postulate of a general market equilibrium in real terms determining relative prices. Expelled from the exchange process, the only logical way money can intervene in the economy is as a stock, a reserve holding. It is therefore a good demanded for its subjective utility, even though it is not a use-value produced in the real economy. The result is that money can intervene in the economy only by way of the *real* cash balances. Money thus acts on the system of relative prices when the real stock changes. But it is not determined by economic relations. Let us suppose, in fact, that the quantity of money doubles or triples, and that prices are uniformly multiplied by two or three, while real monetary stocks remain unchanged, so that the real

[1] D. Patinkin, *Money, Interest and Prices*, New York, 1965.
[2] See B. Schmitt, *Monnaie, salaires et profits*, Paris, 1966; M. Parguez, 'L'analyse macroéconomique de la monnaie', *Economica*, 1975.

equilibrium is unaffected. The effect of the real stock of money thus does not make it possible to determine the quantity of money. This is an exogenous factor, for simple reasons of logic. Hence the illusion that the monetary authorities control the amount of money and consequently the rate of inflation. The absence of a theory of the commodity based on objective value leads to a welter of sophisms. Only such a theory makes it possible to grasp the autonomy of the monetary system without making the monetary constraint disappear. The role of the state can then be conceived without being idealized. The state is the bearer of the monetary constraint. It can displace the effects of this constraint in time and modify the way in which they are experienced in the economy; but it is not in its power to substitute itself for the law of value. If the monetary constraint is to be suppressed, it is necessary to abolish the commodity economy.

Something vital is therefore at issue in any analysis of the monetary system, in other words of how the general equivalent is formed. It is all the more important in that the complete dematerialization of money within nation states since the First World War, or at least since the Great Depression, has strengthened the illusion of a money completely manipulated by the state. This has been cultivated by the amalgamation of money and credit in the framework of the quantitative theory, by way of the monetary multipler. But to understand how the monetary system is organized, it is essential to see that money and credit are *qualitatively* different, even though credit arises out of money. The solution to this mystery lies in the fact that money is created as a token of credit within the banking system, but acquires its attributes of general equivalent outside this system, when these tokens of credit are utilized within commodity production. This fundamental point is so foreign to orthodox monetary theory that we intend to argue it in two steps. First of all we shall establish the relationship between money and credit, when the natural form of money is a material commodity, and consequently distinct from credit for all to see. Then we shall investigate the way in which this relationship is transformed when money comes to assume its full capitalist attributes, by dematerializing and seeming to melt into credit.

1. The General Attributes of Money: the Significance of the Monetary Constraint

We have so far spoken of credit particularly in connection with the financing of accumulation and financial centralization. We now need to be far more precise and establish the theoretical relationships between different concepts. To this end, we must first of all distinguish strictly between money as the general equivalent in commodity exchange; the monetary token of credit or *bank money*, as an original act of monetary creation that qualitatively distinguishes banks from all other financial institutions; and the gathering and allocation of money capital. This latter operation, analysed in Chapter 4, signifies that money already formed can be detached from the general circulation of commodities and become capital by way of a financial circulation involving operations of lending and borrowing, purchases and sales of titles to property.

(a) The status of bank money in the commodity economy. Let us start from simple exchange $C - M - C'$. The monetary constraint means that each participant in exchange has to sell his commodity, in other words prove by obtaining money that this particular commodity gives him disposal over a fraction of total social labour. Having satisfied this obligation, he disposes of a social purchasing power over the sum total of commodities thanks to which he can purchase any use-value that he chooses within the limit of the relationships of equivalence, in other words any use-value that represents an identical fraction of social labour. If purchases and sales are regularly interconnected, then money seems to be a purely technical means of circulation. Its role as general equivalent is expressed abstractly in the posting of prices of commodities. But money does not have to be present in circulation as a material commodity. It can be replaced by a token of value, which equally well performs the function of a means of circulation. This token may be paper, on the express condition that there is no doubt in anyone's mind that it represents the general equivalent value for value. To put it another way, the x dollars shown on the note stand for x units of the general equivalent, the unit being a certain quantity of

the specific commodity that gives the general equivalent its physical substance.

But there is no reason why purchases and sales should always interconnect. The metamorphoses of value can be halted by an interruption in buying and selling. Someone who has sold, in fact, and thereby acquired money, is in possession of a general and permanent purchasing power which does not require him to buy immediately. Money can make an exit from commodity circulation and exist as a *store of value*. Moreover, when commodity circulation has reached a sufficient degree of centralization and permanence, the money commodity or its paper representative has no need to be present in circulation at the actual moment of exchange. Commodities are sold *on credit*, and purchase anticipated. These actions transform the social relation between buyer and seller into a private debtor-creditor relation sealed by a contract. This transformation does not suppress the necessity of the monetary constraint, but it shifts it in time. It is also no longer expressed as an effective equivalence of commodities in money terms, but rather as a *convertibility of credit into money*. This convertibility marks the limit of private contracts. The need for settlement, however, does not always arise for each particular credit. The development of credit contracts leads to their concentration, and enables payments to balance each other to an extent that credit itself tends constantly to enlarge. Chains of credit transactions arise, in which money appears only abstractly as money of account. But when credits and debts no longer balance, when gaps in the duration of contracts tend to interrupt the chain of compensations, then it is necessary to settle credits in money, the real commodity. For this to be possible, reserve funds of means of payment must have been formed. Thus when money becomes a *means of payment* for settling credits, its role as a store of value is no longer an accidental hoarding, but rather a necessity of commodity circulation. When institutions are created for centralizing their customers' credits and organizing their mutual balancing, they also receive and rearrange the monetary deposits that temporarily fall out of circulation.

These developments in the functions of money promote a great expansion of commodity circulation. But they only begin

to make real headway with the reversal of the metamorphoses of
value into the specific articulation of capitalist circulation
$M - C - M'$. This latter becomes a closed cycle in which money
is both the origin and the destination. This holds for each
individual capital. The general circulation of commodities
becomes a series of interconnected cycles that encompass
production. As a result, production presupposes either a preliminary accumulation of money or else an act of credit.
Production credit is very different in nature from the formation
of credit in commodity circulation. But since capitalist circulation forms a whole, these different acts of credit are united
together into a credit system. This system includes agencies
able to unify the various different forms of credit, i.e. the banks.

The taking in of money and advancing of it for productive
investment means the formation and loan of a money capital.
This loan is in no way a credit on existing commodities, with the
simple purpose of accelerating their circulation and advancing
payment in time. It is rather an assignment of the ownership of
future commodities. The industrial capitalist commits himself
to provide the lending capitalist, at a future date stipulated by
contract, with the equivalent for the money immediately spent
plus an addition taken from the profit to be realized, i.e. the
interest on the loan. This he can do if his capital functions in
normal conditions of production, because the sale of his
commodities at the price of production brings in a normal profit.
But the scale of industrial capital formation, its turnover
period, the risks arising from transformation of the conditions
of production and exchange, all generally prevent the broad
mass of lenders from personally running the risks of capitalist
production. This is why the credit system has to centralize the
money that exists outside the sphere of circulation by making
its destination irrespective of the circumstances of its origin.
This is done by the construction of a stratified series of financial
operations conducted by specialized financial agencies. This
stratification by category of risk and time of investment to a
certain extent disconnects the lenders' requirements of security
from the needs and risks of capitalist production. The result is a
relatively stable spread of interest rates for creditors and
debtors, the difference between these providing the profit of the
financial intermediaries.

Since the act of loan which sets production in motion by making it possible to purchase the elements of productive capital is an assignment of a future value, it does not imply the preliminary accumulation of money capital. The capital advance, determined by the fundamental and calculable character of capitalist production, which is to produce surplus-value, can issue from the *creation of bank money ex nihilo*. It is essential to note here that this creation of bank money is a completely original economic act. As against circulation credit, it is not a private agreement between two exchanging parties, concluded to remove the need for the delivery date of a commodity to coincide with the payment for it. As against financial intermediation, the creation of bank money is not the assignment of a money capital previously accumulated by way of savings deposits. This creation is *ex nihilo* because it does not presuppose the existence of a disposable monetary base. As against paper money in circulation, it is not an immediate representative of the general equivalent, but a token of credit that has to give proof of its monetary character.

What is original in bank money is that while it is an act of credit, with its origin therefore in a private relationship, the token that expresses it subsequently acquires a social character, as distinct from any other private credit, by circulating as a representative of the general equivalent before returning to the bank and being destroyed. The agreement between industrialist and banker, therefore, cannot be analysed as a private contract between debtor and creditor. It is true that the industrialist stands in relation to the banker as debtor to creditor. But the banker is not the industrialist's creditor by his possession of a commodity, or because he already is the depositary of a money capital he is charged with employing productively. *What the banker creates by his issue of bank money is a debt against himself.* He hands the industrialist a promise to pay which he does not have to honour simply to this particular industrialist. The industrialist rather makes use of his credit with the bank just as if this really were the general equivalent, and injects it into the productive economy. It is the relationships of exchange equivalence that determine whether or not the bank money has acquired the attributes of the general equivalent. This verification is effected according to modalities which we shall soon proceed to analyse, and which form the concrete realization of the monetary constraint.

Let us note right away that the banks are not subject to this constraint as creditors who will see their private contracts validated or not according to whether the debtors have been able to meet their debt under the conditions laid down. The banks are subject to the monetary constraint in relation to society as a whole, since they are responsible for the convertibility at any moment and without any limit of their particular bank monies into the money commodity. *This general and permanent convertibility at par value is the proof that bank money has the attributes of the general equivalent.* It is only possible if the banks are closely integrated into a banking system subject to a specific regulation.

The above exposition enables us to understand why the banking system is the kernel of the credit system. Thanks to their original role of money creation, the banks combine all the functions of credit. In order to be able to satisfy the transformation of their monetary tokens into the general equivalent, the banks have to spread themselves over a large number of cycles of capitals and circuits of private expenditures so as to profit from the return of temporarily idle money and form money capitals. They necessarily combine, therefore, the function of financial intermediary with that of money creation. The latter, moreover, is not confined to the opening of production credit. By their discounting of commercial bills, the banks substitute their own bank money for the credit proceeding from commodity circulation. To the extent that their acceptance corresponds to the general conditions these commercial bills have to respect, and to the extent that these conditions can be codified, the banks procure for these credits a far larger space of circulation than if these bills had to circulate exclusively between private producers reciprocally acknowledging their debts to one another.

(b) The expression of the monetary constraint. Credit tends permanently to enlarge the current limits of commodity production, by anticipating its further development. With the issue of bank money, credit frees itself from the limits imposed by the gathering of savings. But credit does not modify the funda-

mental character of commodity production, whose social necessity cannot be taken for granted in advance. Credit can defer the social validation of private labours, but not suppress it. The credit system is an immense source of instability for the realization of exchange-value, because bank money makes credits liquid and tends to unify the space of circulation. This is why the validation of bank money as general equivalent, i.e. the solvency of the banking system, becomes the knot where all the contradictions of capitalist accumulation are tied together. Every crisis in the realization of exchange-value assumes a global character and appears as a *financial crisis*. It affects financial circulation as a whole, but its epicentre is necessarily the banking system as the site where private credits are given liquidity.

We have seen that the realization of total exchange-value takes place via the formation of a general rate of profit. The latter governs the relationships of equivalence between the different categories of commodity as the foundation of a system of norms of production and exchange. An ever greater portion of individual commodity exchanges take place in bank money as the credit system develops relative to the expansion of commodity production. It is easy then to fall into the illusion, when everything is going well, that the realization of total value is *ipso facto* satisfied. But it is not so at all. The real exchange of commodities into the general equivalent is simply displaced to a specific point where the validation of bank money as general equivalent is effected. This point is the *money market*, the arena where the credit system and the monetary system are connected and where final settlements are made. The manner in which these settlements occur is crucially dependent on the nature of the monetary system.

When the monetary system is based ultimately on the production of a commodity that is used as money, the monetary expression of the working hour follows directly from the social conditions of production of this commodity, which we can take for the sake of example as gold. Gold production, as a specific branch, forms part of the system of norms of production and exchange. The monetary unit is legally defined as a certain weight of gold. On the basis of this legal definition, gold that is produced at home or purchased abroad is coined in response to the social demand for gold as a means of settlement. This demand depends on the organization of the credit system, which gives the banks empirical experience of an average demand for settlements in the monetary tokens which they themselves issue. This demand does not stand in any quantitative connection with the volume and intensity of commodity transactions. The monetary constraint is a relationship of equivalence which involves a qualitative problem. What is essential is that the convertibility of bank money into gold is *reputedly possible* at any moment, and to an unlimited extent. This is why it was held in 19th century England, when the British financial system enjoyed world hegemony, that the gold standard was the monetary system which most economized gold. In effect, so long as confidence in the banking system was unimpaired, no private economic agent had any interest in the sterile possession of sums of gold with a fixed nominal value.

The problem of solvency affects the banking system as a whole. It is essential that a threat of insolvency which affects a few banks should not shake confidence in the convertibility into gold of bank money as a whole. It was only very slowly, and on the basis of the lessons learned from recurrent financial crises, that banking arrangements were established able to limit the scope of financial crises or at least avoid a general destruction of bank money. These arrangements presuppose certain structural conditions that form procedures for integrating the banks into a single money market. On top of the formation of a dense network of connections, this integration has given rise to a *central bank* playing the pivotal role in the money market. Under the gold standard, the central bank may still be private in law. But it is none the less charged with a social function that sets it apart. It is a leading bank whose money can serve to settle credits between commercial banks. The role of the central bank is then to organize the process of convertibility of bank money by manipulating the conditions under which it issues its own money. The most celebrated example was the use of the Bank of England's rediscount rate before 1914.

The experience of 19th century America, by contrast, provides evidence of the gigantic disturbances engendered by a fragmentation of the banking system.[3] The liquidation of the

---

[3] M. Friedman and A. J. Schwartz, *A Monetary History of the U.S.*, Cambridge, Mass., 1963; Staff of the Federal Reserve Board, *Banking Studies*, 1940.

colonial past and the strong hostility of the frontier populations towards the financial powers of the Northeast prevented any successful attempt to set up a central bank. The Free Banking Act of 1838 put the banks in the same position as any other commercial undertaking, removing any specific obligations on how banks could be established and managed. The proliferation of small banks was even further multiplied by the strict limitation on the area over which branches could be opened. The result was that money issued by these banks, in particular by banks in the new and expanding states, was accepted only locally, or at best regionally. The credit needs kindled by the euphoria of frontier expansion, moreover, incited the banks to issue money and discount credits on extremely dubious business ventures. The convertibility of bank money was thus completely insecure. Money from certain banks was not accepted at face value even in times of normal business. Every financial crisis was immediately transformed into a panic, leading to a general run on precious metals and the collapse of a number of banks. As soon as the crisis ended, new banks were set up and provided fuel for the same disorder. The state's need for credit during the Civil War finally led to the National Bank Act, passed by Congress in 1863, which defined the financial basis and conditions of current management that banks had to fulfil in order to qualify for the status of national banks. A monetary control service was set up under the Treasury Department to check these conditions. But the absence of a central bank continued to prevent the formation of a unified money market. Financial panics continued to arise with every crisis in the realization of exchange-value. Overburdened by financial commitments, the banks would find themselves suddenly faced with demands for payment which could only be met with monetary instruments that they could not themselves create. The absence of a central money that could be accepted in the settlement of their reciprocal commitments meant that the strains they experienced were communicated from one bank to the next. Any sign of potential insolvency shook the confidence of depositors, who demanded conversion into gold. The banks' gold cover was rapidly lost, and payments then ceased. This monetary chaos culminated in the extremely severe financial panic of 1907, which provoked a political reaction that induced Congress to set in motion a monetary reform to create a central bank. The

Federal Reserve Act of 1913 finally established this new agency. From our analysis of the monetary constraint, when the monetary system refers to a material form of the general equivalent, we can draw a basic result as to the relationship between money and credit. All private bank money is subject to a sanction of gold equivalence, directly and without limit. This is why *private bank money bears the weight of commodity realization crises* in the form of insolvency when confronted with demands for settlement in gold. But the relationship between money and credit is not akin to inflation. This is not to say that there may not be periods when the general price level rises. Rises of this kind can come about in two circumstances. Firstly, the conditions of gold production may be transformed (the discovery of new mines in which extraction requires less labour-time, or the improvement of production methods leading to the same result). The fall in the value of gold, if it is significant, leads to a far-reaching change in the social conditions of production. But in all cases the fall in the value of gold means a rise in the exchange-value of commodities, other things being equal. A price rise of this kind may stimulate a new phase of accumulation. This is what happened with the discovery of the Californian gold mines in 1848–49, and the inception of the Transvaal mines in 1896.

Secondly, credit gives the movement of prices in the trade cycle a systematic and general character. Accumulation is accelerated by the anticipations to which credit gives rise. The expansion, imbrication and acceleration of the circulation of credits leads to a swelling of demand which is only effective if credit is given, and adds to it a precautionary demand which increases the stocks of commodities. The price rise has two effects, which interact dynamically: on the one hand, a rise in all costs, on the other hand, the acceleration of demand due to stockpiling against a more rapid rise in prices. These two connected processes generate an increasing demand for bank credit which fuels the acceleration in the price rise, particularly by way of a rise in interest rates. The credit system thus comes adrift from the monetary constraint. But in the context of a monetary system governed by metallic money, this can have only one result: the financial crisis which has already been discussed. Production anticipations fuelled by advances of credit come up against the market's capacity for absorption. The indebted producers can no longer meet their payment dates, at the very moment when costs are at their highest. Their demand for credit grows, while receipts from sales decline. This phenomenon becomes general through the intertwining of exchange relationships. The banks find themselves in the presence of an increased demand for credit, while there is no longer any repayment of earlier credits. Since everyone needs liquidity, settlement demands flow in from all sides. The debt chain breaks at several points where the banks are no longer able to meet their commitments. A financial crisis breaks out and credit contracts, while money appears in its function as a store of value. The sudden devalorization of credits gives rise to bankruptcies and destruction of capitàl. Market prices then fall at an even faster rate than they previously rose. This price movement is combined with the regulation by unemployment and fluctuations in the nominal wage which we described in Chapter 3 as characteristic of the regime of predominantly extensive accumulation. The mode of cohesion of this regime is completed by the effects of the monetary constraint that we shall now investigate.

2. The Capitalist Attributes of Money: the Formation of a National Money

In studying the development of the functions of money, we showed how it gave rise to credit and its systematic organization. Credit takes hold of commodity circulation, which is no longer directly subject at each of its links to the monetary constraint. But we constantly stressed the fact that the law of exchange equivalence was a social law governing the realization of total exchange-value. With credit, the polarization inherent in the general equivalent between commodity and money is expressed in the possibility of the credit system becoming separate and autonomous from the monetary system. This is why money as a commodity could be expelled from exchange in the course of history, to become simply an objective reference into which bank money has to be convertible so as to be exchangeable and actually satisfy the law of equivalence. The monetary constraint, therefore, as it is exercised on the money market, is not only not removed by the existence of credit; it proves to be the unifying principle of the credit system. Financial crises are a reminder that the tendency of the credit system to become self-contained is necessarily checked in a commodity economy. When bank credit unleashes anticipations of output and sales that are incompatible with the objective movement of the norms of production and exchange, the assignments of future value that are issued by the banks have no chance of being cashed in terms of concrete value realized. The apparent transgression of the monetary constraint leads to the brutal confirmation of this constraint in the eruption of a financial crisis.

Yet the expression of the monetary constraint that we have been examining up till now is not the only one possible. Its form is a confrontation of bank money, and via this the entire pyramid of credit, with a universal commodity which by its very nature is not a credit. This is why the weight of financial crises falls necessarily on the private credit agencies. It is no less true, however, that in itself the monetary constraint is a social relation that may assume different forms. Like all other social relations so far investigated, it evolves through the transformation of the structural forms in which it presents itself. The monetary system based on metals has a history rooted in the original form of money, the sole compatible with a rudimentary commodity circulation. Credit developed slowly over a long historical period, modifying the relation of the monetary system to commodity circulation, but without changing the actual form of the system itself. Its bullion basis remained unchanged in all capitalist countries with the exception of short periods of wars or revolutions. But the regime of predominantly intensive accumulation gave rise to a new structural form which is now a lynchpin of its cohesion, closely linked to the others we have already investigated. This form of the monetary system drives metallic money out of the national economic space once and for all; it is based on the *issue of a central money with enforced currency*. Enforced currency is a coercive practice of the state, imposing the unrestricted social acceptance of the monetary tokens issued by the central bank. The central bank money replaces the commodity form of the general equivalent within the national economic space of the nation. The national money market is no longer an arena where private monetary tokens are validated by reference to a universal commodity. It becomes an arena where all bank money is unified by the central money. This unification forms a *national money*. To study how the monetary constraint functions, it is necessary to understand how and within what limits the national money that proceeds from credit can acquire the attributes of the general equivalent.

(a) Integration and disintegration of bank money. It is important to grasp that in modern capitalism bank money is more than simply the support for private credit and the unifying factor of the credit system. We must therefore come back to the overall reproduction of the wage relation as formally depicted in Diagram 9 (Chapter 3), taking into account our findings so far on the laws and forms of social regulation. We have frequently stressed that labour-power is not a commodity like any other. It is a commodity to the extent that the capitalists acquire disposal of it so as to incorporate it into productive capital under their exclusive direction. But it is not a realized or realizable exchange-value. It is impossible to possess labour-power so as to sell it on the market and extract a monetary equivalent. Labour-power is bought only because its use is the creation of value, abstract labour itself. This is why the maintenance cycle of labour-power has a certain autonomy in relation to the cycles of expanded reproduction of capital in the two departments of production. This autonomy is of decisive theoretical importance. The free workers, themselves constrained to purchase their own conditions of existence as commodities, have to receive payment of their wages in money. For the purchases indispensable for the reconstitution of labour-power to be made regularly in the general circulation of commodities, *money must function fully as general equivalent in the hands of the workers*. This condition is all the more fundamental in that the formation and regular development of the social norm of consumption, involving the inflexibility of the nominal reference wage, is the core element in the cohesion of the regime of predominantly intensive accumulation. Now there is no close link between the rhythm at which the wage-earners repeat their expenditures, and the turnover times of capitals, which are themselves very different from one another.

There is thus a double advance between capitalists and workers: on the one hand, from workers to capitalists in that workers are paid only after having worked for a certain time, a time that corresponds to the average renewal of their expenditures; on the other hand, from capitalists to workers in that the money received in payment of their wages is not linked to the value that these workers create, since its production and realization time depend on different labour processes and more or less favourable exchange conditions.[4]

We can understand then how bank money must be endowed with new characteristics when it does not circulate in the circuit of capital, by way of relations between exchanging capitalists, but rather in the autonomous cycle of the maintenance of labour-power. In the first case, bank money has only a potential purchasing power, which is socially confirmed or otherwise according to the ability of the banking system to have its credit tokens validated in the general equivalent. In the second case, bank money must offer a social purchasing power as soon as wages are paid. The systematic advance of wages in bank money, in the context of the formation and development of the social norm of consumption, thus poses new problems for the articulation of the credit and money systems. A considerable theoretical difficulty now appears. Bank money is created, as we have previously shown, in a private relationship between the banker and the commodity producer. It cannot claim to be national money as soon as it is created. All it is, in fact, is a private money, money x, y or z. But it must become national money as soon as it leaves this private relationship when wages are paid. It must now immediately acquire a social purchasing power. No one can say what this will be quantitatively, if wages are not spent.But it must exist qualitatively, in such a way as to permit the maintenance cycle of social labour-power to continue.

The contradiction we have just noted will later lead us to define modern inflation as a phenomenon specific to the regime

[4] This dual character of the wage contract has been acknowledged by the Keynesian school. See in particular M. Kalecki, *Theory of Economic Dynamics*, London, 1965. But because it lacks any connection with a theory of the production of value, their analysis fails to take into account the problem posed by the unity of the different functions of money in the cycle of monetary income. It ends up identifying credit and money.

of intensive accumulation, whose conditions of possibility lie in the transformation of the monetary system peculiar to the latter. But it is necessary first of all to investigate the metamorphoses undergone by bank money in the general circuit of payments. We shall then examine the way in which the monetary constraint is transformed to render these metamorphoses possible.

The production process gives bank money a social purchasing power because it is a net creation of value, the formation of a new abstract labour. When a capitalist pays wages on the basis of an advance made by his banker, he transforms the private monetary token into money income. Projected into social production, *money integrates a social purchasing power.*[5] This follows from the very meaning of abstract labour. The social purchasing power is not acquired because the banker's advance is used to valorize an individual capital; this may or may not happen according to the fate this individual capital encounters in competition. It is acquired because every wage paid in the course of any period whatsoever is a fraction of a homogeneous quantity of monetary rights remitted to the social labour-power that creates the new abstract labour of this period. When it leaves the sphere of production this abstract labour is fragmented, since it is incorporated into a mass of commodities that have to realize their exchange-values. It is because the products of labour are already commodities, i.e. economic objects in a homogeneous value space, that the bank money integrated at the opening of the act of production can continue to bear a social purchasing power. It does not lose this when it leaves the hands of the wage-earners as they spend their incomes. It keeps it in the sum total of acts of commodity circulation which realize abstract labour in the form of total income. This realization is effected according to the pattern of the expanded reproduction of the social capital. It is why profit can appear as an appropriation that accrues to the firm as an excess of receipts over running expenses previously advanced.

[5] The notion of the integration of bank money into the productive economy was developed by B. Schmitt, *Monnaie, salaires et profits,* op. cit. But for lack of any reference to abstract labour, Schmitt fails to take into account those conditions of commodity exchange that involve a monetary constraint. This is why he conceives bank money as spontaneously unified, and does not investigate the way in which the division of different bank monies is overcome.

Commodity circulation does not consist of the exchange of a pile of heterogeneous objects for a certain quantity of monetary tokens. When the products of labour enter the sphere of circulation, they already have a price by virtue of the fact that they are exchange-values. The monetary tokens acquired a social value when they were integrated into production in the payment of wages. But this value is not yet confirmed. It must be confirmed by commodity circulation, which combines the dissociated elements of the exchange relation. Qualitatively, the monetary tokens preserve their purchasing power in the sphere of circulation, even though the expenditure of income detaches them from the initial integrative act for another fraction of income. Quantitatively, however, it is the overall realization of exchange-value that decides on the transformation of the newly created abstract labour into total income, and consequently on the magnitude of the monetary expression of the working hour. When the abstract labour has been completely realized, the tokens of bank money have flowed back to the firm and are detached from any element of income. In proportion to the expenditure, in fact, the income element that occasioned the expenditure is destroyed in the course of exchange, since the corresponding exchange-value has been socially validated and the commodity is now going to be used as a use-value. But this expenditure realizes another fraction of income, and the tokens of bank money are transferred to this, occasioning a new expenditure, and so on. When, however, the total abstract labour for the whole period is realized, the entire income is spent and therefore destroyed.[6] *The bank money has then disintegrated*. It has flowed back entirely into the hands of the capitalists, having lost its social purchasing power. It becomes

---

[6] No duplication can exist in the relationship between total income and total expenditure. Money is integrated only to the extent that it realizes the newly created social labour in expenditure. This latter derives in the short run from company plans, according to the principle of effective demand. When the money has financed the series of purchases and sales that constitute the social validation of production, the income is then destroyed. Income and expenditure are two forms of value which are related to the same abstract labour and are converted into one another in complete respect for the principle of equivalence. The multiplier is necessarily equal to unity. To believe the contrary is to make analysis of value production impossible and to accept that income can survive expenditure. What the circuit of income and expenditure indicates is not a multiplier but the magnitude of the monetary expression of the working hour.

once more a mere token of credit by which the companies cancel their debts towards the banks by sending back the monetary tokens that the banks have issued. After having disintegrated, bank money is destroyed. It has accomplished the full cycle of its circular course, marked by successive acts of creation, integration, disintegration and destruction. A new cycle can then get under way by a new creation *ex nihilo* of bank money followed by the formation of a new monetary income.

(b) The conditions of possibility for inflation. The distinction between bank money and monetary income, which are linked by a process of integration and disintegration of the social purchasing power conferred by abstract labour, is one of the fundamental capitalist attributes of money. It gives concrete expression to the transformation of abstract labour (VA) into income (VP), inasmuch as $m = VP/VA$. But the fact that bank money is the bearer of income and is thus radically distinguished from a simple private credit, is an insufficient condition for the formation of a national money. The relationship recalled above can be spelled out only if we can give a meaning to the monetary expression of the working hour, despite the fact that this is no longer directly determined by the social conditions of production of a commodity taken as general equivalent. Bank money must therefore be totally unified, so that each economic agent is permanently certain of the following condition:

1 dollar from bank X = 1 dollar from bank Y = 1 dollar from bank Z = ... = 1 dollar.

Now this condition is not immediately implied by the analysis of the integration and disintegration of bank money as income. What is needed for this is a far-reaching transformation of the monetary system, centred on the establishment of a central money with enforced currency.

The unification of bank money becomes, in effect, the form of the monetary constraint in the space of the nation. This is so because the different bank monies become the means for a confrontation between two different time dimensions, a social dimension and a private dimension, which the very nature of commodity production prevents from coinciding. New abstract labour is continually created by production. It is possible therefore to speak of the formation of income for a certain period which integrates bank money into social purchasing power. But the expenditure of income which realizes this abstract labour can be extended over a shorter or longer interval, and the bank money can be annihilated only after the income is actually spent. Only then can the credits originally issued by the bankers be cancelled. Now these credits were issued in the private relationships between the bankers and their clients, the capitalist producers. Their issue can in no way take into account the social process of the formation and expenditure of total income. Bank money is issued in the form of assignments of the future realization of the particular exchange-values of the capitalists in question. These realizations occur at the most varied intervals and are subject to all the hazards of competition. Yet only these realizations can cancel the credits originally issued.

The incompatibilities between the objective process of integration and disintegration of social purchasing power by bank money, on the one hand, the particular advances on the future values to which different bank monies are attached, on the other, are reflected within the banking system itself. The circulation of private bank money, in effect, when this serves to bear income over the different phases of social expenditure, gives rise to monetary deposits held by bank X in bank Y, and vice versa, without there being any automatic compensation. Let us suppose that bank Y holds a credit on sight with bank X. This is necessarily a credit in money X. Bank X is unable to settle it in money Y, since on our hypothesis there is no compensation and all that bank X can create *ex nihilo* is its own money. It may happen, of course, that Y gives credit to X, i.e. defers the settlement of the credit on sight until later. It is the role of the money market to establish a specific circulation of credits between banks, so as to make these dates overlap. But theoretical analysis cannot stop here.

Let us suppose that there is a far-reaching discrepancy between the social process of the formation and expenditure of income and private advances, with the result that certain banks, disposing of large amounts of credits against their clients which cannot be settled in the short term, cannot meet their own commitments. Is a financial crisis going to break out, destroying the monetary character of the credit tokens issued by the banks, as when the monetary system functioned by reference to gold? This cannot be the case when the bank money is the bearer of income and particularly of the fund for wages, the regularity of whose formation and expenditure is the central condition for the cohesion of the mode of accumulation. A crisis of this kind would jeopardize capitalism itself. It is necessary to safeguard the system's solvency no matter what the cost. This can only be achieved if the debts among the banks themselves are settled in a common money, that issued by the central bank. The latter then acts as *lender of last resort*. But the central bank money is itself nothing more than a credit which this bank issues against itself. To be accepted in all circumstances as the means of settlement in the economic space of the nation, particularly in a crisis situation, this central money must be vested with a legal power, the enforced currency imposed by the state.

The articulation between the monetary system and the credit system then becomes a new structural form. In the United States this emerged after the collapse of the banking system during the Great Depression. In this new form, the central bank manages the constitution of the general equivalent within the national territory, whereas previously it simply organized the confrontation between bank monies and an objective and universal general equivalent. This management involves a whole series of practices comprising the regulation of banking operations, the guaranteeing of deposits, the surveillance of banks in trouble, and the adjustment of the central money. It becomes a monetary policy, since it cannot be reduced to an organized set of techniques. In effect, *the state becomes the bearer of the monetary constraint*, with the result that its management is permanently subjected to a political sanction which is more or less evident according to the scope of the contradictions that have to be surmounted in order to realize the unification of the national money. On the one hand, the state has no part in the origin of bank money. As issuer of the means of common settlement to the banks, and as lender of last resort, the central bank gives a social validation to private advances. On the other hand, the state is guarantor of the national money. It cannot afford to overcome the division between different bank monies by destroying the social purchasing power which these all sustain. The central bank must therefore impose an overall monetary constraint.[7] This is why monetary policy is always a compromise. The ease or difficulty of realizing this compromise is always related to the greater or lesser acuity of the internal contradictions of the law of accumulation. Since the monetary constraint makes itself felt by way of practices of quantitative management that govern the proportions to be respected in the composition of bank assets, the obligatory reserves to be deposited with the central bank, and the greater or lesser purchases and sales that the central bank makes of government bonds on the money market, it is possible to have the illusion that the central bank actually determines the amount of money. Since in periods of crisis the task of safeguarding the solvency of the banking system forces the central bank to settle government debts on a more massive scale and to play its role of lender of last resort as a priority, it can seem that its monetary laxity is the cause of the crisis.

But the real relationship between the credit and monetary systems has nothing to do with any quantity theory of money. The form assumed by the monetary constraint, in the obligation to accept the central money, is a sufficient condition for inflation. In effect, by ensuring that banks meet their commitments even though there is no effective settlement by disintegration of bank monies and cancellation of credits, the central bank operates a *pseudo-social validation of private labours*.[8] The convertibility of private bank monies into central money with an enforced currency is guaranteed prior to the conversion of commodities into money. In a crisis situation, it may still be guaranteed even though the assignments of future values which the bank money anticipates will never materialize. We may say that commodity circulation is weakened by a relaxation of the monetary constraint. The general equivalent is reconstituted

---

[7] Thus it is because there is an objective monetary constraint that monetary policy is in certain situations restrictive. It is not a restrictive monetary policy defined outside of the economic system that creates the monetary constraint. If in a particular set of circumstances the state is able to modify the intensity of the monetary constraint, it still does not suppress it, but simply shifts it in time, postponing to some future date current problems in the realization of value.

[8] See S. De Brunhoff and J. Cartelier, 'Une analyse marxiste de l'inflation', *Chronique sociale de France*, no. 4, 1974.

by the permanent unification of different bank monies. In this way a monetary expression is formed for the working hour, at any point in time. But the pseudo-social validation of a fraction of commodity production is expressed in a perpetual slippage in this quantity, an erosion of the national money. This erosion is expressed statistically as a rise in the general level of prices. In the regular course of accumulation, there is a creeping inflation which reflects an irreversible weakening of the monetary sanction for commodities within the national circulation space. In periods of financial crisis, when the credit system tends to cut loose from the monetary constraint, the latter no longer finds brutal expression in the form of a demonetization of the credit tokens issued by the banks. On the contrary, the pseudo-validation of the different bank monies as central money extends, and the erosion of the national money is accelerated. Creeping inflation is transformed into galloping inflation. The financial crisis becomes a protracted monetary crisis.

II. Financial Crises as Necessary Aspects of Capitalist Regulation

Despite the creation of the structural forms we have identified, and their capacity for progressive transformation, the antagonism of the wage relation prevents capitalism from achieving the mechanisms for a harmonious regulation. There exist historical phases in which the conditions for expanded reproduction of the capitalist relations of production are not fulfilled. The balance of forces which makes the law of capital accumulation a general movement of value expansion is then broken. The cohesion of the structural forms whose overall operation canalizes and fragments the class struggle, displacing the points at which tensions arise in such a way as to reduce them by financial flows, is undermined. Such a situation is a *crisis*. It is clear that a crisis of this type is always social in character, in the sense that it is born out of the relations of class society. But it can have differing effects on the forms in which these relations exist. Such a crisis always has a more or less sharp effect on economic relations, but it does not necessarily change political relations.

The confrontation between classes does not explicitly challenge the state power of capitalist society, in other words threaten the ability of the capitalist class to manage society from its unified vantage point in the state. A crisis of this sort, which has occurred in the past, is now again under way in the United States. The general ideological principles that legitimize capitalism in the popular consciousness, principles which exploit the peculiar features of American national history and are diffused in a variety of forms by an extremely dense network of cultural and religious institutions, are sufficiently powerful to perpetuate the hegemony of the capitalist class. The American bourgeoisie had and still has the necessary room for manoeuvre to absorb new social transformations and yet safeguard what is essential to it: disposal of the forces of production by means of the wage relation.

In the course of this book we have expounded the theoretical elements that make the economic aspects of social crises intelligible. The root of these crises is always the upsurge of class struggle in production, which jeopardizes the expanded creation of surplus-value on the basis of the prevailing organization of the labour process. This is why the outcome of social crises can only be a major transformation of the labour process and the conditions of existence of the wage-earning class which are indissolubly linked to it, to permit the emergence of new social conditions of production and exchange. But the very nature of commodity production imposes the ubiquity of monetary quantities and the fragmentation of capitals, whose relations are expressed in the laws of competition. The overall character of the social crisis is revealed by monetary flows, because capitalist circulation encompasses production. On top of this, the capitalist response to the first symptoms of a crisis is always to act on these flows in an attempt to defuse the rise of tensions in production, by manipulating the exclusive control that the capitalist class wields over the credit system, with its ability to displace the monetary constraint. This is why the visible eruption of the crisis always takes the form of a financial crisis. Having already investigated the underlying determinants of these crises and their formal expression in terms of the interaction between credit system and monetary system, we can now go on to examine the phenomenon of financial crisis itself.

1. The Over-Accumulation of Capital

The term 'over-accumulation' of capital may seem paradoxical. Since accumulation is the alpha and omega of capitalist societies, how can capital be over-accumulated? Is not any accumulation beneficial, even if its conditions have deteriorated and the rates of profit to be realized are lowered? From the standpoint of the individual capitalist, which the majority of economists adopt and extrapolate to society as a whole, the crisis can come in many guises: inability to sell goods, absence of prospects for new investment, lack of financial resources to operationalize investment plans. Since these different situations may either follow on from one another or exist simultaneously according to the economic sector concerned, extrapolations from micro-economic indications to macro-economic evolution can only lead to confusion. The financial crisis reveals in a negative way the organic unity of the capitalist mode of production. It renders directly visible the fact that market adjustments are modalities of regulation subordinate to the law of accumulation. This social law involves an antagonism that makes global disequilibrium possible. When such a disequilibrium arises, no market mechanism can get rid of it. The financial crisis is a process of purgation of the disequilibrium through which entirely new conditions of accumulation are created. To put it another way, the law of accumulation can in no way authorize the definition of a configuration of stable equilibrium. The most it can do is establish the condition of a metastable balance of forces. The dynamic of the evolution, break-up and reconstitution of metastable states has nothing in common with the dynamic of so-called balanced growth. A financial crisis represents a rupture in the process of accumulation. The concept of the over-accumulation of capital is the key to understanding financial crisis.[9]

(a) Definition of over-accumulation of capital. In seeking to give a rigorous definition of this concept, we can elucidate a

[9] The concept of over-accumulation of capital has been developed and applied to the study of crises by P. Boccara, *Études sur le capitalisme monopoliste d'État, sa crise et son issue*, Paris, 1974.

controversy that is very long-standing but still of current
importance. This is the question of the tendential fall in the rate
of profit. This controversy should not really exist at all, since it
lacks either a logical or an empirical substance. It simply
reflects the lack of understanding among economists of the
materialist dialectic, even that displayed by a good number of
those who profess it. What are the terms of this controversy?
Marx declared that the tendency of the rate of profit to fall was
the most basic economic law of capitalist society. Two objec-
tions are customarily made to this. The first, empirical objection, comes from those who define an average rate of profit,
work out a chronological series for this average over a century
or so, plot this on a curve, and without bothering themselves
with any more detailed analysis, conclude that this curve does
not display any significant decline. The second, theoretical
objection, accepts that contrary influences act on the rate of
profit, but maintains that when some tend to become preponderant, counter-balancing mechanisms reinforce others, in such a
way that the rate of profit can remain permanently stable. The
combination of the empirical and the theoretical objection
leads to the conclusion that balanced growth, a simple expansion of the economy with all proportions constant, is in fact the
rule; no importance is attached to the historical pattern of
variations in these proportions. At best, these trends form part
of theories of cycles resting on the most heteroclite hypotheses.
In any case, such theories are independent of the theory of
balanced growth, which is supposed to be a unitary process and
is conceived as the perpetuation of an equilibrium over time on
an expanding scale. This is the neo-classical position.

The controversy is not a genuine one, because the notion of
balanced growth belongs to the theoretical universe of general
equilibrium which is totally foreign to the law of capitalist
accumulation. So far as the empirical objection is concerned, it
already sows confusion inasmuch as it gives a false idea of the
transition from the abstract to the concrete. For as we have
shown throughout our study, this transition must proceed from
concept to concept, and not by juxtaposing *ad hoc* empirical
observations with a normative option for equilibrium.

Yet the problem still remains. How should the tendency of the
rate of profit to fall be interpreted? Let us recall here certain of

our earlier findings. When we studied the conditions for the formation of the general rate of profit in Chapter 5, and maintained that they could be interpreted as a balance of forces, we did not thereby rejoin traditional conceptions of equilibrium. For the latter, in effect, forces such as supply and demand are supposed to depend on exogenous parameters that are mutually independent. The forces do not interact in their actual formation. This is why a process of adjustment that is external to the parameters on which they depend can modify their valency until they balance one another. An equilibrium of this kind may be stable or unstable, but it is in any case mechanical. The forces involved in the formation of the general rate of profit are completely different in kind. *They are polarized by one and the same social process.*[10] This process is the production of relative surplus-value. It involves a transformation of the conditions of production that radically alters the relations of exchange between the two departments of production but can nevertheless lead to a rise in the rate of surplus-value only if strict proportions are respected in the macro-economic exchanges between them. This is why we have said that the general rate of profit is associated with the realization of total income by the social expenditure deriving from organic exchanges between the two departments of production. We expressed this as the compatibility between the macrostructure of production and the distribution of total income. In as far as this condition is met, the unity of the social process of production and circulation is maintained. But this compatibility is maintained only by accumulation. Any idea of a static equilibrium is quite inconceivable. The wage relation can only be reproduced if the mechanization of labour is pursued ever further, with an ever greater saving on living labour. But for the department producing means of production not to block the realization of the total product by its own expansion, the wage relation has to spread at a sufficiently rapid rate.

Since the existence of the general rate of profit cannot be

[10] There is a basic logical difference between an adjustment in two forces defined prior to the adjustment procedure, and a division determining antagonistic poles that constitute one and the same relation. In the first case, it is possible to conceive of a state of immobility; in the second the very existence of the relationship results from the inequality and qualitative difference in the poles.

taken for granted, but rather poses a problem, the concept of over-accumulation of capital follows directly from this problem. *There is an over-accumulation of capital when the constraint of the full realization of the value newly created by society can no longer be effected by way of the organic exchanges between the two departments of production.* The polarization of forces promoting the uneven development of the two departments can no longer be neutralized by expanding the space of commodity production through accumulation. This uneven development then assumes a qualitatively new guise. A macro-economic imbalance is created, rupturing the social unity of capitalist production and circulation. The process regulating the external relations between individual capitals breaks down, giving way to a violent struggle among them to preserve their independence.

The law of the tendency for the rate of profit to fall thus has the following meaning. It asserts that a phase of apparently regular accumulation does not contain self-correcting mechanisms that can perpetuate it indefinitely. The tendency to uneven development is a macro-economic feature of the law of accumulation. It imposes itself on relations of market competition, and can only be neutralized by social transformations that depend on the evolution of the class struggle. This is why it is legitimate to speak of a metastable equilibrium in characterizing the constraint of the full realization of value. The over-accumulation of capital marks the rupture of this equilibrium. It opens a phase of major disturbances in the form of a financial crisis. The new social conditions of production that arise from this crisis cannot be theoretically added on to the old conditions by a simple shift in the equilibrium. In a financial crisis, the articulation of structural forms that gives the regime of accumulation its cohesion is dislocated. The global morphology of economic forms must be rearranged. The law of the tendential fall in the rate of profit is thus very far from indicating the peaceful evolution, upwards and downwards, of a rate of profit whose formation is unproblematic and whose purely quantitative movement governs displacements of an equilibrium.

(b) The development of the financial crisis. It is very clear that in this rearrangement qualitative phenomena dominate quanti-

tative trends, since there is no longer a continuity in the reproduction of relations capable of giving them direction. All financial crises have certain common features. Yet the fundamental changes in the monetary system that arose from the Great Depression have decisively modified the relations between money and credit. This is why we intend first to examine the development of financial crises when the monetary constraint is exercised in gold terms – which conferred common features on the great American financial crises of 1873, 1894, 1907 and 1929. We shall then deal with the essential differences between these old-style crises and the contemporary crisis that takes the form of the inflation process. In the general spirit of this work, we shall not be able to go into detailed description. We shall simply seek to demonstrate the essential determinants that follow from the concepts we have introduced earlier and to complete our general theory of capitalist accumulation.

The necessary starting point is a proper characterization of the onset of the crisis. This is what the concept of over-accumulation of capital permits us. The crisis begins with a transgression of the requirement that newly created value should be fully realized. When the general equivalent is formed by bank money expressed in gold, then the monetary expression of the working hour remains defined by the social conditions of gold production. But we know that the realization of commodities in money terms does not mean that exchange actually takes place in the money commodity. It does so through the credit system that is articulated to bank money. The condition of full realization of the product signifies that final settlements within the banking system, needed to guarantee the monetary character of the credit tokens issued by the banks, are made without dangerous strains. This absence of strains is attested by the stability of the rate of interest that governs the money market. Transgression of the full monetary realization of the social product, on the other hand, is initially expressed by strains in the credit system.

Here we touch on a decisive point for understanding financial crises. Transgression of the requirement of full realization does not result from a failure of the capitalists to innovate, as Schumpeter would have it, or from a gradual decline in the 'marginal efficiency of capital', following Keynes, that stifles opportunities for investment. It results rather from an uneven development that generates a macro-economic imbalance which imposes itself on the individual capitalists. In its initial phase, this overall imbalance is expressed not in a lack of investment opportunities but on the contrary in an accelerated development of the department producing means of production. *The financial crisis begins with a business euphoria.*[11] The imbalance in the schema of the expanded reproduction of capital sets in behind the backs of the individual capitalists. The latter, encouraged by the results of the earlier valorization that were so easily obtained, anticipate better results in the future, and speed up their investment programmes all the more, since they now dispose of substantial monetary reserves. They are able to do so because they do not immediately feel the monetary constraint. When it becomes impossible to realize the social product in money, this still remains possible on credit. The credit system thus escapes the monetary constraint in so far as credit permits the pursuit and even acceleration of social expenditure in this phase of business euphoria, even though the proportions between the two departments of production that are needed to make final settlements no longer exist. Hence the habitual signs of degeneration towards a speculative boom.

In the economic movement that led to the Great Depression, the overall imbalance resulting from the uneven development of the two departments of production existed below the surface from the mid 1920s. Throughout this decade, income distribution shifted rapidly to the detriment of the wage-earners. Between 1920 and 1929, in fact, incomes received in the form of profit, interest and rent increased by 45%, wage incomes only by 13%.[12] The increase in the rate of surplus-value that made possible this distortion of income distribution fuelled the uneven development of the two departments of production. From 1923 to 1926 the output of producer goods increased at something like double the pace of industrial production as a whole. But the ever greater inequality of incomes led to the market for consumer durables peaking in 1926. Under these

[11] A.F. Burns and W.C. Mitchell, *Measuring Business Cycles*; J. Lescure, *Les crises générales et périodiques de surproduction*, Paris, 1938.
[12] *Fortune*, 'The Great Depression and its Consequences', February–March, 1955.

structural conditions, the sudden upsurge in business activity of 1928–29, after the temporary dip in 1926–27, could be no more than an artificial euphoria bound up with the circulation of a great mass of money capital in the hands of American capitalists, augmented by a massive influx of capital fleeing from the increasing monetary instability in Europe.

The accelerating credit demand addressed to the department producing means of production, and particularly to the sector producing intermediate goods of circulating capital, absorbs excess production capacity. Relative prices for these products rise, and delivery dates are pushed back. These conditions of exchange precipitate strains on these markets, since all capitalists, fearing a lack of supplies, create an additional demand by seeking to build up stocks. These stocks have to be financed on credit, since they go beyond current flows and the receipts that these bring in. Debt therefore increases and becomes ever shorter in term. It swells all the faster in that the renewal of stocks has to be financed at rapidly rising prices. This again inflates demand, by adding speculative purchases, on the expectation of a further rise in prices, to precautionary purchases to guard against a lack of supplies. Commodity speculation spreads across the whole money market, with dealers seeking to get short-term commercial credits discounted or guaranteed in bank money. Short-term interest rates rapidly rise, preceded by the rediscount rate of the central bank, which attempts to restrain bank refinancing. At the same time uneven industrial development creates artificial differences in the apparent financial results of firms, which are realized only on credit. These differences favour speculative gains on the financial market. One section of disposable monetary resources is distracted from productive employment and fuels speculation in stocks. Financial circulation begins to exhibit an autonomous movement of its own, and proves ever more attractive to money capital, which only increases the lack of money for the financing of production. The movement of stock prices on the financial market loses any contact with the valorization of productive capital. It gives rise to purely speculative gains and losses, according to the way the financial intermediaries mount operations of merger or set up fictitious companies.

This speculative process was particularly clear in the development of the financial markets after 1925. Savings and investment companies were created and proliferated at an extraordinary speed. The nominal value of their assets rose from 100 million dollars in 1924 to 1800 million in 1929. The promoters of these companies launched into all kinds of manipulation of the savings entrusted to them, setting up pyramids of holding companies to be able to display artificial financial profits by the exchange of shares controlled by 'insiders'.[13] This method of accelerating the turnover of share portfolios was supplemented by ever more rapid mergers between industrial firms. Financial circulation acquired a dynamic all of its own, losing any relationship with the valorization of productive capital. The Dow Jones index for shares quoted on the New York Stock Exchange doubled between the beginning of 1927 and the beginning of 1929, rising by a further 50% again in the first eight months of that year. Bank loans in support of share dealings rose from 2.5 billion dollars in January 1927 to 7.8 billion in October 1929. This very short-term debt was the basis of a rise in interest rates from 5% to 20% – rates which could only be paid by speculators seeking capital gains of 100% or more. By attracting all economic agents holding monetary reserves to this form of credit, the rise in interest rates led to the build-up of an international tower of debts in the course of 1929.

At the peak of the speculative boom, the runaway momentum of credit brought about a general imbalance on all markets. Debt instability was at its height. The initial imbalance was immensely augmented, and became a general tension felt acutely by all capitalists. The banking system supported a pyramid of debts representing commitments which it had become impossible to settle. The turn from speculative boom to financial panic was therefore necessarily brutal. It was precipitated by the general scarcity of liquidity, given the requirements of settling on-sight credits, which the banks were unable to extend further forward as the impossibility of converting credits into money crystallized over bank money. The final weeks of the speculative boom that preceded the financial panic had something unreal about them. It had already proved

[13] U.S. Senate Committee on Banking and Currency, *Investment Trusts and Investment Companies*, 76th Congress, 3rd session, 1940.

difficult to sell commodities. Investments had come to a halt and stocks were rising. All money reserves had been drawn on, so that the bank vaults were empty. Current receipts only managed to sustain the continuity of production cycles thanks to a section of debts being deferred in time. The final weeks of the speculative boom were thus marked by a plateau in economic activity. But debtors, feeling themselves caught in a trap, tried in every way to get their credits to circulate and obtain nominal gains on the financial market. Speculation thus reached its peak. In this situation, any chance event, even an alarmist rumour, could provoke a financial panic.

Such a panic expresses the violent eruption of the monetary constraint in the form of a *liquidity constraint* that dislocates the whole tower of credit. If the initial expression of an over-accumulation of capital is business euphoria, financial panic is the initial expression of a massive devalorization. All creditors try to obtain immediate payment of outstanding debts. The first bank failures cast suspicion on all bank money, and bank insolvency spreads in a chain reaction. Even if the state decrees the provisional suspension of gold payment, it is too late for the central bank to exert its function of lender of last resort on the scale required, all the more so since the mode of articulation of the credit system and the monetary system render it impossible. Financial panic, therefore, as the initial phase of a depression, unleashes a destruction of one section of credits, a collapse of stock quotations, more or less widespread bankruptcy of financial institutions, the ruin of a significant number of speculators and the brutal contraction of incomes derived from savings. The subsequent result is a decline in effective demand on the consumer markets, on top of a financial situation that has already very much deteriorated for the firms involved. This fall in demand sets under way a chain reaction of cancellations of orders and attempts to dispose of stocks which spreads upstream, amplifying as it goes. The one concern of firms is now to avoid bankruptcy, to spin out settlement of debts as long as possible, and if feasible to consolidate them and recreate reserves.

The financial panic that inaugurated the Great Depression began in the United States on October 22nd, 1929. Within three weeks, the Dow Jones index had fallen from 327 to 199. Shares in financial concerns became unsaleable. More than half these companies disappeared within a few weeks, with savers losing some 90% of the nominal value of their supposed assets. The financial crisis had four immediate consequences whose chain effects played a major role in propagating the economic depression:

(1) A savage reduction in consumer expenditure following from the losses experienced by the higher income categories. Out of a disposable income of 82.5 billion dollars, the financial collapse alone meant a fall of 4 billion in expenditure.

(2) A precipitous fall in industrial investment due to the collapse of effective demand and for financial reasons. Gross capital formation (gross investment and variation in stocks) decreased from 16 billion dollars in 1929 to 10 billion in 1930, 7 billion in 1931, to fall below 1 billion in 1932 and 1933.

(3) A drastic contraction of credit and the collapse of bank assets, as credits became irrecoverable at the moment when depositors struggled to withdraw their assets in money. Since the banks were very greatly indebted to one another, the result was several waves of bankruptcy which reacted immediately on private consumption and investment expenditures.

(4) Losses and flights of foreign capital which led to a deterioration in the balance of payments. American insolvency vis-à-vis foreign creditors generated in return a contraction of American exports and dislocated the international payments system. On top of this, the reduction in foreign assets that followed the deterioration in the balance of payments and the settlement of short-term debts provoked a contraction in the quantity of money at the worst possible moment, which in the monetary system of the time could not be compensated by an issue of central bank money with enforced currency.

These disruptive forces unleashed a spiral movement, with falling levels of stocks chasing the reduction in effective demand, and unemployment rising sharply. This spiral continued so long as firms found no threshold of resistance. This threshold was a level of production where by compression of costs and reduction of activity firms could achieve a combination of expenditure flows and current receipts capable of generating a gross cash flow again, making it possible to reduce short-term debt.

In the course of the Great Depression, this phenomenon was exceptionally pronounced, since new waves of massive devalorization of credits and insolvency of financial institutions showed successive levels of provisional resistance to be unstable. The threshold reached in 1931, for instance, could not stand up to the inconvertibility of sterling, which was itself a response to the intensification of the international financial crisis that followed the bankruptcy of the major credit institution of Central Europe. The financial crisis in the United States increased in severity to a point where the most solid banks in the major financial centres were threatened by the massive withdrawal of the reserves deposited with them by the weaker banks. The situation deteriorated so dangerously from December 1932 onwards that on 6th March, 1933, the president of the United States ordered all banks to close. Emergency measures were hastily taken by the Congress, authorizing the central bank to advance funds to those banks that formed part of the Federal Reserve system in exchange for a vast spectrum of stocks. The banks were authorized to open their counters again after their assets had been scrutinized. In June 1933, public confidence in the banking system began to build up again, once all banks who were members of the Federal Reserve system had their deposits compulsorily insured.

The deepening of the financial crisis had a disastrous effect on production and exchange. In this phase, the devalorization of capital took the form of the definitive failure to sell one portion of production, which was physically destroyed, and the sale of the remainder at reduced prices, often below the long-term costs of production obtaining before the crisis. Everything happened as if firms had to buy their own products in order to pay the expenditures involved in their production. These products were not socially validated and firms had to absorb their private costs, leading to operating losses. One way in which these losses were financed was by suspending the renewal of plant and equipment, which spread the devalorization to fixed capital.

We have already noted the virtual disappearance of gross investment, in other words the suspension of any renewal of the means of production. In three consecutive years net profits gave way to losses for the industrial sector as a whole. The gross rate of profit fell from 12.8% in 1929 to 7.2% in 1930, then to 3.5% and

1.3% in the two following years. Cash flow was only resumed at a level of activity compatible with the maintenance of the exchange-value of the capital stock at new prices depressed by four years of decline and after the definitive destruction of one section of the means of production. The corresponding flow of gross investment was so low that firms began to build up liquidities reflected in rates of self-financing of 320% in 1932, some 230% in 1933 and 160% in 1934. The adjustment in nominal prices and wages was compatible with the table given at the end of Chapter 3. A fall in prices at an annual rate of 6% between 1929 and 1932 was accompanied by a fall in nominal wages at a somewhat slower rate, with the result that real hourly wages increased at 2% per year. But the decline in the total wages as a result of the fall in working hours and massive redundancies led to an official rate of unemployment of 25% of the active population in 1933.

It is important to grasp that a resolution of the financial crisis is insufficient by itself to create a new compatibility between the macrostructure of production and the distribution of total income capable of launching a new cycle of accumulation. This resolution represents a moment in the social crisis at which class confrontations can no longer be canalized by the previous structural forms, and give rise to a process of social creation which may be prompted by shifts in political forces, as with the New Deal. Such class struggles can then generate, in a political and ideological climate that does not threaten capitalism itself, those major transformations in the social organization of labour which alone can provide the basis for the conditions of a new and lasting accumulation.

In the United States, the two major transformations involved the creation of new structural forms for regulating the nominal reference wage on the one hand, and the monetary expression of the working hour on the other. These were the establishment of collective wage bargaining and the reform of the monetary system and financial intermediaries. The two major legislative charters of the latter were the Securities Exchange Act of 1934, which regulated financial circulation, and the Banking Act of 1935, which increased the powers of the Federal Reserve Board, after the establishment of enforced currency, and gave it the instruments needed to conduct monetary policy.

But these qualitative changes were only the basic conditions for canalizing the class struggle into forms capable of creating a new regime of regular accumulation. They were not as such proofs that such a regime was already established. In fact, the depression had profoundly altered the distribution of total income to the detriment of the capitalist class, and the upsurge of the labour movement had consolidated this shift. Between 1933 and 1937 the basic nominal wage rose by 41%, with the result that total net profits after taxes were still 43% lower in 1937 than in 1929. New structural forms had to be instituted to regularize the expansion of a new long-term social demand which would support new relations of exchange in place of those that the Great Depression had dislodged. Now such an expansion was not possible so long as the capitalist class had not managed to redress the division between wages and profits, by achieving a significant increase in the rate of surplus-value. This is why the second half of the 1930s was a period of transformation in the organization of labour far more than one of an expansion in productive capacity. In 1937, for instance, apparent labour productivity was 15% above that of 1929, even though the volume of non-durable goods consumed was only 10% higher, while the consumption of durable goods was still 6% below the 1929 figure, housing construction 40% below and factory construction 50% below. The peak of recovery in 1937 still saw 7.5 million unemployed, and in 1938–39 a new recession set in. It would be a vain task to speculate by what paths the regime of intensive accumulation might have been established if the Second World War had not intervened. What is important is to understand that there is no automatic mechanism of escape from a general crisis of the regime of accumulation.

2. The Process of Inflation

The process of inflation is the form taken by the financial crisis under the regime of predominantly intensive accumulation established after the New Deal, when the monetary constraint is expressed as the formation of a national money with an enforced currency. The theoretical foundations of inflation are thus the same as those of financial crises. The process of inflation is also an expression of the over-accumulation of capital. Sequences of the 'classical' financial crisis can be detected in it. Yet it displays certain original characteristics. Not the least of these is that the crisis is at once far less violent yet much more protracted in time: it appears to become endemic with recurrent phases of deceleration and acceleration of price rises, and an irresistible erosion of the national money. These original characteristics evidently relate to the specific cohesion of the regime of accumulation that we have referred to as Fordism. For it is in the nature of this cohesion that the schema of expanded reproduction of capital in its normal operation, that compatible with the formation of a general rate of profit, involves creeping inflation. The fact that it is possible to speak of inflation in a latent or endemic state, as a characteristic of the regulation itself, is due to the relationships between the credit and monetary systems through which the general equivalent is formed in the national space defined by the legal sanction which enforces the currency of the central money. The articulation of this permissive condition with structural conditions is what produces creeping inflation. The latter is the resultant of the functioning of the whole series of structural forms that regulate the regime of predominantly intensive accumulation.

Contrary to the customarily accepted opinion, it is not the process of cumulative inflation that is hard to understand, but rather the permanent existence of creeping inflation as an organic characteristic of the regime of predominantly intensive accumulation. Once this is grasped, it is easy to see how the over-accumulation of capital takes the form of an inflationary process.

(a) The existence of creeping inflation. Creeping inflation is manifested in an endemic rise in prices despite a marked growth in the apparent productivity of labour. But this rise is neither general nor cumulative. Taken by themselves, however, such observations can only be misleading. If inflation is identified with its statistical expression, and attention is focussed on the inflexibility of individual prices or averages of prices for different categories of commodities, the inevitable result is to make monopolistic competition responsible for inflation.[14] It is

---

[14] See in particular J. L. Dellamagne, *L'Inflation capitaliste*, Paris, 1972.

true that monopolistic competition defines certain relations between autonomous capitals that are indispensable for the cohesion of the regime of intensive accumulation. But these relations are themselves determined by the mode of interaction between the two departments of production, which arises from the formation and development of a norm of social consumption embodied in the conditions of production. The roots of creeping inflation can therefore only be found by studying the formation of the general rate of profit when the organic exchanges between the two departments are determined by the predominant importance of relative surplus-value and a concomitant perpetual transformation of the mode of consumption. Creeping inflation explains the rigidity of prices under monopolistic competition. But these prices do not explain creeping inflation.

We have defined inflation as the loss of value of the general equivalent produced by a weakening of commodity circulation. It is necessary now to explain this crucial point in more detail. Under modern capitalism, bank money bears the sum total of the social income. We know that money is created *ex nihilo* by the banks creating a credit on themselves which they project into production by advances they make to the capitalist producers. This money is integrated into potential purchasing power as soon as wages are paid. This purchasing power is confirmed by the expenditure into which the integrated money successively circulates the different fractions of social income. When all this income is spent, the purchasing power of the money is abolished. It is then disintegrated with its return to the firms. The firms can then cancel their credits by returning the tokens of bank money, now deprived of purchasing power, to the same point at which these were issued. The general equivalent is therefore constituted in a temporal circuit of formation and realization of social income. This circuit is the unity of capitalist production and circulation, through which the labour spent in production is socially validated. This validation is integral, and the social purchasing power of the money is preserved when the flow of money that is integrated as the bearer of newly created income exactly purchases what in commodity circulation corresponds to the value added by the new social labour. In this case the relationship $m = VP/VA$ is satisfied without any systematic increase in m.

Short-term fluctuations may arise from temporal gaps in the

effective realization of the values anticipated by the capitalists, while the banks have daily to meet the condition of convertibility of their monies. An extension of the monetary circuit, which is made up of the intertwining of a multitude of circuits created separately, may delay the disintegration of the money and oblige the banks to receive a temporary and supplementary injection of central money. But if the full realization of total income is not threatened, these fluctuations will balance out and have no implications for the value of money. They are expressed in the oscillations of the general price level over the course of the year that can always be noted. In the same way, if a policy of discontinuous revision of the nominal wage is practised (for example step by step rises in the legal minimum wage), a sudden change occurs in the monetary flow integrated into income, while the social labour that the society spends remains unchanged. The monetary expression of the working hour rises discretely, and after some fluctuation it stabilizes at a new level.

The problem of creeping inflation can now be defined in the following way. How is it possible for there to be a systematic erosion in the value of money while the requirement of a full realization of newly created value is still satisfied? Let us note that the formation of total income and its realization by social expenditure are contained in the schema of the expanded reproduction of capital. The value newly created can only be realized if the sum total of production conditions is renewed by organic exchanges between the two departments of production. Now these latter also involve the realization of constant capital, which obviously takes place through monetary exchange, or more precisely through exchange on credit monetized by the banking system. The question raised above can now admit of only one logical response. The full realization of the value newly created can be compatible with a systematic and permanent erosion of the national money only if one section of the monetary flow which should be devoted to the realization of constant capital goes instead to sustain the expenditure of total income. *The money that buys the products of society's new labour is thus perpetually greater than that integrated in the formation of income.* Since the flow of integrated money must necessarily equal the reflux of disintegrated money, given that both derive from the same bank credit which must be cancelled after the income is realized, the addition in the course of the circuit of income of a monetary flow derived from the realization of constant capital bears on the same product of labour and has to realize the same value. The solution to this contradiction is clear enough: the adaptation is made by raising the monetary expression of the abstract working hour, i.e. by lowering the value of money. This adaptation is only possible owing to the unification of the different bank monies into a single national money which the central money establishes on the money market.

We have now given the logical solution to the problem of creeping inflation. The question which is then immediately raised is whether, under the regime of intensive accumulation, there exists a characteristic of the schema of expanded reproduction of capital that generates this addition of money in the course of the circuit of income. The answer to this is positive, and we have already provided it in establishing the structural conditions of inflation. We showed that relative surplus-value depends on an integration of the two departments of production which spreads the transformations in the forces of production of Department I in such a way as to develop the social norm of mass consumption. This linkage between the two departments involves a permanent devalorization of fixed capital, which is incorporated in the formation of new capital. This is realized by the creation of a depreciation allowance, obviously advanced on credit since it is incorporated into current expenditure, which does not correspond to the realization of any past labour, since the corresponding elements of constant capital are devalorized by obsolescence. But this depreciation allowance enters the circuit of income to purchase newly created means of production.

In national accounting, matters can be presented in the following way. The money integrated into social purchasing power by the formation of income is such that $m = VP/VA$. But this social purchasing power must be confirmed by expenditure. Now a flow of depreciation allowances F is added on for purchasing the product of the same living labour VA. The expenditure of income thus involves a decline in the value of money defined by $m' = VP + F/VA > m$. But the inflexibility of the nominal reference wage is essential for the continuous development of the norm of social consumption. The new cycle of income formation consequently includes a wage payment that integrates the new quantity m'. The process is repeated on this basis, leading to $m'' > m'$ and so on. The slippage in the value of the national money can be continuous, since the formation of the nominal reference wage integrates the magnitudes m, m', m'' ... via a procedure of temporal lags, as we showed in Chapter 3. All the structural forms are thus involved in creeping inflation as an ongoing process: collective bargaining which plans the development of the nominal reference wage; the centralization of capital in industry and finance, permitting the formation of depreciation allowances as the counterpart of an anticipated obsolescence; the articulation of the credit and monetary systems that authorizes a total dematerialization of money within the national territory. The close dependence of the accelerated erosion of money on the accelerated devalorization of capital, noted earlier in the combination of a rise in the general price level and an increase of amortization provisions within cash flow, follows directly from the preceding analysis. The rate of monetary erosion accelerates or decelerates according to whether the ratio F/VP rises or declines – the latter depending on the pace at which real social wage costs decline, in other words the relative ease of production of relative surplus-value.

(b) Cumulative inflation and its limits. The transition from creeping to cumulative inflation does not present any theoretical difficulty after our analysis of the sequences of a financial crisis. It is sufficient to apply the results obtained from the concept of over-accumulation of capital to the structural conditions of the regime of intensive accumulation. We do not intend here to give a detailed description of the process of inflation. We shall simply note the differences between this type of financial crisis and the 'classical' financial crisis presented above, by comparing the characteristic features of the Great Depression and the contemporary crisis in the United States.

The financial crisis opens in the same way, with a phase of business euphoria extended into a speculative boom when uneven development occurs in the exchanges between the two departments of production, to the point of making the effective realization of the total product no longer possible. This realization takes place on credit. But in the case we are concerned with here, the process of inflation is more advanced and more prolonged because bank money never breaks free from the monetary constraint to be transformed into mere credits which will later be brutally demonetized. On the contrary, it is the monetary constraint that weakens, because the central bank can in all circumstances ensure the unity of the bank monies by issuing its own money. By doing so in a situation in which bank money is the bearer of assignments of future values that are ever more hazardous, the central bank effects a pseudo-social validation of income. This is why the cumulative debt total that develops in this phase of financial crisis, growing far more rapidly than the exchange-value of the total product and becoming ever more unstable, is expressed in an accelerated loss of value of the national money.

The concept of an *unstable debt structure* is central to the inflationary process. It is important to understand how this arises. Contrary to the situation in the 1920s, the first symptoms of the new organic crisis of capitalism were not the result of a limit on the expansion of consumer markets. They showed themselves in the form of a long-term faltering in the rate of growth of apparent labour productivity, and a halt in the fall in real social wage costs. As our investigation of the structural conditions of inflation has shown, these indicators were the symptoms of a crisis of Fordism – whereas the outcome of the Great Depression was precisely the expansion of Fordism. In the crisis that opened in 1966–67, the inflexibility of the norm of consumption forms part of the stability of the conditions of production. It is guaranteed by the structural form in which the wage relation is reproduced. This form imposes both the relatively regular advance of nominal wages and a collective reaction against the extension of unemployment as soon as it starts to jeopardize the standard mode of family consumption. Thus, contrary to the 1925–29 period, the second half of the 1960s was characterized by a movement in the division between profits and wages to the detriment of the capitalist class. This development is illustrated by Diagrams 10 and 12.

The reduction of profit margins and net rates of profit, in a situation in which any brutal contraction of the wage bill is ruled out, tends to prolong the initial phase of the crisis, that of business euphoria, because the capitalist reaction to the situation involves the formation of new capital as the decisive instrument of competition in the regime of intensive accumulation. The formation of new capital seeks to re-establish the rate of surplus-value by generating changes in the conditions of production of which one essential component is the intensification of technological obsolescence. This means that the formation of new capital must involve a considerable transfer of one portion of total profit through the modalities of competition. This transfer is all the more difficult to effect inasmuch as the increase in total profit is sharply restrained by the crisis of productivity in those sectors which were previously the motors of growth. In these sectors the valorization of the capital invested, although declining, is still sustained by the rigidity of social demand to a point where it obstructs the centralization of the money capitals needed for the investments that bear the new organization of labour. The inert mass of past labour to be valorized represents an obstacle to the conquest of new domains of valorization by an evolution of the division of labour. This is the fundamental meaning of over-accumulation of capital. It expresses the fact that the specific rhythm of the capitalist relation of production associated with the recovery of the capital invested comes into violent conflict with the living labour-time of the society, which creates the new conditions of the future. As the economic forms of capitalist social relations induce a transformation of the constraints imposed on the space of value in the field of monetary magnitudes, the conflict of these two time dimensions is expressed in a dysfunctioning of the financial markets. A persistent scarcity of the financial resources available for new capital formation reflects the incompatibility between the requirements for the financing of accumulation and the reaction of financial circulation to the over-accumulation of capital.

We have seen how inflation is defined as a decline in the monetary expression of the abstract working hour which is engendered by the formation of circulating monetary funds that do not form part of the integration of money in total net income but are added on to this income to purchase the net product newly created by social labour. The dysfunctioning of the financial markets leads to a rapid growth in these funds relative to the increase in total net income. The consequence is an accelerated loss of money value, as the formal expression of cumulative inflation.

The anarchic proliferation of monetary funds which are not the result of the realization of income – but which still finance the formation of new capital, press on the production of producer goods, inflate the capital to be valorized and thus increase its nominal value – is the result of several processes. The first of these, which we have already investigated, is the generation of reserve funds through a growth in amortization allowances and a reduction in the apparent economic life of plant and equipment. The financing of new investment in this way is not the result of an accumulation of profit but rather of an incorporation into the costs of current exploitation of the devalorization of capital previously invested. It thus represents an attempt to solve the conflict mentioned above between the two time dimensions. This solution, however, is the source of creeping inflation. We have seen, moreover, how the share of these depreciation allowances in cash flow increases at times when the conflict is exacerbated. Even if the fall in the rate of cash flow can be restrained in this way, the formation of these monetary resources in the firm is still conditioned by past investments. The growth in depreciation allowances, setting aside the discontinuities permitted by changes in legislation, is subject to an inertia due to the age composition of fixed capital. It can be accelerated by faster renewal only to the extent that such renewal increases the weight of recent investments. But this increases the demand for the formation of new capital, a flow relation, far more rapidly than it modifies the temporal composition of the invested capital stock on which the increase in amortization provisions depends. This is why the more amortization provisions increase, the more they precipitate a rapid increase in the monetary cost of future investments to be realized. An ever greater share of the financing of capital formation has to absorb price rises for plant and equipment, and this share must be covered by credit. The growth in cash flow on the basis of the devalorization of capital thus generates a *cumulative increase in debt*, the central fulcrum of the financial conditions of inflation.

The increase in debt is more rapid than that of cash flow. For each dollar of cash flow, firms' net annual debt came to 0.65 dollars in 1965. In 1969, under the first push of cumulative inflation, it rose to 0.95 dollars. After falling to 0.75 in the recession of 1970–71, the ratio advanced to 1.60 in 1974. These steep increases, as soon as new capital formation is on the rise, express the enduring lack of available money capital for investment, given future uncertainties. An effect of the discrepancy between the macrostructure of production and the distribution of total income, the scarcity of available funds for the transformation of the conditions of production is aggravated by the inert constraint of the valorization of the enormous mass of capital already invested. This scarcity seriously alters the allocative function of the financial markets, by increasing the threat of financial crisis – in other words a risk whose scope and probability of occurrence can by its very nature not be estimated. The reaction of the big financial intermediaries that agglomerate savings is to resort to quantitative rationing and to compensate for the rise in risks by an increase in profit margins. The result is a distortion of the range of interest rates away from the hierarchy of real returns that guarantees a balanced growth of assets, and a great instability of returns that upsets the calculations of savers in relation to their liquidity preference and the individual risks they agree to run. This distortion and instability leads to contradictory movements of precautionary and speculative behaviour which sweep through financial circulation and aggravate every imbalance. On the one hand, the mass of savers see their assets devalued, the captives of fixed nominal rates of interest which do not respond to the progress of inflation. On the other hand, those dealers who have concentrated large amounts of capital at their disposal turn away from productive investments to engage in operations that generate rapid nominal gains. A stock market fever results, analogous in principle to the euphoria of the late 1920s, but less damaging owing to the regulation now in force. This is what led to the wave of conglomerate mergers of 1967–68 and the speculative construction boom of 1971–72.

The insufficiency of cash flow and the shortcomings of the stock markets give the banking system a pivotal role in the financing of accumulation and make monetary creation the obligatory instrument for ensuring the continuity of productive processes. As soon as the process of cumulative inflation gets under way, the demand for bank credit is necessarily met, because it is advantageous for all the parties involved. It is so for those firms for whom new capital formation is a weapon of competition and the principal means to reverse the unfavourable development of the distribution of income in a situation of strong demand. It is also so for the banks, who see the opening up of a field of loans favoured by the dysfunctioning of the stock markets. The strains on these markets lead them to anticipate a future rise in short-term interest rates, inducing them to offer short-term credits that will rapidly be repaid. Bank credit fuels the inflation process in the two ways we isolated theoretically. On the one hand, it ratifies the previous decline in the monetary expression of the working hour, by taking into account the nominal growth in income and anticipating its future increase when bank money is integrated into the sequential reproduction of the income circuit. On the other hand it closes the income circuit by an adjustment in its nominal level to resolve the antagonism between the distribution of income and the allocation of social labour between the two departments of production that is expressed in the relationship between total income and total expenditure. The more acute the conflict between the change in the division of labour needed for present expenditure of abstract labour to yield a growing rate of surplus-value, and the competitive need to safeguard spaces of valorization for capitals rapidly growing in monetary value, the more intense the need for bank money. The credit pyramid then rests ever more on the indebtedness of the banking system.

An unstable debt structure now forms in the relationship between banks and industrial firms. Shifting forward into the future the conflict between the valorization of past labour and the creation of new productive forces by society's living labour, credit reinforces this conflict by modifying the composition of assets held by private agents. Credit renewed on a rapidly growing scale and sustained ever more by the issue of bank money constrains balance-sheets ever more severely. Between 1964 and 1974, the non-financial companies as a whole saw their ratios of fixed capital to debts fall by half, with a similar development of liquid assets in relation to short-term debt. The banks now needed to borrow ever more liquid funds in order to top up reserves that were stretched by the expansion of credit. This indebtedness of the banks on the money market has increased far more rapidly than their assets, the ratio growing from 2.3% in 1967 to 13.3% in 1974. In these conditions, the formation of an unstable debt structure is not the result of an abstract norm that represents the external limit to the development of debts. It is entirely endogenous. *The unstable debt structure is a threshold effect generated by the outstanding asset-liability structure.* It plays a pivotal role by setting off a change of phase in the process of inflation. It is at the origin of the outbreak of cumulative inflation.

For non-financial companies, the unstable debt structure finds expression in the priority given to the struggle against deteriorating liquidity ratios, as the risk of insolvency puts these companies at the mercy of an untoward hiatus in the interconnection of payments and monetary receipts. Liquidity shortage in turn derives from the overwhelming predominance that short-term debt assumed in the course of the inflationary process. During this process, the continuity of production in a conjuncture of strong demand leads to deferment of delivery dates and anticipation of price rises in the elements of circulating capital: firms respond with precautionary stock-piling. This type of demand increases very rapidly as turnover of capital is accelerated. The debt structure proves unstable once the short-term credit needed for the anticipated financing of stock comes cumulatively to surpass the rate of growth in current receipts deriving from the conversion of the stock already formed into effective demand. This phenomenon emerged in the middle of 1973. While production started to stagnate under the combined effect of the decline in household demand due to the erosion of real wages, the precautionary increase in the money reserves of firms, and the bottlenecks in certain upstream sectors because of the strong demand for intermediate goods, company demand assumed a clearly speculative aspect. At the beginning of 1974, the ratio of stocks to GNP was far higher than at any time since the war, while fixed capital formation declined with the disappearance of cash flow and the total lack of long-term funds for borrowing, and the expansion of short-term credit brought interest rates on the money market to a historic maximum. In such conditions there is no longer any room for expansionist anticipations. The increase in credit and monetary flows can now only absorb the growing cost of those commodity exchanges necessary for the continuance of production cycles. Emergent liquid assets are already absorbed by the renewal of previous commitments, which places the whole economy in a potential liquidity crisis.

For the banks, the unstable debt structure now leads to a decline in their profits following hard on the heels of large inflationary gains, as well as a rapid increase in irrecoverable credits. This unfavourable development results from a combination of assets, with a certain proportion imposed by the past of credits with a fixed rate of return and repayment date, and liabilities, now burdened with the need to borrow from day to day growing liquid sums on the money market if their credit is to be sustained. When the banks have developed their activities to a point where assets with a fixed rate of return can no longer be entirely financed by low interest deposits, they begin to finance assets that are less sensitive to money market conditions by resources which are highly sensitive. In these conditions they can no longer control their profits, which begin to fluctuate with interest rates on the money market, and are vulnerable to a possible crisis of confidence. At the peak of the speculative boom, the rise in interest rates on the money market leads large depositors to withdraw their deposits and place these in short-term stocks. To draw in the liquid assets which they need, the banks have to borrow back the money draining from them at very high rates of interest. When these rates are higher than the base rate for bank credit, the banks suffer losses on the marginal reserves which they borrow. They must necessarily then contract their creation of money.

It is thus clear why the process of inflation does not just substitute a regular rate of inflation for financial crisis. It leads to financial crisis by its cumulative character, via the formation of unstable debt structures. When these structures are generalized to involve the economy as a whole, the monetary constraint asserts itself brutally in the form of a constraint on liquidity. The next phase is one of a deflation in short-term debt, similar to that described earlier in connection with the Great

Depression. What is important to note here is that the entire structure of modern capitalism functions in such a way as to avoid this phase degenerating into financial panic. This cannot happen without an interruption of the deflation process of the debt pyramid. The economy thus finds a threshold of resistance at the point at which stocks are exhausted and short-term debt starts to be consolidated; for the banking arrangements authorized by contemporary financial centralization, whose cohesion is guaranteed by the central bank, make it possible to avoid a general destabilization of the financial system which would lead to massive destructions of fixed capital. In the severe recession of 1974–75, industrial production fell by 9% in real terms, while the purchasing power of total wages fell by 11%. There was indeed a deflation of certain industrial prices which had taken off in the speculative boom, but no general deflation. The general price level, which had been rising at an annual rate of 14%, stabilized after a few oscillations at a new rate of creeping inflation of the order of 5.5 to 6%.

The operation of the structural forms explains the contemporary pattern of successive phases of rapid expansion and cumulative inflation on the one hand, and phases of creeping inflation accompanied by a stagnation in investment on the other, and the linkage of the two by the formation of unstable debt structures succeeded by a deflation of short-term debt. The organic crisis of capitalism continues with the recurrence of this conjunctural pattern. But between each cycle and the next there is a rise in the average level of unemployment from its low point in 1969, and an acceleration in the average rate of price increases. The central bank's role of lender of last resort is decisive in this dynamic, as it organizes the settlement of bank debts in its own money. The problem which remains is whether this recurrent economic crisis will generate new social conditions for another epoch of enduring accumulation, or whether, as in the 1930s, the interaction between internal imbalances and international disturbances provoked by the disappearance of a universal means of settlement will end by precipitating a catastrophic depression. The phases of stabilization in a regime of creeping inflation certainly shift the division between wages and profits to the advantage of the capitalist class. The restoration of profit seems consolidated with each successive crisis, thus reversing the deterioration of the late 1960s. But this re-establishment of conditions more favourable to capital has not yet been sufficient to restore its previous portfolio positions. Debt already incurred constantly contributes to maintaining the scarcity of capital for the future; hence the great sensitivity of the inflationary process to any renewal of capital formation. This vicious circle can be broken only if companies enjoy a stabilized economic environment to develop long-term plans. To obtain this extension of temporal horizon and reduction of generalized uncertainty in a society of class struggle, capitalism has once again to impose its own conception of time: the domination of the time of the valorization of things over that of the enhancement of human capacities.

General Conclusion

To conclude this book I should like to sum up very briefly the most basic findings of the theory of capitalist regulation developed above. The contribution I have sought to make to such a theory, which by its very nature must always be in process of development, has drawn on a historical analysis of capitalist accumulation in the United States. It was necessary to identify the major social transformations that have so far taken place in the 20th century. On the basis of the general theory of capitalism founded by Marx, I have tried to elaborate the concepts of the historically determinate social relations that make it possible to conceive these transformations. Finally, in a movement from the abstract to the concrete, we have proceeded from one concept to the next with the aim of organizing them into a theory of social regulation under the dominance of the basic relationship which defines capitalism: the wage relation.

This experimental procedure has led us to draw on certain contemporary elements in the critique of political economy. But it has kept us at a distance from the major debates which excite the different tendencies of Marxist thought. We have done no more than make discreet allusions to them here and there. It is evident enough, however, that the lessons of the interaction between historical analysis and conceptual development in this work are not without a bearing on these debates. Our conclusion, therefore, must set out the political consequences of our theoretical investigation. We shall put these forward under two rubrics: the theory of capitalist regulation as the basis for the concept of state monopoly capitalism, and the problem of the general conditions for a capitalist resolution of the crisis in the United States.

1. The Theory of Capitalist Regulation as a Basis for the Concept of State Monopoly Capitalism

So far we have refrained from using the term 'state monopoly capitalism'. Neither have we used the term 'monopoly', except in the rigorous sense of relations of monopolistic competition defined in Chapter 5. These omissions were intentional, due at once to the logic of our exposition and to reasons of a fundamental theoretical order. If the expression 'state monopoly capitalism' has any meaning, it is the concept of a structured social totality, denoting a mode of articulation of relations which are themselves complex. This concept can therefore only be produced at the end of an analytic procedure which has elicited the general laws of capitalist regulation and the manner in which these laws develop historically.

The demands of logical coherence indicate the rationale of our theoretical abstention. State monopoly capitalism can in no way be defined simply on the basis of relations of competition. We have shown that the laws of competition are determined by the law of capital accumulation, and not vice versa. The proper conceptual order, moreover, is no mere intellectual game. It is very important that not all concepts are of the same level, but enter into a complex process of production of concrete knowledge. For it is this that enables us to identify those aspects of the inherent social contradictions of capitalism that are principal, i.e. universal and permanent, and those that are secondary, i.e. transformable, even if in certain conjunctures the latter can become the most acute.

It is legitimate to speak of state monopoly capitalism if the organic unity of the conditions of expanded reproduction of the wage relation modifies the expression of the laws of capitalist regulation to the point of producing historically new phenomena. The major changes marking the thirty years between 1915 and 1945 were certainly of this kind. The new mode of cohesion of capitalist relations of production made possible a gigantic upsurge in accumulation after the Second World War. The basis for this upsurge was the long-run fall in the social cost of reproduction of labour-power, which generated a growing capacity for accumulation and produced a great expansion of the wage-earning class. Capitalist relations of production were further generalized by the interaction of two determinants that transformed the conditions of existence of the wage-earning class. On the one hand the social organization of labour developed and deepened the principle of mechanization. On the other hand an intrinsically capitalist mode of consumption was formed and structured by the mass production of standardized commodities. The interaction between these two forces was the principle governing the correspondence of value relations between the two departments of production.

We used the term 'Fordism' to refer to the regime of predominantly intensive accumulation based on these historical transformations. Fordism necessarily influenced the stratification of social classes and the modalities of their struggle. It accentuated those tendencies latent in the unification of the wage-earning class and the centralization of capital. These tendencies profoundly altered relations of competition by generating an organized workers' movement within the system of economic relations and by multiplying complex relationships of mutual influence between separate capitals, which have modified the exercise of proprietary control. The capitalist class cannot maintain its position in the relations of production and direct the social process of accumulation unless it can institutionalize the class struggle in the economic sphere and create new divisions within the wage-earning class, while at the same time mitigating the destructive internal struggles caused by the centralization of capital. We have shown how transformations in the forms of class struggle can be interpreted with the concept of structural form. This concept refers to the organic unity of a complex of forces in a space structured by relations subject to the principles of qualitative difference and unequal influence. Structural forms enable us to understand how the field of capitalist social relations is neither a nebulous space of functional interdependencies nor a space of indeterminate relations of forces. It is a complex whole structured by the domination of the wage relation and perpetuating it.

Each of the principal structural forms acts on the law of accumulation in a decisive area. The procedure of collective wage bargaining guarantees the inflexibility of the nominal wage that is needed for the regular development of the mode of consumption, while the system of social security is designed to maintain workers deprived of their jobs in their position as consumers. The giant corporation and the financial group are forms of centralized capital adapted to the pursuit of that competition for investments which hastens the obsolescence of the conditions of production, while transferring the ensuing losses onto society as a whole. The monetary system unifies bank monies into a single national money under the guarantee of enforced currency, and socially validates the waste of resources, to the detriment of society as a whole, by a permanent erosion of the social purchasing power of money.

None of these structural forms can play its role in the mitigation of social contradictions without the simultaneous operation of all the others. But this simultanous operation is in no way something inherent in the logic of accumulation. On the contrary, the structural forms are separate from one another and each cover a specific field within the overall space of capitalist social relations. The contradictions of accumulation affect them all, and the dysfunctioning of one tends to de-stabilize the others as well. They can only form a complex structured whole, able to reproduce itself and evolve in an orderly manner, by their hybrid location, both within economic relations and outside these relations – in other words within the state. It is in the state, and there alone, that the cohesion of these structural forms can be assured, permanently jeopardized and as permanently reproduced by the fluctuating compromises of economic policy. State monopoly capitalism is the mode of articulation of the structural forms engendered by Fordism.

2. The General Conditions for a Capitalist Resolution of the Crisis in the United States.

The general conditions for a capitalist resolution of the crisis of Fordism can be understood in the context of the laws of capitalist regulation because they satisfy the principle of invariance which is the common basis of these laws – that is, the reproduction of the wage relation. The crisis whose beginnings can be seen in the mid 1960s is an organic crisis of capitalism because its roots lie in a threat to the foundations of Fordism. It can be summarily defined as a reversal of the long-run tendency of a falling social cost of reproduction of labour-power. On the one hand, the development of work organization in the direction of an ever more intensive application of the principle of mechanization tends to exhaust its productive potentialities and renews the class struggle in production. On the other hand, the stability of the mode of consumption based on the mass consumption of private goods and the stratification of the wage-earning class is ever more dependent on collective goods and disturbed by the fact that Fordism drives the production of these collective goods to the margins of capitalist accumulation. Their cost increases dramatically with a rise in social demand. The operation of the structural forms of state monopoly capitalism prevents a total breakdown in the cohesion of the regime of intensive accumulation. But this is at the cost of a severe disturbance in the principles of their articulation in economic policy, determining a general weakening of the monetary constraint which is expressed in the process of overt inflation.

The crises of capitalism form part of the laws of its regulation, as moments of a general transformation of the conditions of production and exchange that are necessary for the law of accumulation to perpetuate itself. But state monopoly capitalism is a mode of articulation of the structural forms which prolongs the social crisis in time. The crisis is still a developing process. The deep recession of 1974–75 gives an indication of its maturing, by revealing the limits of the process of inflation as a procedure for delaying settlements. The inflationary process makes it possible to dissociate two temporal rhythms, whose telescoping together was the reason for the brutal character of earlier crises: on the one hand the rhythm of major transformations in work organization and the conditions of existence of the wage-earning class; on the other hand the renewal of the schema of expanded reproduction of capital, which requires the preservation of a compatibility between the macrostructure of production and the distribution of total income. This is why the financial aspects of the social crisis assume a different guise today. The traditional crises exhibited a sequence of over-accumulation followed by a massive devalorization of capital. The contemporary crisis of state monopoly capitalism incorporates these devalorizations into the inflation process and staggers them in time. It takes the form of a succession of phases of cumulative inflation followed by phases of ever more severe over-production, which however only slow down the process of inflation without giving rise to deflation. Each phase of over-production is the occasion for an advance of new conditions of production that is sufficiently partial to avoid a dislocation of the relationships of exchange between the two departments of production.

Capitalism can escape from its contemporary organic crisis only by generating a new cohesion, a Neo-Fordism. This cohesion must be compatible with the wage relation, the principle of invariance of the capitalist mode of production. Such compatibility is possible only if specific transformations of the infrastructure give rise to a new and protracted fall in the cost of the social reproduction of labour-power, the basis for intensive accumulation. We have sought to identify these transformations in the course of this investigation. A major advance in socialization cannot but restructure the mode of consumption profoundly, by focussing it on collective means of consumption. The cost of the latter will have to be massively reduced by a decisive transformation in their conditions of production, to enable commodity relations to flourish in this new field. This transformation is only possible by the generalization of a new mode of work organization in which the principle of mechanization is subordinated to the principle of information, with fragmented work giving way to the semi-autonomous work group and the procedure of hierarchical directives to the overall constraint of production itself.

The coming massive socialization of the conditions of life will destroy free enterprise as the pillar of liberal ideology. Its development under the domination of the wage relation will certainly change the structural forms inherited from Fordism. It is already possible to indicate certain lines of development here. The two most fundamental are a contraction of public initiative in the production of collective goods and services and a correlative reduction in the role of budgetary expenditure as a direct instrument for assuring due proportionality between the two departments of production. The decline of so-called Keynesian budgetary policies is the necessary consequence of a far-reaching restructuration of the norm of social consumption in which so-called collective resources no longer simply provide the framework for the upsurge of standardized commodities but become a major field in their own right for the expansion of commodity relations in the department producing means of consumption. The scope of the changes in the conditions of existence of the wage-earning class that are necessary for creating a new coherence in the regime of accumulation implies a new deployment of state influence within the structural forms. The ever more complete articulation of social relations within the state is, in effect, the only response compatible with safeguarding the wage relation when the socialization of the conditions of life comes into conflict with the modes of stratification by which the division of the proletariat was previously ensured. The future will tell whether the development of the modalities of regulation is such that we may speak of a transformation of state monopoly capitalism into state capitalism. But if this latter term has any meaning, it cannot denote a withering away of commoditity relations, but on the contrary their greatest possible extension, obtained at the cost of a new progress in the unification of the wage-earning class.

This overall organization of society within the state, by which modern capitalism attempts a solution at the political risk of universalizing its social conflicts, evidently gives rise to a strong totalitarian tendency under the ideological cover of liberalism. The socialization of the conditions of life can be a support for accumulation only if the leading fraction of the capitalist class succeeds in imposing an overall management of labour-power by binding the conditions of its reproduction in a tight network of social controls. One important element of these controls would be the recasting of the various institutional systems of insurance and social security in the direction of a guaranteed minimum income with uniform application to all social situations. A further essential element would be a coordinated expansion of both collective and private means of consumption; the social dimensions inherent in the former will necessitate a system of minimal norms – both quantitative and qualitative – in their production. Finally, the direct influence of the scale, duration and collective risks involved in the financing of individualized investments on the stability of the mode of consumption, will call into being state guarantees and a reinforced financial centralization with tighter controls on the stock market.

The tendencies summarized above will give the structural forms a well-defined direction of development. Collective bargaining, even if it keeps its legal autonomy, will be ever more subject to an overall wages policy imposed by state authority. The development of automatic systems of production and management control is the decisive weapon of finance capital in centralizing proprietary control at a level and in forms that permit it to confront the tendency towards a unification of the wage-earners. The considerable growth in monetary flows at the free disposition of the private economy that will result from the reduction of transfer payments in favour of a guaranteed minimum income and from the decline in budgetary expenditure will give state management of the money supply an ever greater importance. The predominance of monetary over fiscal policy, which can already be discerned in broad outline, will be definitively established. This predominance expresses the domination of the state by finance capital. It will become more than ever before the decisive instrument in the articulation of the structural forms.

Postface to the New Edition[1]

Capitalism at the Turn of the Century: Regulation Theory and the Challenge of Social Change

A Theory of Capitalist Regulation was written more than twenty years ago. The new edition perhaps testifies to the longevity of the ideas it sought to communicate. These two decades, however, have not been kind to anyone trying to make sense of the erratic and sometimes disconcerting development of contemporary societies. Here, I should like to say how the ideas contained in the book have stood this test, and how they can be modified or extended so that we can try to understand the dramas we are witnessing and the hopes of renewal we cherish as this twentieth century draws to its close.

A Theory of Capitalist Regulation has been the source of an approach to the analysis of economic phenomena which has gained widespread acceptance, in the sense that a wide range of studies and analyses have seized upon its ideas and have developed them in many different directions. We must speak of an approach rather than a theory. What has gained acceptance is not a body of fully refined concepts, but a research programme.

When the theoretical positions defended in *A Theory of Capitalist Regulation* were elaborated, ambitious synoptic studies were ideologically appealing as interpretations of the economic system. They were intellectually seductive because of their capacity to grasp the economic system as a whole. On the basis of so-called first principles, they developed consistent concepts reconciling micro-economics and macro-economics, microscopic and macroscopic phenomena. Yet this could not take place without a postulate of homogeneity that gave these theories, however mutually antagonistic, a peculiar epistemological congruity.

<hr>

[1] This is an edited version of the postface to the new edition of my *Régulation et crises du capitalisme*, Odile Jacob, coll. Opus, October 1997.

In Search of Homogeneity

The neo-classical theory inspired by liberalism, which amounts to a representation of the system as a pure economy in a natural state of equilibrium, stretches the postulate of homogeneity to its very limits. Not only does the axiom of rationality assign the same identity to all individuals in pursuit of their goals by defining an economic behaviour pattern that can be applied to any domain of social practice, but the characterization of the whole system as an equilibrium created by perfect competition implies that each player is totally aware of the web of their relations with all other players, and that this web presents itself to the individual in the form of constraints on the use of their resources.

Marxism, as an economic theory, is built upon a radical separation which explains capitalism by rejecting the postulate of homogeneity. Not only is market exchange no longer perceived as a symmetrical relation between contracting parties; the labour force is also put on one side of a basic social division which sets one class of individuals against the other. Nevertheless, the Marxist view of the economy remains strongly homogeneous because capitalism is supposed to move in accordance with general laws which lead to its overthrow, whatever the nature of the society in which it develops. Furthermore, the overthrow of capitalism heralds the coming of a transparent and homogeneous system of perfect planning.

The debate that raged in the 1930s on the relative merits of a market economy and a planned economy culminated in the demonstration by Oskar Lange that perfect competition and perfect planning were identical. If the economic system is homogeneous, there can be no real decentralization. A general economic equilibrium is a completely centralized system, either because the characteristics of the system are in the minds of all individuals, who act like a single representative individual – the hypothesis of rational expectations – or because the coordination of individual plans is guided by an explicit or implicit planner – the omniscient invisible hand in Léon Walras's general equilibrium model.

The Enigma of the Economic Quanta

Advances in economic thought have been made against the postulate of homogeneity, but they run into a formidable difficulty. Where heterogeneous features are taken into account in the behaviour of micro-economic players, the coherence of the entire system becomes a puzzle. micro-economics and macro-economics become estranged because it is no longer possible to postulate a uniform system of co-ordination. This state of affairs is not unique to economics. In the physical sciences and life sciences, it is known that microscopic and macroscopic phenomena cannot be described with the same formal tools. Macroscopic regularities have their own autonomy. However, it is in economics that the philosophy of methodological individualism is found at its most virulent. The desire to found macro-economics on micro-economic principles is such that the prevailing inclination is to overlook such obstacles and hence to perpetuate the postulate of homogeneity against all empirical evidence. Thus, the macro-economy is no more than a micro-economy enlarged to full size by means of the hypothesis of the representative agent. Another approach is simply to deny that macro-economics is in any way relevant. It is evident that this type of fundamentalism has serious consequences for economic policy. We have experienced the paradox of ideological ossification at the very time when theoretical progress has revealed the complexity of relations between the levels at which economic phenomena are perceived. But this progress has forever tainted the purity of the great paradigms.

In fact, for a quarter of a century, exploration of this complexity has produced a splintered image of economic science. A key dimension of the heterogeneity of economic phenomena relates to information. Costly, incomplete, unbalanced and organized into structures that are far from being exclusively markets, information creates asymmetries in terms of influence, giving some economic operators power over others. Information is processed by intermediaries situated between the micro-economic and the macro-economic levels, organizations which are not themselves aggregations of micro-economic agents but sets of non-market relationships which help to create consistencies within the 'global' economy.

Another dimension of this complexity is the discovery of the extent of the role played in economics by externalities, in other word, of any type of interdependence that is not incorporated into prices. The greater the role played by externalities, that is, the less markets themselves are the sole co-ordinators, the more ambiguous and fallible will be the use of a market equilibrium to represent the system in its entirety. Externalities have undermined the dichotomy between public and private goods, have emphasized the role of collective action in the achievement of economic efficiency, and have made a considerable contribution to better understanding of the process of growth.

In a world in which information is an issue and in which externalities are laden with significance, there is no such thing as a general equilibrium of perfect competition. Nor is there any reason why maximum competition should be the best possible form of relationship between economic agents, for competition in these contexts entails the adoption of behavioural strategies, the effects of which could be socially and even individually disadvantageous. This is the environment in which the problems of regulation arise.

Regulation theory is concerned with heterogeneous economic processes in which necessity and contingency, the constraint of the past and the creation of the new are intertwined. It deals with processes that emerge, are reproduced, then wither away under the effects of the unequal development inherent in capitalism.

Accumulation and Cohesion

A mode of regulation is a set of mediations which ensure that the distortions created by the accumulation of capital are kept within limits which are compatible with social cohesion within each nation. This compatibility is always observable in specific contexts at specific historical moments. The salient test for any analysis of the changes that capitalism has undergone is to describe this cohesion in its local manifestations. It also involves understanding why such cohesion is a short-lived phenomenon in the life of nations, why the effectiveness of a mode of regulation always wanes. And it requires grasping the processes that occur at times of crisis, confusion and changing behaviour patterns. Lastly, it involves trying to perceive the seeds of a new mode of regulation in the very midst of the crisis afflicting the old one.

Here I shall begin by returning to certain fundamental concepts used in *A Theory of Capitalist Regulation* with a view to examining them in the light of the developments in economic theory that have occurred over the past twenty years. I shall then present a summary of the forces behind the great post-war boom, in which I shall include both the American experience and that of Western Europe. Thereafter I shall study the demise of the mode of regulation known as Fordism and the profound social changes of the last twenty years. Finally, I shall address the open question of the emergence of a new mode of regulation, the promise of a new age of the wage society.[2]

---

[2] Translation note: 'Wage society' is a translation of the term 'la société salariale' by which is meant 'a society which develops under the impulse of capitalism and in which wage – labour – by far the preponderant form of employment – is also the predominant source of total demand. It follows from this that the compatibility between wage costs and income has to be regulated by social institutions' (author's definition).

Theoretical Problems

If we reject the paradigm of the pure economy, as established by the rational expectations school, this raises the problem of the social fabric. Economic relations cannot exist outside a social framework. It is quite clear that in democratic societies individuals can pursue their own objectives within markets, subject to a wider range of constraints than just scarce resources. These constraints include lack of knowledge, moral considerations and institutional or organizational restrictions. Even such a general formulation is already far removed from the pure economy. What is being hinted at here is an evolutionary theory of micro-economics with imperfect information, a system in which processes of learning and adaptation are of the essence. The question that then arises is what kind of macro-economics goes with it – a conception of the global system compatible with a representation of individual behaviour that goes beyond assuming the individual's desire and capacity to achieve the best possible deal under an exogenous set of constraints.

Individualism, in fact, has little to do with the logic of utilitarianism. Contrary to the claims of an instrumentalist perspective, goals are not exogenously given, merely forming part of the social background to economic relations. The goals themselves, and not only the means used in their pursuit, help to form economic relationships and are influenced by such relationships. Some outstanding economists of the past have given a great deal of thought to the way in which individual behaviour influences the economic climate and vice versa. Joseph Schumpeter portrays individualism in the figure of the entrepreneur. Entrepreneurs are far from being profit-maximizing automata. They are innovators. By venturing into the unknown, they enable society to reduce its dependence on existing structures. But they do not do so without causing social damage; they are destroyers as well as creators. Keynes depicts the infernal intertwining of the industrialist and the financier. They do not have the same perception of time or the same evaluation of profit, yet they are linked by a web of financial obligations. The inevitability of debt also binds them inexorably together in conflict. That relation is preordained by the power relationships which derive from this financial bond – asymmetric information, as it is termed nowadays in the sanitized language of economists. Keynes shows that economic development depends on which is the dominant force, the entrepreneur or the financier. However, which has the upper hand itself depends on the prevailing situation.

Thus, in a society in which individualism reigns, individual goals take on economic form by asserting themselves in the pursuit of interests. These do not necessarily embody collective aims when they are formulated and revised. But these interests come into contact with each other. They may be mutually antagonistic or mutually reinforcing, depending on the nature of the social links which they are helping to change. Those links, however, function primarily as vehicles for the formulation and pursuit of individual interests, because the successful pursuit of these interests depends on society's acceptance or rejection of the result of the actions to which they give rise. The social fabric appears first and foremost as a problem of collective belonging, in the form of a system or systems in which individual interests are validated by the results they produce.

The Division of Labour, Money and Debt

The regulation approach assigns an important role to money, which, since the original publication of *A Theory of Capitalist Regulation*, has constantly been reaffirmed. Money is the primordial social link in market economies.[3]

Let us underline the importance of this hypothesis. It means that, logically and historically, money precedes exchange. There can be no starker statement of the contrast between this hypothesis and that of the pure economy, in which money is regarded as a development of barter. In the pure economy, money is a particular means of exchange which springs from the spontaneous coordination among rational individuals. In the social-link model, money is the collective pivotal point in the relationship between the individual and society. A relationship between two individuals may be termed 'commercial' because it is conducted through the institution of money. Individuals do not have to make their mutual interests compatible via the price mechanism before actually exchanging commodities. They may express their interests independently and perhaps these interests will conflict, for the individuals' actions must respect one social constraint, namely the need to settle their prior debts in money. Money is

[3] This conception of money, which is not absent from the works of Karl Marx and which is also one of the foundations of Keynesian economics, was explicitly mentioned as part of the very definition of a market economy by C. Benetti and J. Cartelier, *Marchands, salariats et capitalistes*, Paris 1980. A compatible formulation may be found in M. Aglietta and A. Orléan, *La Violence et la monnaie*, Paris 1984.

thus the key to membership of the market society of individuals who are free to pursue their own ends without having to co-ordinate their actions through the determination of equilibrium prices. The underlying rationale that gives coherence to the system of market exchanges is the settling of debts, not the determination of prices.

If money is the basic social link in market economies, and if it means that individual actions are validated by the obligation to settle debts, we still need to know why such great importance is attached to debt. This is because debt is the type of relationship between the individual and a society which rests on the division of labour. Individuals pursuing their own ends are no less a part of society, for they are necessarily incorporated into the division of labour. The division of labour creates reciprocal indebtedness between each individual and society in general. To translate their goals into an autonomous activity, economic agents must invest, in other words, take resources from society. They are thus indebted to the community and responsible for the resources borrowed. But society, for its part, owes a debt to individuals insofar as the use they make of these resources helps to reconstitute the division of labour.

What is better understood is how money serves as the fundamental institution in any market economy. When individuals pay off their debt, they are proving that they have helped to renew the division of labour. But they can only do this because of the income earned through their activity. By transferring money through someone buying the fruits of a particular individual's labour, society has given the individual what it believes he or she has given it. But the apparent reciprocity of this relationship is illusory, since individuals' valuation of their input will not necessarily match society's valuation when it pays them. This disparity is reflected in unpaid debts, the deferment of which can cause problems. Society may therefore exist in a state of financial disequilibrium. The state of individual accounts and of the obligations they entail under the prevailing financial rules is what creates the potential for conflict between individual goals and social constraints.

As the primordial institution of market exchange, money is consubstantial with value. Indeed, economic value is the anonymous judgement passed by the market society – all other individuals – on the economic act of each individual. This judgement is ratified by the system of payments. It is the form in which societies with autonomous economies reward the contribution of each individual to the reconstitution of the division of labour. Money, as the operator of value, is the regulatory institution par excellence, because payment is prescriptive. Money logically precedes exchanges, because it is the unit in which prices are defined. As a basic social norm, it proceeds from sovereignty. It is the temple of the common faith of individuals in the markets, because it is through money that they belong to the market economy. The economy, then, is not pure, because its very foundation, the monetary standard, is an extraneous factor.

Capitalism and the Working Classes

How do money and debt relate to capital and the labour force? There is no doubt that capitalism, in the eyes of both Marx and Keynes, is a monetary economic system. If wages create social division, establishing the power of one social class over another, that power is the power of money. To be more precise, it is the power of those who have the initiative to create money in order to transform it into a means of funding; it is their power over those whose only access to money is the sale of their capacity to work. This power is exercised with a view to accumulation. Transforming money into capital means sharpening the contrast between the goods produced by individuals' activity and money itself. As Marx himself said, 'If ordinary items of merchandise are considered, money presents itself as the only adequate incarnation of their value.' But the money that is accumulated as capital is money that is not extinguished in the settlement of debts. Accumulation of capital is one side of the equation, but the other side is necessarily the development of indebtedness.

Trying to accumulate money for its own sake as the aim of economic activity means seeking power over others, because money is the basis of the social fabric. The accumulation of power, however, is a limitless desire. This is what makes capitalism a force that cuts across society, a dynamic that takes control of the division of labour to continually transform it. But capitalists are part of the division of labour, too. They cannot accumulate the power of money without an input and hence without incurring debt and submitting to the judgement of society. That is why the employer–employee relationship is an intensification of the link between the individual and society, the illusory reciprocity of which we emphasized above. Marx made much of the antagonistic aspect of this relationship, placing it in the context of an unrelenting class struggle that would result in the demise of capitalism itself

Nevertheless, it is theoretically possible to alter this illusory reciprocity within capitalism. It can be altered if the dynamism of capital also improves the living conditions of the labour force and develops a wage society. This is the theoretical option that the regulation approach has pursued and that this book has explored in order to interpret the development of American society as a model for the Western societies of the twentieth century. This involves a clear definition of the relationship between employers and employees.

Wagering on the Future

The employer–employee relationship is the separation which renders a body of free individuals incapable of becoming private producers within the market economy. The withdrawal of resources from society by the agents in the market economy turns these resources into the means of producing goods autonomously. Employees are also individuals who are free to pursue their own ends, but this pursuit is subject to the constraint of the privation of property. Their access to money is obtained through an employment contract whereby they sell a number of hours' work in return for a wage or salary. Subordination to the capitalists occurs in the realm of production, which is not a place of exchange. The fact is that the labour contract entitles capitalists to have their employees work under their control. Enterprises are therefore specific kinds of organizations, since hierarchical power is exercised there to produce goods with a view to accumulating money.

It follows that the dichotomy of the individual and society is not seen in the same way by employees and capitalists. Collectively, employees have a common status; the key to their subsistence is work under the authority of those who own the means of production.

Individually, employees are free to hire out their labour to any capitalist. They are also free to spend their pay as they see fit. There is therefore a twofold mobility that can act as a regulator on the accumulation of capital: the mobility of the employees themselves which is a source of unemployment, and the mobility of their consumption habits.

Collectively, the capitalists depend on employees' consumption in the market to honour their financial obligations and realize their monetary profit. Individually, they are competing to accumulate capital. Capitalist enrichment is private, in the sense that the debts incurred by capitalists are wagers on the future which are not mutually compatible, for reasons clearly identified by Schumpeter. To accumulate capital, each capitalist tries to free himself from the constraints of the existing division of labour. That is what makes capitalism a dynamic force for technical change which drastically alters the division of labour. As it takes some time for society to validate or invalidate these wagers, the evaluation of capital at any given moment includes a specific process of buying and selling debts and rights to capitalist property. The capital owned by individual capitalists is evaluated in financial markets. This evaluation itself amounts to speculation on the future. It comprises wagers placed by the financial community, in other words by other capitalists, on the success or failure of the gambles taken by each individual capitalist. The financial evaluation of capital introduces the ambivalent solidarity between industrialists and financiers to which Keynes refers. The incoherence of the capitalists' wagers on the future division of labour is illustrated by the solvency problems affecting their debts. Doubts about solvency provoke drastic revisions in these evaluations of capital, which trigger financial crises. These crises are the expression of the monetary constraint that reveals the incoherence of individual interests whenever these interests take the form of capital accumulation.

The Importance of Mediation

The essential idea of *A Theory of Capitalist Regulation* is that the dynamism of capital represents an enormous productive potential but that it is also a blind force. It does not contain a self-limiting mechanism of its own, nor is it guided in a direction that would enable it to fulfil the capitalists' dream of perpetual accumulation. To put it another way, capitalism has the inherent ability to mobilize human energy and transform it into growth, but it does not have the capacity to convert the clash of individual interests into a coherent global system.

The abstract form of the link between the individual and society represented by the buyer-seller relationship itself depends on the basic social institution of money. But a virtual economy comprising only buyer-seller relationships would be regulated exclusively by the system of payments, that is, by a coherent set of monetary rules and by an institution which is the guarantor and executor of that system. The same no longer applies to capitalism. We have just seen that the evaluation of capital already presupposes an entire financial system. Moreover, the employer–employee relationship is fundamentally hierarchical within the enterprise, even though it assumes the guise of an exchange that is formalized by the employment contract. Since it is spurred on by the limitless desire to accumulate money, capitalist management of the production process can degenerate into a power capable of destroying the labour force it has subjugated, as the tragic history of proletarianization demonstrates.

To manage an ordered productive force, namely one that is capable of preserving the working potential at its disposal, capitalism must be hemmed in by constraining structures. Such structures are not the fruit of capitalist reasoning or the spontaneous result of competition, but rather emanate from the creation of social institutions, legitimized by collective values from which societies draw their cohesion. This cohesion is the product of social interactions that take a variety of forms: conflicts, some of which may be violent, debates that find their way into the political arena, associations that lend collective strength to groups of employees and legislative provisions that institute and enshrine social rights.

Within its own ranks, capitalism unleashes conflicts which obstruct its own development. But it also summons up forces opposed to its desire for accumulation, forces which find a way to channel this opposition into social mediation. In a historical context, it is this mediation that makes actual the notion of the wage society. Thanks to this mediation, processes of capital accumulation can also improve employees' living conditions. Technical progress can be converted into social progress. That is no more, of course, than a possibility; everything depends on the creation of mediatory mechanisms and their effectiveness as regulators.[4]

Against the Primacy of State or Market

The regulation approach is therefore related to numerous critical views of the orthodoxy that presents capitalism as a spontaneous development, and progress as the direct and continuous effect of technical development. It affirms the belief that market mechanisms must be supplemented or supplanted by collective action. This action is expressed in social mediation. But the regulation approach is distinct from two mutually contradictory conceptions: first, the idea that rules and institutions are products of the convergence of private decisions; second, that any non-market force

---

[4] In *A Theory of Capitalist Regulation*, written at a time when the term 'mediation' was not really established in this sense, these mechanisms are referred to as 'structural forms' or 'institutional forms'.

that has a global effect on the development of capitalist economies must proceed from the state.

Mediation mechanisms, in the regulation approach, are genuinely intermediary structures that modify the relationships in which tension between individuals and society plays a part. Mediation mechanisms are present in the context of private actions. For instance, an industrialist will decide to invest on the basis of the financial community's opinions, the credit lines his banker is prepared to open and any tax incentives available. But there are other matters for consideration: the impact of the investment on the social hierarchy in the company and of the changes which new technology – if involved – might have on the pay scale, on the status of categories of worker and on promotion opportunities. This context is socially constructed by an intermingling of mediation mechanisms. They have their own inertia, they perpetuate behavioural routines, but they also develop at different rates – the markets' opinion of the value of the capital being affected by the intentions of an industrialist and developing more rapidly and in a more volatile manner than the change in the organization of labour necessitated by the realization of these intentions.

The overall context, however, does change along with the collective interests that are activated by the interaction of the various wills within these mediating mechanisms.

From another point of view, this mediation creates global processes that are types of macro-economic sequences. *A Theory of Capitalist Regulation*, for example, provides ample demonstration of the ways in which collective bargaining alters the development of pay structures and how the advent of the large enterprise transformed the price system. In short, this whole mediatory structure helps to shape a mode of regulation. The life expectancy of a mode of regulation is that of the compatibility of the mediation mechanisms that lend it coherence. This approach leads us to reflect on the role of mediation mechanisms in regulation theory compared with the more general approach of institutional economics.

The question of mediation mechanisms is that of the passage from the micro-economy to the macro-economy in a situation in which the economic players and their behaviour patterns are heterogeneous. The unsatisfactory nature of the concept of utility maximization as the sole universal goal within the framework of limited resources makes it impossible to imagine the macro-economy as a projection based on a representative individual. Even if this view persists in macro-economics and claims to represent the system on the basis of primary micro-economic principles, it is incompatible with the new micro-economy.

Institutionalism as Pragmatist Minimalism

In the face of this insurmountable obstacle in the present state of knowledge in the social sciences, and particularly within economics, the pragmatic position consists in taking note of the separation between microscopic and macroscopic phenomena. The investigations and theoretical propositions applicable to individual players are not regarded as relevant to the study of economic systems. We should state that this approach is very familiar to experimental scientists. Everyone knows that some physical laws possess only statistical validity since it is impossible to account for observed patterns on the basis of a complete explanation of the interaction between elementary physical units Similarly, without seeking to enter the philosophical debate between holism and individualism in the study of what a society is, we can recognize regular macro-economic patterns. There is therefore a field of macro-economic study that is closely linked to economic policy. It consists in examining the relationships between the global factors involved in these patterns, in identifying the conditions under which they will remain stable, in making projections and in studying the global effects of budgetary or monetary responses.

Institutional economics is critical of this minimalist approach. It acknowledges the existence of a multitude of rules, agreements, customs and norms. It studies their appearance, their effect on the elementary economic agents and their defects. Compared with the micro-economics of the rational individual restricted by scarcity, institutional economics emphasizes a variety of relationships. These create more or less extensive co-ordination systems among micro-economic players, favour certain behaviour patterns, conclude agreements and combine individual objectives into collective aims. The institutions therefore perform mediatory functions

But in its burgeoning development, modern institutional economics, with its strongly evolutionary tendency, does not solve the problem of macro-economic coherence. The problem essentially consists in the perception that institutions are the products of behavioural interactions among micro-economic agents.[5] According to this definition, however, traffic lights, product labels,

[5] One good example of this approach may be found in A. Schotter, *The Economic Theory of Social Institutions*, Cambridge 1981.

the rules of etiquette, social security and central banks can all be called institutions! The ways in which the institutions are linked, dovetailed, hierarchically organized, and so forth, to form subsystems are not dealt with systematically. This institutional approach does shed some very important light on the collective factors that condition the behaviour of individual economic players and, by extension, on the environmental changes produced by the interaction of players trying to loosen constraints. But it cannot explain the existence, coherence or incoherence of macro-economic patterns by this method.

Theory of Conventions

The theory of conventions explicitly admits the existence of collective entities that are not the results of the behaviour of individuals under bounded rationality. The collective entities have an existence of their own, the analysis of which is rooted in the cognitive sciences. The theory of conventions therefore offers a wide variety of models in which institutional forms are studied.[6] But the transition to the macro-economy is almost totally absent. It is this transition that regulation theory seeks to establish by linking the mediation mechanisms to the fundamental relationships of capitalism, namely money and employer–employee relations, as defined above. There is, however, some common ground between regulation and convention theories which reconciles these viewpoints with regard to evolutionary neo-classical economics. The latter regards institutions merely as contracts between economic players. Convention theory and regulation theory explicitly perceive institutions as mediatory mechanisms. Enterprises are the co-ordinating organizations between the micro-economy and the macro-economy, since rules of payment, flows of goods and money and financial relationships are linked into a hierarchical structure where deals are struck between various categories of stakeholders with claims on the collectively produced added value. The conceptual division of the enterprise into product markets, labour, and capital, in neo-classical economic theory obscures the essential point, namely the existence of structured links that are not markets, links without which the overall coherence of the economic system is unintelligible.

---

[6] Some of the texts on which the economics of conventions is based appear in J. P. Dupuy et al., eds, 'L'Economie des conventions', in *Revue Economique*, special issue, March 1989. See also the collective work edited by A. Orléan, *Analyse économique des conventions*, Paris 1994.

There are, though, differences between convention theory and regulation theory on the role of mediation mechanisms as a means of accounting for macro-economic patterns: they are apparent in views of the formation of the collective entities through which these mediation mechanisms operate. Convention theory, like the ideas of the neo-Austrian school inspired by Friedrich von Hayek, tends to see these as spontaneous processes emerging from the dynamic interaction of individuals pursuing their interests. Regulation theory, by contrast, emphasizes the organized establishment and pursuit of collective interests. The creation of institutions is an essentially political act, and politics is never an individualized pursuit. Government intervention, industrial disputes and the formalization of compromises by the legislature must be considered in order to take account of changes in institutions as well as to describe the hierarchical structure of their relationships. The mode of regulation manages the tension between the expansive force of capital and the democratic principle. This principle is the source of the mediation mechanisms that lead to regular macro-economic patterns in which the accumulation of capital can be made compatible with social cohesion.

The Advent of the Wage Society

The twentieth century has been an era of social upheaval on an exceptional scale.[7] In these closing years of this century, when Europe has fallen prey to chronic stagnation, pessimism has become fashionable among some intellectuals. As they review the key events of the century, they delight in focusing on its tragedies. This nihilism, or, at best, scepticism, contemplates history and judges it absurd. Whether they invoke the curse of the human condition or the empty abyss that lies beyond the acquisition of freedom, these pessimists thrive on a metaphysical theory in which the notion of progress has no place. Such a point of view is not part of the regulation approach, which postulates that the thread

---

[7] *A Theory of Capitalist Regulation* describes how the wage society developed in the United States and why it has served to regulate the accumulation of capital. In the following pages, these results are generalized by reference to the experience of European countries. Special attention is given to the crucial mediation mechanisms within the accumulation system, their relative importance as part of the mode of regulation and their effect on individual preferences. Emphasis is also placed on the importance of the nation as the crucible of institutions creating a greater degree of social cohesion during the period of rapid growth.

running through the history of the twentieth century is that of the advent of the wage society.

It was suggested above that capitalism is a force motivated by the individual's desire to accumulate money. This force is converted into a dynamism that transforms the division of labour. Since it is intrinsically a creator and a destroyer, capitalism can only achieve progress for society if sets of mediation mechanisms, forming a mode of regulation, establish coherence among the imbalances inherent in the capitalist system. The cumulative effect of this coherence, once it has been achieved, is the establishment of a régime of growth.

The advent of the wage society is the product of changes in the employer–employee relationship in the first half of the twentieth century: the integration of the labour force into the process of the circulation of wealth produced under the stimulus of capitalism. This integration has established constraints on the accumulation of capital which have given a collective purpose to the pursuit of interests, thereby legitimizing both parts of the dichotomy between individual goals and membership of society. On the one hand, constraints on the accumulation of capital have opened up markets created by the integration of the labour force. On the other hand, the subordination of the labour force to the production process has been normalized by the acquisition of social rights giving employees access to the wealth they produce. This historic transformation gives rise to the following proposition: *the modes of regulation in the wage society are legitimate to the extent that they permit social progress.*

The Age of Large Organizations and Stable Social Hierarchies

Political debate is indispensable as a means of transforming the aspirations that stem from experiences that individuals undergo in particular economic situations into social aims which can be supported by broad sections of the population. After all, political deliberation, whether it influences legislative work or whether it results in agreements between organizations representing interests that are both mutually opposed and mutually dependent, has always been party to the creation of the major social mediation mechanisms. It is in this sense that it was true to say that the rights of employees at work, the collective negotiation of pay rates and social protection are institutionalized compromises. They do not derive from the spontaneous progress of capitalism but from an institutionalization of relations between employers and employees. The mode of regulation that established the Fordist system, whereby the constraints imposed on capital corresponded to the degree of integration of the labour force, was the fruit of the institutionalization of economic relations.

From the capitalist point of view, the twentieth century has been the century of organization. Capitalism based on organization in the industrial and financial sectors has become the main engine of accumulation in place of Schumpeter's individual entrepreneurs. It is also organized capitalism that has structured the masses employed in industry into hierarchical strata, ranging from the specialized worker to the engineer, to replace the mosaic of trades that coexisted in the factories of the nineteenth century.

Organized capitalism developed from the end of the nineteenth century and blossomed after World War II. The major companies, the public institutions administering social infrastructures such as schools, urban facilities and transport systems, the social institutions and the intermediaries involved in the circulation of capital – large commercial businesses and the financial system – grew rapidly as the full-time employment wage contract became the norm.[8] All of these organizations enable markets to function while they themselves operate according to their own rationale – that of an organization. The form of organization which divides the work force into functional strata is preordained because it is effective in the wage society. This hierarchical stratification reduces uncertainty about the behaviour patterns expected of those who occupy a position within the structure. The organizations rebuild a sense of belonging to society on the ruins of the traditional forms of social life that capitalism destroys.[9]

The large organization is integrated by stratification, because the staffing system it entails is robust enough to withstand the shocks of the market economy. In the Fordist model, uncertainty was relegated to the margins of capitalist accumulation, to small

[8] In the countries of the Western world, 80 to 95 per cent of the active population were wage-earners in 1970, compared with less than 50 per cent at the start of the twentieth century.

[9] That is why we come across overstated pessimism in the sociological approaches inspired by Karl Polanyi. While Polanyi provides an admirable analysis of the ways in which capitalism destroys the forms of social life inherited from the pre-industrial era, he undoubtedly underestimates the capacity to recreate the social fabric generated by social conflicts, provided that these can be shifted into the political arena, thanks to the democratic principle which encourages political groups to express their common interests through collective channels.

subcontracting businesses, agriculture, small traders, Third World countries, and so forth. In this way, the large organization legitimized its growth by sucking into the labour force non-wage-earning populations on the periphery of capitalism and giving them the chance of integration into the mainstream economy. The transformation of the employment structure, involving migration into paid employment and stratification of the labour force into socio-professional categories, was the driving force behind the growth that followed World War II.

Establishment of a Growth Regime

The large organization not only drew new social strata into itself. It also provided them with a framework and a code of member-ship: a steady wage, job security, the prospect of climbing a visible promotion ladder and rules governing upward mobility. The employees integrated into the organization were thus able to give meaning to their aspirations by pursuing the goal of social mobility.[10] This is why certain sociologists were able to say that the wage society was turning class struggle into a struggle over status. These aspirations extended across generational bound-aries and addressed a powerful demand to schools, which became the producers of human capital, striving for equality of opportunity. In fact, schooling was a selection process, and schools had to adapt to the limitations on social mobility that the hierarchy imposed to ensure that the large organizations oper-ated in the interests of capital accumulation. This is what mediation mechanisms do effectively: find acceptable compro-mises between forces that are diametrically opposed but inextricably linked.

Another conclusion drawn from this connection between the major enterprise or administrative apparatus and the school is that the various mediation mechanisms are dovetailed to form the framework of a mode of regulation. This dovetailing does not happen automatically because each of these organizations has its own rationale, the integrity of its own structures that makes it persevere in its perceived social role. That is why the coherence of a mode of regulation does not conform to any pre-established gen-eral law. It is a historically unique entity that may be called a growth regime. By contrast, the symptoms of exhaustion of a growth regime, heralding a period of uncertainty, crisis and change,

10 M. Pages et al., *L'emprise de l'organisation*, Paris 1981.

must be sought in malfunctions of the interaction between mediation mechanisms.

In this coherence that ultimately turns into malfunctioning, it must never be forgotten that mediation mechanisms are charged with the tension that exists between the individual and society. The compatibility between mobility and security provided by the large organization – as long as there is a coherent mode of regulation – reinforces individualism, for the hierarchical principle is at work there. This is how a collection of functions is articulated through a set of rules. Authority can no longer be legitimized by a symbolic figurehead or by the invocation of a transcendent moral value or religious belief. The large organization considerably alters the nature of our sense of belonging. We are citizens with all sorts of cards – identity cards, national insurance cards, credit cards. We are able to join all sorts of associations. In short, we belong to many things. But none of these memberships implies any particular emotional commitment. Scope for autonomous action, unthinkable only a few decades ago, has become available to a multitude of individuals.[11]

The rise of individualism, which released a prodigious amount of energy that large organizations succeeded in harnessing, also ran into opposition in the events of 1968, which were experienced more or less intensely throughout the Western world. While the large organization gives rise to individualism, it must also limit that individualism in order to play its mediatory role. The large organization limits mobility and innovation, because the stability of its constituent rules does not allow it to accommodate more than a limited margin of flexibility in its operating conditions. Large companies, for example, in opting for a form of technical progress and trying to control the pace of that progress, will make use of employees' initiatives but will channel them through company mechanisms. These limitations preserve capitalist power over the production process but this power comes into conflict with the increasing autonomy of individuals. The quest for an enterprise culture aims to rediscover emotional commitment in order to cement employees' sense of belonging to a purely objective type of organization. The failure of these efforts in the 1970s was one reason why productivity ran out of steam, inflationary pressures built up and the rate of growth declined.

---

[11] G. Mendel, *54 millions d'individus sans appartenance*, Paris 1983.

The Economic Principles of Regulation in the Fordist Model

The exceptional quality of this mode of regulation, which achieved maximum coherence during the 1960s, may be illustrated with reference to a number of stylized economic facts.[12] The core of the mode of regulation was the reconciliation of rapid increases in productivity with the growth of real income and with stability in its distribution. Real wages increased regularly because they were linked to productivity growth. The functional division of income into wages and profits remained stable, because the increase in money wages was linked to the price index. This made the improvement in the standard of living of the workforce compatible with the constancy of the rate of profit and hence with the steady accumulation of capital. This set of stylized facts depicts the macroeconomic process whereby the labour force was integrated into capitalism.

To the first pillar of the growth regime, namely the distribution of wealth, was added another, comprising a high level of investment, the increase in the labour force, stable employment structures and a low unemployment rate. The positive interaction between the distribution of income, on the one hand, and investment and productivity, on the other, was a result of the dynamism of demand. Thanks to the very broad redistribution of the fruits of increased productivity among the labour force, popular demand, based on mass consumption by an urban and suburban society, lent impetus and a sense of direction to technical progress. The result was endogenous growth, as it is called nowadays. The long-term development of employees' consumption demands ensured a rapid and very steady rate of technical progress. The steeper the long-term growth curve, the greater progress was achieved in the domain of productivity. These dynamically increasing returns on a macro-economic scale more than offset the diminishing marginal return on investments as the stock of productive capital increased. The interacting dynamics of consumer demand and technical progress steadily extended the limits of technical efficiency in the production process, thereby preventing any reduction of profit rates. It also continually created

---

[12] *A Theory of Capitalist Regulation* analyses these in detail as they relate to the United States. They can be generalized, with variations to reflect specific national circumstances. Such variations, however, cannot cast doubt on the fundamental fact that all Western countries benefited from a common growth regime.

new activities to absorb the labour force that productivity growth had made superfluous.

Along with self-sustaining long-term growth – which lasted for almost three decades – another remarkable property of Fordism was the way in which the growth regime could cushion the fluctuations of the business cycle. Such is the efficiency of the regulation mechanism. The coherent dovetailing of the mediating institutions played a decisive role here. First of all, a steady rise in real wages was guaranteed by collective pay bargaining and by the expansion of social transfers, which served as a powerful anti-cyclical instrument. In the event of a transitory drop in sales, large companies could foresee that the trend in demand was not altered. Working on a longer timescale than that of the trade cycle, they invested on expectation of future demand growth ahead of the present shortfall, thus sustaining global demand.

The financial system and its close links with monetary policy formed a second line of defence to guarantee the durability of growth. Within a framework of rules that legislated in their favour, banks could administer interest rates so as to safeguard their profit margins. They therefore competed with each other over credit volumes. The credit system was a buyer's market, with rigid interest rates and high elasticity of supply. This enabled companies to invest in growth and technical progress at minimum financial cost, which created a high leverage of borrowed funds over companies' own capital. This credit supply function certainly tended to fuel cyclical tensions. The sustained pace of capital accumulation resulted in demand outstripping supply, thereby creating inflationary pressures. However, the way in which these pressures were eased, namely by increased productivity, explains the creeping inflation that dogged the era of Fordism.

Monetary policy was therefore mainly directed towards the avoidance of inflationary excesses. Its chief problem was to limit the liquidity of banks by quantitative measures, which were toughened whenever signs of excessive demand became widespread – mandatory reserves, limits on borrowing to the central bank, credit restrictions. For all that, the recessions which this monetary policy might have provoked were fairly mild and short-lived, for the reasons given above. The dynamics of income, demand and investment ensured that sales always picked up again.

Government and Nation

Relations between governments and national economies have always been the source of bitter ideological strife. The dominant view in the 1960s was that long-term growth depended only on supply and that the macro-economic influence of the government depended solely on demand. So the state had to regulate the business cycle to match the long-term trend as closely as possible in order to maintain full employment, using a combination of budgetary and monetary measures. This, at least, was the Anglo-Saxon idea of a synthesis of the neo-classical and Keynesian schools. It was attacked in the 1970s by the ultra-liberals, who did not see any reason for macro-economic intervention by the state, and by the monetarists, who regarded it as no more than nominal price stabilization.

There have certainly been other economic histories and other political cultures in Europe. The Scandinavian Social Democrats put the state at the heart of the collective bargaining process, as a mediatory third party in a centralized system of income control. The German form of welfare-state capitalism – the 'social market economy' – developed a tradition of close collaboration on a regional scale by the public, private and cooperative sectors to create the technical and human environment that would best promote the competitiveness of small- and medium-sized businesses. In France the role of government was to counteract the division of the union movement and the archaic attitudes of employers. The renewal effort in France after World War II was led by a central administration, which succeeded in converting the mercantilist tradition established by Jean-Baptiste Colbert into a force for progress, thanks to the renewal of the élites. The French model of state direction of the economy had a strong public presence in the production system and entailed tight control of the financial system.

The use of mediatory institutions therefore took on a national hue, allowing the development of national varieties of the Fordist growth regime. The coexistence of these variants was permitted by the international monetary system, which left scope for national autonomy in the choice of their mode of regulation. In fact, the modest share of GDP that foreign trade contributed at that time, the limited degree of financial integration resulting from the restrictions on international capital movements and the ability to devalue the currency in a system of fixed but adjustable exchange rates offered some room for manoeuvre in the formulation of economic policy. In those post-war years, governments were able to coordinate the various mediation mechanisms. Economic policy determined how the macro-economy was to be regulated. We have seen that this coherence affected the relationship between progress in productivity, wage increases, social transfers and domestic demand. The pivotal point of this coherence was therefore the total amount of wages and salaries in its dual role as production cost for firms and consumer spending power. That is why it was possible to speak of a national wage standard to describe this mode of regulation in a nutshell. The state asserted its responsibility in this domain by stabilizing the national business cycle. In that way, it created a chronological perspective for all economic agents and increased the predictability of the climate in which private agents conceived and pursued their ventures.

Apart from macro-economic coherence, which is the Keynesian heritage recognized by the Anglo-Saxon tradition during the era of Fordist regulation, the regulation approach underlines the more structural government inputs into institutions. This idea is nurtured by the experiences of continental Europe. These forms of state input may be characterized by the aims they seek to achieve: building up collective production bases; stimulating technical progress, overcoming the collective risks inherent in the financial system; and promoting an equitable distribution of income.

The Institutional Base

The importance of the school in the emergence of the wage society has already been indicated. The same applies to energy, transport and urban planning. All these investments are far more profitable to society than to a private investor, because their full collective value cannot be translated into a pricing system. The resources that need to be raised to fund such collective capital are enormous, and the amortization periods are very long. These infrastructural amenities are the social foundations of productivity.

Technological innovation also depends on collective factors – basic research, scientific knowledge and skills – which yield fewer returns for a private investor than for society as a whole. When the state withdraws from this domain, some of the collective factors that lend impetus to technical progress are missing, and the pace of innovation slackens. The more available these factors are, the more beneficial external effects they have on the production of market goods and services, encouraging greater diversity. This process is at the root of the increasing returns from capitalist production which preserve the stability of the rate of profit. State intervention can take various forms. Where purely collective factors are concerned, factors which cannot be privately appropriated – general scientific knowledge – the state must undertake to produce them in public laboratories. Where the factors of innovation can be produced privately – records of industrial research – because their use is a source of revenue to those who produce them, the state may restrict itself to encouraging invention. It may offer tax incentives, relax the rules governing patents or involve itself directly in associations of public laboratories and private companies.

It was indicated above that the financial system was a system of capitalist mediation. It involves evaluating wagers on the accumulation of future profits, redistributing risks in order to spread them more widely, and acquiring and investing funds drawn from the savings of the general public. But financial activity implies certain risks that cannot be spread because the financial markets are incomplete, because the information flow is imperfect and because attitudes to a particular risk are changeable. The result of this is a contagious effect which produces collective behaviour patterns, generating waves of optimism and pessimism in the course of which financial values can undergo huge fluctuations. These disruptions can trigger financial crises, the social cost of which is far higher than the cost to private investors. That is one of the key reasons why governments intervene in the financial sector to prevent crises if possible, or at least to limit their disastrous social consequences.

Regulating the Financial System

Under the Fordist regulation system, national governments have generally been strongly interventionist in financial matters. They have established rules in favour of concentrated banking systems, often differentiating between banks and other financial institutions. They have controlled interest rates to avoid excessive variations and have concluded agreements with their respective central banks to ensure that commercial banks in temporary difficulties have enough liquid assets to guarantee bank deposits at all times.

The development of social transfers creates moral hazards similar to the financial risks. These transfers, in fact, are inspired by solidarity and the need to cover social risks that cannot be spread. They are not therefore regulated by private insurance contracts but by social rules. The moral hazard lies in the fact that the system of social protection has no control over the social costs for which it is liable. It administers a form of passive solidarity in which responsibilities are diluted. The ways in which states have tried to resolve that contradiction vary widely. But the principles of equity underlying these systems of social protection derive from a common philosophy. A purely individualist society cannot exist; there must be a common basis of solidarity. This common basis comprises first and foremost the fundamental necessities of which no-one should be deprived and which must therefore be provided by public or publicly guaranteed systems. It also implies social justice in the form of a system of taxation which redistributes wealth while maintaining the hierarchy of incomes within generally accepted limits.

Equity is thus an important dimension of the reconciliation of capitalist interests with social progress in the wage society. By preventing exclusion, it reinforces citizenship and hence identification with the economic system. By preserving homogeneity in the distribution of income, it encourages the widespread adoption of modern lifestyles and hence the development of markets for mass consumer goods, the very development that served as the main engine of capital accumulation.

The Globalization of Capitalism and Crises in the Wage Society

When A *Theory of Capitalist Regulation* was written, the Fordist system was just beginning to malfunction. With twenty years of hindsight and within the theoretical framework presented here, we might venture to suggest an understanding for the many changes, jolts and convulsions that have marked the crises of this period. To that end, we must reconsider the two contradictory faces of employer–employee relations which brought forth the wage society.

Let us recall the hypothesis that underlies the regulation approach, namely that capitalism is a force for change which has no inherent regulatory principle; this principle is provided by a coherent set of mechanisms for social mediation that guide the accumulation of capital in the direction of social progress. The capacity of these mediation mechanisms to absorb the effects of change in a manner compatible with the global growth rate is limited in two ways. First, the effectiveness of organizations lies entirely in the stability of their internal rules, but these allow them limited scope to respond to variations in the conditions governing the accumulation of capital. Second, the institutionalized compromises between interest groups, whether they are contractual or enshrined in law, only reduce uncertainty by virtue of their rigidity. The causes for the malfunctioning of the growth regime must be sought in the distortions between the changes unleashed by capitalism and the impotence of the existing institutions to deal with them in the framework of the established macro-economic regulatory system. Many such changes have occurred over the past twenty to twenty-five years: the extension of the wage society as capitalism spreads across the world, financial globalization, the technological revolution and the renewal of individual interests. These upheavals affect employment, employees' lifestyles and the substance of social progress in the countries that were previously the main beneficiaries of growth and mass consumption.

What is Globalization?

The term 'globalization' has become a catch-all word for journalists, politicians and the business community. It is the horizon for all our hopes and the source of all our ills. In continental Europe it is accused of having caused chronic unemployment. In the Anglo-Saxon countries it is blamed for the fall in average real wages and the spectacular widening of the income gap.

These concerns are dismissed by the liberal economists who emphasize the primacy of global competitiveness. Free trade is not a zero-sum game but rather an engine of growth. The acceleration of global growth in the 1990s, after the previous decade had been one of decline and stagnation in many developing countries, has introduced hundreds of millions of people to the era of mass consumption.

Above all, globalization means the spread of paid employment which has enabled capitalism to penetrate into the very heart of non-Western societies. This is happening because the international division of labour offers the prospect of profit. Most importantly, the cost of transferring up-to-date technical knowledge is falling sharply. An increasingly wide range of activities has been profitably included in the international exchange of more highly skilled work in the more developed countries for lower-skilled work in the less developed countries. This two-fold dynamism, broadening and deepening the division of labour, is stimulating the growth of productivity. In the most advanced capitalist countries, the service sector is being revolutionized by the upsurge in intellectual work on concepts, symbols and forms – technical and financial consultancy, design, know-how, information and communication. In the developing countries, the intensity of capitalist activity is increasing with the production of capital goods, the growth of processing industries and the expansion of financial services. The intensification of the international division of labour is therefore equivalent to an increase in productivity.

There is another dimension of the international division of labour which looks set for a promising future at the start of the next century, and that is the exchange between generations. The savings of the ageing active population of the developed countries will be exchanged for flows of future income earned by the young labour force of the newly industrialized countries. This type of integration is based on solid demographic trends. The average age of the population of the developed countries is bound to rise because of the declining fertility rate among women aspiring to greater independence, and because of increased life expectancy. Furthermore, the declining birth rates that are now being registered in more and more regions of the world will result in a relative increase in the size of the labour force as a percentage of the whole population. The transfer of savings that results from this really did take off during the 1990s. It is a key factor in the pursuit of financial globalization, although the latter phenomenon dates much farther back.

This transformation of the division of labour on a planetary scale is a source of capital accumulation which is fuelling a new growth regime. However, as has always been the case in the history of capitalism, this technological revolution is not self-regulating. The policies, mentalities and institutions which interfere with the determinant factors of capital accumulation do not develop at the same rate as techniques, working methods and markets.

The European Dimension

So the new accumulation system that is establishing itself is not that dreamed of by the theorists of free trade – a global economy unified by the market. Although economic policy has shifted towards liberalism, it has not returned to the competitive capitalism of the nineteenth century. Nevertheless, the institutions of Fordism have found it very difficult to adapt. The regulations that proved effective in the 1960s have become largely inadequate. This does not, however, alter the fact that the twentieth century has seen the rise of the wage societies. In these societies, social rights are a constituent element of citizenship; they are the cement of social cohesion. The organization of the work process has increasingly become a collective process which depends on investments in the infrastructure and human capacities. And so the globalization of the economy is leading neither to the disappearance of nations nor to a minimalist state. But the need to formulate regulatory principles that can guide the accumulation of capital into a new era of wage societies calls for changes in many institutions. Nation-states are required to redefine which social rights are truly fundamental and to strengthen the collective bases of their competitiveness.

The rates of growth and the unemployment trends over three decades suggest that the changes in the social mediation mechanisms are posing more serious problems in Europe than in the United States. There has not been a long-term slackening of growth or increase in unemployment, and the economic policy options have not been radically changed, in the United States. In Europe, by contrast, discriminatory divisions have emerged. Britain has seen the overthrow of the regulatory system, resulting in the intrusion of competition into industrial relations. Yet the Germanic model of negotiations and compromise between organized interests has remained unchanged. The rampant growth of social inequality in the British model, which matches similar American developments, and the relentless rise of unemployment in the Germanic model both underline the difficulties facing wage societies that have experienced Fordism when they try to equip their institutions to establish a new compatibility between the accumulation of capital and social progress. To arrive at a better understanding of this tension, it will be useful to describe the numerous forms taken by the globalization of capital.

Economic Integration

Globalization is a multiplicity of distinct but interconnected processes. Occurring at different speeds, in different sequences and in different places with varying degrees of intensity, these processes are far from coherent. They take root in the main areas of change in the international division of labour. But by interacting with existing regulation models they create various types of disruption in the economic, financial and monetary fields.

Economic integration is a process that has increased in scope since the 1960s. The most obvious measure of its development is the fact that world trade has been growing at a consistently faster rate than world GDP. This trend has proved robust enough to withstand the financial crises and structural shocks that have studded the history of the last three decades. Economic integration generated by trade has not been homogeneous. The establishment of regional economic areas, where the greatest increases have occurred in foreign trade, has been a particularly conspicuous development in Europe, but the trend has not left Asia or America untouched. However, spectacular though the development of trade may be, it does not account for the processes that are transforming the conditions governing the accumulation of capital. It does not satisfactorily explain why such severe and lasting damage has been done to the macro-economic equilibrium of the countries of Europe. To do that, we must focus on the forms of competition to which the technical progress of our age has given rise and which feature in the international division of labour.

International competition has been extended to broad areas that were shielded from it under the Fordist system. These include public transport, communications, information systems, television networks, energy distribution and financial services. This amounts to a decisive shift in the dividing line between markets and public services. The social shock has been all the more deeply felt in countries where public services were successfully supplied by national public monopolies in which the workforce had enjoyed special conditions of employment. In countries where a high percentage of the labour force had the status of civil servants, the labour contract in the public services used to have a strong influence on wages and prices in the whole economy. That is why the impact of competition is causing considerable upheaval in those countries.

This upheaval is amplified by the effect of the exchange between skilled and unskilled labour resulting from world-wide expansion. The expansion of markets for mass consumer goods and services in the newly industrialized countries is establishing a production base with low wage costs relative to those in the more developed countries. However, thanks to the low cost of technology transfer and to dynamic increasing returns to scale, productivity is high. The result is a distortion of the wage structure in advanced capitalist countries, with upward pressure on the price of skills required to produce goods and services with a high added value, and downward pressure on the cost of labour in industries where there is competition from foreign manufacturers.

Besides the growing quantitative inequality, the distribution of income has been affected by the disappearance of the rules that guaranteed its stability during the Fordist era. The more technical skills become available to companies throughout the world, the greater is the extent to which the cost of the various types of labour is determined by competition on a supranational scale. If specialized workers and engineers have their income determined in supranational markets, their interests will split. Collective bargaining, which used to maintain a stable wage structure accompanied by a steady increase in real income, is no longer underpinned by a common interest in the upward shift of the whole wage ladder.

Weakened Collective Bargaining

The globalization of corporations has undermined the stability of wage structures. As long as the exchange of goods was the predominant form of international interdependence, the labour of one country could be exchanged for the labour of another without the core of the domestic price system being significantly affected by such external transactions. When firms become integrated networks of plants located throughout the world, their competitiveness does not depend decisively on the comparative advantage in a particular country. They are concerned with global profitability and the centralization of cash flows which are means of their strategic decision-making on capital accumulation. Because the interests of multinationals no longer coincide with those of their country of origin, collective bargaining ceases to be the pivotal element in the system of national macro-economic regulation.

Labour standards linked to full-employment equilibria, determined themselves by multi-year collective bargaining, were the economic linchpins of wage societies during the Fordist era. Cyclical adjustment of economic policies, discretionary devaluations and exchange controls were sufficient to reconcile the national autonomy of these regulations with international trade. By contrast, present-day economic integration is forcing companies to compete on labour costs, to make employment the residual variable and to adjust their profitability to tight financial requirements. Financial integration has become the leading force of globalization. It is in the financial sphere that there have appeared some of the key institutional forms of the new growth regime.

The nature of international competition changes when the interests of companies cease to coincide with those of their respective countries of origin. The competitiveness of enterprises depends on their ability to organize flows of goods, production factors, engineering and finance throughout the world. The production and distribution of economic value by corporations are becoming detached from their territory of origin. Since the coherence of the Fordist mode of regulation lay in the relationship between productivity and distribution in a national context, there is a feeling that the institutions which monitored these adjustments are in disarray. Indeed, real wages and productivity increases have been disconnected, weakening unions and emptying the content of collective bargaining.

The other side of the coin is that the globalization of enterprises intensifies competition, and hence the preponderance of capitalist interests, throughout the entire social fabric of each nation. 'Whatever moves in the world economy puts competitive pressure on factors that do not move'.[13] The set of mediation mechanisms that maintained the delicate balance between private interests and social cohesion has been broken, which has enabled private multinational interests to break out of confinement. Capitalism is engaging entire societies, and the individuals who live in them, in competition without any longer being subject to the constraints that formerly channelled the quest for capital accumulation in the direction of social progress.

The Opening of Financial Markets

Unlike economic integration, which has been proceeding at a steady pace for more than thirty years, the opening of financial markets was a discontinuous regime change arising from deregulation and financial innovation. Finance, after all, is a key mediation mechanism in the regulation of capital accumulation.

Financial intermediaries shape the structure of assets and liabilities which give rise to objective commitments stemming from the idiosyncratic endeavours of entrepreneurs. The logic of finance confronts uncertainty to establish the economic horizon in which capitalist projects can be implemented and to assume liability for specific risks arising from the great diversity of company wagers. This mediation has three functions. The first is the production and circulation of information. Financial logic is threatened by vicious circles and self-fulfilling processes, because finance produces

---

[13] A. Brender, in *L'impératif de solidarité. La France face à la mondialisation*, Paris 1996.

information from information. This process can always degenerate into pure speculation, detached from the real world of production, and create disruptive phenomena: speculative bubbles, sunspot equilibria, overshooting, heterogeneous expectations and shifts in beliefs.

These disruptions have repercussions on the second function, namely the evaluation of the financial assets that determine the direction in which accumulation is guided and the allocation of savings by internal means (self-financing) and by external means (credit and share issues). The quality of the first two functions conditions the third, which is the supervision of the use of savings. This third function is a means of exercising proprietary rights over enterprises. It can either be done centrally on the basis of judgements arrived at by the financial markets or in a decentralized manner through bilateral relations between companies and financial intermediaries.

Since these three functions of finance are not independent of each other, it is the type of combination between them that defines the financial regime of macro-economic regulation. During the Fordist period, accumulation on a national basis was supported by the mobilization of national savings, courtesy of intermediaries competing within an oligopoly. This competition was contained and channelled by a detailed set of rules governing market activities and conditions. The strict control of international movements of capital added to the coherence of that system.

The opening of financial markets was the result of the crisis of Fordism coming into conjunction with the increase in economic integration. This brought about an abrupt change in the financial system, followed by the slow emergence of new forms of macro-economic regulation. This discordance produced the banking crises and the upheavals within the finance markets which punctuated the 1980s and 1990s.[14]

There are numerous links between the opening of financial markets and economic integration. They affect the three functions of the financial system described above. The crisis of Fordism resulted in an economic slowdown, the severity of which varied between developed countries, resulting in differences between countries in the way in which the balance between savings and investment shifted. The United States, for example, became a net debtor and Japan a net creditor, a polarization that became ever sharper as time went

---

[14] For a definition of the financial systems and a description of the characteristic features of the various crises, see M. Aglietta, *Macroéconomie financière*, Paris 1995, chs. 4, 5.

on. Even so, the globalization of enterprises led to the mobilization of international financial resources. These forces brought about the dismantling of controls on movements of capital on a country-by-country basis. As a result, we have seen the beginnings of a disconnection between domestic savings and domestic investments.

The Rise of the Institutional Investor

This disconnection is one reason for the international diversification of financial wealth but it is not the only reason. The other powerful force derives from the change in savings themselves. The relative decline in savings in the form of bank deposits and the prodigious rise in institutionalized savings have led to a demand among savers for higher returns. The institutional investors have become the instruments of the diversification of financial wealth. But the management of a portfolio makes very different demands than those made by banks in terms of transparency of information, ability to manage risks, evaluation of financial assets by the markets and forms of proprietary control of enterprises.

The system of market finance, with its predominance of institutional investors, has therefore replaced the financial system administered by the banking oligopolies. The new system has decisively changed the constraints on the accumulation of capital by changing the way in which proprietary control is exercised. The old form of managerial control accepted pay deals based on stable distribution of the added value of the firms. Long-term stability of accumulation was the management objective. Institutional investors with holdings in a company, by contrast, insist on the performance criteria as evaluated by the financial markets. They compel firms to maximize their equity value in the short term, under the constant threat of hostile mergers and leveraged buyouts. This form of company management breeds an obsession with cutting wage costs and shedding jobs to boost share prices without much thought for future development.

Another characteristic of market finance derives from innovation in the management of risks. The enormous increase in the volume of trading in securities and the extraordinary boom in derivatives are entirely the fruits of this revolution. Instead of being exclusively administered by the banks, which hold claims until they fall due, the risks associated with market finance are divided into elementary components. These are formalized by financial instruments which make them negotiable – in other words, redistributable to anyone who is able to take them over with profit. A large number of interdependent market segments have combined to provide the elements of a wholesale market in global liquidity. Currencies are exchanged there, the risk and time profiles of portfolios are remodelled, and barriers between banking and non-banking activities are removed. These micro-economic innovations have spectacular macro-economic effects. A complex web of financial interdependence is being woven between countries through the arbitrage of interest rates, through currency speculation and international creditor and debtor positions. This financial configuration is spreading gradually across the whole world as the new capitalist countries make their currencies convertible and deregulate their financial systems. This is the dominant mediation mechanism in the establishment of the new growth regime.

Technical Progress, Exaggerated Individualism and Identity Crisis

The globalization of economies is far from being the only profound change that wage societies have undergone. They are also subject to the forces of individualism that strike at the social fabric and threaten it with disintegration. Individualism can develop in societies where the main social bond is money. It is only under capitalism that this factor can become a drive that determines individual goals as well as a generalized behaviour pattern. This is the case because, under capitalism, money becomes more than just the standard by which everybody's place in the division of labour is judged. Money becomes a form of wealth that is sought for its own sake, not out of some pathological craving, but as evidence of the social recognition accorded to individuals. By integrating the wage-earning and salaried population into the circulation of wealth, because their incomes exceed the levels required for the mere perpetuation of existing lifestyles, the wage society has given individualism a massive boost.

We are all well aware of the extent to which the generalization of wage labour during the post-war boom contributed to the financial autonomy of individuals. We are also aware of the extent to which it changed the nature of the family by allowing individual aspirations to be fulfilled outside the constraints of the family unit. Although some of the dynamics of consumer demand were generated by efforts to improve the living conditions of the family as a group, changing lifestyles diverted another part of this dynamism into the satisfaction of individual desires.

Nevertheless, individualism does intensify the contradiction inherent in the relationship between the individual and society. There is a positive and a negative side to individualism.[15] The positive side consists in emancipation from the shackles of a system of social allegiance, from personal subordination, loyalty and observance of rituals legitimized by a symbolic order. This emancipation serves as the key to rational economic behaviour, opening the door to the pursuit by monetary means of the individual aims we call interests. This also sustains the dynamics of effective demand by causing constant diversification of supply, an innovation which capitalist enterprises can turn to account in order to renew their profitable investment bases.

The negative aspect of individualism, however, is that membership of society, in other words the legitimization of individual acts, has to be constantly reclaimed. Taken to extremes, individualist demands tend to dissolve the social fabric from which such demands derive their validity. Or else, the impact of globalization on organizations makes individuals unsure of their identity within society and destroys the bonds of solidarity that once allowed the collective expression of individual experiences. Individualism is then a negative force in the sense that it results from the failure of the mediation mechanisms to produce social cohesion.

Fordism more or less provided the conditions in which individuals could vie to assert their individual aspirations in the legitimate belief that they were contributing to social progress. These conditions were visible in the hierarchical struggles within large organizations. They reconciled upward social mobility, which was limited by structural constraints but was not negligible, with the stability of a hierarchy of social strata based on professional rank. This was reflected in an income structure that developed slowly, opening up until the early 1960s and closing thereafter. The integration of individuals, the process within which these hierarchical struggles were waged, was guaranteed by the steady increase in each individual's real wages, the low unemployment level and the short periods of unemployment.

From Crisis to Technological Revolution

When the mass-production-based productivity boom in the United States ran out of steam, this triggered the crisis of Fordism. In the

---

[15] J. P. Fitoussi and P. Rosanvallon refer to positive individualism and negative individualism in *Le nouvel âge des inégalités*, Paris 1996.

course of that crisis, the struggle waged by enterprises to halt the decline in their profitability gave rise to innovations that explored new technological frontiers. Some observers see in the introduction and subsequent widespread use of computers a third industrial revolution, because they believe that information technology, which has played its own part in promoting the international division of labour, is also transforming the organization of the work process. This is seen in research into artificial intelligence, in human genetics triggered by the social cost of increased life expectancy, the challenges related to the degradation of the biosphere, the pursuit of space exploration and the revolutionizing of the food chain by genetic engineering.

Where capitalism captures these frontiers of knowledge, it develops a compartmentalized system to incorporate the new activity into its structures – product design, graphic design, information, communication. The consequences are drastic for the hierarchy of qualifications inherited from the stage of mass production. The productive capacity of collective work performed through co-operation by highly skilled teams cannot be measured by a common yardstick with the contribution of each individual identified separately. Yet, one single lapse on the part of a team member can have the gravest of consequences for production processes that are highly vulnerable to breakdowns or accidents. This means that the individual marginal productivity of labour loses all significance, as does the principle 'to each according to his labour'. From another point of view, the applications of new technology are changeable and therefore uncertain, so they are far from leading to the systematic development of the kind of product ranges that resulted from the invention of electricity or the motor car. The fact is that the present rules of social life, the various forms of cultural resistance and public institutions are out of tune with present-day possibilities for technical progress.

The disappearance of the link between individual earnings and the marginal productivity of labour, like the uncertainty surrounding the fate of businesses that engage in innovation, is leading to the break-up of wage scales. These hesitations in the accumulation of capital are also causing extensive and abrupt fluctuations in the demand for labour. The result is an individualization of career patterns. Employees who have undergone identical initial training may have entirely different pay levels and careers, depending on the companies or collective activities into which fortune or misfortune has led them.

The Uncertainty of the Employee

Under the impact of technological change, the economic ground rules within companies have been overturned, since the mobility of capital has created competition between social systems, that is, the body of institutions and rights on the basis of which employer–employee relations were regulated nationally. Moreover, the overthrow of the rules within companies has destabilized the socio-professional hierarchy. The disappearance of the standards that had helped stabilize struggles over rank, as well as the waves of reorganization which have resulted in redundancies among formerly protected categories of employees, have caused uncertainty about what tomorrow will bring. Increasing numbers of employees cannot find their place in the division of labour. The destruction of functional identities turns out individuals without any sense of belonging, individuals for whom the question of social identity poses a problem. That is a measure of the depth of the malaise which has gripped wage societies in these trying times. The very principle of the integration of labour into the corporate structure, the progressive force behind the post-war boom, is now under threat. This malaise eats into the individual psyche when the energy that used to be channelled into work is converted into fear of an unforeseeable future.

This profound identity crisis leads to splintering of the inequalities that are no longer stratified by common standards and to collective demands for which the political process can no longer assume responsibility. It also causes a general decline in solidarity. The result is a loss of legitimacy among trade unions and political parties, which can no longer clearly portray the social fabric as one within which conflicts can be managed and compromises negotiated.

The fragmentation of inequalities is penetrating every socio-professional stratum. No longer do qualifications, seniority or hierarchical responsibility guarantee recognized positions in organizations. A patchwork of individual destinies is emerging as unforeseeable changes plunge one person into redundancy, another into precarious employment and yet another into work for which he or she is over-qualified. The state of social helplessness is reflected in the feeling that these anarchic inequalities are not the transient effects of a remodelling of the division of labour in the light of technical progress and global competition. They are perceived as chronic symptoms of exclusion, in other words of backsliding into a form of capitalism in which the integration of the labour force is no longer on the agenda. This profound and sustained erosion of the social mediation mechanisms of the Fordist age has left its imprint on the economy in many different ways.

The Economic Symptoms of Crisis

The spectacular fall in growth rates and the inexorable rise in unemployment are the most evident symptoms of crisis for the population of Europe. This twofold phenomenon derives from a weakening of the dynamics that once powered the accumulation of capital, namely the maintenance of a balance between technical progress and the expansion and diversification of consumer demand. This dynamism had sustained both the steady progression of real wages and the redistribution of labour among the various fields of economic activity.

The joint effect of the slowdown in productivity and in final demand in Western countries was so spectacular as to undermine the industrial relations that had developed during the boom. In the United States, economic liberalism decisively weakened the unions and the collective bargaining process, decentralized the determination of wages and created very fierce competition among job-seekers in the labour market. A growth rate based on very small labour productivity gains has established itself. Standards of living have deteriorated for many social strata. Two or three sources of income are necessary for families to sustain a lifestyle that was previously financed by one wage. The growth provided by small productivity gains absorbed a 55 per cent increase in the labour force, in other words a net gain of 40 million jobs, between 1971 and 1993!

At the same time, the employment structure has been transformed, thanks in part to a very considerable wave of immigration and to the shortcomings of the education system. The competition from this new unskilled and non-unionized labour force in decentralized labour markets has led to the creation of a huge number of precarious and low-paid jobs in the non-industrial sectors. The result of this dramatic reshaping of the employment structure is the anarchic patchwork of disparities, with extreme individualization of pay structures and differences in pay and conditions between employees with the same qualifications in the same occupation.

In Europe, the growth regime has been far more seriously undermined. There seem to be two main reasons which explain this difference. First, industrial relations in Europe are more rigidly structured by contractual mediation mechanisms, and direct market influence in the regulation of wages is weaker. In particular, the system of social protection is considerably stronger. For several years after growth had been slowing down, these mediation mechanisms defended the social benefits of those to whom they had previously been granted. A dichotomy developed within the labour force. In the 1970s, an 'internal labour market' preserved the existing bargaining mechanisms and their corollary, the organizational stability of companies. Where high wage costs were a barrier to employment, businesses had recourse to the 'external market', passing on their problem to a workforce that was not protected by collective agreements. From the 1980s onwards, and at different times, depending on the state of their respective economies, all countries experienced the repercussions of the strategies whereby companies sought to free themselves of obligations deriving from past pay agreements, which had become millstones around their necks in the context of international competition. The more bitterly this assault on labour costs was contested, the more serious was the impact on employment.

Europe Versus the World

Second, the countries of continental Europe had to respond to the globalization of enterprises to safeguard the construction of Europe. The solution that was adopted, after Europe had run the risk of marking time until the mid-1980s, was to move towards economic and financial integration (the Single Market project) then to proceed to monetary integration (the EMU project). Consequently, the mode of regulation based on strong national autonomy which had guaranteed post-war prosperity, was completely destabilized, but the political initiative that might have established new mediation mechanisms for a fully integrated market was not forthcoming. The result was a vacuum in the content of collective bargaining. The system of national labour standards that prevailed during the Fordist era has been replaced by a European monetary standard.[16]

The monetary criterion is becoming predominant. Instead of relatively autonomous national price systems that are harmonized with each other by means of exchange-rate variations, the target –

[16] R. Boyer, 'D'une série de National Labour Standards à un European Monetary Standard', *Recherches économiques de Louvain*, vol. 59, nos. 1–2, 1993.

at least in France – is a set of homogeneous national price systems subject to the constraint of fixed exchange rates. Wages are expected to become once more the 'variable capital' of which Karl Marx spoke. Because the labour force is less mobile than companies, its price has to adjust to financial constraints. This requirement for wage flexibility is made all the more imperative by the fact that European governments have proved incapable of co-ordinating their macro-economic policies, despite their professed desire to establish a monetary union. The contradiction between the respect of monetary targets and the persistence of former pro-cedures of wage bargaining has produced the worst possible result: pressure on wages and chronic mass unemployment.

In the absence of political management, the problem posed by the need for wage flexibility has been exacerbated by the partial dismantling of established institutions in the wake of macro-economic difficulties without their being replaced by other collec-tive systems linking income to productivity. The result was an unseemly rush to abolish obstacles to dismissal on economic grounds, to undermine the statutory minimum wage in some coun-tries, to end the indexing of wages, to embrace an extreme and arbitrary individualization of wages and salaries that would oblit-erate any relation between pay and productivity, and to make the system of unemployment benefits increasingly restrictive. The remodelling of wage structures is therefore part of the hidden agenda of the European construction process and is an area of con-frontation rather than collaboration between governments.

The State and Debt

The other main dimension of the sustained crises within wage societies is a result of financial constraints. These are a direct product of the malfunctioning of the former mode of regulation. Because of the weakening of the dynamic relationship linking pro-ductivity, income and employment, the value added on which social transfers were levied has increased more slowly since the 1970s. At the same time, the transfers necessitated by the social rules in force have risen far more sharply as unemployment has increased. This meant that all countries, each at its own pace, incurred budget deficits and increased the ratio between public debt and GDP. The quest for means of funding this debt, along with the globalization of enterprises and the upheaval in the international currency markets resulting from the oil crisis, was one of the main reasons for the transformation of the financial systems. Debt has once again become the predominant factor in economic policy. Debt implies the obligation to settle. It creates a situation of potential rivalry between debtors and creditors, a situation in which money plays an intermediary role.

In the 1970s, the debate on monetary doctrine was raging. But, in practice, monetary policy favoured the debtor as long as the system of tightly regulated finance was still in force. To safeguard growth as far as possible, the monetary authorities left a great deal of leeway for bank credit by mitigating the effects of inflation on nominal interest rates. The subsequent decrease in real interest rates triggered a revolt among creditors anxious to preserve the real value of their financial assets. Financial innovations began to proliferate on the initiative of financial agents, who offered effective investment instruments to beat inflation and compelled the main commercial banks to follow suit.

The two other forces for change in the financial structure were the need of governments to finance the public debt by non-inflationary means and the recycling of oil revenues. This situation resulted in the creation of new financial markets in which interest rates became far more sensitive to variations in the rate of inflation. In the late 1970s, the international development of these markets had already created a network of financial interdependence which caused disorders in exchange-rate movements. A vicious circle developed between the depreciation of certain currencies and the acceleration of inflation in other countries, between the appreciation of some currencies and loss of competitiveness in other countries. These macro-economic disorders forced monetary policies to change radically. Since the US dollar is a key currency in the international monetary system, it was the global crisis of confidence in the dollar in the late 1970s which raised widespread doubt about the ability of monetary management to resolve situations of financial antagonism. By encouraging a general escape into inflation, these antagonisms imperilled the monetary foundations of capitalism. The time had come to re-establish monetary discipline.

Defending the Creditor

As logic dictated, it was the US Federal Reserve which initiated the shift in the balance of monetary constraint in favour of the creditors' interests by radically changing its monetary policy at the start of the 1980s. This sudden and unexpected change of course resulted in the insolvency of a string of sovereign debtors in the developing countries. It also caused the other Western countries to vie with each other to produce the most restrictive monetary policies. Interest rates rocketed, the recession spread across the world, and the unemployment rate scaled heights unknown since the Second World War. By accepting exorbitant transitional social costs, reinforced monetary restraint had succeeded in conquering inflation by the mid 1980s. But it had done much more than that. It had transformed the rules of the financial system by opening the door to liberalized financial markets.

The stabilization of inflation at low levels and the maintenance of high interest rates greatly increased the cost of indebtedness. Public debts became highly onerous, and debt-service obligations perpetuated budget deficits. The high interest rates encouraged financial investments with prospects of a high short-term return. And so, the flow of credit into productive investments involving industrial risks virtually dried up in favour of speculation on the prices of the existing instruments of private wealth – shares, the property market, building land and so on. The capitalist economies, rediscovering in this the characteristics of the Edwardian era, became sensitive again to credit cycles and to the price of property holdings. Where the nominal base value is guaranteed by a low and stable inflation rate, variations in interest rates set the tone for macro-economic adjustments. The tensions that have emerged with regard to the settlement of debts are also affecting the rhythm of production and investment which is becoming more erratic. These fluctuations are occurring in the context of a steady discharging of company debts but also of government debts. Judged against the imperative of financial rigour, expenditure on social protection has to be reduced. The twofold vigilance of financial markets and central bankers has pared away means of funding the public services. The impotence of political action has combined with the problem of individualism to put the cohesion of the social fabric under serious threat.

Towards a New Age of the Wage Society

The wage societies of the developed world are trying to cope with the triple challenge of the globalization of capitalism, the disintegration of social identity and the shrinkage of the state. I have tried to show how these three ills are closely interlinked. The same applies to the encouraging trends, the initiatives and aspirations that might bring forth new mediation mechanisms capable of redefining the regulatory system. These are more visible in some Western countries than in others.

The fact that several types of wage society were able to coexist with Fordism testifies to the diversity of modes of regulation. These are coherent sets of mediation mechanisms, not a standard universal tuning system for all markets. The type of regulation system depends on the dominant mediation mechanisms. It was possible, for example, to distinguish an Anglo-Saxon form of capitalism, in which the markets and the state interacted within a framework of active economic policies, and a so-called Rhenish-type capitalism, where collective interests were organized and social compromises were negotiated and capable of making accumulation of capital and social progress consistent.

Globalization, technical changes outside the domain of mass production, and the proliferation of individualism had different effects on the different types of wage society. In the Anglo-Saxon versions, the incompatibility of these trends with Fordism manifested itself sooner in the form of contradictions which the markets intensified – inflation and financial innovations – and for which drastic monetary cures were prescribed: the monetary shocks experienced under Paul Volcker in the United States and Margaret Thatcher in the United Kingdom in 1979. The decline of manufacturing industry and the rise of the service sector were very rapid. The polarization between precarious jobs with no prospect of social mobility and highly valued jobs in the worlds of finance and multinational business was sharpened.

Parliamentary majorities adopted an intransigent economic liberalism that eroded the economic position of employees who had formerly enjoyed statutory protection. Excessive deregulation of public services in the United States and the headlong rush into privatizations in the United Kingdom wrought radical changes to the structure of industrial relations. These relations became highly competitive once more, resulting in violently fluctuating unemployment rates as the trade cycle turned. In the United States, the demand for labour varied greatly with cyclical changes. In the United Kingdom, the trade cycle mainly affected the supply of labour, the activity rate of the population having become far more sensitive to economic fluctuations. The essential feature of this type of labour regulation is the high turnover of staff in jobs. In the United States, unemployment was not a step on the road to exclusion, but disparities in income and education levels were such that the promise of upward social mobility, the essence of the American Dream, was seriously compromised.

Segmentation of the Labour Market

In Europe, deals negotiated between organized collective interests play a far greater part in the functioning of markets. Social rights strongly affect wage costs. The dominance of a hard core of major shareholders, the presence of employees on company boards or the control of enterprises by their own management create a variety of corporate models. The long-term continuity of the enterprise, the stability of the rules governing its operation and the maintenance of competitiveness are aims pursued by those who hold economic power in this form of capitalism. The style of personnel management that results from this favours the existence of an 'internal' labour market within firms, protected against competition from the 'external' market. This segmentation is an integral part of the organized capitalism that flourished in the Fordist era. That is the main reason for what was termed the rigidity of the European labour market.

Serving as the basis of a virtuous circle as long as growth was strong and steady, this segmentation was also at the root of the degradation of the employment structure that occurred under the impact of the radical change in the growth regime. One of the segmentation factors was certainly that of formal qualifications. Thus the steady increase in unemployment in France during the 1970s and 1980s essentially affected unskilled labour. Moreover, the existence of in-house labour markets produced hysteresis – effect lagging behind cause. Wage negotiations do not depend on the aggregate level of unemployment but on its variation. The terms under negotiation do not, in fact, depend on the potential competition from the dole queue, since segmentation has eliminated that, but on the threat to existing jobs. Whatever the level of unemployment, as soon as it is stable, the pay of the 'insiders' can be increased. When this happens, companies have to make other workers redundant to reduce their wage bills. Once unemployment has struck, once a person in France is in the 'external' labour market, the odds against finding another job within three months are four to five times greater than in the United States. As periods of unemployment lengthen, with the accompanying deterioration of working capacity and demoralization, the segmentation of the labour market condemns people to exclusion. The attempt to overcome this exclusion through many forms of assistance, often in the guise of recruitment incentives, ultimately foundered on the rock of massive public deficits.

The question of the future of the advanced wage societies is as follows: the factors we have analyzed that plunged the Fordist system into crisis were sufficiently powerful to lay the foundations of a new accumulation system. This system has borrowed from Anglo-Saxon capitalism the emphasis on competition, the control of companies by institutional shareholders and the place of profit and market value as the key criteria of success. But this type of capitalism is no less dependent on wage societies in their entirety, even though companies and financial institutions are less attached to any particular nation. But, in wage societies, the legitimacy of capitalism lies in the social progress that its dynamism sustains. The crisis of Fordism halted and even reversed social progress in the countries of continental Europe where it had flourished most abundantly. But market capitalism, even in conjunction with economic policies designed to maintain a high level of employment, cannot justify its existence in the absence of adequate regulation of social inequalities. Is it possible that the contradictions inherent in European societies will be resolved, that the enormous changes required to enable Europe to benefit from the new growth regime will be made and that a mode of regulation will emerge which is able to reconcile market capitalism with a renewed principle of solidarity?

Without claiming to answer such a vast question, we can state that it coincides with the renewal of the social-democratic blueprint for Europe. How can this blueprint be explained? According to regulation theory, it is necessary to identify the social mediation mechanisms which, in combination, will form the required mode of regulation. These mechanisms must be such that they work together to guide the accumulation of capital in the direction of a redistribution of income that will re-establish solidarity. A few propositions can be advanced, propositions which have profound implications and which may help to analyze the demise of Fordism as well as the new sources of growth.

Corporate Governance, Institutional Savings and the Redistribution of Income

Given the problem presented above, the viable mediation mechanisms are those that reconcile efficiency and equity. As the population ages, one crucial dimension of equity is that of fair treatment of different generations. But it is also a source of financial power through institutional savings. The institutional investors can surely be identified as the most important mediators in the new growth regime. The political implications attaching to institutional savings still have to be emphasized.

In the logic of Anglo-Saxon capitalism, the role of institutional investors is considered from an individualist and purely financial point of view. These bodies privately administer a fund made up of individual savings. Investment funds are numerous and competition between them is fierce. Performance criteria are relative, the aim of each being to produce a better average return than its competitors. Pension funds have developed into a portfolio structure in which shares predominate, because their long-term yield is superior to that of other financial assets. Because institutional savings have been advancing more rapidly than any other form of saving, these intermediaries acquire stakes in companies, which induce them to exercise influence, albeit passively, on company strategy. They impose the criterion of financial profitability. They insist on transparency of information, the suppression of corruption and the prevention of insider dealing. They do not hesitate to sell blocks of shares and reinvest in rival companies. In short, they are the agents of market discipline, ensuring that companies' sole concern is the profitability of capital.

But that idea is inadequate. It does not incorporate the financial dimension of industrial relations. Far from being only the intermediaries of individual saving, the institutional investors are also the potential agents of shareholding employees. The whole question, then, is who ultimately holds the companies' shares as a result of this mediatory mechanism. What may emerge through the mediation of the institutional investors is a capitalism of consolidated individual funds, the socialized ownership of enterprises. If this development is given political backing, it may lead to a wage society that is very different from Anglo-Saxon-style market capitalism while also abandoning the European models of corporate capitalism that marked the Fordist era.

If the trade unions are to regain the power to influence the distribution of income, they must realize that the battle to be fought and won is the battle for control of company shareholdings. The development of employees' funds will be the paramount mediation mechanism that will enable the capitalism of continental Europe to remain distinct from the Anglo-Saxon variety of capitalism.

The Primacy of Pension Funds

In fact the conversion of contractual savings into property rights in respect of companies implies a decisive change in the way companies are run. Companies are controlled to an ever-diminishing extent by their own organization in the manner of the managerial capitalism of Fordism and to an ever-increasing extent by pension funds. These funds impose criteria in terms of financial returns which determine the nature of investments and the distribution of the value added by the company. Anglo-Saxon pension funds, spurred on by competition and by the purely financial demands of their clients, require companies to achieve a very high yield – about 15 per cent – from their own funds. Since this performance standard is considerably higher than the real long-term risk-adjusted interest rate, it is reflected in the tremendous increase in equity market values. To comply with this financial constraint, companies invest primarily in information technology so as to minimize the cost of unskilled labour through quality control and on-line processes. In this way, individual savings patterns are becoming the main engine of the distribution of income via the institutional investors' governance of company behaviour.

So there are regulation principles that are now shared by all wage societies: the predominance of the financial link, in other words, of profit-sharing and shareholding, in income inequalities; the fact that the supranational, multi-product company has superseded the branch or industrial sector in the national economy as the unit within which the rules of income distribution are applied; the primacy of the profitable use of the company's own funds, dictated by financial globalization, instead of the negotiated sharing of the fruits of productivity gains in accordance with national standards governing increases in real wages.

In this mode of regulation, corporate governance is decisive. The rise of a shareholding labour force to assume control of the pension funds could alter the balance between the interests of savers and those of the workers. That would suit the trade unions of continental Europe. Their history calls on them to transcend the corporate interests of individual trades and to voice the needs of the entire labour force. In employees' funds they would find the mediation mechanism to influence the rules of profitability. Instead of a maximum short-term yield, they could demand a guaranteed long-term rate of return for a stable ownership of company assets, protecting the management from hostile take-overs. With a greater prospect of economic stability, companies could regain the room for manoeuvre to negotiate productivity contracts with their employees, which would include provision for linking real wage and productivity increases and adjustments in working hours. The opening of this window of opportunity on the European continent would have the advantage of hastening the advent of supranational collective bargaining in the enterprises whose activities are spread across the whole territory covered by monetary union. After these bad times, when national collective bargaining structures are being destroyed, a more hopeful phase may follow, in which the reorganization of industrial relations on a European scale can be launched in line with the needs of the companies themselves.

Government, Social Investment and macro-economic Regulation

To assess the globalization of capital, we must first recognize that enterprises are no longer the main generators of social integration within a nation. Enterprises create competition between the national collective factors of productivity: the general level of education, the scientific basis for technical progress and the infrastructural amenities in each country. Enhancing the collective basis of productivity growth to sell at a high price the fruits of expensive labour is the only acceptable solution for developed wage societies. It is the only way to entice companies concerned with global profitability to locate plants which create a high level of added value. But, since the collective sources of productivity are exploited for the accumulation of capital by enterprises that have played little part in their creation, a heavy burden of responsibility rests with governments. Reform of the state, of its aims and of its means of action, so that it becomes an investor in the living forces of productivity, is essential if the nation is to reclaim its place as the cradle of common values of social cohesion. In this respect there is no contradiction between competition among nations within the global competitive framework and improvements in national living standards.

If the separation between work, unemployment and inactivity is to be overcome, a means must be found of according social recognition to the idea of full activity throughout a person's working life. This implies considerable organizational changes of the type that have been explored in the Netherlands and the Scandinavian countries. Since employees' attachment to their companies loosens with the globalization of capitalism, it must be accepted that enterprises are not the only places where professional skills can be acquired and maintained. In the Fordist era the education system, besides determining the general level of education, also established the hierarchy of formal qualifications which held the key to recruitment and starting levels in companies and defined the scope for promotion during the working life of an employee. The education system must become far more involved in training human capital throughout the working lives of individuals. The investing state is the one that offers employees the means of acquiring evolutionary and mobile skills – in other words, skills that can be transferred from one company to another through a system of periodic reversion to a formal learning process.

This is the first aspect of reduced working hours we should consider – namely a reduction of the individual's entire working life in order to enhance the productivity factors that he or she embodies. This basic concern must become an essential component of the social contract within nations, although there must also be scope for a very wide range of ways in which this principle can be put into practice.

Towards a Mobile Labour Force

Individuals who are less dependent on particular companies for the acquisition of specific skills can take advantage of the tendency to organize production processes in a more flexible manner, reconciling size and diversity. As we have seen, the Fordist enterprise had a vertical structure supporting a functional hierarchy. Conversely, the mobility of capital encourages companies to adopt a network structure. It favours a subtle mix of cooperation and competition between units belonging to the same enterprise. It alters the types of inducement offered to employees. Less attached to a particular enterprise, employees will largely tend to look for employment contracts in which their mobility is not penalized. The development of negotiable skills is a fundamental asset. But so are the availability of broader and more precise information about potential future jobs and working hours that enable the individual to seek new employment while working in his or her present job without having to endure a period of unemployment.

The relational aspect of work should also be able to operate in the domain of socially useful services in the regions and local communities. Collective and individual services are becoming front-line social issues in today's wage societies. It is imperative that the state should be the planning body, because the population will depend increasingly on the reliability and quality of a closely-woven network of services which shapes our living environment. It is up to regional and local authorities, with the support of central government, to develop combinations of public and private funding in order to fuel a latent demand which has enormous job-creation potential.

Commitment of the state to the training, preservation and

renewal of human resources could not be further removed from the ideology of the minimalist state that was all the rage in the 1980s. The investing state is the natural ally of technical progress. The germs of growth lie in the creative capacity of brainwork. But forming the factors of innovation is a collective business, since the social return on that investment is greater than its private return. The impetus of the state in education, research and the social infrastructure, far from excluding private investment, actually complements such investment. It is a growth-enhancing input. This does mean, however, that governments have to invest with a view to improving the employability of the whole population rather than creating jobs in specific competitive sectors. Information technology, after all, has taken the market economy into areas hitherto regarded as non-commercial. And so the state is no longer called upon to provide, either directly or through intermediary companies, transport, telecommunication, postal, electricity and municipal maintenance services, and so forth. The concentration of budgetary expenditure on investments with wide-reaching external effects is one of the main aspects of the new mixed economy.

Refocusing the State

If the state were to refocus its activities on the development of the collective productivity factors, budgetary practices would have to be modified. Neither public accounting nor parliamentary procedures are conducive to investment. Depreciation is part and parcel of any type of capital. But that concept is absent from the principles of public accounting. Equally, no investment can be made without an evaluation of the return it is likely to yield. Those who produce analytical forecasts and public economic assessments should come out of the ivory towers of economic science and add their views to the political debate. There cannot be investment in the most basic factors of growth without a clear long-term perspective. The investment in research and the resources for higher education must be protected from the vagaries of the business cycle by means of laws establishing long-term programmes.

State responsibility for maintaining the rate of technical progress is the way to influence long-term growth. But the steady-state growth is also important. It implies political responsibility for anti-cyclical measures, which monetarism had denied. The first reason for this stems from the growth factors themselves. Where technical progress is chiefly linked to the experience of workers who gradually raise the productivity of their teams as they work together in the production process, recessions have adverse effects on growth patterns, because they diminish the employability of redundant workers, especially if they are lengthy and recovery is slow, as has been the case in Europe. Consequently, structural policies designed to improve the quality and flexibility of jobs cannot function independently of macro-economic policies designed to stimulate growth. If structural measures are taken in a context of stagnation, and if macro-economic policies remain neutral or restrictive, the increased mobility of labour only serves to convert a structural unemployment into Keynesian unemployment. The structural measures do nothing to improve productivity or growth.

A second reason for an active anti-cyclical policy relates to deflation in a globalized financial environment. Monetarist doctrine rationalized the monetary policy of the 1970s at a time when administered financial systems showed obvious signs of malfunctioning. The extreme elasticity of the supply of bank credit and the widespread indexation of wages and prices in national economies handed the initiative to debtors. Monetary policies generally consisted in restricting the liquidity of banks by curbing the supply of money from the central banks. This line of approach was rationalized by reference to the notion of a 'natural' equilibrium level of unemployment rate as expressed in the long-run vertical Phillips curve. Since long-term growth was independent of inflation, it was not the concern of monetary policy to respond to real shocks, so employment did not have to be treated as a policy aim.

The error made by governments in Europe, by contrast with the United States, was to treat this doctrine as axiomatic, whereas the extent to which it was true depended on a very specific set of financial circumstances. Let us recall that A. W. Phillips demonstrated a long-term inverse relationship between increases in money wages and unemployment.[17] This relationship was particularly clear-cut in the half-century prior to World War I. From the point of view of financial adjustments, conditions in that period are considerably more relevant to us than those which prevailed twenty years ago. It was an era of financial globalization, of international competition, of changes in the division of labour resulting from the second Industrial Revolution. In the economic structures of that period, the financial markets themselves contained mechanisms for the

[17] Phillips's original study covered the relationship between wage inflation and unemployment over almost a century. 'The Relationship Between Unemployment and the Rate of Change of Money Wage Rates in the UK, 1861–1957', *Economica*, November 1958.

correction of nominal price increases, which they accomplished by setting long-term interest rates. There could be no sustained inflationary trend in the form of a self-perpetuating price spiral. But that type of economy is vulnerable to international shocks, which destabilize the short-term relationship between inflation and unemployment. One reason for this instability is the behaviour of economic agents when inflation is close to zero.

Equilibrium and Unemployment

During periods when inflation is very low, many individual company prices should fall. But some key money prices are fixed by agreement or by the dictates of logic. Money wages do not fall spontaneously, nor do nominal interest rates become negative. This means that companies under pressure from their competitors, and forced to lower their money prices, are compelled to respond to the decimation of their profit margins by cutting jobs and reducing their debts. The net result of these adjustments is that unemployment becomes sensitive to the general level of prices in an equilibrium situation with very low inflation. It is the task of central banks to avoid this type of inefficient equilibrium and hence to seek the balance between inflation and unemployment that will best promote steady growth in the long run.

A third reason for closely involving the monetary authorities in economic regulation is concern for the stability of the financial systems. In a globalized financial structure the prices of financial assets are subject to considerable fluctuations. The behaviour patterns of financial operators may be affected at any moment by a burst of frenzied speculation. It is illusory to believe that prudential regulation and supervision of institutions will be enough to shore up the banks if the financial markets are unstable and the business cycle is substantial. Fragile banks will, in turn, impair the macro-economic efficiency of monetary policy. They may neutralize the effect of a precautionary cut in monetary interest rates by not reflecting the cut in their own lending rates. They may offset the effect of an increase in the money supply by destroying some money in an effort to reduce their debts. And so, in globalized financial systems, central banks cannot separate monetary policy and prudential policy. One of their responsibilities is to ensure that waves of speculation in the financial assets markets do not assume dangerous proportions, as was the case in the late 1980s.

Statement of Social Rights and Fiscal Reform

The principles of regulation that have been suggested so far are compatible with the globalization of economies, the primacy of market competition and the mobility of labour, because they come into play before the price system and affect the global economic equilibrium. Before the price system enters the equation, it is the institutions which influence the control of enterprises and the employability of the labour force. As for the global level of regulation, which is governed by macro-economic policy, it is justified by the existence of multiple equilibria and by the incapacity of market adjustments to achieve a satisfactory equilibrium in a spontaneous manner.

These principles, however, cannot of themselves resolve the problems resulting from the widening disparities and diminishing solidarity that have been experienced since the start of the 1980s. Solidarity is not guaranteed by commercial insurance policies. It is a set of rules through which a nation assumes the risks that threaten life in society. According to this solidaristic rationale, the ultimate foundation of solidarity is the impossibility of a purely individualistic society. Democracy cannot be vital and active unless concern for the res publica is incorporated into the aspirations of the people. This implies a quality and variety of social interaction through which individuals attain effective freedom, and that quality depends on universal membership of society. That is why real freedom within a society is measured by the resources of its poorest members. A highly inegalitarian society, consumed by the excesses of individualism, is liable to drift towards totalitarianism. The totalitarian temptation derives from endemic violence and from a loss of involvement in the democratic process. This drift can be an insidious development and may not lead all the way to the establishment of a totalitarian order. Marginalization of minority groups, segregationist ideologies, aggressive assertion of the rights of ethnic or cultural minorities, tax revolts and systematic denigration of the state under some tawdry libertarian banner – these are some of the symptoms of an ailing democracy.

Retrieving Citizenship

In the major Western countries these ailments developed with the decline of the Fordist mode of regulation. The disintegration of the cohesive social fabric occurred at the same time as capitalism was being freed from every constraint. It is high time that political discussion recovered some of its former vigour to set about redefining the standards of social justice, after years of open hostility or indifference to such standards in the name of economic liberalism. To establish a shared concept of social justice, and to ensure that it is incorporated into the rights which it is the duty of the state to enforce, is to give meaning once again to the notion of citizenship. In the Fordist age, social rights were formulated on a basis of occupational solidarity. They developed with collective bargaining and were implemented by an increasingly complex and inscrutable system of social transfers. The redistributive element, designed to redress the disparities inherent in the struggle over rank, was combined with mechanisms affording protection against risks, the funding of which involved non-redistributive levies, particularly in France. The malfunctioning of the regulation structure provoked a deluge of urgent calls for action to mitigate the effects of the rise in unemployment and to finance spiralling health costs. The responses to these demands, entailing one extra cost after the other, increased the tax burden but also caused people to lose sight of the justification for the payment of tax. That is why redefining social rights also means being committed to the rehabilitation of the levy principle. The cohesion of a society may be judged by its acceptance of tax for what it should be, namely the reciprocal commitment of the citizen and the nation to provide highly productive work in return for a good quality of life. That is how social progress can be renewed in harmony with a regulatory principles which must strengthen the nation so that it can take advantage of the opportunities offered by global capitalism.

The reciprocal commitment of the individual and society cannot be renewed unless there is a moral imperative which clearly distinguishes moral rights from a purely passive form of solidarity. To an extent, it is a right of membership, the right not to be excluded, which must become the supreme value, as well as the kernel of the political debate. Freedom from exclusion must become the minimum right enshrined in the social contract, and hence the categorical imperative for the state. However, this aim, which ought to be at the heart of any new version of the social-democratic blueprint, is difficult to achieve, for changes in the work process have divided the wage society into three interest groups: those who benefit from technological modernity and globalization, those whose economic positions are still protected by statute or by their clientele, and those who are excluded. The last of these groups will inevitably remain a minority with no economic leverage. A policy for the promotion of solidarity cannot therefore derive from the interaction of economic forces. It cannot be driven by the occupational interest groups which fostered the development of social rights in the course of the Fordist era.

Democracy and Solidarity

The reaffirmation of solidarity today depends on the rehabilitation of politics as the main agent of social cohesion. The meaning of democracy must be rediscovered at its very roots: solidarity as a collective value without which the individual cannot develop. That is the only way to make the imperative of social cohesion compatible with the opening of the wage societies to globalization. Such an approach avoids the type of identity search which, though creating collective values, is also susceptible to the snares of populism and nationalism.

If the political blueprint succeeds in restating the need for solidarity the economic resources required for its implementation will lead, especially in France, to the institution of a process of radical tax reform and to a redefinition of social rights. By the end of this process, the welfare state will have been completely overhauled.

Today's wage societies are characterized by a loosening of the link between pay and the per capita marginal productivity of labour, but also by continued regard for work as the paramount criterion of integration into society. Consequently, the fight against social exclusion means increasing the demand for labour while endeavouring to enhance the employability of the labour supply. It also means defining and gaining acceptance for the principle of equity in the distribution of revenue, so that employees receive a reasonably fair share of the total value added. Proper regulation of the division into wages and profits depends on the briskness of demand and the pace of investment. Governments can act on these two aspects of revenue distribution through the tax structure and redistribution.

When a comparison is made for each country between the structure of budgetary expenditure and the tax system with the aid of OECD statistics, two characteristics emerge. France and Germany devote far smaller amounts than the United States and Japan to public investment but allocate larger percentages to social transfers and operating expenditure. These two European countries derive a particularly small amount of their fiscal revenue from capital duties, which account for 12 per cent and 13 per cent respectively of all taxes levied compared to almost 30 per cent in the United States and Japan. In more general terms, in all the

Anglo-Saxon countries, where acceptance of capitalism and the primacy of the market is widespread in all strata of society, there is a far heavier fiscal burden on capital than on the European continent. This burden is offset in different ways – by lower excise duties in the United States, and even in Japan, or by lower income taxes in the United Kingdom and Australia.

Reforming the Tax System

These great disparities underline the fact that taxation systems are not carved in tablets of stone. Ambitious reforms are possible if they are guided by a clear focus on solidarity. As far as France and Germany are concerned, the urgent priority is to seek reductions in the welfare charges levied on the wages of unskilled workers. The modest start that has been made over the past few years ought to be developed a good deal further. But whatever else happens, we must not fall into the demagogues' snare by reducing the overall tax burden. As we saw above, governments have a crucial role to play in the new regime of growth. They need substantial resources to recover some room for manoeuvre, whilst getting to grips with the excessively high levels of public debt.

There is no miracle remedy that will remodel the tax structure in such a way as to turn activities with lower marginal revenue products into profitable ventures. It will no doubt be necessary to increase the tax burden on capital in countries such as France where it is unduly light. The French Government must scrap the arrangement whereby income tax is subordinated to demographic considerations through a system of child allowances. All individual income, whatever its origin, must be made taxable. If the tangle of benefits accorded to certain categories of person is eliminated, it will be possible to increase the revenue from income tax while preventing marginal rates from becoming excessive in the higher strata. Incidentally, the transparency resulting from a sensible tax reform would be part of a national policy of solidarity which would redefine the spectrum of social rights.

It is high time that part of the burden of charges levied on low wages was transferred to the widest possible range of other taxes. In substituting a universal welfare levy and VAT taxes for social security contributions on wages, a momentum can be created in favour of solidarity and the fight against exclusion. If taxes on wages are replaced by higher taxes on consumption, employees who are victims of international competition could share the benefits derived from this competition by the population as a whole through the import of consumer goods. It is enough to tax staple items at a lower rate to meet any fears that such a measure might ultimately run counter to the aim of redistributing wealth.

The logic that consists in using taxation to fund welfare benefits not covered by national insurance contributions is a result of the way in which the modern wage societies have developed. The political philosophy which regards solidarity as an attribute of citizenship is replacing the concept of social solidarity based on occupational categories, which has been undermined by the destruction of the corporatist fabric under the impact of technical progress and globalization. The result is that social rights must never again take the degrading form of state handouts, and that the aid currently given to companies should be focused on people. France is surely the country that has made most use of employment incentives, peppering companies with a variety of subsidies throughout the 1980s. This method was part of an extension of Fordism, based on the premise that the enterprise was still a vehicle of social integration. The French government persisted in this approach at the very time when companies were discarding unskilled labour and loosening their territorial roots. It is hardly surprising, then, that such aid has had little effect. What is more serious is its blind adherence to this practice in the course of the 1990s. Its illusions, however, have now been dispelled. The employment and poverty traps that this array of assistance schemes creates are being denounced from all sides. The time has come for a political blueprint for a radical reform of the redistribution system. It is a matter of establishing a guaranteed minimum income that will provide individuals with the economic resources on which the exercise of their inalienable rights depends. That is a mechanism designed to combine economic efficiency and social justice.

A Guaranteed Minimum Income

Economists have often made this type of proposal.[18] The advantage of a guaranteed minimum income is that it proceeds from a universal understanding of taxation as an incentive to work rather

[18] It is mischievous to portray the right-wing economist Milton Friedman as the inventor of this proposal. It was put forward in France by L. Stoléru in the same vein, in other words, from a liberal perspective in which redistribution played a strictly limited role. The idea was incorporated into a completely different approach by P. Van Parijs and an entire post-Keynesian school for whom the development of collective productivity completely separates income from work

than a deterrent. Because this income is granted to everyone of working age, it avoids any discrimination between those who are on benefits and those who are not. Because this income is maintained whether the individual is in or out of work, it does not create a poverty trap. Finally, this income is an aid to individuals, not to companies. It corrects the disparities that result from huge pay differentials and makes it possible to employ low-skilled workers with limited marginal productivity.

This redistribution mechanism consists in determining the amount of a fixed-rate transfer without means testing. At the same time, a standard tax rate is set and is deducted at source from every type of income. Finally, an element of progressive taxation is introduced in the form of a surtax on large incomes. The average rate of taxation is assessed in such a manner as to ensure a net balance between receipts and expenditures. The minimum income can then replace the existing social transfers – child benefit and housing benefit in France – which amount to less than the minimum income; where such benefits exceed the minimum income, the excess amount of benefit would remain payable. With the same amount of income of whatever type being subject to the same amount of tax, this mechanism can be linked with the universal social levies, health insurance contributions and the remaining vestiges of child benefit.

The stage is therefore set for a political debate. The real challenge is certainly not to dismantle the welfare state or even to erode its benefits. On the contrary, there is a particularly pressing need for social cohesion. The purpose of the political debate is to devise a means of giving expression to people's social rights so that the new growth régime can put wage societies back on the road to social progress.

Translated courtesy of Eurostat

This essay was first published in *New Left Review*,
No. 232, November–December 1998

(see Van Parijs, *Sauver la solidarité*, Paris 1995). A guaranteed income is the logical conclusion of a hypothesis according to which work is no longer a form of socialization of individuals. We, on the contrary, believe that work is still the principal means of social integration, and we subscribe to the pragmatic approach recently set forth by F. Bourguignon and P. A. Chiappori, *Fiscalité et redistribution*, Notes de la Fondation Saint-Simon, Paris 1997.

Index